THE AMERICAN EXPRESS POCKET GUIDE TO FLORENCE AND TUSCANY

Sheila Hale

PRENTICE HALL PRESS
NEW YORK

The Author
Sheila Hale, the author of *The American Express Pocket Guide to Venice*, was formerly a staff writer for *Vogue* and the *Telegraph Sunday Magazine*. She was born in New York, but has lived in Italy and England since 1962, working as a writer and journalist. Her work appears in several newspapers and magazines, including *Connoisseur*, the *New York Times*, the *Observer* and *Harpers & Queen*.

Contributor
Burton Anderson (Tuscan wines)

Acknowledgments
The author and publishers would like to thank the following for their invaluable help and advice: Burton Anderson, Professor Andreis of the Italian Institute of Culture, Lisa Beveridge, Julia Crosse, David Ekserdjian, Caroline Elam, Rosaria Falivene, Pamela Fiori, J. R. Hale, Italian State Tourist Department, Countess Aloisia Rucellai, Stella Rudolph; and for the revised edition: Sally Hood, Charles Hope, Monica Loni, Nicolai Rubinstein.

Quotations
The author and publishers are grateful to those listed below for their kind permission to reprint the following extracts: Phaidon Press Ltd. (UK and US) for the quotations from *Piero della Francesca* by Sir Kenneth Clark (p127 and p177); Laurence Pollinger Ltd. and the Estate of the late Mrs Frieda Lawrence Ravagli (UK) and Viking Penguin Inc. (US) for the quotation from *Aaron's Rod* by D. H. Lawrence (p46).

Few travel books are without errors, and no guidebook can ever be completely up-to-date, for telephone numbers and opening hours change without warning, and hotels and restaurants come under new management, which can affect standards. While every effort has been made to ensure that all information is accurate at the time of going to press, the publishers will be glad to receive any corrections and suggestions for improvements, which can be incorporated in the next edition. Price information in this book is accurate at the time of going to press, but prices and currency exchange rates do fluctuate. Dollar amounts appearing in this book are at exchange rates in effect in mid-1986.

Series Editor   David Townsend Jones
Editor of first edition (1983)   David Arnold
Art Editor   Eric Drewery
Designer   Sarah Jackson
Illustrators   Jeremy Ford (David Lewis Artists), Illustra Design Ltd, Illustrated Arts
Production   Androulla Pavlou

Edited and designed by
Mitchell Beazley International Limited
Artists House, 14–15 Manette Street,
London W1V 5LB

© American Express Publishing
Corporation Inc. 1983
New revised edition © American Express
Publishing Corporation Inc. 1987
All rights reserved including the
right of reproduction in whole or
in part in any form
Published by Prentice Hall Press
A Division of Simon and Schuster Inc.
Gulf & Western Building
One Gulf & Western Plaza
New York, New York 10023
Maps in 4-color by Clyde Surveys Ltd, Maidenhead, England
Typeset by Vantage Photosetting Co. Ltd, Eastleigh, England
Printed and bound in Hong Kong by Mandarin Offset International Ltd

Library of Congress Cataloging
in Publication Data.
Hale, Sheila.
The American Express pocket
travel guide to Florence and Tuscany.
(The Simon and Schuster/American
Express pocket travel guides)
Includes index.
1. Florence (Italy)—Description—
1981—Guide-books. 2. Tuscany
(Italy)—Description and travel—
Guide-books. I. Title. II. Series.
DG732.H24 914.5′504928 82-3217
ISBN 0-13-025032-5   AACR2

Contents

How to use this book

The American Express Pocket Guide to Florence and Tuscany is an encyclopedia of travel information, organized in the sections listed on the previous page. There is also a comprehensive **index** (pages 213–224), including a **street gazetteer** for Florence, and there are full-color **maps** at the end of the book.

For easy reference, all major sections (**Sights and places of interest, Hotels, Restaurants**) and other sections as far as possible are arranged alphabetically. For the organization of the book as a whole, see *Contents*. For places that do not have separate entries in *Sights and places of interest*, see the *Index*.

Abbreviations

As far as possible only standard abbreviations have been used. These include days of the week and months, points of the compass (N, S, E and W), San, Santa or Santo (S.), Santi or Santissima (SS.), Saint (St), C for century, and measurements.

Bold type

Bold type is used in running text primarily for emphasis, to draw attention to something of special interest or importance. It is also used in this way to pick out places – shops or minor museums, for instance – that do not have full entries of their own. In such cases it is usually followed in brackets by the address, telephone number, and details of opening times.

Cross-references

A special type has been used for cross-references. Whenever a place or section title is printed in sans serif italics (for example *Bargello* or *Basic information*) in the text, this indicates that you can turn to the appropriate heading in the book for further information. For added convenience, the running heads, printed at the top corner of the page, always correspond with these cross-references.

Cross-references always refer either to sections of the book – *Basic information, Culture, history and background, Planning* – or to individual entries in **Sights and places of interest**, such as *Accademia* or *Uffizi*. Ordinary italics are used to identify sub-sections. For instance: see *Calendar of events* in *Planning*.

How entries are organized

Belvedere *(Forte di Belvedere)* ▥

☎ 287055. Map **3**E4 ◻ Open Tues–Sun 8:30am–1:30pm, exhibitions 9am–8pm. Closed Mon. Main entrance from Via del Forte di S. Giorgio.

Crowning the hill of S. Giorgio is the ruthlessly practical Belvedere fortress surrounding its elegant shoe-box-shaped Mannerist palace, both built by Buontalenti in 1590–5 for Grand Duke Ferdinand I. The terraces are now used for modern **sculpture exhibitions** ▨ which are only occasionally worthy of a setting commanding some of the most magnificent views of Florence and the surrounding hills and valleys. At the top of the Costa di S. Giorgio is the S. Giorgio gate (c.1260), reduced to about half its original height, embellished with a fresco of the *Madonna and Saints* by Bicci di Lorenzo. The relief carving of St George is a copy of the original now in the *Signoria*.

Floors

To conform with local usage, "first floor" is used throughout the book to refer to the floor above the ground floor, "second floor" to the floor above that, and so on. The floor below the ground floor is the basement.

Map references

Each page of the color maps at the end of the book has a page number (2–16), and each map is divided into a grid of squares, which are identified vertically by letters (A, B, C, D, etc.) and horizontally by numbers (1, 2, 3, 4, etc.). A map reference identifies the page and square in which the street or place can be found – thus **Siena** is located in the square identified as Map 11G6.

Price categories

Price categories are denoted by the symbols ⬚ ⬚⬚ ⬚⬚⬚ ⬚⬚⬚⬚ and ⬚⬚⬚⬚ which signify cheap, inexpensive, moderately priced, expensive and very expensive, respectively. In the cases of hotels and restaurants these correspond approximately with the following actual prices, which give a guideline at the time of printing. Although actual prices will inevitably increase, in most cases the relative price category – for example, expensive or cheap – will be likely to remain more or less the same.

Price categories	Corresponding to approximate prices	
	for **hotels**	for **restaurants**
	double room with bath and breakfast; singles are usually one third less	*meal for one with service, tax and house wine*
⬚ cheap	under $40	under $10
⬚⬚ inexpensive	$40–60	$10–15
⬚⬚⬚ moderate	$60–80	$15–25
⬚⬚⬚⬚ expensive	$80–230	$25–50
⬚⬚⬚⬚ very expensive	over $230	over $50

— Bold blue type for entry headings.

— Blue italics for address, practical information and symbols, encapsulating standard information and special recommendations. For list of symbols see p6.

— Black text for description.
  Bold type used for emphasis.
_ Sans serif italics used for cross-references to other entries.

Entries for hotels, restaurants, shops, etc. follow the same organization, and are usually printed across a narrow measure.
In hotels, symbols indicating special facilities appear at the end of the entry, in black.

Rigatti
Lungarno Generale Diaz 2, 50122 Firenze ☎ (055) 213022. Map 5E4 ⬚⬚ 28 rms ▭ 15 ═ ▭ obligatory.
Location: On the Arno, between the Uffizi and S. Croce. A superb position on the top two floors of the Palazzo Alberti, with spacious, uncluttered rooms, an elegant drawing room hung with old brocade, and an outstanding view from the terrace.
🍴 🐾 🌱 *on roof* 🔥

5

Key to symbols

☎	Telephone	≪	Outstanding views
⊤	Telex	⇌	Swimming pool
★	Not to be missed	⇌	Good beach nearby
☆	Worth a visit	♒	Tennis court(s)
✿	Good value (in its class)	✓	Golf course
i	Tourist information	✿	Riding facilities
⊶	Parking	⊶	Fishing facilities
⇌	Hotel	✿	Conference facilities
⬛	Simple (hotel)	⊟	Restaurant
🏨	Luxury (hotel)	☕	Simple (restaurant)
▢	Cheap	◿	Luxury (restaurant)
▯	Inexpensive	▱	A la carte available
▥	Moderately priced	▰	Set (fixed price) menu available
▥	Expensive		
▥	Very expensive	▬	Good for wines
▱	Rooms with private bathroom	⊜	Open-air dining available
▤	Air conditioning	🏛	Building of architectural interest
▱	Residential terms available	†	Church or cathedral
AE	American Express	▣	Free entrance
CB	Carte Blanche	▣	Entrance fee payable
◉	Diners Club	▣	Entrance expensive
▣	MasterCard/Eurocard	✖	Photography forbidden
VISA	Visa	✗	Guided tour available
▱	Secure garage	✗	Guided tour compulsory
▱	Meal obligatory	▣	Cafeteria
◠	Quiet hotel	✦	Special interest for children
⬍	Elevator		
♿	Facilities for disabled people	⅋	Bar
▢	TV in each room	●	Disco dancing
▱	Telephone in each room	◢	Nightclub
		✿	Casino/gambling
🐕	Dogs not allowed	♫	Live music
⚘	Garden	❧	Dancing
		≋	Revue

6

Before you go

Documents required
For citizens of the USA, EEC and British Commonwealth, a
passport is the only document required for visits not exceeding
three months. For longer visits, and for most other nationals, a
visa must be obtained in advance in the country of departure.
Vaccination certificates are not normally required, but if you
are traveling from the Middle East, Far East, South America or
Africa, you should check when buying your ticket.

To drive a car in Italy, you need an International Driving
Permit, obtainable from the AAA. If you are bringing your car
into the country, you must carry the vehicle registration
document (logbook) and an insurance certificate or
international green card.

Travel and medical insurance
It is advisable to travel with an insurance policy which covers
loss of deposits paid to airlines, hotels, and tour operators, and
the cost of dealing with emergency requirements, such as
special tickets home and extra nights in a hotel, as well as a
medical insurance policy.

The IAMAT (International Association for Medical
Assistance to Travelers) has a list of English-speaking doctors
who will call for a fee, as well as having member hospitals and
clinics in Italy. Membership of IAMAT is free.

For information and a directory of doctors and hospitals that
are members, write to: IAMAT, Suite 5620, 350 5th Ave., New
York, NY 10001.

The nearest American hospital which accepts certain US
medical insurance is in Rome. Always consult your own
insurance company for advice when going abroad.

Money
The monetary unit is the lira (plural lire). There are coins for
50, 100, 200 and 500 lire, and notes for 500, 1,000, 2,000,
5,000, 10,000, 20,000, 50,000 and 100,000 lire. You may not
take more than 200,000 lire in or out of the country without
official clearance, but check this amount with your bank before
you go. There are no restrictions on other currencies or
travelers cheques taken into the country, but if you intend
exporting more than 200,000 lire-worth of any currency you
should complete form V2 at customs on entry.

Carry cash in small amounts only. Travelers cheques issued
by all major companies are widely recognized. Make sure you
read the instructions included with your travelers cheques. It is
important to note separately the serial numbers of your cheques
and the telephone number to call in case of loss. Specialist
travelers cheque companies such as American Express provide
extensive local refund facilities through their own offices or
agents. Eurocheque encashment card holders can cash personal
checks in most banks. The principal cards accepted in Florence
are American Express, Diners Club, Eurocard and Visa.
Outside Florence, you are usually expected to pay cash.

Customs
Any items clearly intended for personal or professional use may
be brought into the country free of charge.

In the following list, the figures in brackets are the increased
allowances for goods obtained duty and tax paid in the EEC. In

7

all cases the allowances apply only to travelers over 17 years.
Tobacco   If you live in an EEC country, you are allowed 300
cigarettes *or* 150 cigarillos *or* 75 cigars *or* 400g tobacco. If you
live outside Europe, you are allowed 400 cigarettes *or* 200
cigarillos *or* 100 cigars *or* 500g tobacco; however, if you live in a
non-EEC European country you are allowed half this amount.
Alcoholic drinks   1(1.5) liters spirits (over 22% alcohol by
volume) *or* 2(3) liters of alcoholic drinks of 22% alcohol or less;
plus 2(4) liters still wines.
Perfume   50g/60cc/2 fl oz (75g/90cc/3 fl oz).
Other goods   You may bring goods to the value of $500 ($200)
from the USA.

When returning, you can export up to 1,000,000 lire's worth
of goods. To export works of art, apply to the Export
Department of the Italian Ministry of Education.

Getting there

By air: The most convenient airport for all destinations in
Tuscany is Pisa. The small airport at Bologna also receives some
European flights. Unfortunately, Florence Airport is too small
to serve overseas aircraft. Passengers from outside Europe will
have to make a transfer stop or fly direct to one of the large
international airports at Milan or Rome. Pan Am, TWA and
Alitalia fly USA–Rome, and the two latter USA–Milan also.
Flight time to Rome from the eastern USA is about 8hr.
By train: The two main trans-European trains to Florence are
the Palatino from Paris (couchettes and sleeping cars only) and
the Italia Express from London stopping at Lille, Strasbourg,
Basel, Milan and Bologna. Both carry first- and second-class
passengers and reservation is obligatory.
By road: Two highways (autostrade) enter Tuscany from the
N: the A12 along the coast from France via Genoa, and the A1
over the Apennines from Milan and Bologna, which continues s
to Rome.

Climate

The weather in Florence is more variable than in most Italian
cities. The temperature ranges from a brisk average of
42°F(5.8°C) in Dec, Jan and Feb to a sticky 77°F(25°C) in late
July and Aug. It can rain at any time of the year but rarely for
prolonged periods in summer. The wettest months are Jan, late
Nov, Oct and Apr, in that order. Winters are much milder on the
Versilia than in Florence.

Clothes

Be sure to pack one comfortable pair of shoes for sightseeing. In
summertime light, loose clothing is essential for comfort. In
spring and autumn bring a sweater or light coat and umbrella.
In winter you will need full protection as it can become cold,
particularly at night. Florentines are justly famous for their
sense of fashion, but their style is extremely understated.
Informal day clothes will take you virtually anywhere. Italian
men do tend to wear ties on most occasions, but there is no rule
about wearing ties in restaurants. Evening dress is rarely seen
these days except in private houses.

General delivery

Correspondence marked *Fermo Posta* plus the name of the town
and province will be held at the central post office. A small
charge is payable on collection; you must show your passport.

Getting around

From the airport to Florence
At Pisa incoming and departing flights are served by direct trains to and from Florence station at S. Maria Novella; the journey takes about 1hr. Taxis are available for the journey but are expensive.

Public transport
Buses
City and inter-city buses are cheap and efficient. In Florence the city lines, run by the ATAF bus company, are explained in the Yellow Pages telephone directory. One ticket is good for up to 70min of travel. For most buses, tickets must be purchased in advance from bars or tobacconists, in the form of a *biglietto semplice* (single ticket) or a *biglietto multiplo* (book of eleven tickets). There are also new buses which accept exact change only; these are marked by a hand holding a coin. There are two main bus companies operating outside Florence.

LAZZI Piazza Stazione 4–6 ☎(055) 294178 (serves Tuscany and Liguria)

SITA Via Sta Caterina da Siena 15 ☎(055) 211487/214721 (serves most parts of Italy)

Railroad services
The Florence station at Santa Maria Novella is one of the busiest and best connected in central Italy. The information office is open from 7am–10pm ☎(055) 278785. There are stations at or near all the provincial capitals. Fares are quite reasonable by European standards but they do vary according to the speed and type of train. Trains are classified as follows.

Super-Rapido: Luxury first-class-only trains running between the main Italian cities; a special supplement is charged and seat reservations are obligatory. The Super-Rapido trains stopping at Florence are the *Settebello* and *Ambrosiano* (Milan, Bologna, Florence, Rome), and the *Vesuvio*, which continues to Naples.

Rapido: Fast inter-city trains. Some carry only first-class coaches; a supplementary charge is made. Seat reservations are sometimes obligatory and for this too there is an extra charge.

Espresso: Long-distance express trains stopping only at main stations and carrying both first- and second-class passengers.

Diretto: Trains stopping at most stations; both classes.

Locale: Trains stopping at all stations; both classes.

Taxis
Taxis do not usually respond to being hailed but it is worth trying. There are stands in most of the main squares of Florence, and taxis can always be called by telephone. For radio taxis in Florence ☎4390 or 4798. Extra charges are made for this service, also for each piece of luggage, for journeys made between 10pm–7am, and on Sun and public holidays. The driver is not required to take you outside the city limits; if he does, the fare increases. It is customary to give the driver a 10% tip.

Getting around by car
Having a car in Tuscany is obviously a great advantage but be prepared to cope with Italian driving, which is skillfully aggressive. International road signs are in use and vehicles drive on the right; unless signposts indicate otherwise, cars must give way to traffic coming from the right. It is obligatory to carry a

warning triangle (which may be rented at the frontier), to be placed in emergency 55yd (50m) behind the stationary car.

The condition of the roads is variable. Tolls payable on the autostrada (highway) can be a considerable expense, but this is partly compensated for by the high standard of such roads. Maximum speed limits are 50kph (32mph) in built-up areas, 110kph (70mph) on country roads and 140kph (85mph) on highways. Heavy, on-the-spot fines are strictly enforced for breaking these limits. Gas stations often close between noon–3pm and after 7pm.

Tourists who have rented cars elsewhere in Europe are entitled to petrol coupons and highway vouchers. These can be bought in the country in which the car is rented and at Italian frontier points from the Italian Automobile Club (ACI) – but not within Italy. They can be refunded only by the issuing office.

Florence is served by highways in four directions. They are: the A1 running N to Bologna and SE to Rome via Arezzo and Chiusi; the Florence–Siena link which is due to be extended to Rome in the 1980s; and the A11 for Pistoia, Lucca, Pisa and the sea. The stretch of highway, A12, along the coast from Marina di Carrara to Livorno, will eventually be extended to Rome. For traffic information ☎ (055) 577777.

It is wise to leave your car outside the historic center of the city you are visiting. Most cities are provided with attended parking lots for this purpose. Many centers are now zoned against traffic; where traffic is allowed it is directed through one-way systems that baffle even the natives.

The ACI will give free assistance to members of affiliated touring clubs such as the AAA, AA or RAC.

Renting a car

The major international companies have branches in most cities and airports, and offer various reduced-rate schemes for cars booked in advance and paid for outside Italy. Companies can arrange to have a car waiting for you at your point of arrival. Cars rented from local agencies are often still somewhat cheaper, by up to 25%; these agencies can be traced through hotels or tourist offices.

Basic insurance is normally included in the rental rate with extra cover optional at fixed charges, and some companies require drivers to be over 21. Most firms require a deposit equivalent to the estimated total cost of rental. Value Added Tax (IVA) at 18% will be added to the final bill.

Mopeds

Mopeds can be rented in many towns if you have a driver's license. Ask at the *Azienda Autonoma* for a list of local companies.

Getting around on foot

All Tuscan towns and cities, including Florence, are small enough to be seen on foot; and many have now created traffic-free zones (*zone pedonale*) in parts of their centers. Traffic where unrestricted can be a nuisance, especially in Florence. In Italy, as elsewhere in Europe, pedestrians have precedence over vehicles at uncontrolled crossings.

Walking in rural Tuscany, where some of the prettiest landscape and monuments have been bypassed by the modern road network, is still a delight, See *Sports, leisure, ideas for children* for information.

10

On-the-spot information

Public holidays
Jan 1; Easter Monday; Liberation Day, Apr 25; Labor Day
(*Festa del Lavoro*), May 1; Assumption of the Virgin
(*Ferragosto*), Aug 15; All Saints Day (*Ognissanti*), Nov 1;
Conception of the Virgin Mary (*Immacolata*), Dec 8; Dec 25
and 26. Shops, banks and offices close on these days. Feast days
in honor of local patron saints are not official bank holidays, but
many shops close in Florence on the Feast of St John the
Baptist, June 24.

Time zones
Italy is 6hr behind Eastern Standard Time, and from 7–9hr
behind the other time zones in the USA.

Banks and currency exchange
Banks are open Mon–Fri 8:30am–1:20pm, and closed on Sat,
Sun and national holidays. You will need your passport when
cashing travelers cheques. Personal checks may be cashed by
Eurocheque Encashment Card holders. Most hotels cash
travelers cheques, but the rate is less favorable than at a bank.
Bureaux de change (*cambio*) are open during office hours.

Shopping and business hours
Shops are normally open 9am–1pm, 3:30 or 4–7 or 7:30pm.
Not all shops close Sun. In winter most shops in Florence close
on Mon morning, except for food stores, which close on Wed
afternoon. In summer some bigger shops close all day Sat, but
remain open on Mon morning.

Post and telephone services
Stamps may be bought from tobacconists (indicated by a 'T'
sign) and hotels as well as at the post office. The central post
office in Florence can be found at Via Pietrapiana 53–55.

Mailboxes are red and marked *Poste* or *Lettere*; collections
may be erratic outside towns.

Telegrams can be sent from post offices or over the
telephone; if writing in English it is safest to send the telegram
yourself from a post office.

Public telephones, to be found in post offices, tobacconists,
bars and at some newsstands, are operated by *gettone* (tokens
obtained from tobacconists and bars but often used as currency)
which must be inserted when the caller answers. Each province
has its own code which must be used if ringing from outside that
province (see *A–Z* entries for codes); the Florence code is 055.
Long-distance calls can be dialed direct from boxes marked
Interurbano.

Public rest rooms
In Florence there are public rest rooms in the basement of the
Palazzo della Signoria, off the courtyard of the Pitti and in the
station. Otherwise, don't rely on them; they hardly exist. Most
of the larger bars have toilets which may be used in exchange for
the price of a coffee. *Signori* means 'men' and *Signore* 'women.'
Leave a tip.

Electric current
Electricity in most places is 220V AC. The standard two-
pronged plugs or adapters can be purchased in most countries.

Laws and regulations
Italy possesses one or two unusual bureaucratic laws. One of the

11

most important is registering with the police within three days of entering Italy, which then entitles you to stay in Italy for three months; if you are staying at a hotel this will be done for you. There is a strictly enforced requirement that passports should be produced when registering at hotels.

If you are driving do not leave the vehicle registration book or rental agreement in the car; if the car is stolen or towed away the police will not co-operate unless you can produce proof of your right to drive the car.

If you leave your bill behind in a restaurant the waiter may run after you into the street and press it into your hand. This is because a new law requires that each customer leave the premises with evidence that a taxable sum has been paid.

Topless sunbathing is illegal but is nevertheless common in many resorts; if you see topless Italian girls you can assume it is acceptable.

Customs and etiquette

When visiting churches, it is important to remember that they are not museums and it is offensive to interrupt services even in the cause of seeing a major masterpiece. Women may wear trousers but are expected to cover their shoulders.

Tuscans pride themselves on their egalitarian manners. In restaurants and hotels, a friendly handshake and even the clumsiest effort to speak Italian will often work wonders. Children are welcome even in the smartest restaurants; indeed they often get better service than adults.

At times, Italian friendliness can be rather a nuisance, particularly when directed towards women traveling on their own. A firm but courteous rebuff (*Va via, per favore*) is the most effective way of dealing with such attentions, which are generally just playful and rarely sinister.

Tipping

In a restaurant, if service is not included on the bill, leave 15%; if service is included, a small note per person is an adequate supplement. The usher who takes you to your seat in the cinema, theater or opera will expect a tip. If a sacristan or custodian does you any special favor, such as opening parts of a church or museum which are normally closed, you should be more generous. Porters, hairdressers and taxi drivers also appreciate small tips.

Disabled travelers

Unfortunately, Italian legislation regarding premises for the disabled is not enlightened. Many hotels are located in old buildings not equipped with elevators, but the Italian State Tourist Office (ISTO) publishes an *Annuario Alberghi D'Italia*, which marks suitable hotels for disabled visitors with the wheelchair symbol.

Some major galleries, like the *Uffizi*, are accessible to wheelchairs, but many are not. Remember that marble floors can be hazardous for crutches or calipers, and cobbled streets are not ideal for wheelchairs. Most restaurants are happy to accommodate wheelchairs with advance notice.

For further information and details of tour operators specializing in tours for the handicapped, write to the Travel Information Service, Moss Rehabilitation Hospital, 12th St. and Tabor Rd., Philadelphia, Penn. 19141, or to the Director of Education, Easter Seal Society for Crippled Children and Adults, 2023 W Ogden Ave., Chicago, Illinois 60612.

Local publications
The daily newspaper of Florence is *La Nazione*. The
bimonthly magazine *Firenze Oggi/Florence Today*, available
free from the *Azienda Autonoma* and many hotels, is written in
both Italian and English and contains useful local information.

Useful addresses

Tourist information
American Express Travel Service Universalturismo, Via degli
Speziali 7 ☎(055) 217241, is a valuable source of information
for any traveler in need of help, advice or emergency services.
The *Azienda Autonoma di Turismo*, Via Tornabuoni 15, 50123
Firenze ☎(055) 216544/5, provides city maps and information
about special events and opening times in the city. The *Ente
Provinciale Turismo*, Via Manzoni 16, 50121 Firenze
☎(055) 2478141, provides information about the province of
Florence. The other eight provincial capitals, Arezzo, Grosseto,
Livorno, Lucca, Massa Carrara, Pisa, Pistoia and Siena, have
their own provincial tourist information boards.
Arezzo   Piazza Risorgimento 116 ☎(0575) 20839
Grosseto   Viale Monterosa 206 ☎(0564) 22534
Livorno   Piazza Cavour 6 ☎(0586) 33111
Lucca   Via Vittorio Veneto 40 ☎(0583) 46915
Massa Carrara   Piazza 2 Giugno 14 ☎(0585) 70894
Pisa   Piazza del Duomo ☎(050) 23535
Pistoia   Via 27 Aprile 13 ☎(0573) 21622
Siena   Via di Città 5 ☎(0577) 47051

Renting a cottage or villa
Agriturist, Via del Proconsolo 10, 50123 Firenze, provides
information about old houses with character for rent or sale.

Airline companies
Alitalia   Lungarno Acciaioli 10–12, 50123 Firenze
☎(055) 263051/2/3. Reservations ☎(055) 2788.
Via Veneto 9/10, 50047 Prato ☎(0574) 29220/33220
British Airways   Via della Vigna Nuova 36–38, 50123 Firenze
☎(055) 218655
Pan Am   Lungarno Acciaioli 10, 50123 Firenze
☎(055) 282716
TWA   Piazza S. Trinita 1, 50123 Firenze ☎(055) 284691
   Florence's flight terminal is at Piazza Adua. International
inquiries ☎(055) 214721; internal inquiries ☎(055) 296102.
Pisa Airport ☎(050) 25188

Automobile organizations
Automobile Club d'Italia (ACI)   Viale Amendola 36,
Firenze ☎(055) 27841

Post offices
Central Post Office (Posta Centrale)   Via Pietrapiana 53–55,
50121 Firenze ☎(055) 212305; and at Via Pellicceria, 50123
Firenze ☎(055) 216122

Tour operators in Florence
American Express   c/o Universalturismo, Via Speziali 7,
50123 Firenze ☎(055) 217241
CIT   Via Cerretani 57–59, 50123 Firenze ☎(055) 294306
Wagons Lits/Cook   Piazza Strozzi 14–15, 50123 Firenze
☎(055) 218851

Basic information

Major libraries in Florence
Biblioteca Nazionale Centrale Piazza Cavalleggeri 1,
☎(055) 287048
British Institute Library Lungarno Guicciardini 9
☎(055) 263334
Vieusseux Library Palazzo Strozzi, ☎(055) 215990

Major places of worship in Florence
St James's (American Episcopal Church) Via Rucellai 9
☎(055) 294417
St Mark's (Church of England) Via Maggio 16 ☎(055) 294764
Synagogue Via L.C. Farini 4 ☎(055) 210763

Consulates
Austria Via dei Servi 9, 50122 Firenze ☎(055) 215352
Belgium Via dei Conti 4, 50123 Firenze ☎(055) 294276
Denmark Via dei Servi 13, 50122 Firenze ☎(055) 211007
France Piazza Sta Trinita 1, 50123 Firenze ☎(055) 213509
Netherlands Via Cavour 81, 50129 Firenze ☎(055) 475249
Norway Via Sassetti 4, 50123 Firenze ☎(055) 27621
Spain Piazza di Salterelli 1, 50122 Firenze ☎(055) 212173
Sweden Via della Scala 4, 50123 Firenze ☎(055) 296865
Switzerland Via Tornabuoni 1, 50123 Firenze
☎(055) 216142
UK Lungarno Corsini 2, 50123 Firenze ☎(055) 284133
USA Lungarno Amerigo Vespucci 38, 50123 Firenze
☎(055) 298276

Australia, Canada, Germany, Greece, Ireland, Japan, New
Zealand and South Africa are countries not represented in
Florence; for help and information contact the consulate in
Rome.

Conversion tables

Length		
cm	0 5 10 15 20 25 30	
in	0 1 2 3 4 5 6 7 8 9 10 11 12	
meters	0 0.5 1 1.5 2	
ft/yd	0 1ft 2ft 3ft(1yd) 2yd	

Distance		
km	0 1 2 3 4 5 6 7 8 9 10 11 12 13 14 15 16	
miles	0 1 2 3 4 5 6 7 8 9 10	

Weight		
	(¼kg) (½kg) (¾kg) (1kg)	
grams	0 100 200 300 400 500 600 700 800 900 1,000	
ounces	0 4 8 12 16 20 24 28 32	
	(¼lb) (½lb) (¾lb) (1lb) (1½lb) (2lb)	

Fluid measures		
liters	0 1 2 3 4 5	liters 0 5 10 20 30
imp.pints	0 1 2 3 4 5 6 7 8	imp. gallons 0 1 2 3 4 5 6
US pints	0 1 2 3 4 5 6 7 8	US gallons 0 1 2 3 4 5 6 7

Temperature chart		
°C	−15 −10 −5 0 5 10 15 20 25 30 35 36.9 40 100	
°F	0 10 20 30 40 50 60 70 80 90 100 105 212	
	32 98.4	

14

Emergency information

Emergency services

Police	☎113.
Ambulance	You will be asked which service
Fire	you require.

Hospital casualty departments in Florence

Camerata   Via Piazzola 68 ☎(055) 575807
San Giovanni di Dio   Borgognissanti 20 ☎(055) 278751
Santa Maria Nuova-Careggi   Ponte Nuovo ☎(055) 27741

Other medical emergencies

If your complaint does not warrant an ambulance,
telephone the *guardia medica* (doctor on call)
☎(055) 477891. A list of English-speaking doctors and
dentists is published in *Firenze Oggi*. The police can also be
telephoned on 4977.

Late-night pharmacies

Every *farmacia* (pharmacy) has the late-night roster of
druggists on call displayed in its window. This information
is also published in *La Nazione* or ☎110.

Automobile accidents

— Do not admit liability or incriminate yourself.
— Ask any witness(es) to stay and give a statement.
— Remember to use your warning triangle.
— Exchange names, addresses, car details and insurance
  companies' names and addresses with the other driver(s).
— Report the accident to your insurance company.

Car breakdowns

— Put on flashing hazard warning lights and place warning
  triangle 50m(55yd) behind the car.
— ☎116 and tell the operator where you are, with plate
  number and type of car. The ACI will bring assistance.

Lost passport

If you lose your passport you should immediately report the
loss to the police and contact your consulate (see *Consulates
p14*) for emergency travel documents.

Lost travelers cheques

Notify the local police immediately then follow the
instructions provided with your travelers cheques, or
contact the nearest office of the issuing company. Contact
your consulate or American Express if you are stranded
with no money.

Lost property

If you lose anything it may be handed in at the lost property
office ☎(055) 216341. If you do not find it, report the loss
to the local police, as many insurance companies will not
recognize claims without a police report.

Emergency phrases

Help!   *Aiuto!*
There has been an accident.   *C'è stato un incidente.*
Where is the nearest telephone/hospital?   *Dov'è il
  telefono/l'ospedale più vicino?*
Call a doctor/ambulance.   *Chiamate un
  dottore/un'ambulanza.*
Call the police.   *Chiamate la polizia.*

15

Tuscans in Tuscany

Tuscans quite properly regard themselves as the most civilized of Italians. They speak the purest Italian, their culture is the oldest in Italy, and they were responsible for creating the first Renaissance. They will also admit to being the least cosmopolitan of Italians and the most afflicted with *campanilismo*, the Italian word for provincialism which means, in the literal sense, excessive attachment to everything within sight of one's native bell tower.

Florence, the little city which helped to transform Western European civilization and which still possesses many of its supreme artistic achievements, is capital of a region which is predominantly rural. That harmonious trio, the vine, the olive and the cypress, climbs up to the walls of many Tuscan towns and villages and slips into the conversation of the most sophisticated city dwellers. "They argue endlessly about *language*," observed the French writer Stendhal, who understood the Tuscan character better than most foreigners; "they argue no less about the price of various oils."

The Accademia della Crusca, the academic body which watches over the purity of the Italian language, sees its function in agricultural terms: it exists to sift the wheat from the chaff and its emblem is an agricultural flour sieve. Puccini was in all ways the prototypical Tuscan. His nights were spent composing for the great metropolitan opera houses of the world; but by day, as the guide will tell you if you visit his house at Torre del Lago, it was *la caccia* – the hunt!

Tuscans neither romanticize their countryside nor do they create artificial barriers between city and country. There is no Tuscan tradition of landscape painting or landscape gardening. If you come across an ornamental tree or herbaceous border in a suburban garden, the chances are that it was planted not by a native but by a homesick foreigner, probably English-born.

Two-thirds of mainland Tuscany is hilly, one-fifth mountainous, one-tenth plain. The cultivated land is extraordinarily productive thanks to naturally fertile soil and an abundance of both sunshine and rain. Farming in modern Tuscany is nevertheless not without its problems. Methods have changed drastically in the last 30yr: the white oxen which pulled the plows until 10yr ago have been replaced by machines in all but the most remote areas; the feudal *mezzadria* system by which the landowner gave a tenant farmer tools, seed and half the profit in exchange for labor died out in the 1960s and has not yet been satisfactorily replaced. The cost of agricultural labor today makes the wonderful Tuscan olive oil nearly as expensive as the liquid green-gold it resembles. In the industrialized vineyards beyond Pontassieve and above Siena disease-proof concrete vine supports have proliferated like tombstones. Elsewhere, wine growers, suffering the consequences of over-production, have turned their fields over to easy crops, like tobacco and sunflowers.

Such changes are esthetically regrettable, but they have not fundamentally altered the appearance of a landscape which has been ordered over centuries by collaboration between man and nature. Tuscans have imposed their own character on their countryside: their methods are conservative, enlightened and motivated by a not unnatural desire to make a profit. The result is that the ecological balance remains relatively undisturbed and that Tuscany still looks, as Goethe noticed almost 200yr ago, the way Italy ought to look, and promotes a sense of well-being in most Northern Europeans.

The countryside still shelters a profusion of rare wild flowers, butterflies, birds and indigenous animals. The *macchia*, the dense Mediterranean scrub characteristic of the Tuscan coast, is now officially protected in designated areas, where it acts as a sanctuary for migrating birds, roebuck, deer, partridge and wild boar. In the wild mountains on the Umbrian border you may still sometimes hear the lethal moan of a wolf or the cough of the hoopoe. Some of the noble mountain forests of fir and beech have been maintained by monastic foundations for centuries. Elsewhere the woods are protected by their very utility. The chestnut trees which attain magnificent proportions on the lower mountain slopes produce chestnuts for flour; the beech trees which grow at high altitudes shed mast on which pigs are grazed; pine trees produce pine nuts; and the scented yellow *ginestra* is used to make brooms. In late summer and autumn the forest floor is a treasure trove of luscious mushrooms and white truffles.

Below the surface of this productive landscape is a wealth of minerals, mineral springs and building materials. The soil of Elba contains 150 different minerals and its iron mines produce much of Italy's total requirement. The hills which form a ridge running toward the coast from just below Siena are called the Colline Metallifere after the copper, zinc and lead they contain. Monte Amiata is one of the major sources of mercury in the world, and half a million tons of Carrara marble are quarried each year from the Apuan Alps. Then there are the colored marbles – red from the Maremma, dark green from Prato, yellow from the Montagnola hills w of Siena, which have supplied the festive dressing for many great Tuscan churches.

Tuscan towns are made out of the Tuscan countryside. No one town or village or city is like another because the shape, color and texture of each is determined by the contours and building materials of its particular site. Siena is built of burnt-Siena bricks from the clay hummocks that its SE, Cortona is a brown sandstone city, Volterra is honeyed limestone, and Florence is gray-brown *pietra forte* with its interior spaces often marked out by the soft, lead-colored *pietra serena* quarried from the Fiesolan hills.

Tuscans themselves are, as they were in the Renaissance, hardworking, inventive and commercially tough-minded. If you visit a busy, well-kept town such as Prato or Arezzo, you will see the consequences of modern prosperity, negative as well as positive. The center may be clogged with tourist buses, the old walls may have been torn down to make way for beltways with factories and industrial suburbs beyond. In Florence there is a drug problem, a traffic problem, and far too many shoe shops and *pizzerie* to tempt and console the tourist. Arguments rage in the press about yet more new building on the outskirts.

Tuscans are also conservative, campanilistic and tied to the land. The young people who take part in those picturesque historic spectacles – jousting, flag-waving, playing soccer in medieval costume, racing horses around the town square – are not doing so just for the sake of tourists. These young people are beginning to buy back farmhouses of the kind gratefully abandoned by their parents after World War II. Their weekend pleasure is to tend the vine and the olive; and when they return to the town on Monday, there will be more vines and olives, growing right up to the walls of the factories where they work.

17

Time chart of Tuscan history

8th– 4thC BC	Area called Etruria after the Etruscans, the most ancient of the indigenous Italian tribes, skillful artisans and seafaring tradesmen.
6thC BC	Etruscan civilization reached from Po valley to Bay of Naples; federation of autonomous kingdoms or 'lucomonies' included Arezzo, Cortona, Chiusi, Fiesole, Populonia, Roselle, Vetulonia, Volterra.
351 BC	Etruria annexed by Rome.
3rd– 2ndC BC	Roman roads (the Aurelia, Clodia, Cassia and Flaminia) built across Etruria; Roman colonies included Ansedonia, Fiesole, Roselle and Volterra.
91 BC	Roman citizenship extended to Etruscans, whose cultural identity was gradually absorbed.
570 AD	Tuscany occupied by the Lombards, a Germanic people, whose dukes ruled from Lucca.
774 AD	Tuscany annexed to Charlemagne's empire and administered, still from Lucca, by a succession of imperial margraves. The countryside was held by feudal landlords, lay and ecclesiastic; the Benedictine Abbadia S. Salvatore was the most powerful of the religious foundations.
11thC	First crusade opened trade with eastern markets and stimulated religious feeling; city life revived with formation of new class of merchants and artisans. Reforming religious orders founded at Vallombrosa and Camaldoli. Powerful warlords, such as the Guidi, Aldobrandeschi and Malaspina, still held large tracts of country in fee.
1115	Countess Matilda, the last of the Germanic margraves, died, leaving her lands to the Pope. With Papacy and Holy Roman Empire locked in conflict, the nascent Tuscan cities asserted their independence; experimental republican governments were administered from public buildings fortified against the unrepresented majority and jealous feudal landowners. From the end of the 12thC, a magistrate or *podestà*, usually a foreigner, was responsible for law and order. The most prosperous early communes were Arezzo, Florence, Pisa, Pistoia and Siena; a strong economy developed based on commerce, especially the cloth trade, and banking.
1125	Florence took Fiesole, the first, most violent conquest in gradual takeover of Tuscany.
1215	Tuscan participation in long-standing conflict between Pope and Emperor was sparked off by a feud between the Buondelmonti and Amadei clans, according to legend. The words 'Guelf' and 'Ghibelline', for supporters of the Pope and Emperor respectively, were not used for several decades. By 1266 the Guelfs prevailed in Florence, with the two main factions after 1300 named the 'Blacks' and the 'Whites'.
1293	The Ordinances of Justice consolidated the political power of the major guilds, excluding from government the nobility.
1338	The chronicler Villani recorded Florence's population as 90,000. It was Europe's richest city. The Palazzo Vecchio, the churches of S. Maria Novella and S. Croce had been built; the Duomo begun. Internal

politics in the merchant oligarchy were chronically unstable. Dante's comparison of his native city to a sick woman tossing and turning in her bed, searching in any direction for rest and relief, still held.

1342   First of the Florentine bankruptcies after King Edward III of England defaulted on large debts. To reconcile civil factions, a foreigner, Walter of Brienne, Duke of Athens, was granted executive authority, but expelled within the year.

1348   The Black Death killed off more than one-third of the population of Tuscany.

1378   Armed uprising in Florence of the *ciompi*, the lowest-paid employees in the wool industry, seeking guild representation. After initial concessions, the result was a tightening of the merchant oligarchy.

1384   Arezzo fell to Florence which, although at war with Milan and Naples, continued its imperial expansion, gaining Montepulciano (1390), Pisa, the great prize (1406), Cortona (1411) and Livorno (1421). Chroniclers increasingly referred not to Tuscany but to the 'Florentine Empire.'

1434   After a brief exile, Cosimo de' Medici, from a rich business family, became unofficial leader of Florence, initiating a period of unprecedented stability, prosperity and achievement.

1469   Lorenzo the Magnificent, although only 20, was called upon to take charge of the city after the brief reign of Piero, Cosimo's son.

1478   Francesco and Jacopo Pazzi, encouraged by Pope Sixtus IV, made an ill-judged bid for power by plotting the assassination of Lorenzo and his brother Giuliano at High Mass in the Duomo. Giuliano was stabbed to death, Lorenzo escaped. The Pazzi family and its supporters were exiled or executed with the enthusiastic backing of the Florentine public. Sixtus served an interdict on Florence, and excommunicated Lorenzo.

1492   Death of Lorenzo.

1494   Charles VIII of France invaded Italy, took rebellious Pisa under his protection, and entered Florence. The Medici were expelled, and Florence governed according to a new, broader-based republican constitution supported by Savonarola, Dominican prior of S. Marco and a puritanical preacher. Some 3,000 citizens were enfranchized.

1498   Savonarola burned at the stake in the Piazza Signoria as a heretic, with the connivance of the Borgia Pope, Alexander VI.

1502   The democratic constitution proved an inefficient instrument at a time of unremitting war. Piero Soderini was elected head of government for life.

1503–4 Leonardo and Michelangelo commissioned to fresco the walls of the council chamber of the republic with representation of past Florentine victories, but neither work has survived.

1509   Reconquest of Pisa.

1512   The Medici were reinstated as leaders of Florence, and their control subsequently fortified by two Medici Popes, Giovanni as Pope Leo X, and Giulio as Pope Clement VII.

1525	Accademia degli Intronati, the first of the modern literary academies, founded in Siena.
1527	As imperial mercenaries sacked Rome, Florence again expelled the Medici and reinvoked the Savonarolan republican constitution.
1530	Florence besieged by imperial forces. Alessandro de' Medici installed as head of the defeated republic.
1531	Alessandro created first Duke of Florence.
1532	First (posthumous) publication of Machiavelli's *The Prince*.
1537	Cosimo I, from a lateral branch of the Medici family, created Duke of Florence, after assassination of Alessandro. He ruled until 1574.
1555–9	Florentine conquest of Siena and its territories. The concept of Etruria was revived to emphasize the cultural and political unity of Cosimo's enlarged empire.
1563	The Accademia del Disegno, the first fine arts academy in Europe, founded with Cosimo I as its patron.
1569	Cosimo I created Grand Duke of Tuscany by Pope Pius V. Of the six grand dukes who succeeded Cosimo, only his grandson, Ferdinand I (reigned 1587–1609), inherited his gift for leadership.
1582	The Accademia della Crusca, a scholarly body responsible for the purity of the Tuscan language, began work on a definitive Italian dictionary.
1589	Galileo demonstrated the first principles of dynamics at Pisa.
1593	The free port of Livorno, established by Cosimo I, was opened to all immigrants.
1610	Galileo discovered the satellites of Jupiter, the 'Medicean Planets,' and was made court mathematician to Cosimo II.
1737	Gian Gastone, the last of the Medici, died without an heir; the Tuscan grand duchy passed to the house of Lorraine, under whose enlightened rule Tuscany became known as a liberal oasis in a Europe otherwise suffering from despotic and inefficient governments. Administrative procedures and religious foundations were reformed and rationalized; agricultural improvements included draining swampy coastal plains and the Valdichiana.
1753	The Accademia dei Georgofili was founded and supported an agricultural economy.
1799– 1814	French occupation interrupted rule of House of Lorraine, now head of Austrian Empire.
1815	Restoration of Ferdinand III of Lorraine, who continued to implement progressive policies. The Congress of Vienna ceded Monte Argentario, Piombino and Elba to Tuscany. Lucca and Massa Carrara were still separate duchies.
1847	Lucca ceded to Tuscany.
1848	Uprisings spearheaded by middle-class radicals. Leopold II retired to Gaeta but was recalled in a year.
1860	Tuscany voted to be annexed to the united Italy emerging from the wars. The following year, a United Kingdom of Italy was officially proclaimed.
1865 –71	Florence capital of Italy. Part of the old city rebuilt as Piazza della Repubblica.
1944	German bombs destroy Por S. Maria, Ponte Santa

Trinita and Borgo San Jacopo. Outside Florence the most severe war damage was inflicted on Grosseto, Livorno, Pisa and along the 'Gothic Line' from the Versilia through the Mugello into Romagna.

1966   Florence suffered its most severe flood in recorded history. The low-lying Santa Croce area was the worst affected. Some 1,000 paintings and 500 sculptures were damaged or destroyed.

The Renaissance

The first writer to popularize the idea that art was reborn in central Italy shortly after 1300 was Giorgio Vasari in his *Lives*, first published in 1550 at the end of the period he was describing. According to Vasari's anthropomorphic chronology, each art had its own life cycle: in painting Giotto was the representative genius of vigorous youth, Masaccio of early maturity, Michelangelo and Leonardo of perfected prime. Vasari contended that with these late Renaissance masters, art, hitherto devoted to reproducing the appearance of the real world, had finally triumphed over nature and become its own master.

It was not, however, until the publication of the French historian Jules Michelet's *La Renaissance* in 1855 that the word 'renaissance' was applied not only to art but to an entire historic period. Michelet was, in fact, describing 16thC France; but 5yr later Jacob Burckhardt picked up the term and attached it to the spirit of Italian history from 1300–1550. And there, dazzlingly and maddeningly, it has stuck ever since.

The word is out of favor with modern historians. They argue that all period labels are misleading because history is a continuum, not a series of neatly packaged 'ages,' and that this particular label is worse than most because it refers to the activities of an unrepresentative elite minority.

A common reaction to all clinical historiography of the Renaissance is rather like that experienced by the character in E.M. Forster's novel *Where Angels Fear to Tread*. He was forced to think of a dentist operating among the medieval towers of a Tuscan hill town, and found it painful and disgusting to accept "False teeth and laughing gas and the tilting chair at a place which knew . . . . the Renaissance, all fighting and beauty!" The Renaissance is a sensitive subject because it contains the roots of our own civilization; yet we do need the dentist-historians because it is also one of the most complex of historic periods.

Fighting and beauty, yes, but also crises within municipalities, wars between city-states, invasion from without. Deference to the ideas and achievements of ancient Rome and Greece set standards which stimulated every form of thought and practical endeavor. Through the weight of investment, the technique of business practice, and the geographical reach of commerce, capitalism emerged in something very like its modern form.

If to these developments we add transformation in the arts – music and literature as well as painting, sculpture and architecture – then we have a revolution. But a revolution cannot last for 250yr. So we use a label: the Renaissance. Modified, the label came to describe the outward flow from Italy: the English Renaissance, the French Renaissance, and so forth. Inwardly, however, the pulse rate had certainly been set by Tuscany.

Tuscan architecture

Etruscan

Few non-mortuary buildings survive, but evidence suggests Etruscan origins for the atrium, the central courtyard of the Roman house, and a remarkable similarity between the Etruscan villa type and that of 15thC Florentine palaces. The Tuscan order was characterized by plain rounded columns and capitals. Sections of city walls built with huge irregular blocks remain at Volterra, Cortona and other Tuscan towns. Outside the walls, rock-cut underground tombs were constructed.

See *Route 4* in *Planning*.

Roman

The Romans, superb engineers, developed the Tuscan arch as a central structural element – Classical Orders were used mainly for decoration. They were master town-planners, and the most complete city remains are at Fiesole, Roselle and Cosa (now called Ansedonia), one of the earliest and most extensive colonies, still under excavation. Ruins of patrician villas can be seen on Elba, Giannutri and near Porto Santo Stefano.

Romanesque *(11th – 12thC)*

The most influential single building was the Duomo at Pisa, with its tiers of open arcades, a mixture of Lombard and oriental stylistic elements imitated in country churches and at

Etruscan urn (left) in the shape of a house (6th – 3rdC BC), rare evidence about domestic architecture of the period.

San Miniato, Florence (above). The Romanesque facade dates from c.1090.

Duomo, Pisa (left). Begun in 1064, the tiered facade was added in the 12thC.

Monteriggioni. The 13thC walls (below) were built by the Sienese.

Carrara, Pistoia, Prato and Lucca. Florentine churches – the Baptistry, Santi Apostoli, San Miniato – remained more strictly within the Classical tradition; the Collegiata at Empoli marks the western limit of the Florentine influence. The Benedictine Abbey of Sant'Antimo, built in local alabaster but in a style imported from northern Italy, is one of the most incandescently lovely religious buildings in Italy.

Medieval towns bristled with defense towers; those of San Gimignano and Monteriggioni are the best preserved.

Gothic *(13th–14thC)*

Gothic architecture was first introduced into Italy by the French Cistercians who built San Galgano around 1218. A native variation of the Burgundian model emerged first in Florence with the preaching churches of Santa Maria Novella and Santa Croce, and reached its noblest expression there with Arnolfo di Cambio's Duomo. The two loveliest Gothic structures in Florence are the Loggia dei Lanzi and the church of Orsanmichele, also originally a loggia. Civic buildings were conceived as fortresses: the Palazzo della Signoria at Florence is the most imposing of these republican strongholds, the Palazzo Pubblico at Siena the most graceful.

Renaissance *(15thC)*

The innovative genius of Brunelleschi (1377–1446) was nourished first by Florentine Romanesque church architecture,

Palazzo Pubblico, Siena. The most graceful Gothic civic building in Tuscany, built from 1297–1342.

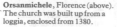

Orsanmichele, Florence (above). The church was built up from a loggia, enclosed from 1380.

Loggia dei Lanzi, Piazza della Signoria, Florence (right). Built from 1376–82.

Innocenti loggia, Piazza SS Annunziata, Florence (below). Completed in 1426, an inaugural building of the Renaissance.

Culture, history and background

later by Byzantine and Classical Roman engineering principles. His Innocenti loggia in Florence is the first building of the Renaissance, and his cupola of the city's Duomo its outstanding engineering achievement. Brunelleschi's genius reached its maturity in Florence with the Pazzi Chapel and Santo Spirito.

Of equal caliber but less influential in the Florence of his own day was the Genoese architect Leon Battista Alberti, whose Rucellai Palace and Chapel are elegant and scholarly restatements of Classical themes, and whose facade of S. M. Novella was later imitated all over Italy.

Michelozzo's Medici Palace in Florence remained the prototype for domestic building in Tuscany until the end of the century; there are fine Renaissance palaces at Pienza and Montepulciano. Perhaps the most magnificent of all Medici villas is Giuliano da Sangallo's symmetrical Poggio a Caiano, with its Classical arcaded basement.

High Renaissance and Mannerist (16thC)

The initiative passed to Rome. Michelangelo's first architectural works, the Laurentian Library and New Sacristy at Florence's San Lorenzo, were Medici commissions, built after he had worked for some years in Rome. His dynamic flouting of Classical order and constructional principles provided inspiration for the later Florentine Mannerist architects, Ammannati and Buontalenti.

Santa Maria Novella, Florence (above).

Rucellai Palace, Florence (above), built from the 1450s.

◀ **Medici Riccardi Palace**, Florence (left), built from 1444–64.

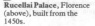

Villa Medici, Poggio a Caiano (1480–85), Giuliano da Sangallo's adaptation of the antique Roman villa type.

24

The classicizing influence of the Roman High Renaissance style, founded by Bramante, is most evident in Antonio da Sangallo the Elder's domed church of San Biagio at Montepulciano, with a Greek cross plan.

Two 16thC Medici villas near Florence, Artimino and Petraia, were built by Buontalenti for Ferdinand I, and Giuliano di Baccio d'Agnolo's Palazzo Campana at Colle di Val d'Elsa shows Mannerist architecture at its most elegant.

Baroque and Neoclassical (17th–18thC)

The swirling theatricality of the Baroque was created in Rome, but Florence boasts some fine church facades: G. Silvani's San Gaetano is the most beautiful, and Ferdinando Ruggieri's San Firenze the largest and boldest. The master of Italian Baroque, Bernini, added the Chigi Chapel to the Duomo in Siena. Interesting palaces in Florence include the *trompe l'oeil* Cartelloni in Via S. Antonino, the Capponi in Via G. Capponi, and the Corsini on the Lungarno Corsini.

Modern (19th–20thC)

The seafront at Viareggio is lined with splendid Liberty-style hotels, and in Florence the Villino Broggi, Via Scipione Ammirato 99, is another delightful example of Liberty architecture. The 19thC cast-iron arcades of the Mercato Centrale show the use of new materials which culminated in the functionalist Florence Station and Nervi's Stadium.

Laurentian Library steps, San Lorenzo, Florence (left), by Michelangelo (1550s).

San Biagio, Montepulciano (above), designed by Antonio da Sangallo the elder, built 1518–45.

◀ **San Gaetano**, Florence (left), the best Baroque church facade in Florence, built in 1648.

Central Station, Florence (below). The first functionalist station in Italy, built in 1935.
▼

Tuscan sculpture

Etruscan

Etruscan sculpture was broadly Greek-based, but more vigorous and less rational in character. The finest examples in Tuscany are in the Florence Archeological Museum, but exceptional pieces do remain at Chiusi, Cortona and Volterra; and the museum at Grosseto is a beautifully organized introduction to the subject.

See *Route 4* in *Planning*.

Roman

Roman humanism led to a new emphasis on portraiture, and the Uffizi possesses one of the most distinguished collections of Roman busts in the world. The sarcophaghi in the Pisa Camposanto affected the new sculptural art created by the Pisani in the 13th–14thC, and Roman columns and capitals were often incorporated into Romanesque churches.

Romanesque

Romanesque figure sculpture developed relatively late in Tuscany. In Florence the work is mainly decorative, with Classical or Oriental motifs, as illustrated in San Miniato and the Baptistry.

Pisa emerged as the leading center in the late 12thC and produced the first named Tuscan sculptors: Guglielmo, whose ornate style is demonstrated in the decorations of the Pisa Duomo and Baptistry; and Bonanno, famous for the bronze doors of the Pisa Duomo. Followers of the Lombard Master Antelmi worked in Arezzo, the Casentino, Massa Marittima and Volterra. The wealth of Romanesque sculpture at Pistoia includes the more austere and highly individual work of Gruamonte.

The Pisani and the Gothic

Nicola Pisano and his son Giovanni (active 1258–1314) created a realistic and expressive figure style which looks modern even today. Their four famous pulpits in Tuscany are in the Pisa Duomo and Baptistry, the Siena Duomo and in the church of Sant'Andrea at Pistoia. Giovanni also carved the figures for the facade of the Siena Duomo which have now been removed to the Museo dell'Duomo, as well as a *Madonna* in the Pisa Duomo and a *Madonna and Child* in the Prato Duomo. They and their immediate successors, Andrea and Nino Pisano, and Tino da Camaiano, established Pisa and Siena as the most active centers, although Andrea is best known for the first doors of the Florence Baptistry. Tino's works are scattered, but well represented in the Duomos of Pisa and Siena and the Bardini Museum, Florence.

The exquisite relief carvings of another Sienese sculptor, Goro di Gregorio, on the tomb of St Cerbone in the Massa Marittima Duomo, demonstrate the continuing influence of illuminated manuscripts on Gothic sculpture despite the example of the Pisani. The most important Florentine Gothic sculptors were Andrea Orcagna, whose principal works are the relief carvings of the Orsanmichele Tabernacle in Florence, and Nanni di Banco, whose sinuous relief of the *Assumption* over the Porta della Mandorla of the Florence Duomo and the classical *Four Crowned Saints* on the facade of Orsanmichele point gently but firmly toward the dawning Renaissance.

15thC Renaissance

The richest collection of Renaissance sculpture is in the Florence Bargello, where, among many key pieces, are the

Donatello and Verrocchio *Davids*, and works by the Della
Robbias, Desiderio da Settignano, Antonio Pollaiuolo and
Antonio Rossellino, demonstrating the variety of
interpretations of the ideals and proportion of Classical
sculpture. The two best places in Florence to study the
evolution of Florentine sculpture from Gothic to Renaissance
are the exteriors of the Baptistry and Orsanmichele. Lorenzo
Ghiberti's first set of Baptistry doors, on the N, are still late
Gothic; the second set, on the E, are fully of the Renaissance.
Ghiberti is represented on the facade of Orsanmichele, as is the
transitional work of Nanni di Banco. Donatello's St George
predella, the earliest example of perspective in relief carving, has
now followed the St George into the Bargello.

Donatello, who infused feeling and tension into Classical
forms, was the dominant genius of 15thC sculpture. To
appreciate his full range one must visit the Duomo Museum and
the churches of Santa Croce and San Lorenzo as well as the
Bargello.

The greatest master outside Florence was the Sienese Jacopo
della Quercia whose animated works in Siena include the
original carvings from the Fonte Gaia in the Palazzo Pubblico.

16thC Renaissance

The Florentine Michelangelo held that sculpture was the
highest art form, and his work in this medium has an
unprecedented expressive range. Important works at Florence
include his first carvings in the Casa Buonarroti and his last in
the Duomo Museum, as well as the *David* and *Slaves* in the
Accademia and the Medici Tombs in San Lorenzo.

Michelangelo's overpowering genius has caused his
contemporaries and Mannerist successors to be seen in an
unfair light in the eyes of posterity. A recently arranged room in
the Bargello is designed to show his influence on, as well as the
individual talents of, Andrea Sansovino, Vincenzo Rossi,
Vincenzo Danti, Giambologna and, most impressive,
Benvenuto Cellini. Outside Florence, the most exciting works
are Domenico Beccafumi's uncharacteristically restrained eight
bronze angels in the Siena Duomo.

Baroque and Rococo *(17th–18thC)*

The ivories in Florence's Argenti Museum express all the
inherent fantastication of the Baroque and Rococo spirit, and
Ferdinando Tacca's tomb sculptures in the San Lorenzo
Cappella dei Principi convey its authoritative courtliness.

The greatest Baroque sculpture was created and mostly
remains in Rome, although there are some Berninis in the
Bargello, Florence and the Siena Duomo. The Florentine
Pietro Tacca, sculptor to the grand dukes, produced a number
of notable works including the lovable and much-patted
Porcellino Fountain in the Florence Mercato Nuovo, and the
strange, wicked fountains in Santissima Annunziata. His four
Moors at Livorno are strenuous but empty of meaning. G.B.
Foggini, one of the most prolific Florentine Baroque artists,
both as sculptor and architect, is increasingly admired,
especially for his decorative stucco reliefs in the Carmine and
Santissima Annunziata.

19th–20thC

There is a revival of interest in early 19thC sculptor Lorenzo
Bartolini, whose work has a smoothly accomplished feel. There
are works by Marino Marini in his native Pistoia and at Florence
in the Alberto della Ragione Collection in the Piazza Signoria
and in the new Marini Museum next to the Rucellai Chapel.

Tuscan painting

Etruscan

The only Etruscan painted tombs now in Tuscany are in the
Florence Archeological Museum and at Chiusi.

The Byzantine Manner (12th–13thC)

Each center developed the so-called Byzantine Manner in its
own way, as one can see from the many painted crosses in
Tuscan churches. Panel paintings of other subjects are now
more usually in museums, although Bonaventura Berlinghieri's
St Francis has been left in San Francesco, Pescia. Other Tuscan
masters were Giunta Pisano and the St Martin Master,
represented at the Museo Nazionale at Pisa, Margarito
d'Arezzo, at the Galleria, Arezzo, and Guido da Siena, on show
at the Pinacoteca Nazionale, Siena.

Towards the end of the 13thC iconic stylization began to give
way to the more vigorous monumentality of Cimabue and the
Gothic grace and humanity of the Sienese master Duccio.
Cimabue's famous *Crucifixion* is in the S. Croce Museum,
Florence; he is also represented in the Uffizi and at
S. Domenico, Arezzo, and the mosaics he worked on are in the
Florence Baptistry and Pisa Duomo. Duccio is on show in his
hometown in the Museo dell'Opera Duomo and Pinacoteca
Nazionale, and at S. Francesco in Grosseto and the Uffizi.

Giottesque Realism and the International Gothic (14thC)

At the turn of the 13thC Giotto introduced a new kind of
painting, representing solid forms placed in three-dimensional
space and conveying the humanity of its subjects. His example
determined the course of Florentine painting through the High
Renaissance. His principal works in Florence are in the Bardi
and Peruzzi Chapels of S. Croce and in the Uffizi.

Two schools dominated Tuscan painting: Giottesque
Realism from Florence, and the International Gothic from
Siena. Giotto's successors include Taddeo Gaddi, Bernardo
Daddi, Giottino, Agnolo Gaddi and Spinello Aretino: they
refined his settings, but never quite matched his psychological
power. Two Florentine painters who rejected Giotto's example
and worked within the graceful but two-dimensional Gothic
tradition were Andrea Orcagna and Lorenzo Monaco. In
Florence 14thC painting is best represented in the churches of
S. Croce and S. M. Novella.

The great Tuscan interpreter of the International Gothic was
the Sienese master Simone Martini, whose major works are in
the Palazzo Pubblico and Pinacoteca Nazionale at Siena, the
Museo Nazionale in Pisa, and the Uffizi. Along with the Horne
Museum, Florence, these galleries also house works of the
Sienese Lorenzetti brothers, Pietro and Ambrogio, who
combined elements from both styles.

The Renaissance (15thC)

The astonishing story of Florentine *quattrocento* painting is best
told in the Uffizi, where portable works from the Medici
collections and Tuscan churches are arranged chronologically,
enabling one to follow the various innovations, preoccupations
and influences: perspective, light, anatomy, Neo-Platonic and
Christian symbolism, and the first contact with Flemish
Realism.

Fortunately, more masterpieces have remained outside this
didactic sanctuary than can be listed here. They include, in
Florence, the Carmine Masaccios, the Medici Palace Gozzoli
cycle, the S. Apollonia Castagnos, the S. Marco Angelicos, the

S.M. Novella Uccellos, and the Ghirlandaios in Ognissanti, S.M. Novella and S. Trinità.

The greatest masterpieces outside Florence are the Piero della Francescas at San Francesco, Arezzo, in the little church at Monterchi, and, at Sansepolcro, the *Misericordia* altarpiece and *Resurrection*. Filippo Lippi's outstanding works are the lovely frescoes in the Prato Duomo. The Museo Diocesano in Cortona possesses one major Angelico and a number of Signorellis. There are delightful narrative cycles at San Gimignano by Ghirlandaio in the Collegiata and Gozzoli in San Agostino.

High Renaissance and Mannerist (16thC)
Florence lost its artistic supremacy. The two greatest Tuscan geniuses, Michelangelo and Leonardo, left Tuscany after the first few years of the century. Only one painting by Michelangelo and three by Leonardo remain in Tuscany, all in the Uffizi, where there are also fine works by other 16thC masters including Andrea del Sarto and the early Mannerists.

The disturbing, highly intellectual style later called Mannerism was the last original Florentine contribution to mainstream Italian painting. The leading Tuscan Mannerist painters were Rosso Fiorentino, Pontormo, Bronzino, Salviati, Sodoma, Beccafumi.

The richest collection of 16thC paintings in Tuscany is at Florence in the Pitti's Palatine Gallery, where Cristoforo Allori's ravishing *Judith* sums up many of the achievements of the century, and where masters from other Italian centers compete for attention with Florentines, including Andrea del Sarto, Fra Bartolommeo, and the Mannerists.

At Arezzo, Vasari decorated his own house with allegorical frescoes which have a freshness and charm lacking in his official work. The great Pontormos outside Florence can be seen within a day. They are in S. Michele at Carmignano, at the Certosa Pinacoteca, Galluzzo, and at Poggio a Caiano. The Rossos are farther flung and are to be found at the Galleria, Arezzo, at S. Lorenzo, Sansepolcro; and one of his most stirring works, the *Deposition*, is housed in the Galleria Pittorica at Volterra.

Baroque and Rococo (17th–18thC)
The Baroque, like the Gothic, was a style Florentine artists never embraced wholeheartedly. The most splendid Baroque decorations are in the Pitti Palace, where the first rooms of the Palatine Gallery were frescoed by Pietro da Cortona, and in the ground-floor rooms of the Argenti Museum by A.M. Colonna and Giovanni da S. Giovanni.

The Florentine Rococo painters were not original but cannot be ignored. Their decorations, mainly frescoes, can be seen in many churches, notably San Firenze, the Badia and Ognissanti.

19th–20thC
The Pitti Gallery of Modern Art displays a vast collection of 19thC academic paintings. Several rooms there are devoted to the Tuscan school, known as the 'Macchiaioli' after their Impressionistic 'blotted' paintings, which reacted against the academic style. Also in Florence, the Alberto della Ragione Collection in the Piazza Signoria contains some interesting 20thC figurative pictures by Tuscan artists.

At Livorno, the Museo Civico possesses several works by Modigliani, who was born here, and by the Macchiaioli, for whom the town was a major center. The Futurist Gino Severini was born in Cortona, where a room in the Museo dell'Accademia Etrusca is devoted to his life and work.

Tuscany and literature

The great period of Tuscan literature began prodigiously, with three writers whose words have since been the chief shaping influence on the Italian language. Dante (1265–1321) was hounded out of his native Florence in 1302 into an exile during which he wrote the greatest work in the language, the *Divine Comedy*, a comprehensive vision of this and the next world. He signed himself "Dante Alighieri, a Florentine by birth but not by character," and his love-hate feelings for the beautiful city which ejected him are especially pungent in the first two parts of the poem, *Inferno* and *Purgatorio*. Spiritualized love is represented by the figure of Dante's Beatrice. Laura was the love of Italy's second greatest poet, Petrarch, born in Arezzo in 1304 to a father who had been exiled in the same purge as Dante. A good translation conveys the meticulous delicacy of his vastly influential love sonnets. His close friend Boccaccio, born in Certaldo in 1313, is the third of the 14thC Tuscan triumvirate. The hundred tales of his *Decameron* start with a description of Florence during the Black Death of 1348.

The traveler who has gone to Italy to study the tactile values of Giotto, or the corruption of the Papacy, may return remembering nothing but the blue sky and the men and women who live under it.

E. M. Forster, *A Room with a View* (1908)

The next burst of Tuscan vernacular literary talent came late in the 15thC with the subtle, polished poetry of Pulci, Poliziano and Lorenzo de' Medici; little has been worthily translated. Thereafter it was chiefly in prose that Tuscans of genius expressed themselves. Machiavelli's brief *The Prince* (written 1513) still retains the incandescence of its conviction that politics is not about morals but about getting things done, and the *Maxims* of his friend Guicciardini (1483–1540) conveys the realistic appraisal of human affairs Tuscans have prided themselves on ever since. *Storia d'Italia*, Guicciardini's account of the wars and crises of 1492–1534, has been called the most important work to have issued from an Italian mind.

The poems of Michelangelo, unusually troubled and ecstatic for the period, offer a balancing vision not only of his work but also of his times, as does the marvelously picaresque and direct self-revelation of Cellini's *Autobiography* (1558).

It was a scientist, Galileo (1564–1642), who was to be the last great writer of Tuscan prose. Since his *Dialogue Concerning the Two Chief World Systems* and *The Two New Sciences*, Tuscany has contributed little to the mainstream of Italian literature apart from two exceptional 20thC Florentine novels: Aldo Palazzeschi's *Sorelle Materassi* (1934), about genteel poverty in a Florentine suburb; and Vasco Pratolini's *Cronache di Poveri Amanti* (1947), a picture of working-class life in Santa Croce.

In the early 19thC Tuscany began to play a different literary role. Florence, the city which had exiled its own greatest geniuses, was now capital of a region which Shelley, in his famous letter to Medwin of 1820, described as the "paradise of exiles." Dostoevsky (1821–81) was one of these literary exiles, but mostly they were British or American, often taking refuge in Tuscany because the living was cheap, the climate healthy and the peace and order of its landscape and depth of its history cast a spell on the foreign imagination.

Many writers discovered in Tuscany their ideal working environment. Mark Twain, working on *Pudd'nhead Wilson* in Settignano in the 1890s, claimed he had written more in four months than he could in two years at home. Henry James pronounced the atmosphere of Florence better for mental concentration than Venice. D.H. Lawrence wrote *Lady Chatterley's Lover* (1928) sitting on the grass outside his villa at Scandicci, inspired, so his friends said, by contact with a sympathetic alien culture. Nathaniel Hawthorne, James Fenimore Cooper and Arnold Bennett all enjoyed productive visits to Florence.

Yet the many foreign poets and novelists who have attempted to write *about* Tuscany have generally failed. Elizabeth Barrett Browning's long verse polemics about the Risorgimento (1847–61) and George Eliot's novel *Romola* (1863) about Renaissance Florence are among the most ambitious and most unreadable efforts. William Dean Howells' *Indian Summer* (1886) is one of the more delightful of novels set in Tuscany; Anatole France's satire *Le Lys Rouge* (1894) is perhaps the sharpest and funniest; E.M. Forster's *Where Angels Fear to Tread* (1905) and *A Room with a View* (1908) are the ones which are still widely read.

Much of this fiction takes place within the foreign community, a large various group of cultivated aliens given to making crucial excursions into a landscape where the senses and intellects of the repressed Northern European may open and flower. Italians, when they appear at all, are often lazy opportunists or forces of nature. Stendhal (1783–1842) was unusual as a foreigner who really did want to understand how Tuscans of all classes lived and thought. The others, even those passionate 'Italophiles' the Brownings, didn't often meet real Italians, and their fictional treatments of Tuscany suffer from what Charles Greville, writing about Florentine society in 1830, described as "no foundation of natives."

The only novelist who turned the Florentine foreign community into the subject of truly great literature was Henry James (1843–1916). James did not wish to be regarded as one of the crowd of 'local' novelists, and disguised or sublimated his source material. Nevertheless, there is something of Florence in most of his Italian novels, and many of his characters are based in whole or part on Florentine acquaintances. *The Aspern Papers* is a notable example – although set in Venice, it was inspired by the story of Jane Clairmont, mother of Byron's daughter Allegra and stepsister of Mary Shelley, who spent her old age in voluntary exile in Florence in possession of many of Shelley's papers. James' concern with the experience of exile and the meeting of cultures gives us perhaps the truest impression of Florence as a paradise of exiles.

Reading list

In addition to books mentioned above, Giorgio Vasari's *Lives of the Painters, Sculptors and Architects* is still the essential basis of all the art history. Guidebooks: Eve Borsook's *Companion Guide to Florence* (revised 1985) is readable, learned and full of fascinating detail; also, the Touring Club Italiano guides *Firenze e Dintorni* and *Toscana*. J.R. Hale's *Florence and the Medici* is the clearest account of how and why the Medici took control; Harold Acton's *The Last Medici* closes the story. Judith Hook's *Siena* is a short account of the history and art. Mary McCarthy's *The Stones of Florence* is a vivid, personal essay. Also recommended: Iris Origo's *The Merchant of Prato*, on Renaissance commerce, *The World of San Bernardino*, on religious life, *War in Val d'Orcia*, on occupation and liberation.

Orientation map

Pontremoli

LUNIGIANA

A15

A12

Cp

Carrara

Massa

Apuan Alps

GARFAGNAN

13

A11/12

Monte
T

Viareggio

14

A12

Lucca

1

A11

P

N

* **Pisa**

R. Arne

67

A12

1

Livorno

Castiglioncello

15

1

Sandy beaches

1   Versilia
2   Gulf of Barratti
3   Riva del Sole to Principina a Mare
4   La Cannelle
5   Spiaggia di S. Libertà
6   Spiaggia La Feniglia
7   Ansedonia to Lago di Burano
8   Elba
9   Giglio

Skiing

10   Abetone

Spas

11   Montecatini Terme
12   Chianciano Terme

Resorts

13   Forte dei Marmi
14   Viareggio
15   Castiglioncello
16   Elba
17   Punta Ala
18   Castiglione della Pescaia
19   Monte Argentario
20   Giglio
21   Ansedonia
*   Towns of major artistic/scenic interest

2

Piombino

Elba 16

8

8

8   8   8   8   8

km
0   20   40   60   80

miles
0   10   25   50

Autostrade
Principal roads

Apennines

325

Pistoia ✳
A1
Prato
A11
MUGELLO

FIRENZE

69

CASENTINO

✳
Empoli

Bibbiena ●

Pratomagno Hills

429

CHIANTI

A1

Gimignano
Poggibonsi

Arezzo ✳

erra ✳

71

Colle di
V. d'Elsa

2

Siena ✳
326

Lucignano ●
Cortona ●

a Marittima
✳

Valchiana

A1

Montepulciano ✳
■ 12

223

Pienza ✳

MAREMMA

R. Ombrone

1

Monte Amiata
2

Grosseto ●

1

Pitigliano ✳

ate Argentario
5

1
4 6 2 1 7

siglio
9
20

19

Ⓒ
Giannutri

33

Calendar of events

January/February

Viareggio. *Carnevale*. The most colorful of Tuscan carnivals, in the weeks before Lent, culminating on Shrove Tuesday. Masked processions, fireworks, and soccer matches

March

Florence. Italian and international high fashion collections shown in the Sala Bianca of the Pitti Palace

April

Easter Day. Florence. *Scoppio del Carro* (Explosion of the Cart). A cart laden with flowers and fireworks is drawn by three pairs of white oxen to the Duomo. At noon mass, during the Gloria, a firework rocket in the shape of a dove is lit at the high altar and whizzes the length of the nave along a wire attached to the cart

　　Florence. Crafts exhibition at the Fortezza da Basso. Continues through May

　　Florence. Flower display in Piazza Signoria and Uffizi. Through to June

　　Lucca. Sacred music festival in the churches. Lasts until late June

May

Florence. Iris show in Piazzale Michelangelo. The largest European collection of the symbolic 'lily of Florence'

　　May 20 or next Sun. Massa Marittima. *Balestro del Girifalco* (Joust of the Falcon). Procession, flag-waving and crossbow shooting at mechanical falcon in Piazza d.Duomo, all in 15thC costume. Again in Aug

　　Mid-May to late June. Florence. *Maggio Musicale*. Opera, ballet and concerts

June

Fiesole. Summer festival. Concerts, ballet, theater. Through to Sept

　　June 17. Pisa. *Regata di San Ranieri*. The buildings facing the Arno are illuminated with torches the evening before the boat race

　　June 24. Florence. Feast of St John the Baptist, patron saint of the city. Fireworks over the Arno from Piazzale Michelangelo. *Gioco del Calcio Storico*. The traditional rough soccer game in 16thC costume in Piazza Signoria

　　June 28. Florence. Second *Gioco del Calcio*

　　June 28. Pisa. *Gioco del Ponte*. Mock 16thC battle

July

July 2. Siena. *Palio*. The most serious of all historic spectacles. The bareback horserace around the Piazza del Campo is fiercely contested. Before the event there are processions and rehearsals. Again in Aug

　　Siena. *Accademia Musicale Chigiana*. Music festival

August

Torre del Lago Puccini. Festival of Puccini operas

　　2nd Sun. Massa Marittima. *Balestro del Girifalco* (see May)

　　Aug 15, Assumption Day. Florence. *Festa del Grillo*. Caged crickets are sold in the fair in the Cascine

　　Aug 15–16. Montepulciano. *Il Bruscello*. Folklore and song festival

　　Porto Santo Stefano. *Palio Marinaro*. Parade in the square and rowing race

　　Aug 16. Siena. Second *Palio* (see July)

September

1st Sun. Arezzo. *Giostra del Saracino*. Eight horsemen in 13thC costume joust against a mechanical Saracen, in the Piazza Grande

　　1st week. Greve. Chianti Classico wine fair

　　Sept 7. Florence. *Festa delle Rificolone* (Lantern Day). On the eve of the Nativity of the Virgin children race through the streets carrying colored paper lanterns. The following evening the Via dei Servi is lined with candy stalls and the children parade carrying lanterns from the Duomo to SS. Annunziata

　　2nd Sun. Sansepolcro. *Palio della Balestra*. Crossbow competition in medieval costume

　　Sept 14. Lucca. *Festa della Santa Croce*. On Holy Cross Eve, a miraculous wooden effigy of Christ is carried from the cathedral to the church of S.Frediano and back

　　Florence. Alternate years. Antiques fair at Palazzo Strozzi. Through to Nov

　　Sept 28. Florence. On St Michael's Eve, at the beginning of the hunting season, hunting equipment and birds of every kind, from hawks to owls, are sold at Porta Romana

October

Prato. Season opens at Teatro Metastasio. The home company is one of the liveliest experimental theater groups in Italy. Until April

Florence. Winter fashion collections shown in Pitti

Mid-Oct. Impruneta. Agricultural fair of St Luke

Last Sun. Montalcino. *Sagra del Tordo*. Traditional shooting and eating of thrushes

November

Florence. Opening of main concert season at Teatro Comunale. Through to mid-Dec

December

Florence. Opening of opera season at Teatro Comunale. Through to mid-Jan

See also *Public holidays* in *Basic information.*

When and where to go

May and Sept are the ideal months to visit Florence; cool enough for vigorous sightseeing, summery enough for leisurely day trips into the hills. The countryside in May is radiant with wildflowers, scented with blossoms and young grasses. For the grand tourists of the 18th and 19thC, Sept was the start of the Florence season, and a very sensible time it still is, a little warmer and drier than May, and less crowded than Aug, which is in every way the most uncomfortable month.

In fact, those who do not wish to share their vacation with what seems like half the world should avoid Florence, a city ill-suited to mass tourism, in the week before and including Easter and from June through to the end of Aug. Overcrowding, as regular visitors know, can render the narrow medieval streets barely tolerable. However, if you must go in the high season, be sure to book a hotel in advance.

Whatever the season, the day will come when Florence seems too much: too much art, too much noise in the narrow streets, a stony maze from which one longs to escape. This is the day to go to Siena, gently dreaming on its landlocked hills, or to Lucca, proud and independent in its star of intact fortifications, the two most likeable provincial capitals.

Pisa should be visited for its churches and pictures as well as for the famous Duomo complex. There is pre-Renaissance sculpture in Pisa, Prato and Pistoia, and Renaissance churches in Prato and near Cortona and Montepulciano as fine and important as anything in Florence. The Renaissance paintings which stir the modern soul most profoundly are the Piero della Francescas in and near Arezzo.

Then there are the smaller hill towns, each with its own distinctive shape and character: San Gimignano still bristling with medieval watchtowers; windy Volterra; Romanesque-Gothic Massa Marittima; Pienza and Montepulciano like miniature Renaissance cities. In fact, there is hardly a town or village in Tuscany that is not worth visiting.

The Tuscan countryside is as elusive to the would-be categorizer as it is inspiring to native and visitor alike. Geographically there is no such thing as one Tuscany. Each of the valleys, mountains, plains and stretches of coast has its own beauty, and, as often as not, its own micro-climate. The best-laid plan for visiting Tuscany is the one that leaves room for spontaneous exploration and personal discovery.

Area planners and tours

Historically, Tuscany has been dominated by Florence since the late Middle Ages, but the region's constituent areas have in no way surrendered their individuality to their presiding sovereign. The names of these areas can often baffle foreigners because they have no administrative significance and no precisely defined geographical boundaries. For Tuscans they sum up everything, from the climate and landscape to the character of the native population and the local food and wine. Six of the most enticing are described here.

The Casentino The remote upper valley of the Arno, to the N of Arezzo, enclosed by wooded mountains. The magnificent specimen forests of beech, fir and chestnut, and the green pastures where white oxen can still occasionally be seen, are loveliest in spring and remain cool even in high summer. The monastic sanctuaries of Camaldoli and La Verna are good bases for walking, picnicking, and gathering wild strawberries and mushrooms. Hotels are few and simple.

The Chianti The heart of Tuscany and the landscape that matches many people's ideal of the way Italy ought to look. The area that originally gave its name to the wine has expanded over the centuries to include everywhere the wine is produced, which is now from a little to the N of Florence down to Siena. May is the best time, but in high summer, when Florence is hot and full of tourists and the Tuscan coast is crowded with Florentines, there is much to be said for basing a vacation on the Chianti. Alternatively, you could spend a long winter weekend riding or walking along the Etruscan roads which crest the hills, tasting and shopping for wine. Many villas, castles, abbeys and farmhouses have been converted into hotels or residences.

The Garfagnana The landscape of the upper valley of the fast-flowing Serchio and the valleys of its tributaries is one of the most fascinating in Tuscany for the variety of climate and vegetation. The chilly marble peaks of the Apuan Alps contrast with the lower slopes of the Apennines, wooded with magnificent chestnuts and luxuriant vegetation, and the mild, humid air of the lower altitudes. Lucca is just to the S, and Barga is the prettiest hill village.

The Maremma The word means coastal plain, but it is now most often associated with the province of Grosseto, including the coast known as the Costa d'Argento (between Alberese and Ansedonia), the promontory of Monte Argentario and, inland, the foothills of Monte Amiata. The Etruscan-red soil is wonderfully fertile, producing vegetables, fruit, grain, flowers and vines in colorful abundance. The many Etruscan sites remind one that the Maremma was probably more densely populated in the pre-Christian era than it is now. The natives, physically tough and independent-minded, regard themselves as the wild westerners of Tuscany; the local cowboys, less often seen than they were, are known as *butteri*. Apart from the Etruscan and Roman sites, you should at least visit Massa Marittima, Pitigliano and the nature reserve of Monti dell'Uccellina. There are very few hotels except on the coast, but some excellent country restaurants.

The Mugello In the early Renaissance the river basin of the Sieve, the homeland of Giotto and the Medici, was considered to be the healthiest and most beautiful of the rural areas near the city of Florence. Protected by the Apennines to the N and well-watered by mountain springs, the climate of this lovely

gentle green valley is more temperate than that of the Arno.
The Versilia This coastal strip in northern Tuscany boasts the region's longest uninterrupted stretch of white sandy beach, and has an even, balmy climate with mild winters and light rainfall. Forte dei Marmi is fashionable with Italians; Viareggio's prime is past, but it still has a certain decaying period charm. Some of the other resorts are squalid. There are a staggering 690 hotels, some excellent, and plenty of good fish restaurants.

Route 1: Pisa to Florence
Uninitiated visitors to Tuscany, automatically whisked from Pisa Airport to Florence, are often left with a dim impression of the intervening country, which does not reveal its treasures from the autostrada. Apart from three of the most artistically important Tuscan cities – Lucca, Pistoia and Prato – this slower, more interesting itinerary embraces Romanesque churches, Medici villas, radiant mountain landscapes, and some of the best restaurants in Tuscany. It is well worth the luxury of a rented car. Anyone unfamiliar with the highlights of the trip could allow two or three days. Otherwise, sections of the route could be followed as day excursions from Florence by taking the autostrada as far as Pisa, Lucca or Pistoia and then returning along the suggested roads.

Leave *Pisa* by the SS12 for *Lucca*, via S. Giuliano Terme and S. Maria del Giudice, where there are two Romanesque churches. From Lucca's Porta Elisa follow the SS435 for *Pescia*, turning off for the Romanesque church of S.Gennaro and for *Collodi*, on the left. After Pescia the road descends alongside River Pescia to *Montecatini Terme*. Heading now for *Pistoia*, one passes the remains of medieval fortifications at Serravalle. Take the *Empoli* road from Pistoia's Porta Leonardo da Vinci; it winds over Monte Albano, commanding ravishing views of the Arno valley as it approaches *Vinci* through woodland and olive groves. From Vinci, turn left on to the pretty *Carmignano* road which runs for 16km (10 miles) along the s flank of the Albano mountains through pine woods, olives and the vineyards which produce some of the finest Tuscan wines, and past the Romanesque church of S.Giusto. There is a tempting view of Florence from Carmignano, but don't miss the opportunity to visit the Etruscan tombs near Comeana, the village and Medici villa of *Artimino*, and another Medici villa at *Poggio a Caiano*, all within 10km (6 miles) of Carmignano. *Prato* is 8km (5 miles) N of Poggio a Caiano. Aiming now for Florence, eschew the autostrada and choose instead the Roman road along the base of the Calvana and Morello mountains, for *Sesto Fiorentino* and *Castello*.

Route 2: The Chianti

In May, when the landscape of the Chianti is at its loveliest, this short journey into the heart of Tuscany is one of the essential pleasures of a Florentine holiday: all year round, it is a uniquely Tuscan delight. Blue signs point to the wine growers who will be happy to let you taste their produce and will sell wine, beautifully packaged, by the bottle or cellarful. Since there are some 250 producers in the Chianti Classico zone selling wine under their own labels, it can be difficult to select the best; see *Tuscan wines* for suggestions.

Visitors who want only one leisurely day's outing from Florence can simplify the itinerary by taking the Chiantigiana to Siena and returning to Florence on the SS2 or the autostrada. The whole circular tour can be made to fit into a busy day.

The starting point from Florence is Piazza F. Ferrucci. Take the 18thC wine road, the Strada Chiantigiana, SS222, the classic route into the Chianti which it bisects lengthwise. After Grassina the vista opens on to a hilly landscape punctuated by medieval towers. Shortly after passing the splendid Baroque Villa Ugolino, you are ushered in by a large notice into the Chianti Classico wine zone. The road now descends to *Greve*. Just to the s, on the road for Lamole to the left, is the privately owned Renaissance Villa Vignamaggio, which appears in the background of an early drawing by Leonardo and where some romantics like to imagine the *Mona Lisa* was painted. At *Castellina* you can turn left onto SS429 into the historic center of the Chianti for *Radda* and *Gaiole*, and then approach *Siena* by the old Chiantigiana, SS408. Otherwise, continue s via Fonterutoli towards Siena, which you will enter close to the station. If you do not intend to visit Siena, turn right N of the city on to the SS2 for *Monteriggioni*, taking care to avoid the motorway entrance. After Monteriggioni, turn left for *Colle di Val d'Elsa*, *San Gimignano*, and *Certaldo*, each rising up one after another like medieval mirages. From Certaldo a sound but unspectacular road carries you NE across the Elsa and Pesa valleys for 23km (14 miles), past the castles of S.Maria Novella and Lucardo to *San Casciano*, at the NW limit of the Classico zone. Admirers of Machiavelli will want to rejoin the approach road to Florence by way of S.Andrea in Percussina (see *San Casciano*). After a stop at *Galluzzo*, one re-enters *Florence* by the *Porta Romana*.

Route 3: Florence to Arezzo by the Pratomagno and Casentino

The drive to *Vallombrosa*, less than an hour from Florence, is a favorite Florentine family day outing. By allowing two days for this route to Arezzo you would have time also to visit the remoter monastic retreats of *Camaldoli* and *La Verna*.

From Florence, follow the SS67 along the N bank of the Arno, pausing at Sieci to admire the view of the Arno from the weir and the church of S. Giovanni Battista a Remole, with its splendid Romanesque campanile. After crossing the Sieve at *Pontassieve*, take the narrower road, SS70, signposted to Consuma, which climbs through vineyards and olives and soon passes the castle of Nipozzano on the left. Owned by the Frescobaldi family, its vineyards produce an outstanding Chianti Riserva. Just past Borselli, a short detour to the left passes the Romanesque church of Tosina on the way to Pomino, another of the Frescobaldi properties, where the grapes for the excellent Pomino white wine are grown. Back on SS70, the road now climbs more steeply through beech, fir and pine woods towards Consuma. Just 1km (0.6 miles) before the village a right turn leads to *Vallombrosa*, secluded in its dense beechwood on the eastern slope of Monte Secchieta.

Those who wish to return to Florence may vary the route by returning to Pontassieve via Tosi and Pelago. Otherwise, return to the SS70 and turn right towards Poppi, crossing the Pratomagno range through the Consuma pass. Descending into the Casentino you can see Monte Falterona, where the Arno has its source, on the left, and ahead the castle of *Poppi*, like a transplanted Palazzo Vecchio. Fork left 10km (6 miles) after Consuma for the castle of Romena, the Romanesque church of Romena on a parallel road, and *Stia*. From there turn right onto the SS310 via Pratovecchio, where Paolo Uccello was born in 1397, and along the E bank of the Arno, past Campaldino, where Dante fought in the battle of 1289 against Arezzo, to *Poppi*. The road for the monastery and then the hermitage of *Camaldoli* is on the left just beyond Poppi. Then descend via Serravalle onto SS71 to *Bibbiena*, where a left turn onto the SS208 leads to the famous Franciscan sanctuary of *La Verna* high up in the mountains which separate the Arno and Tiber valleys. The road from La Verna via Chitignano, which rejoins the SS71 for Arezzo at Rassina, is rough in places but worth choosing for the views of the Pratomagno hills ahead as you descend. After Giovi, where the Arno curves away toward the W, you emerge from the Casentino into the suburbs of *Arezzo*.

Route 4: Tracking down the Etruscans
Traces of the elusive and intriguing Etruscans remain all over Tuscany. The tourist who enjoys walking or riding, or who takes shortcuts along unpaved byroads, will sometimes discover tombs and trails which are not necessarily signposted or identified. However, to appreciate the Etruscans' achievements in the arts and crafts one must also visit museums; some outstanding objects have been allowed to remain in the local museums on the following itineraries.

If you wish to test your interest in Etruscan sites before embarking on a longer journey, begin with *Fiesole*, Comeana (see *Artimino*) and *Sesto Fiorentino*, all within easy reach of Florence. Or, if you are making an excursion to San Gimignano, go on to *Volterra*, a lovely drive only 27km (17 miles) to the SW. The two densest concentrations of the major centers are in the Valdichiana and the Grosseto Maremma, most conveniently visited separately.

a) The Etruscan sites of eastern Tuscany

In the pre-Christian era when the River Chiana was navigable, the Etruscan cities of the Valdichiana were both prosperous and artistically sophisticated thanks to fertile farmlands and trade with other civilizations.

Start at *Arezzo*, the city Livy called the capital of the Etruscan people. Then take the SS71 for *Cortona*, stopping just to the N of the city for the tombs at Sodo. Have a look at the extraordinary bronze lamp in the Etruscan Academy in Cortona and, on the way S, visit the tomb near the station at Camucia. The quickest way to *Chiusi*, which has one of the most important Etruscan museums outside Florence, is by autostrada. Alternatively, take the SS71 along the shore of Lake Trasimeno. From Chiusi station, loop S and then NW to visit the minor rural centers of Cetona, Sarteano, *Chianciano* and *Montepulciano*, all of which preserve interesting Etruscan fragments. Perugia and Orvieto, outside Tuscany, are nearby.

b) The Etruscan sites of southwestern Tuscany

This is a much longer journey, requiring about three days, and it differs in that many of the major sites were abandoned by later civilizations. The necropoli are often in dense woods or cultivated fields, so wear stout shoes and be prepared to take the car over unpaved roads.

Start at *Volterra*, allowing at least half a day for the walls, gate, necropoli and the museum, with its 600 funerary urns and miniature votive bronzes. After perhaps spending the night here, *Populonia*, on the coast, is a 1½ hr drive to the SW, and *Vetulonia* another hour farther on. The second night could be spent on the coast at *Punta Ala, Castiglione della Pescaia* or Principina a Mare. From Vetulonia continue along the Aurelia (SS1) and turn left after 15km (9 miles) for *Roselle*, following the signs *'ruderi'* for the access road. *Grosseto* is 10km (6 miles) to the s and worth visiting for the material excavated from Roselle, Vetulonia and other local Etruscan sites, featured in the Archeological Museum. Now travel inland by the SS322 via Scansano to Montemerano, where you turn left for *Saturnia*, and then *Sovana*; you might spend the third night in either. To complete a tour of the major sites, journey s into Lazio, for Vulci, Tarquinia, Cerveteri, and Veio.

Route 5: From Siena to the Valdichiana

This itinerary SE from Siena could be accomplished in one long day, but the variety and unfaltering beauty of the landscape of the *crete*, the Val d'Orcia and the Valdichiana, and the importance of the churches and hill towns, which include some of the finest examples of Renaissance architecture and town planning outside Florence, justify at least one overnight stop. Food and wine produced in this radiant countryside and served in the best of the restaurants is of exceptional quality.

One day Leaving Siena by the Porta Romana, the Via Cassia, SS2, follows the River Arbia through a strange, furrowed landscape of infertile clay hummocks known as the *crete*. After Buonconvento the Cassia begins to twist dramatically, and the view becomes more spacious with *Montalcino* and *Monte Amiata* visible on the right. From *San Quirico d'Orcia*, on its high plain overlooking the valleys of the Orcia and the Asso, take the SS146 which travels E to the Renaissance hill towns of *Pienza* and *Montepulciano*. The superb High Renaissance church of S. Biagio is on the left 2km (1.25 miles) before Montepulciano. Those who are returning to Siena should leave Montepulciano by the Porta al Prato, stopping briefly after 1km (0.6 miles) to admire the simple Mannerist facade of the church of S. Maria delle Grazie on the left, then proceeding N to Nottola, where you join the SS326 for Siena via Torrita di Siena and *Sinalunga*.

Two days Follow the route described on the previous page, and then make diversions to take in at least some if not all of the following excursions.

a) At Buonconvento turn left on the SS451 for *Monte Oliveto Maggiore*. Then continue for another 2km (1.25 miles) on the road for S. Giovanni d'Asso as far as lofty Chiusure, for the magnificent panorama of the moonlike landscape below. On the return drive to Buonconvento there are fine views of the *crete*, the Ombrone valley and *Monte Amiata*.

b) 10km (6 miles) S of Buonconvento, at Torrenieri, turn right for *Montalcino*. Then continue S into the Val d'Orcia for Sant'Antimo, set in an enchanted landscape of wheatfields, flickering olives and dark cypresses.

c) At *Montepulciano* turn right and follow the SS146 for *Chianciano Terme*; the old city can be seen high on the left as one approaches the modern spa. *Chiusi* is 11km (7 miles) farther to the SE, by way of a beautiful undulating road running into the Valdichiana with the tributary of the River Chiana, the Astrone, with glimpses to the left of the lakes of Chiusi and Montepulciano.

d) Returning to Siena from Chiusi take the autostrada A1 as far as the Valdichiana exit for *Sinalunga*. Stay on the SS326 for 14km (9 miles), turning off for *Asciano*, and then returning to Siena on the SS438 through the *crete*, entering the city by the Porta Pispini.

e) Alternatively, leave the A1 at the Monte S. Savino exit, following the SS73 to *Monte S. Savino*, diverging briefly for *Gargonza* on the right, then for Castelnuovo Berardenga on the eastern edge of the Chianti near the source of the Ombrone. Return to Siena either by the SS326 or by the old Chiantigiana road, SS408.

Route 6: A day in the Mugello

In the days of the Grand Tour, travelers from the N crossed the Apennines into Tuscany by the Futa Pass and continued along the Via Bolognese through the Mugello, making a last overnight stop at La Lastra before entering Florence through the Porta S. Gallo. That is still the most dramatic and scenic way to approach Florence – perhaps a little too slow for the modern tourist and even too dramatic in winter, when the pass is often closed.

However, if you are driving in a southerly direction from Bologna on the autostrada A1, do follow part of this itinerary in reverse from the Barberino exit. Otherwise it is a day trip from Florence which may be enjoyed in any or all of the three stages indicated, depending on the desired proportion of driving to sightseeing.

a) This first short itinerary will be long enough for those who wish to visit the great gardens of La Pietra, Petraia and *Castello*; but be sure to check opening times in advance. From Porta S. Gallo, cross the Mugnone by the Ponte Rosso into the Via Bolognese which, once outside Florence, is now officially known as the SS65 della Futa. The road passes some of the grandest Renaissance villas in the environs of Florence. On the right, no. 120, is La Pietra, so called because it is near the old milestone from Porta S. Gallo. Farther on the right, no. 156, is the Villa Salviati, a medieval castle reworked by Giuliano da Sangallo, where, in the 17thC, Jacopo Salviati was given the severed head of his mistress as a New Year's present from his wife. Past Montorsoli at Fontesecca, turn to the left onto the

panoramic road of the Colli Alti (high hills), which twists for
15km (9 miles) along the slopes of Monte Morello, passing
Piazzale Leonardo da Vinci which commands magnificent
views of the Arno valley stretching out as far as the Chianti
Mountains, to *Sesto Fiorentino*, whence you could return to
Florence.

b) Complete only the first 6km (4 miles) of the Colli Alti, as far
as Piazzale Leonardo da Vinci. Returning to the SS65, continue
N past the park of the Villa Demidoff, adapted by Buontalenti
for Francesco de' Medici, but now demolished, to Pratolino.
For the convent of Monte Senario, a 13thC foundation
remade in the late 16thC and worth visiting for its lofty
situation, fork right from Pratolino. From Montesenario
descend into the basin of the Mugello valley via *Bivigliano*
rejoining the SS65 at Vaglia. Taking the left fork at the Novoli
crossroads, you pass on the left two of the earliest Medici villas,
both of which were once fortified castles made into hunting
lodges by Michelozzo for Cosimo il Vecchio: first Trebbio, now
only occasionally open to the public; then Cafaggiolo, now a
hospital, where Poliziano spent the rainy winter of 1478−9
instructing Lorenzo de' Medici's children. To return to
Florence rejoin the autostrada at Barberino. See also *Borgo San
Lorenzo*.

c) Otherwise, take another route and leave the SS65 N of
Cafaggiolo turning right across the Sieve for Galliano, looping
right for Sant' Agata and *Scarperia*, then following the SS503 s
toward San Piero a Sieve. Just before reaching San Piero a
Sieve, turn right for the medieval Franciscan monastery, Bosco
ai Frati, which was rebuilt in the Renaissance by Michelozzo,
where there is a wooden crucifix in the church attributed by
some scholars to Donatello. Take the SS551 from San Piero to
Borgo San Lorenzo. The landscape visible from the road along
this stretch is disfigured by industrial sprawl as far as Vicchio
and Vespignano, after which the road follows the broad curve of
the Sieve through gentle, cultivated country to Dicomano,
Rúfina, center of the smallest and choicest of the Chianti Putto
zones, and *Pontassieve*, where the Sieve joins the Arno. Turn
w on the SS67 for Florence. The road follows the N bank of the
Arno through the industrial vineyards which are controlled by
the Ruffino firm, and passes many interesting country churches
of which the most notable are S.Giovanni Battista a Remole at
Sieci and S.Andrea at Rovezzano situated on the outskirts of
Florence.

Where to stay

Cleanliness is a virtue of Tuscan hotels, and the days when Aldous Huxley described Tuscany as "under-bathroomed and over-monumented" are past: the monuments are now increasingly occupied by hotels, and they have been bathroomed.

Standards and prices are controlled by the Regional Tourist Board: categories are deluxe and first- to fourth-class for hotels, and P1–P3 for *pensioni*. While most Florentine *pensioni* have dropped the meal requirement, half board, where available, is usually good value. Resort hotels often insist on half board in high season.

Rural Tuscany is unevenly supplied with tourist hotels. There is a good choice in the Chianti hills, in the coastal resorts and in spa towns. Elsewhere it is usually possible to find a decent commercial hotel on the outskirts of a large town or near a major autostrada junction.

Hotel breakfasts are sparse and expensive. If you are on a budget, do as the Italians do and take breakfast at the nearest bar. Hotels can also put a heavy surcharge on telephone calls.

'Residences,' service apartments rentable for a minimum of one week, are an increasingly popular alternative to hotels. There are also a number of agencies, including **Villas Italia** *(405 Radnor House, Regent St., London W1 ☎ (01) 439–8547)*, that will find private villas to rent.

Where to eat

Two words Tuscans often use to describe good food are *genuino* and *sano* (healthy). Although the 20thC plague of international junk food has inevitably spread along with mass tourism to Tuscan cities, the majority of *trattorie* still serve wholesome, robust, traditional food that is indeed genuine, as to the ingredients and cooking methods, and healthy, according to modern dietary principles. Thick vegetable soups, simply cooked meat or fish, chewy unsalted bread and only one cheese, *pecorino*, may sound a monotonous regime. But when prepared to ancient recipes, flavored with herbs and aromatic wood smoke and accompanied by a bottle of local wine, these dishes add up to one of the most satisfying cuisines in Europe.

It is basically a peasant cuisine. The best Tuscan restaurants are generally outside cities, often in deeply rural areas, behind doors that may not even be signed. You won't necessarily be offered a menu; the proprietor will tell you what has been prepared that day. This is the kind of restaurant that this book tries to single out. There are, of course, many others, and one way of recognizing them is by their unpretentious appearance.

The culinary glory of Tuscany is, in Elizabeth David's words, "that remarkable *bistecca alla Fiorentina*, a vast steak, grilled over a wood fire, which, tender and aromatic, is a dish worth going some way to eat." The best Tuscan beef is from a steer less than two years old. The citified way of presenting it is as a *gran' pezzo*, a roast sirloin.

Pasta is widely available but is not a Tuscan specialty. The farinacious staple is bread, used to make the bread salad, *panzanella*, and to thicken the excellent peasant soups which vary by area. There are some 100 varieties of *pecorino*, which is eaten with *fave* (broad beans) as an antipasto.

Florence (Firenze)

Map 2–7. 50100 Firenze. Population: 463,000 i Via Tornabuoni 15 ☎ (055) 216544/5. See Basic information.

Florence is the most densely packed urban treasure house in Europe. If you were not detained by the profusion of artistic masterpieces it contains, you could walk across its historic center in half an hour. Only two of the sights recommended are beyond pleasant walking distance of the Piazza della Signoria. It is, then, a city which can be explored according to the taste of the individual visitor.

To make the most of this freedom, however, you must adjust to the rhythm of the city, which rises early and closes down at noon for a long siesta. Churches close for three or sometimes four hours in the middle of the day, but they are often open from 7am and open again in the evening until 7pm or 8pm. As in the rest of Italy, museum opening hours are too short and subject to change. A law that would rationalize opening hours is under discussion. Meanwhile, many museums open in the mornings only, closing at 2pm on weekdays, 1pm on Sun and remaining closed on Mon. Inevitably in a city that possesses so much precious art that is fragile with age, there will always be some works that are withdrawn from the public gaze for restoration and some buildings that are temporarily closed. Strikes and inadequate staffing can also lead to unexpected closure.

Fortunately for the independent-minded visitor, mass tourism does not often penetrate beyond the Uffizi, Palatine Gallery, Bargello and Accademia, the four most visited sights in that order. The churches, chapels, painted refectories and small museums are usually peaceful even in high summer. Although no one will be able to take in all the city has to offer in one short visit – and it would be an exhausting waste of time to try – Florence does reveal its essential urban character to the visitor very quickly. Its narrow streets flanked by medieval and Renaissance palaces are, with very few exceptions, unspoiled as yet by modern intrusions. Since the last building boom under the Medici grand dukes, the fabric of Florence has suffered only four drastic changes.

The first happened in the mid 19thC when Florence disastrously prepared itself for its brief period as Italy's capital by demolishing its old walls and part of its center to make way for the Viale and the Piazza della Repubblica. The second was the destruction toward the end of World War II of Ponte Santa Trinita (subsequently reconstructed) and the areas to the N and S of the Ponte Vecchio. The third was the flood of 1966, the worst in the city's history. The fourth is the traffic which, since the early 1970s, has come to dominate Florence more cruelly than any of its hated tyrant-rulers, turning its beautiful squares into parking lots and roaring through its medieval streets.

Fortunately there is probably no other major city in the world from which escape is so easy and so delightful. Much of the lovely Tuscan countryside immediately outside Florence has been consciously and courageously defended from the worst ravages of modern development, and can be reached either on foot or by a short bus ride.

Postcards and catalogs are not sold in any Italian state museums but can be bought from good bookshops and bookstalls. Street numbers in Florence are organized in two separate systems. Black numbers indicate residential addresses, while commercial establishments are given red numbers.

Sights and places of interest

Florence is so richly endowed with artistic treasures that the following guide is inevitably highly selective and the use of stars (★ ★) has been limited to the greatest and most famous only. This does not mean that they are all that is worth seeing. The city is packed with lesser-known museums, galleries, churches and private collections which are essential to the specialist and which may charm and fascinate many independent-minded tourists. The *Azienda Autonoma* (see p.13) provides a complete list of the sights and their current opening hours.

Accademia *(Galleria dell'Accademia)* ★
Via Ricasoli 60 ☎ *214375. Map 3B4* 🏛 🚶 *Open Tues – Sat 9am – 2pm, Sun and hols 9am – 1pm. Closed Mon.*
In 1563, 70 leading Florentine artists founded the first Academy of Art in Europe. The organizing members were Vasari, Bronzino and Ammannati, and the president was Cosimo I. Thus academic art, like so many modern institutions, was a Florentine invention. First located at *Santissima Annunziata*, the Accademia was moved to Via Ricasoli 66 in 1764. This building, with its spacious 14thC loggia, is now the Florentine Art School and College.

The Accademia gallery nearby at no.60 was founded in 1784 by Peter Leopold I, who donated a collection which was greatly enriched by works brought here from the suppressed religious orders in 1786 and 1808 – 10. Until World War I the Accademia possessed an outstanding collection of early Tuscan masterpieces, the best of which were transferred in 1913 to the *Uffizi*. During the 1970s the display was reorganized and enlarged in order to emphasize the link with the original Academy of Art, and new rooms housing 18th and 19thC academic paintings and sculptures, including hitherto neglected works by Lorenzo Bartolini, were opened in 1982.

Meanwhile, most visitors will come here, as they have for over a century, to gaze up at the *David* of Michelangelo.

Rm I, Sala del Colosso. Dominated by Giambologna's model (c.1582) for the *Rape of the Sabines* in the Loggia dei Lanzi (see *Signoria*). On the walls are 16thC paintings by Fra Bartolommeo, Perugino, Granacci, and others.

The *David* . . . . standing forward stripped and exposed and eternally half-shrinking, half-wishing to expose himself, he is the genius of Florence.

D. H. Lawrence, *Aaron's Rod* (1922)

Rm II, Salone di Michelangelo. Against the walls, which are hung with magnificent 16thC tapestries, are four of Michelangelo's unfinished *Slaves* (c.1519 – 36) ★ first meant for Pope Julius II's unrealized mausoleum in St Peter's in Rome (the Louvre possesses two other slaves). The figures may represent the liberal arts enslaved by the death of their patron, Julius II. On the right wall are also the deeply expressive, unfinished *St Matthew* (before 1505); and the Palestrina *Pietà*, no longer attributed to Michelangelo. It was saved from export in 1940 and brought here from the Church of S. Rosalia di Palestrina in Rome. At the far end of the room, Michelangelo's *David* (1501 – 4) ★ dwarfs and astonishes the perpetual crowds. This tribune was specially built to receive the *David* when it was brought here from the Signoria in 1873. The statue was carved from a block of Carrara marble known as 'the giant,' which had been spoiled by Agostino di Duccio and abandoned in the courtyard of the Opera del Duomo. The *David* established Michelangelo's reputation as the leading sculptor of his day, and has remained the most potent of all symbols of Florentine republicanism. But it has not always been admired: William Hazlitt, one of the many early 19thC travellers who were irritated by Michelangelo's style, described it as looking "like an awkward overgrown actor at one of our minor theatres, without his clothes."

The other rooms are devoted to a study collection of 13th–18thC Florentine paintings, including, in the second of the three rooms to the right of the Salone di Michelangelo, Baldovinetti's important but ruined *Trinity with Saints*. At the end of the corridor to the left of the Tribuna is an elegantly arranged gallery of plaster casts.

Anthropological Museum *(Museo Nazionale di Antropologia ed Etnologia)* Ⅲ
Via del Proconsolo 12 ☎296449. *Map* **5**C5. *Open by appointment Wed, Fri 9am–1pm.*

Opened in 1869, this was the first anthropological museum in Italy. The collection is displayed on the ground floor of the Palazzo Nonfinito (see *Florence/Walk 2*) and is a fascinating documentation of ethnic custom and costume.

Antica Casa Fiorentina, Museo dell'   The house museum of Florence in the *Davanzati Palace*.

Arcetri and Pian dei Giullari
Map **7**E4. *Bus no. 38.*

Florence may be hot and crowded, but half an hour's walk s from the Ponte Vecchio will lift you into the cool, high heart of Tuscany. At no.2 Pian dei Giullari is the **Astrophysical Observatory of Arcetri** with the first solar tower built in Europe (1872). Opposite the entrance is the Villa Capponi, with famous but private gardens. The **Torre del Gallo** is just to the E: this 19thC reconstruction was once owned by the antiquarian robber-baron Stefano Bardini (see *Bardini Museum*). In the adjacent **Villa la Gallina** are Antonio del Pollaiuolo's **frescoes of nude dancers**: persistent or specialist visitors have been known to gain access by appointment.

Pian dei Giullari takes its name from the minstrels who entertained Florentine patricians here from the 12thC. Galileo died in the **Villa il Gioiello** (no.42). On no.48 a plaque sentences to imprisonment anyone who dares to play any ball game within 200yd of the monastery of S. Matteo in Arcetri.

In the Via S. Margherita a Montici, at the Villa Ravà, no. 75, Francesco Guicciardini wrote his histories of Italy between 1537–40. Further on is the church of S. Margherita a Montici commanding stupendous views of the Arno and Ema valleys. Inside are two 14thC panels by the Master of St Cecilia.

(See also *Florence/Walk 4*.)

Archeological Museum *(Museo Archeologico)* ☆
Via della Colonna 36 ☎2478641. *Map* **3**B5 ▨ ✳ *Open Tues–Sat 9am–2pm. Sun and hols 9am–1pm. Closed Mon.*

To say that the Archeological Museum is of outstanding international importance may sound forbidding to the non-specialist. In fact, every visitor will find much here to delight the eye, stimulate the imagination and enrich further sightseeing in Florence and Tuscany. The Etruscan sculptures are an essential and fascinating grounding for those who intend to visit the sites; the Greek and Roman collections will deepen one's understanding of the Renaissance art they helped inspire.

Having suffered appalling damage from the 1966 flood, the museum still has an air of post-crisis impermanence. Many rooms are closed, others badly labeled, and all displays are subject to change, but the finest objects, of which only the highlights are mentioned here, have been brilliantly restored and are on public display.

Ground floor, Rm I. François Vase (c. 570 BC), the earliest known Attic volute-krater, discovered in 1845 by Alexander François at Chiusi. Smashed by a member of staff of the museum into 638 pieces in 1900, the vase was restored in 1972.

Rm II. **Etruscan tomb sculpture** (6th–5thC BC), from Chianciano and Chiusi.

First floor. The **Egyptian Collection** is in Rms I–VIII to the left of the stairs. It consists mainly of objects discovered in 1828–9 during a Franco-Tuscan expedition directed by Ippolito Rosselini and Jean François Champollion. The prize piece is the large **chariot** in Rm VIII, found by Rossellini in a 14thC BC tomb at Thebes.

The **Etruscan, Greek and Roman Collection** is in the rooms to the right of the stairs and continues on the second floor.

Rm X. Etruscan tomb sculpture, including *Urn in the Shape of an Etruscan House* (6th–3rdC BC), no. 5539, from Chiusi, a rare piece of evidence about Etruscan architecture, worth bearing in mind when looking at 15thC Tuscan palaces. *Sarcophagus of the Fat Etruscan* (3rd–2ndC BC), no. 5482, from Chiusi, mentioned by Catullus.

Rm XIV. The greatest Etruscan bronzes, including: *Wounded Chimera* (15thC BC), discovered at Arezzo in 1553 (the two left legs were restored by Cellini); and *The Orator* (c.7th–2ndC BC), a funereal sculpture found near Trasimeno in 1566.

A small section of the ground floor, entered from Piazza SS. Annunziata, is reserved for special exhibitions. The garden and topographical display charting the evolution of Etruscan culture have been closed.

Argenti Museum   Collection of objets d'art in the *Pitti Palace*.

Badia Fiorentina Ⅲ ☆
Map 5C4.

The old Benedictine Abbey of Florence is the only church, besides the Baptistry and S. Miniato, mentioned by Dante, who tells us that he saw Beatrice at Mass here and that the bell tower of the Badia gave Florence the hours. According to Vasari, the abbey, founded in 978, was enlarged by Arnolfo di Cambio, c.1285. This 13thC building was reoriented and radically rebuilt in the 17thC, but the original apse can still be seen from the outside. The hexagonal Romanesque-Gothic **campanile** was completed in 1330.

The **interior** is best lit in the morning. The **portal** (1495) and **vestibule** leading to Via Dante Alighieri were designed by Benedetto da Rovezzano. The noble Baroque **ceiling** is by Matteo Segaloni, architect of the 17thC church. Immediately to the left of the entrance is Filippino Lippi's restless masterpiece, *St Bernard's Vision of the Madonna* (c.1485). Farther to the left is the **monument to Count Ugo**, benefactor of the 10thC foundation (1469–81), by Mino da Fiesole. To the right of the entrance, off the Renaissance Pandolfini Chapel, is the little chapel occupying the site of the church of S. Stefano, where Boccaccio delivered the first literary lecture, on the *Divine Comedy.* Among Baroque decorations elsewhere in the church is Ferretti's fresco over the presbytery of the *Martyrdom of St Stephen* (after 1734).

Oranges were cultivated in the center of the large 15thC cloister, designed by Bernardo Rossellino. The tombs date from the 13thC onwards. There is a nice view of the three towers of the Badia, *Bargello* and *Signoria* from the upper loggia.

Baptistry *(Battistero)*   The city's oldest building, and once its cathedral. See *Duomo.*

Bardini Museum ▥

Piazza de' Mozzi 1 ☎*296749. Map **5**F5.* 🔳 🚗 *Open Mon–Tues, Thurs–Sat 9am–2pm, Sun and hols 8am–1pm. Closed Wed.*

Stefano Bardini (1836–1922) was the leading Italian art dealer of his day, and by 1883 he had amassed a fortune more than large enough to build this palace. He tore down a 13thC church to create the site and, like the American robber barons of the period, incorporated architectural members from older buildings.

The first-floor windows are framed with the altars from a church in Pistoia. The cool, spacious **interior** is embellished throughout with ceilings, door frames and chimney pieces from other earlier buildings. Bardini's taste was almost boundlessly eclectic, and the collection includes, on the ground floor, sculptures and architectural decorations from the Etruscan period to the Baroque.

On the second floor there are pictures, furniture, ceramics, tapestries, musical instruments, arms and armor. The Corsi Gallery is closed pending possible relocation.

Bargello, National Sculpture Museum *(Museo Nazionale)* ▥ ★

Via del Proconsolo ☎*210801. Map **5**C5* 🔳 *Open Tues–Sat 9am–2pm, Sun and hols 9am–1pm. Closed Mon.*

There are a fair number of murderers in the National Sculpture Museum, of which the best known are Donatello's *David*, Verrocchio's *David*, Michelangelo's *Brutus* and Cellini's model for the *Perseus*. Thus Florentine Renaissance sculpture reflected the Florentine obsession with tyranny. It is an ironic coincidence that, during the turbulent period when these sculptures were created, the Bargello was the place where real murderers were tried and sentenced; and the message that crime doesn't pay even if committed in the name of freedom was advertised on the tower walls, frescoed with representations of the mutilated corpses of the condemned. The body of one of the Pazzi Conspirators was hung from a window, where Leonardo made a careful drawing of him, paying special attention to his clothes.

The Bargello was built around an earlier tower in 1255, 5yr after the establishment of the new Florentine Republic, as its first town hall or Palazzo del Podestà. In 1261 it became the official residence of the Chief Magistrate (*bargello*) and it was used also as a law court and prison. The Sculpture Museum, the most important in Italy, has been here since 1859, and was enriched in 1888 by the Carrand Collection of small bronzes, ivories, enamels, goldsmiths' work and ceramics.

The **courtyard** is the most picturesque part of the palace. Its loggia and staircase are 14thC. Among the sculptures are Ammannati's figures from the fountain in the Boboli gardens. To the right of the entrance is the new **sculpture gallery ★** opened in 1975. Moving clockwise, you will encounter, most notably: Michelangelo's *Bacchus* (c.1497), his first large free-standing sculpture, *Pitti Tondo* (c.1504) and *Brutus* (c.1540), which possibly celebrates the assassination of Alessandro de' Medici; and Sansovino's *Bacchus*. There are also terra-cotta sketches by Michelangelo's followers and contemporaries. Works by Cellini include the **four bronze statues** and the relief panel of *Perseus Liberating Andromeda*, now brought here for safekeeping from the Loggia dei Lanzi; also his model for the *Perseus* – he boasts in his autobiography that Cosimo I doubted that anyone had the skill to enlarge it. Of the *Narcissus*, he tells us that a defective block of marble dictated the form. His larger-than-life portrait bust of *Cosimo I* (1557) was made, while he was perfecting his bronze technique for the *Perseus*, for the fortress Cosimo built at Portoferraio. You cannot very well ignore Giambologna's enormous, violent *Victory of Florence over Pisa* (1570), or the splendid **bronze reliefs** by Vincenzo Danti.

Beyond the courtyard are 14thC sculptural fragments, of which the finest piece is Tino da Camaino's *Madonna and Child*.

First floor. The open staircase leads to the **loggia**, with Giambologna's *Mercury* (c.1564) and bronze animals (c.1570) made for the Medici Villa at *Castello*. On the right is the large **Salone del Consiglio Generale ★** On the walls, notice especially: the Madonnas by Luca della Robbia, Michelozzo and Agostino di Duccio; on the far wall, Donatello's *St George* (1416) with its original predella, from the facade of *Orsanmichele*; the two panels of *The Sacrifice of Isaac* by Brunelleschi and Ghiberti, which were competition entries for the second Baptistry doors.

Among the free-standing sculptures by Donatello: the *Marzocco* (1420), the heraldic lion of Florence; *Cupid* (c.1430–40), described by Vasari as "dressed in a rather bizarre fashion"; and the polychrome terra-cotta *Bust of a Man*, probably Niccolò da Uzzano. Compare the swaying elegance of Donatello's early marble *David* (1408) with the late bronze *David* (c.1430), his most famous and titillating boy and the first free-standing nude of the Renaissance. Also two sensitive busts by Desiderio da Settignano. The next rooms on this floor contain a large and heterogeneous collection of European and Islamic applied art, most of it from the **Carrand bequest** of 1888.

Salone del Podestà. This was the law court, frescoed during the brief reign of the Duke of Athens. Off the far end is the frescoed **Chapel of the Condemned** with fine intarsiate choir stalls (1493) and lectern (1490). Next is a room of metalwork, with Cellini's *Ganymede*, and another room devoted to 15th–16thC Italian majolicas.

Second floor. At the top of the stairs is the Sala di Giovanni della Robbia where Giovanni Rustici's huge terra-cotta relief

panel of *Christ and the Magdalen* demonstrates his superiority
to Giovanni della Robbia. Bernini's bust of *Constanza Bonarelli*
is usually displayed in this room. Off one end of the room is a
display of arms and armor. Off the other, the Sala di Andrea
della Robbia leads to the **Sala di Verrocchio ★** In the center
are Verrocchio's *David* (before 1476) and Antonio Pollaiuolo's
small bronze masterpiece *Hercules and Anteus*. Among the
works dislayed on the walls are, clockwise from the entrance: the
marble bust of *Battista Sforza, Duchess of Urbino* (1474–7) by
Francesco Laurana; Verrocchio's *Bust of a Woman* and
Madonna and Child (c.1480) and the bust of *Piero Mellini*
(1474) by Benedetto da Maiano. Portrait busts and relief
carvings by Mino da Fiesole include the tondo of the *Madonna
and Child* (1481). Across the Sala di Andrea della Robbia is the
Sala dei Bronzetti ☆ containing the most important collection
of bronzes in Italy. The magnificent 16thC chimneypiece is by
Benedetto da Rovezzano.

Bellosguardo
*Map **6**D3. No bus connection.*
Bellosguardo is one of the nearest of the hill villages s of
Florence. You can walk it in half an hour either from *Porta
Romana* or *San Frediano*, and will be rewarded for the steep
climb by views as ravishing as the word *bellosguardo* (fine view)
suggests. Via Bellosguardo forks to either side of the piazza. On
the w side is the Villa Belvedere al Saracino (1502) by Baccio
d'Agnolo, and farther along the Via San Carlo is the Torre
Montauto, where Hawthorne stayed. On the E side of the piazza
is the park of Villa Ombrellino, where Alice Keppel, Edward
VII's last mistress, lived from 1925 to her death in 1947. Her
daughter, Violet Trefusis, also died at the Ombrellino.

The best views are from the garden of the Villa di
Bellosguardo, reached by a pretty little road running along the
NE flank of the Ombrellino park.

In the piazza a plaque records the most famous of the
numerous foreign visitors who have lived in and around
Bellosguardo. Aldous Huxley's short story, *The Rest Cure*, is
about a neurotic Englishwoman staying here.

Belvedere *(Forte di Belvedere)* ▥
*☎ 287055. Map **3**E4 ⊡ Open Tues – Sun 8:30am – 1:30pm,
exhibitions 9am – 8pm. Closed Mon. Main entrance from Via
del Forte di S. Giorgio.*
Crowning the hill of S. Giorgio is the ruthlessly practical
Belvedere fortress surrounding its elegant shoe-box-shaped
Mannerist palace, both built by Buontalenti in 1590 – 5 for
Grand Duke Ferdinand I. The terraces are now used for
modern **sculpture exhibitions** ▨ which are only occasionally
worthy of a setting commanding some of the most magnificent
views of Florence and the surrounding hills and valleys. At the
top of the Costa di S. Giorgio is the S. Giorgio gate (c.1260),
reduced to about half its original height, embellished with a
fresco of the *Madonna and Saints* by Bicci di Lorenzo. The relief
carving of St George is a copy of the original now in the
Signoria.

Two interesting buildings in the Costa di S. Giorgio are the
splendid Baroque church of S. Giorgio, modernized by
G.B. Foggini in 1707 and lately restored, with a boudoir-like
oval ceiling frescoed by Alessandro Gherardini, and the house
(no. 19) where Galileo was visited by Ferdinand I.

Boboli Gardens _(Giardino di Boboli)_ ☆

☎ _226587. Map_ **4**_F3_ 👁 💻 ♣ _Open 9am–before sunset. Main gate to left of Pitti; others not always open._

"The most important if not the most pleasing of Tuscan pleasure gardens . . . . because the Boboli is a court garden, and not designed for private use." Thus Edith Wharton explained the curiously lowering effect the Boboli can have on one's spirits. At certain seasons, when roses tumble through the somber plantations of holly and cypress or when Florence is gilded with slanting autumn light, the Boboli would be a fine place for an evening stroll. But as another American novelist, Mary McCarthy, has pointed out, this is just the time when the gates close.

Eleanor of Toledo ordered gardens to be laid out behind the Pitti as soon as she and Cosimo I took possession in 1549. The original designer was Triboli, who died before accomplishing the extraordinary technical feat of taming this wedge of steep quarry. Later alterations by Ammannati, Buontalenti and the Parigi gave the gardens their playful, grandiose complexity.

If you wander freely in the Boboli, the late Mannerist jokes will take you by surprise as they were intended to do. A more purposeful tour should include the following highlights:
1. Statue of _Pietro Barbino Riding a Tortoise_, Cosimo I's favorite dwarf immortalized by Valerio Cioli. 2. **Buontalenti Grotto** (1583–88), a serious joke about nature; the casts of Michelangelo's _Slaves_ replace the originals, now in the _Accademia_, which were installed here for a time in the 16thC. Giambologna's _Venus_ is in the third recess, not always open.
3. The **Kaffeehaus** (1776), for a drink and fine views. 4. The **Amphitheater**, "One of the triumphs of Italian garden architecture" (Edith Wharton). Built from 1618 by the Parigi for spectacular grand-ducal entertainments. 5. **Neptune Fountain** (1565) by Stoldo Lorenzi. 6. **Porcelain Museum (Museo delle Porcellane)**, a small but choice collection of French, Italian, Viennese and German porcelains, formerly exhibited in the Argenti Museum, has now been installed in the airy Casino del Cavaliere. Panoramic views to the s from the terrace. 7. **Cypress Alley (Viottolone)**, lined with statues of various periods, the most famous of which, towards the bottom, are the knowingly rustic 17thC groups of games. 8. **The Isolotto** (1618) by A. Parigi. The shallow pool, the tall box hedges and the pots of oranges and entwined trees on the island provide cooling relief. Rising from the fountain is a copy of Giambologna's _Oceanus_ (the original is in the _Bargello_).

(See also _Pitti Palace_.)

Botanical Garden and Museum _(Orto Botanico, Giardino dei Semplici)_

Via G. la Pira 4 ☎ _284696. Map_ **3**_B4_ 👁 ♣ _Open Mon, Wed, Fri 9am–noon._

In a stony city where most gardens are hidden behind high walls, this scholarly display of the vegetable heritage of Tuscany makes a refreshing change from art galleries and churches. It is also an excellent preparation for those who plan to visit rural Tuscany and would like to be able to identify the native trees and flowers.

The Giardino dei Semplici, as it was originally called because its first function was the cultivation of medicinal plants, was founded in 1545 by Cosimo I. On the second floor of the Botanical Institute is a little museum founded in 1842.

Brancacci Chapel   A chapel in the *Carmine*, containing Masaccio's influential frescoes.

Carmine *(Santa Maria del Carmine)* †
Piazza del Carmine. Map 2D2.

If Renaissance painting was born in Giotto's Arena Chapel at Padua and reached its fullest maturity in Michelángelo's Sistine Chapel, it was in the **Brancacci Chapel ★** of the Carmine (right transept, best seen on a clear evening without electric light) that it made its most innovative and lasting impact. Here, a century after Giotto, the young Masaccio 'rivalled nature' and revolutionized Western art. Most Renaissance painters, from Fra Angelico to Raphael, studied these frescoes, but perhaps none understood them as well as Michelangelo (whose nose was broken by Pietro Torrigiano on the steps of thc Carmine). Many of the greatest 20thC artists continue to draw inspiration from Masaccio's bold, rigorous, uncluttered technique.

The frescoes were begun around 1425 by Masolino, who was joined a little later by his protégé Masaccio and so influenced by the young genius that it is not always easy to distinguish their work. The decoration of the chapel was interrupted when they departed for Rome in 1428 and was completed in 1485 by Filippino Lippi. The 18thC **ceiling** is by Vincenzo Meucci and Carlo Sacconi.

There are seven sections by Masaccio. Facing the altar and starting from the near left wall, the outstanding frescoes are the first two in the upper tier: *Expulsion from the Garden* ★ one of the most tragic images in religious art; and the *Tribute Money* ★ Once you have seen these faces with their quick, watching eyes, you will see them again and again in Florence. Below the *Tribute Money* is Masaccio's last work in this chapel, *St Peter Enthroned*; the left portion of this fresco was finished by Filippino Lippi. On the altar wall, bottom left, is *St Peter Heals with his Shadow*; top right, *St Peter Baptizes the Neophites*; bottom right, *St Peter and St John Distribute Alms*. On the right wall, upper tier, first section of the left, is found *St Peter Heals the Lame Man*; the *Raising of Tubitha* on the right section of this fresco is by Masolino. The Florentine houses in the center background are thought to have been Masaccio's starting point.

The **Corsini Chapel** in the left transept was built in 1675–83 by P.F. Silvani. The splendid relief sculptures (1675–91) on the walls and altar are by G.B. Foggini, and the cupola fresco of the *Apotheosis of S. Andrea Corsini* (1682) by Luca Giordano.

The rest of the church is late 18thC, the original building having been destroyed in 1771 by a fire which spared the Brancacci and Corsini chapels. In a **museum** off the cloister are a number of detached frescoes including fragments by Starnina.

Casa Buonarroti   Built by Michelangelo's family after the artist's death, now the *Michelangelo Museum*.

Le Cascine
Map 6D3. Bus 17.

Surprisingly few tourists make use of Le Cascine, the shady park which runs for 3km (1¾ miles) along the N bank of the Arno W from Piazza Vittorio Veneto. Yet it is one of the few places in the city where you can take the air undistracted by traffic and artistic masterpieces; and the private tennis club and swimming pool are open to foreign nonmembers.

Originally a dairy farm belonging to the Medici, the Cascine became the grand-ducal chase in the 17thC. Shelley composed his *Ode to the West Wind* while striding through the Cascine. Later in the 19thC the park was so full of fashionable carriages that Charles Lever described it as being to the world of society "what the Bourse is to the world of trade."

(See also *Florence/Shopping* for markets and *Sports, leisure, ideas for children.*)

Corridoio   Vasari's aerial link between the *Pitti Palace* and the *Uffizi*, offering superb views as it crosses the Arno. Tours Tues–Sun mornings; book the previous day at the Uffizi.

Corsini Gallery ▥
Palazzo Corsini, Via del Parione 11 ☎*287629. Map 4C2. Open by previous appointment.*

The most important private collection in Florence, with works by Signorelli, Pontormo, Raphael, Rigaud and other Italian and European artists of the 15th–18thC.

The palace (1648–56) which gives its name to this stretch of the lungarno is by Pier Francesco Silvani and Antonio Ferri.

Davanzati Palace and Antica Casa Fiorentina, Museo dell' *(Florentine House Museum)* ▥ ☆
Piazza Davanzati, Via Porta Rossa ☎*216518. Map 4D3* ▨ ⚹ *Guided tours Tues–Sat 9:30am, 10:30am, 11:30am, 12:30pm, Sun and hols 9:30am, 10:30am, 11:30am. Closed Mon.*

The exterior of the Davanzati is the best-preserved of any mid-14thC palace in Florence. Inside, the House Museum offers a rare opportunity to explore an early palace interior and to learn about domestic life in 14th–16thC Florence. If George Eliot had known the Davanzati as it is today, *Romola* would have been a livelier novel. The house was built by the Davizzi family, who lived here for over a century before selling to the historian Bernardo Davanzati in 1578. The interior was badly mishandled in the 19thC after the suicide by defenestration of the last Davanzati, but was rescued and accurately restored by Elia Volpi just after the turn of this century.

Architecturally the building is midway between a medieval defence tower and a Renaissance palace. Apart from the 16thC roof loggia, a replacement of the original battlements, and the Davanzati coat of arms placed here in the 16thC, the facade looks very much like the one you can see in the Masolino-Masaccio fresco of the *Resurrection of Tabitha* in the *Carmine*.

The entrance loggia, initially used for important family celebrations, was converted into three wool shops by the end of the 15thC. The horizontal perches running across the windows were used, as shown in the Carmine fresco, for hanging out washing, or birdcages, and for festive drapes.

The interior is largely a reconstruction, and a very good one, by Volpi. The **courtyard staircase** is particularly worth noting as the only one of its type left in Florence. The well is an unusual luxury for a palace of this date; all five floors were served by a shaft carrying buckets of water by rope and pulley. Kitchens, as always in medieval palaces, are on the top floor. The sanitary arrangements include lavatories which you can see next to the bedrooms on the three upper floors. The house is unusual in having two *piani nobili*, on the second as well as the first floor.

Of the wall decorations, the most attractive and most complete is in the second-floor bedroom where a fresco cycle illustrates the medieval French poem *The Châtelaine of Vergi*.

Duomo 🏛 † ★

*Map **5**B4. Open 6:30am–noon, 2:30–7pm.*

Traffic swarms around the religious center of Florence, shaking
the nerves of tourists and the very foundations of the cathedral.
The Piazza del Duomo is the crossroads of the city's busiest
streets, the headquarters of its ancient voluntary ambulance
service (the *Misericordia*, an original Red Cross) and a magnet
for the modern tourist industry; but it is no place for a
meditative cup of coffee. To appreciate the grandeur and
significance of the Duomo and its attendant buildings, you must
first go away from it, glimpse its flagrant burst of color from
the dark narrow city streets and take your coffee overlooking
it from a rooftop or from the hills above, where you will see how
disproportionately large the cathedral is in the small city.

> The cathedral and its belfry suggested the grotesque similitude
> of a huge architectural zebra and its keeper – the former with a
> coating or skin, consisting of alternate stripes of black and white
> marble, the latter exhibiting, on its exterior, all the colours of
> the rainbow, all the chequers of a gigantic harlequin! Is there no
> mitigation of the penalty due to this gothic and tasteless idea?
> James Johnson MD (1831)

The cathedral (Santa Maria del Fiore) clad in white marble
from Carrara, green from Prato, and pink from the Maremma,
could hardly be more of a contrast with the plain brown
understated city around it. Like the two sides of the Florentine
character: one is measured, conservative, puritanical; the other
excessive, innovating, festive; and both are dominated by the
great cranium-shaped intelligence of Brunelleschi's dome.

Arnolfo di Cambio was commissioned in 1296 to build a
cathedral which would surpass anything produced by the
ancient Romans and Greeks or by Florence's rivals the Pisans
and Sienese. Work was interrupted by Arnolfo's death, began
again in 1331, and after another pause resumed under the
direction of Francesco Talenti from 1357–1364. The nave was
completed in 1380, and the tribunes and the drum of the dome
were finished by 1418.

The problem then was how to raise a dome over a space 42m
(138ft) across and 55m (180ft) above the ground. No dome of
this size had been built since antiquity, and various unlikely
solutions were proposed before Brunelleschi, who had studied
Classical building techniques in Rome, provided the answer.
His dome, realized in 1436, was the supreme engineering feat of
the Renaissance. The lantern was completed in 1461, after

Piazza del Duomo

Brunelleschi's death; the gallery, on only one of the eight sides of the drum of the dome, was begun by Baccio d'Agnolo in 1506 but abandoned after Michelangelo called it "a cage for crickets."

The Neo-Gothic facade of the cathedral is a late 19thC interpretation of the original one. The apse is best viewed from the corner of Via Proconsolo and Via dell'Oriuolo. The s flank is the earliest section of the exterior, but the most beautiful of the doors, the **Porta della Mandorla**, is on the N nave. Above it is Nanni di Banco's lovely relief of the *Assumption of the Madonna* (1414–21).

The cathedral **interior**, the fourth largest in the world, is all the more imposing for the sparseness of detailed decoration. There are only a few major works of art to distract from the sense of echoing space. In the left aisle of the nave are the two famous monuments to *condottieri* (mercenary commanders), which have been cited as examples of Florentine meanness because they imitate marble in *trompe l'oeil* fresco. Both have long since been transferred to canvas: the first, **Monument to Niccolò da Tolentino** (1456) by Castagno; the second, **Monument to Sir John Hawkwood** (1436) by Uccello. Just before the crossing is an interesting panel painting of *Dante Explaining the Divine Comedy* (1465) by Domenico di Michelino.

Access to the vast octagonal **crossing** and the three polygonal tribunes of the apse will be barred until the 1990s while the dome is under restoration. Meanwhile, the question is whether the late 16thC frescoes of the *Last Judgement* on the interior dome by Vasari and F. Zuccari, now covered by netting, should be removed to reveal more clearly Brunelleschi's structure.

The noble octagonal marble **choir enclosure** (1555) beneath the dome is by Bandinelli, as is the high altar over which is a wooden **crucifix** (1495–7) by Benedetto da Maiano. The **bronze doors** to the New Sacristy are the only surviving work in this material designed by Luca della Robbia; they were cast by Michelozzo (1445–69). These doors were slammed on the Pazzi conspirators in 1478 after they had murdered Giuliano de' Medici, and Lorenzo de' Medici escaped through them. In the lunette above is a terra-cotta *Resurrection* (1444), also by Luca. Michelangelo's *Pietà* has been removed from the left tribune to the Cathedral Museum.

Crypt *(Santa Reparata)* 🏛 †
📷 *Open Mon–Sat 9:30am–12:30pm, 2:30–5:30pm, Sun 9:30am–12:30pm.*
This crypt of the earlier cathedral, entered from the left aisle, was excavated in the 1960s, and contains Roman and early Christian sculptural fragments, 13th and 14thC tombs, and the remains of 14thC frescoes.

Ascent to dome lantern
📷 ✱ *Open Mon–Sat 8:30am–12:30pm, 2:30–5:30pm. Closed Sun.*
The ascent should not be attempted by anyone who suffers from vertigo, claustrophobia or weak legs, but those who can manage the steep climb will be rewarded by a panoramic view and an increased understanding of Brunelleschi's constructional method, which involved the erection of two shells, one inside the other, with these maintenance stairs between.

Baptistry 🏛 † ★ 📷 *Open 9am–12:30pm, 2:30–5:30pm.*
Dante's "bel S. Giovanni," the Baptistry is the oldest building in Florence, although it is not as old as Brunelleschi and his

contemporaries liked to believe. In the early 15thC it was thought to have been the Roman temple of Mars, and it was a deeper influence on Tuscan Renaissance architecture than any real Classical building. Its date is still uncertain, but historians agree that it is not earlier than the 4th–5thC AD, and that it was probably built on the site of the old Roman praetorium. The green and white marble cladding belongs to the 11th–13thC, and the rectangular tribune was added in 1202. The Baptistry was the cathedral of Florence for a century before the completion of S. Reparata.

The gilded bronze Baptistry **doors** ★ chart the progress of sculptural style from Gothic to the Renaissance.

The chronological order of the doors is: 1. **South gate**, from a wax model prepared in 1330 by Andrea Pisano. The 20 highest panels relate the story of John the Baptist; the eight below depict the cardinal and theological virtues. The Renaissance **door surround** is by Vittorio Ghiberti. Above the doors is the *Baptist and Salome* (1571), by Vincenzo Danti. 2. **North gate** (1403–24) by Lorenzo Ghiberti and assistants. These are the doors resulting from the competition set in 1401. Brunelleschi's losing entry and Ghiberti's winner can be seen in the *Bargello*. The 20 highest panels illustrate scenes from the New Testament; below are the four *Evangelists* and four *Church Doctors*. Above the doors is *The Baptist between a Pharisee and a Levite* (1506–11), by G.F. Rustici, with advice from Leonardo. 3. **East gate** (1425–52) by Lorenzo Ghiberti. Michelangelo called these doors "the gates of paradise." They opened a new artistic era when sculptural perspective replaced Gothic stylization. The doors are divided into ten panels with Old Testament scenes. The antique porphyry side columns were presented to Florence by Pisa in 1117 in gratitude for help in the conquest of the Balearic Islands. Above is the *Baptism of Christ*, started by A. Sansovino in 1502, finished by V. Danti in 1564.

The exquisite Baptistry **interior** is more apparently Classical than the exterior and incorporates Roman columns and capitals. The 13thC mosaics in the vault—the *Last Judgment*, the *Creation*, the *Story of Joseph* and the *Baptist*—have never lost their magic despite five centuries of periodic restoration. The 13thC tessellated marble **pavement** around the font, representing the Zodiac, is unmatched in Florence, except by a similar example in *San Miniato*. 14thC Pisan reliefs have been applied to the 16thC font. To the right of the tribune is the **tomb of Cardinal Baldassare Coscia** (1421–7), the schismatic Pope John XXIII, by Donatello and Michelozzo.

Ascent of Campanile

▨ ⅋ *Open summer 9am–7pm, winter 9am–5pm.*

The Campanile (1334–1359) ★ is known as 'Giotto's Tower' although Giotto was responsible only for the first story. It was carried on after his death by Andrea Pisano until 1348 and completed by Francesco Talenti. The originals of the sculptural decorations are in the Cathedral Museum. The climb up to the bell tower is relatively easy and the views are spectacular.

Cathedral Museum *(Museo dell' Opera del Duomo)* ★

Piazza Duomo 9 ☎ *213229. Open Mon–Sat summer 9am–8pm, winter 9am–6pm, Sun and hols 10am–1pm.*

The Cathedral Museum contains an accumulation of important works transferred during the last century from the Duomo, Baptistry and Campanile. The palace has been the administrative headquarters of the Duomo since the early 15thC. Michelangelo carved the *David* in the courtyard.

Ground floor. Sculptures from the 14thC cathedral facade; 16thC drawings of the unfinished facade. In a new room is Brunelleschi's death mask, the wooden model for his dome made for the 1418 competition, and tools which were used for its construction. On the mezzanine is Michelangelo's *Pietà* (1550–c.53) ★ here for the duration of the restoration of the cathedral dome. Perhaps his most tragic religious sculpture, it was made for what he planned would be his own tomb. Vasari says the head of Nicodemus is a self-portrait. Dissatisfied with his unfinished work, he broke it up and gave parts away. They were pieced together in the 18thC.

First floor. **Sala delle Cantorie**. Sit down and decide which of the two **choral galleries** ★ makes your heart sing more joyously. They were removed from the cathedral in the 17thC, stored away and forgotten until the 19thC. On the entrance wall is Luca della Robbia's (1431–8) with the original panels displayed below; opposite is Donatello's (1433–9). Underneath that is Donatello's stark, expressionistically penitent *Magdalen* (1435–55) ★ The 16 statues around the walls by Donatello and others are from the niches of the bell tower. The most startlingly realistic is Donatello's *Abakuk* (1434–6), known as 'Lo Zuccone' ('Big Head'), which can be seen on the wall left of the entrance.

Sala delle Formelle ☆ The **relief panels** were brought here from the Campanile in the 1960s. The earliest are by Andrea Pisano, based on designs by Giotto. The series depicts man's spiritual progress by way of labor, art and the sacraments. "Read but once these inlaid jewels," wrote Ruskin, "and your hour's study will give you strength for all your life."

Sala dell'Altare. The **silver altar** from the Baptistry was begun in 1366, then labored over for a century by craftsmen and artists including Verrocchio and Antonio del Pollaiuolo.

English Cemetery *(Cimitero Protestante)*
Piazzale Donatello. Map **3**B5 ▣ *Open Mon–Sat, Apr–Sept 9am–noon, 3–6pm; Oct–Mar 9am–noon, 3–5pm; Sun and hols 9am–noon. Closed Jan 1, May 1, Aug 15. Ring for admission: tip expected.*

In this oval cemetery lie the remains of Protestants who died in Florence in the late 19thC. Many, like Elizabeth Barrett Browning, had come here from the chilly north to convalesce. Walter Savage Landor, Frances Trollope and Jean Vieusseux are among the famous foreigners buried here.

"Firenze com'era" *(Topographical Museum of Florence as it was)*
Via dell' Oriuolo 24 ☎217305. Map **5**C5 ▣ *Open Mon–Wed, Fri–Sat 9am–2pm, Sun and hols 8am–1pm. Closed Thurs.*

The urban development of Florence from the 15th–19thC is traced in this fascinating museum with maps, topographical prints, plans, paintings, photographs. Among the maps of the 15thC city in the first room is an 18thC reproduction of the 1470 'Chain Map' (Carta della Catena); the original is in Berlin. In the following rooms the delightful lunettes painted by Giusto Utens for the Villa Artimino record the appearance of grand-ducal villas and gardens at the end of the 16thC; and 18thC Florence comes alive in Giuseppe Zocchi's prints of churches, palaces and villas. Finally, comes the shameful story of the destruction of the old center and the building of that monument to 19thC insensitivity, the Piazza della Repubblica.

Fortezza da Basso 🏛

Viale Filippo Strozzi. Map 2B3 ✦ ❀ Open for crafts exhibitions only.

The largest historical monument in Florence and the most signposted, the Fortezza da Basso is now a traffic island ringed by the Viale Filippo Strozzi. The fortress was built in 1534–5 for Alessandro de' Medici, the first Duke of Florence. Supported by Charles V, Alessandro's chief purpose was to cow the people of Florence into unquestioning obedience with a citadel, as one contemporary historian described it, "whereby the citizens lost all hope of ever living in freedom." The design is by Antonio da Sangallo the Younger; the carved stones around the entrance depict the Medici emblem.

Within are a school, a restoration center, a barracks, and, since 1978, the **Crafts Exhibition and Merchandising Pavilion**, where some 30 exhibitions are held each year.

Foundling Hospital *(Spedale degli Innocenti)*   One of the
inaugural buildings of the Renaissance. (See *Santissima Annunziata*.)

Fra Angelico Museum *(Museo dell' Angelico)*
Collection of Fra Angelico's work, now housed in *San Marco*.

Horne Museum 🏛

Via de' Benci 6 ☎244661. Map 5D5 ▨ Open Mon–Fri 4–8pm, Sat 9am–1pm. Closed Sun.

The two enduring achievements of the English art historian Herbert Percy Horne (1864–1916) were his pioneering work on Botticelli, then a still undervalued artist, and the collection he installed in this palace where he lived during the last few years of his life.

The palace was built in 1489 for the Corsi family, and the architect was probably Cronaca, whose Guadagni palace in *Santo Spirito* it resembles. The Corsi were cloth merchants and the design of their palace answered the requirements of their trade: a large cellar for dyeing vats, a sunny gallery over the courtyard portico for drying wool. The stone capitals, carved in the workshop of Andrea Sansovino, are among the finest in Florence.

The **museum** contains no major masterpieces. Horne was not a rich man, but he collected at a time when a keen and educated eye could spot real bargains, and there are many small treasures throughout the museum. There are pictures by Daddi, Pietro Lorenzetti, Filippo Lippi, Beccafumi, Dosso Dossi, and others; Renaissance furniture and majolica; and the pre-industrial domestic utensils which were among Horne's special interests.

The world is made up of earth, air, fire and water – but there is another element – the Florentines.

Pope Boniface VIII (c.1300)

Laurentian Library *(Biblioteca Medici-Laurenziana)*
Library designed by Michelangelo in *San Lorenzo*, epitomizing Mannerist architecture.

Medici Chapels *(Cappelle Medicee)*   The Medici
commissioned some superb works of art for their own glorification in these famous chapels in *San Lorenzo*.

Medici Riccardi Palace 🏛 ★

Via Cavour ☎ *217601. Map* **5***B4* 📷 *Open Mon–Tues,*
Thurs–Sat 9am–12:30pm, 3–5pm, Sun and hols 9am–noon.
Closed Wed.

The palace building boom in 15thC Florence was made possible
by the financial and fiscal policies of Cosimo il Vecchio, and his
palace, built between 1444–1464, was a prototype from which
Florentine palace architecture rarely departed until the 16thC.
The exterior of the palace is best seen from the corner of Via
Cavour.

According to one story, Brunelleschi made a model for the
Medici Palace which Cosimo rejected as being too elaborate.
Brunelleschi flew into a rage and either smashed the model or
sold it to Luca Pitti (see *Pitti Palace*). Certainly Cosimo would
not have wanted to build a family house that was too
ostentatious; he was, after all, the unofficial leader of a
supposedly republican government.

In the event it was Michelozzo, the loyal friend who had
accompanied Cosimo into exile, who built the Medici Palace, a
transitional mixture of medieval and Brunelleschian elements:
biforate windows as in the Palazzo Vecchio, arranged
symmetrically; graduated rustication, very heavy on the ground
floor, entirely smooth at the top; the first *all' antica* palace
cornice in Florence, but unsupported by architrave, frieze or
columns. The crenellated garden wall carries the design back,
with a jerk, into the Middle Ages. These walled side gardens
were attached to most new palaces in this area, but this is one of
the few to have survived.

The ground floor windows, enclosing what was originally a
loggia, were designed by Michelangelo, and are the first
appearance in Florence of the so-called 'kneeling windows'
which became such a common feature of 16thC palaces. The
proportions of the palace were radically altered when the
Riccardi, who bought it in 1659, added the seven northernmost
windows on the Via Cavour.

The interior, much altered over the centuries, now houses
the offices of the Prefecture. Vasari described the Medici Palace
as the first to be built for domestic convenience but, inevitably,
some of the great symbolic events of Florentine history took
place in these rooms. It was here that Lorenzo the Magnificent,
when only 21, accepted control of the government, "for in
Florence one lives ill in the presence of wealth without power."
Emperor Charles VIII was entertained here in 1494, and
Charles V of France in 1536.

Uccello's *Battle of San Romano* hung in Lorenzo's bedroom.
Donatello's *David* and *Judith* were both originally placed in the
courtyard. *Judith*, the tyrant-slayer, was taken away to the
Signoria after the Medici were expelled in 1494, and was
followed there 46yr later by Cosimo I the tyrant in person.
When Cosimo I moved out of the Medici's private palace and
into the Palazzo della Signoria, republican government in
Florence was irrevocably finished. Gradually, the old family
palace was stripped of many Medici-commissioned works of art
which are today among the greatest treasures of the city's
museums and galleries.

Medici Chapel *(Cappella di Benozzo Gozzoli)* ★

📷 *Open Mon–Tues, Thurs–Sat 9am–noon, 3–5pm, Sun and*
hols 9am–noon. Closed Wed.

The **Medici Chapel** ★ retained its treasures. Gozzoli's *Journal*
of the Magi frescoes (1459), the artist's most popular and

imaginative works, were commissioned by Piero de' Medici to commemorate his membership of the religious confraternity of the *Three Magi*. Around the walls members of the Medici family process on horseback through a fairytale Tuscan landscape reminiscent of the Fiesolan hill of Vincigliata (see *Tuscany/Fiesole*).

In the first floor **gallery**, reached by the second staircase on the right of the courtyard, is one of the most exhilarating and ridiculous sights in all Florence. It is Luca Giordano's ceiling fresco, the *Apotheosis of the Medici* (1683), commissioned by the Marchese Riccardi as a gesture of gratitude to the Medici whose palace his family had lately bought.

Michelangelo Museum *(Casa Buonarroti)* ☆
Via Ghibellina 70 ☎*241752. Map* **5***C5* ◼◼ *Open Mon, Wed–Sat 10am–2pm, Sun and hols 9am–1pm. Closed Tues.*
Michelangelo never actually lived here. The house was built on a plot of land he bought for his nephew and was later partly decorated in Michelangelo's honor by his grand-nephew Michelangelo the Younger.

Ground floor. The drawings are reproductions; the originals are sometimes shown on special occasions. The unfinished *Venus* and *Prisoner* statues are probably not by Michelangelo.

First floor. In the room to the left of the stairs are the two most interesting pieces in this museum. The *Madonna della Scala* (1490–2), Michelangelo's earliest known work, is extraordinarily prophetic in style, and like so many of his later works it is unfinished. Poliziano suggested the subject for the *Battle of the Centaurs* (1492), made while Michelangelo was attached to the Medici household; the artist's preoccupation with interlocking male figures began here. In the next room to the left are architectural sketches and the **wooden model for the facade of San Lorenzo** (1517), never carried out; the plain architecture, typical of his early period, was meant to be a setting for elaborate sculpture. Running along the left of the courtyard is the gallery frescoed in homage to Michelangelo by Baroque artists. In a room to the right of the stairs is the **wooden crucifix** from S. Spirito, first attributed to Michelangelo in 1962, although not all art historians agree on this point. In the next room is a **large model of a river god**, the only full-scale model by Michelangelo in existence.

Ognissanti � †
Piazza d'Ognissanti. Map **4***C1. Refectory open 9am–noon, 2–4pm. Offering expected.*
The church of Ognissanti was founded in the late 13thC by the Umiliati, the wool-weaving order who taught Florence the skill which was to be the basis of its prosperity. The building was made over completely in 1627 by the Franciscans. A complete restoration was carried out after the 1966 flood. The facade (1637) by Matteo Nigetti is one of the earliest appearances in Florence of the Baroque style. The slender campanile, very like that of *Santa Maria Novella* but simpler, is 13th–14thC.

The interior is decorated in best-boudoir 17th–18thC Baroque. On the ceiling, *St Francis in Glory* (1770), frescoed by Giuseppe Romei. Over the second altar on the right are the restored remains of Dom. Ghirlandaio's fresco, the *Madonna of Mercy Sheltering the Vespucci Family* (c.1472), which gives the only authentic portrait of Simonetta Vespucci, whose funeral was held in this church in 1476, and a probable portrait of

Amerigo Vespucci as a young boy. In the sacristy, entered from the left transept, is a large School-of-Giotto *Crucifixion*, a *Crucifixion* by Taddeo Gaddi, and a fresco of the *Resurrection* attributed to Agnolo Gaddi (its sinopia can be seen in the refectory).

The entrance to the **refectory museum** is to the far left of the church and through the 15thC cloister. At the far end of the refectory is Dom. Ghirlandaio's fresco of the *Last Supper* (1480).

The two frescoes of saints in their studies, Ghirlandaio's *St Jerome* (1480) ★ on the left wall, and Botticelli's more mystic *St Augustine* (1480) ★ on the right wall, were originally in the choir of the church; the realistic detail of both was inspired by Flemish artist Jan van Eyck's *St Jerome in his Study*, which was owned by Lorenzo de' Medici.

Oltrarno

Although Florence is well served by bridges, any one of which is crossed in a minute, Florentines persist in referring to everything S of the Arno as the Oltrarno, or as the *Arno di là* (over there), as though it were still the suburb it used to be in the Middle Ages. The Oltrarno certainly has a very distinctive character, a far richer urban mix than you will find anywhere N of the Arno in that part of the city Florentines call the *Arno di quà* (over here).

It is a working-class neighborhood amid which some of the oldest and wealthiest Florentine families have maintained palaces for centuries. Thus, some of the most fashionable restaurants and food shops are in and around San Jacopo, but you can just as easily choose your lunch from a market stall in Piazza *Santo Spirito* or eat with students and craftsmen in any one of many cheap family-run trattorias. You can buy chic boutique clothes or antiques, or you can have your old shoes repaired in a hole-in-the-wall workshop.

It was a place of refuge for early Christians, and even after the 14thC walls embraced the Oltrarno and it became the S. Spirito Quarter of the enlarged city, it remained a place favored by outsiders and subversives. The nobles took their last stand here in 1343; here the signal was given for the Ciompi Uprising. Luca Pitti, a leading opponent of the Medici, chose to build his palace on this, or rather 'that,' side of the Arno.

In the 16thC, after Cosimo I chose to make the *Pitti* the official ducal palace, the Oltrarno became the most fashionable address in Florence. Its most exclusive street, and still the most interesting for those who like palaces of the grand-ducal period, was Via Maggio, linked to the Via Tornabuoni by Ammannati's beautiful bridge of *Santa Trìnita*.

(See also *Florence/Walk 3*.)

Orsanmichele ⅢⅢ † ★
Via dei Calzaiuoli. Map 5C4.

The name Orsanmichele refers to an oratory, San Michele in Orto, which stood here in the 8thC. Later the site was occupied by a loggiaed grain market, famous for a miraculous image of the Virgin painted on one of its pillars. The grain market burned down and was replaced by a grander loggia used as an oratory and as a trading center by the guilds of Florence. This loggia, which is the basis of the present structure, was erected from 1337 by Francesco Talenti, Neri di Fioraventi and Benci di Cione.

From 1380 the loggia was enclosed by Simone Talenti and used exclusively for religious worship. The two upper stories were added as warehouses for emergency supplies of grain. The decoration of the church was supervised by the nearby Guelf organization which delegated responsibility for each of the outside niches to a guild. It is fortunate that this decorative program, which was planned from 1339, did not actually get under way until the early 15thC when Florentine sculpture, after a dullish period, leapt forward into the age of Donatello and Ghiberti.

Some original statues have been removed. Donatello's *St George*, made for the smiths and armorers guild, is now in the *Bargello*, and his *St Louis*, made for the Guelf organization, is in the *Santa Croce* Museum. However, more than enough remain to make the four facades of Orsanmichele the best place to study the evolution of Florentine freestanding sculpture.

E side (Via dei Calzaiuoli): Ghiberti's still Gothic *John the Baptist* (1414–16); Verrocchio's *Doubting Thomas* (1466–83) and above it the ceramic medallion by Luca della Robbia (1463). S side (Via dei Lamberti): Donatello's *St Mark* (1411–12); the *Madonna of the Rose*, attributed to Piero di Giovanni Tedesco. W side (Via dell' Arte della Lana): Ghiberti's *St Matthew* (1419–22) and *St Stephen* (1428); Nanni di Banco's Gothic *St Eligius*. N side (Via Orsanmichele); Nanni di Banco's *Four Crowned Saints*; bronze copy of Donatello's marble *St George*, with the original predella of *St George and the Dragon* (1417), the first relief carving to achieve perspective.

Interior. The odd but satisfying shape recalls the original secular function of the church. The pillars are frescoed with damaged and restored images of patron saints of the guilds. Orcagna's **tabernacle ★** (1348–59), one of the most beautiful Gothic aedicules in Italy, houses the miraculous image of the *Virgin* (1347), painted by Daddi to replace the earlier fresco destroyed by fire.

The upper stories of the church, the **Saloni di Orsanmichele**, are entered through the restored 14thC palace of the Arte della Lana (Wool Guild) across a connecting bridge. There are splendid views from these imposing rooms, restored in the 1960s.

Palatine Gallery   Gallery in the *Pitti Palace* with an outstanding collection of 16thC Italian paintings.

Palazzo del Podestà   Built as Florence's first town hall, the building now known as the *Bargello*.

Palazzo Vecchio   See *Signoria*.

Pazzi Chapel   Brunelleschi's chapel in the cloister of *Santa Croce*.

Piazzale Michelangelo
Map 3E5.

Piazzale Michelangelo is the traditional orientation point for a holiday in Florence. The outlook over the city embraces some of the most celebrated and photographed views in the world. The **monument to Michelangelo** (1875) in the centre of the piazzale is dominated by one of the city's two reproductions of Michelangelo's *David* (the original is in the *Accademia*).

If you place yourself at the center of the balustrade facing the

Arno and above the tower of *San Niccolò*, you will see, looking
left to right across Florence: the bell tower of the *Signoria*; the
top of the tower of *Santa Maria Novella*; the *Badia* tower and
immediately to its right the cupola of the *San Lorenzo* Cappella
dei Principi; the white marble tower of the *Duomo*;
Brunelleschi's dome; and, farther right, the minaret-like tower of
Santa Croce; the green dome of the Synagogue; and
the concrete tower of Nervi's stadium complex. In the distance,
left to right, are the hills and valleys of northern Tuscany: see
A–Z/Tuscany for hills behind *Pistoia* and *Prato*; the tower of
Petraia at *Sesto Fiorentino*; the three peaks of Monte Morello;
Fiesole, with the hill of S. Francesco and the Mugnone valley to
its left and Monte Céceri, Vincigliato, and *Settignano* to its
right. Further right, on a clear spring day, you can see as far as
Vallombrosa in the E. Back to Florence and moving to the far
corner of the left balustrade and facing W, looking from the
Arno southward, you can see: the dome of *San Frediano*, the
tower of *Santo Spirito*, the silhouetted *Belvedere* and,
dominating the view from the S, the Victorian crenellations of
the restored Torre del Gallo on the hill of *Arcetri*.

A staircase to the right of the restaurant La Loggia (see
Florence/Restaurants) leads to **San Salvatore al Monte**,
begun in 1499 to a design by Cronaca.

Pitti Palace ▥ ★
Piazza Pitti ☎ 287096. *Map **4**F2* ▣ *Tues–Sat 9am–2pm,
Sun and hols 9am–1pm. Closed Mon.*

Luca Pitti's motive for erecting a building so unusually bold for
mid-15thC Florence was partly a bid to outdo his political rival
Cosimo de' Medici. When work began on the Pitti in the late
1450s, the more simply conceived *Medici Palace* was nearing
completion. The design of the Pitti is traditionally, but without
evidence, attributed to Brunelleschi, and it is possible that the
plans carried out by Luca Fancelli could have been those
Brunelleschi supposedly submitted to Cosimo who rejected
them as too ostentatious.

Although the palace as left unfinished at Pitti's death in 1472
consisted of only the seven central bays of the present structure,
both Machiavelli and Vasari commented on the unique size and
splendor of the Pitti. Even now that the palace has been
enlarged and altered, you can imagine the original impact of
these lofty proportions dramatically clad like an Etruscan
building in huge, rough-hewn stone blocks. Nevertheless, the
Pitti Palace, only one room deep and carved into the steep slope
of its own quarry, must have been an uncomfortable living
space for Pitti's impoverished heirs.

In 1549 the Pittis sold their palace to Eleanor of Toledo,
Cosimo I's wife, and in May of the following year the Medici
entourage moved in. Five years later Vasari's **Corridoio** was
thrown across the Arno to connect the old palace, the Palazzo
Vecchio (see *Signoria*) with the new palace which was to be the
grand-ducal and eventually royal residence for the next three
centuries. Ammannati's extensions, the superb **courtyard ★**
and the wings towards the Boboli Gardens, were carried out
between 1558–70.

A lunette by Utens in *Firenze com'era* shows how the Pitti
looked at the end of the 16thC. The facade was enlarged to its
present width in the early 17thC by G. and A. Parigi. The two
front wings were added in the early 19thC after the return of the
bland, good-natured Lorraine dukes (who entertained all

foreigners at their palace regardless of social standing). Possession passed to the House of Savoy in 1860. Victor Emmanuel, who occupied the Pitti without much pleasure while Florence was briefly capital of Italy, installed his throne in a room which is now part of the State Apartments, overlooking the courtyard and the house, marked by a plaque, where the exiled Dostoevsky was writing *The Idiot*.

Palatine Gallery *(Galleria Palatina)* ★
▓ 𝒦 *Ticket also good for Argenti Museum.*

Try to allow the full morning for these two most important sections of the Pitti, the Palatine and Argenti. To reach the Palatine you must climb Ammannati's long, steep staircase to the first floor. The Palatine is famous for its great grand-ducal collection of 16thC paintings of which the supreme treasures are the Raphaels and Titians, mostly portraits; also of outstanding quality are the frescoes by Pietro da Cortona. The tiered arrangement, in keeping with the period of the rooms, is that of a 17thC princely collection; the works are thus placed for decorative effect and not, as in the Uffizi, according to date and school. Thanks to the splendid lighting, the good condition of the pictures and the impeccable taste and knowledge with which they are hung, it doesn't take long to accustom yourself to the lack of didactic guidance. Indeed, after the Palatine, the Uffizi seems dismayingly like a textbook.

From the vestibule you pass through two Neoclassical rooms to the Sala di Venere, where the gallery proper begins. On the ceiling, the bold **fresco allegory** (1641–2) ★ by Pietro da Cortona, which was commissioned by Ferdinand II and executed with the help of Ciro Ferri, begins with the *Ideal Prince Being Torn from the Arms of Venus*; the cycle continues through the next four rooms. In the center of the room is Canova's statue of *Venus*, sent to Florence by Napoleon as a replacement for the looted Uffizi *Venus de Medici*.

Paintings/Titian: *The Concert* (c.1510–13) ★ is an early work which passed as a Giorgione for 250yr after its purchase in 1654 by Cardinal Leopold; *Portrait of Pietro Aretino* (1545) ★ who was the talented, roistering Venetian intellectual who thought so highly of this likeness that he presented it to Cosimo I; and *Portrait of a Lady, 'La Bella'* (1536) ★ with perhaps the same model as the *Uffizi Venus*. Of the two glowing landscapes by Rubens, *Peasants Returning from the Fields* (c.1637) ★ is the finer. The *Portrait of Julius II*, a contemporary copy of Raphael's original, is now in the National Gallery in London.

Sala di Apollo. On the ceiling (1647–60), *The Young Prince Converses with Apollo*, protector of the Arts and Sciences. Paintings: Guido Reni's late masterpiece *Cleopatra*; *Sacred Family* and *Deposition* by Andrea del Sarto; Rosso Fiorentino's *Madonna Enthroned with Saints* (1522), enlarged to its present size when it was bought from the church of S. Spirito. Titian: the intensely romantic *Portrait of a Man* (c.1540) ★ was called 'The Englishman' because the subject was thought to be the Duke of Norfolk; and *The Magdalen* (c.1531) ★ is more ripe than repentant.

Sala di Marte. Ceiling (1645–7): the Medici arms surmounted by the grand-ducal crown dominate the composition. Paintings: Tintoretto's finest work in the gallery, *Portrait of Luigi Cornaro*; van Dyck's *Cardinal Bentivoglio* (c.1623), Papal Ambassador to Flanders and France; Titian's *Ippolito de' Medici* (1532), dressed as a grandee of Hungary and painted 3yr before he was poisoned at Gaeta; Rubens'

Consequences of War (1638), an allegory of the Thirty Years War. Mars, escaped from the arms of Venus, destroys Harmony, The Arts, and Family Life. Rubens himself explained "that grief-stricken woman in black" as "the unfortunate Europe, who, for so many years now, has suffered plunder, outrage, and misery." Also by Rubens, *The Four Philosophers*, a self-portrait with his brother and two scholars.

Sala di Giove, formerly the grand-ducal throne room. The frescoes (1643–6) portray the eponymous god in the center and other gods in the lunettes. Paintings: Raphael's Portrait of a woman, *La Velata* (c.1516) ✫ the virtuoso handling of the sleeve contrasts with the purity of outline which was to influence Ingres; Bronzino's very early *Portrait of Guidobaldo della Rovere*; Andrea del Sarto's graceful *St John the Baptist as a Boy* (1523) ✫ which once belonged to Cosimo I and hung in the Uffizi Tribuna – the background has been damaged by early restoration; Fra Bartolommeo's monumental *St Mark* (1514–16), and *Deposition* (c.1516) ✫ which was his last and greatest work, left partly unfinished; and Perugino's *Madonna Adoring the Christ Child*, known as the 'Madonna del Sacco' after the bolster on which the child is seated.

Sala di Saturno. The last of Pietro da Cortona's fresco sequence (1663–5) was executed by Ciro Ferri. Raphael's *Madonna della Seggiola* (of the chair) (c.1515) ✫ is now, as always, the most popular picture in the Palatine. In the 19thC the waiting list for permission to copy her was 5yr. The legend is that the circular panel was taken from the end of a wine cask, but the more plausible explanation for the tondo is Raphael's wish to master a traditional Florentine compositional challenge. Also by Raphael are portraits of *Agnolo* ✫ and of *Maddalena Doni* (c.1505–6) ✫ which were painted a few years after their marriage (an occasion celebrated also by Michelangelo's *Doni Tondo* in the *Uffizi*). Leonardo's *Mona Lisa* suggested Maddalena's pose. *Portrait of Tommaso Inghirami* (c.1515) ✫ – he was an important figure at the court of Leo X – and the portrait reveals the character of the sitter as much through his hands as face; and the *Grand-ducal Madonna* (c.1504–5), so-called because the Grand Duke Ferdinand III, who bought it in 1799, took it with him wherever he traveled. The beauty of Perugino's *Deposition* (1495) ✫ has been revealed by cleaning.

Sala dell'Iliade. Neo-Classical decorations. Paintings: Justus Sustermans' *Portrait of Waldemar Christian, Prince of Denmark* (c.1662), the artist's best-known work; Andrea del Sarto's *Assumption of The Virgin* (c.1527), based on the similar, earlier composition on the opposite wall; Artemisia Gentileschi's dramatic *Judith*; Raphael's portrait of a pregnant woman, *La Gravida* (c.1504–8) ✫; and Velazquez' *Philip IV on Horseback*, a studio work sent to Florence as a model for an equestrian statue. In centre of room, *Charity* (1824) by L. Bartolini.

Sala dell' Educazione di Giove. Paintings: Caravaggio's *Sleeping Cupid* (c.1608); and Cristofano Allori's *Judith* ✫ – one of the most universally admired 17thC Florentine paintings for its technical perfection and ravishing use of color.

Sala della Stufa. Formerly a bathroom, the **frescoes** (1637–41) ✫ represent the Four Ages of Man and are among Pietro da Cortona's minor masterpieces. Sala di Bagno. An early 19thC bathroom.

Sala di Ulisse. Paintings: Moroni's *Portrait of a Woman*, intensely human; Raphael's *Madonna of the Impannata* (1514) – the *impannate* are the waxpaper-paned windows in the background; and Cigoli's expressive *Ecce Homo*.

Sala di Prometeo. Paintings: Filippo Lippi's *Madonna and Child* (c.1452), the quintessential Early Renaissance picture; Signorelli's *Holy Family*; D. Beccafumi's *Holy Family*. Off the Sala di Prometeo are four rooms decorated in the 1830s. Paintings include landscapes by C. von Poelenburg; Titian's portrait of *Tommaso Mosti* (1526); A. del Sarto's *Stories of Joseph* (1520–23); G. Schalken's *Girl with a Candle*; and fruit paintings by Rachele Ruysch.

Sala del Poccetti, named for the artist whose frescoes glorifying the House of Medici decorate the ceiling. Paintings: Rubens' *Portrait of a Woman*, probably Catherine Manners, Duchess of Buckingham; D. Fetti's two genre-like parables; F. Furini's exuberant *Hylas and the Nymphs*.

Volterrano Wing. Pictures by 17th and 18thC artists, notably Furini, Giovanni da S. Giovanni, Cigoli, Bilivert and Salvator Rosa. First room. Volterrano's *A Trick of the Parish Priest Arlotto* (c.1650) illustrates an anecdote about Arlotto, a jokester priest who lived in the Mugello in the 1440s. Last room. The most complete collection of fruit paintings in existence by 17thC Neapolitan woman artist Giovanna Garzoni.

Argenti Museum ☆
Entrance near left corner of courtyard ▄▄ *Open Wed, Fri 9am–2pm, Sun 9am–1pm.*

Despite its name, this is not primarily a museum of silverware. The exquisite treasures bought or commissioned by the Medici and Lorraine dynasties which it contains form one of the richest displays of luxury craftsmanship in the world. There is no better place to follow the changing taste of Florence's rulers, from the sublime collection of Lorenzo's antique vases to the ridiculous, ingenious opulence that appealed in later centuries. The exhilarating Baroque frescoes of the ground floor apartments, used as reception rooms for important visitors by Ferdinand II, are rare in Florence for their sense of fun.

Sala di S. Giovanni. Frescoed by S. Giovanni (1634–36), Furini (1638–42) and others for the marriage of Ferdinand II and Vittoria della Rovere, this room is one of the final, most exuberant tributes the Medici were to pay to Lorenzo the Magnificent.

Sala Buia. Lorenzo's collection of **antique vases** ★ is the glory of the museum. That a sensitive, discriminating poet-diplomat would have his initials carved on such objects shows the confidence of Renaissance man. Grotticina. Carved wooden relief by Grinling Gibbons given to Cosimo II by Charles II of England. The next three rooms are frescoed with stupendous illusionist architecture and historical or allegorical subjects by A.M. Colonna (1638–44). Sala degli Avori. Baroque ivory fantasies, some beautiful, some bizarre jokes.

First floor. Three rooms left of the stairs contain the silver treasure of the Archbishop of Salzburg, brought to Florence in 1815 by Ferdinand III. In the fourth are examples of the not altogether healthy grand-ducal interest in anthropology. Sala dei Cammei. A wonderful collection of cameos, with a *pietradura* mosaic of the Piazza Signoria (1598). Sala dei Gioielli. **Pietradura exvoto** (1617–24) of Cosimo II, a portrait in precious stones, the ultimate in grand-ducal decadence; and a fine collection of Baroque pearls and engraved classical gems mounted on rings.

Returning to the ground floor the exit is through the former grand-ducal bedroom.

Gallery of Modern Art *(Galleria d'Arte Moderna)*
■ *Tickets at the gallery entrance on second floor.*

In the 19thC when tourists, even more singlemindedly than today, came to Florence to study the work of artists long dead, this is what living Tuscan artists were producing: stuffy, academic paintings, orgasmic nudes, and elaborate furniture. In the middle of the 19thC Italian painters reacted with their own Impressionist movement. They are known as the Macchiaioli, and their work is to be found in Rms XXIII–XXVI, which also afford rare views of the Oltrarno and the nave of *Santo Spirito*. The gallery has recently been reorganized and houses some 2,000 works in its 30 rooms.

    Appartamenti Monumentali. Occupying the right half of the first floor and nowadays usually closed to the public, this apartment, which includes the Savoy throne room, contains no major work of art but is notable for some very fine late Neo-Classical decoration. Most elegant are the oval Queen Margherita's Dressing Room (late 18thC) and the Neo-Classical Sala Bianca, where fashion shows now take place beneath superb stuccowork by G. Albertolli (1776–80).

    Meridiana Palace. Behind the right wing of the Pitti, this sub-palace was the preferred residence of Victor Emmanuel. It houses the fine Contini-Bonacossi Collection of Italian and Spanish paintings, not yet open to the public.

    Coach Museum (Museo delle Berline). Although advertised, the official word is that this is closed for some years.

Ponte Vecchio ★
Map 4D3.

The Ponte Vecchio spans the Arno at its narrowest point and is very likely the site of the Roman bridge which carried the N–S traffic of the Via Cassia. The present structure dates from 1345, when an earlier bridge was rebuilt so solidly that it has withstood all subsequent floods. The jewelers of the Ponte Vecchio were among the first to be notified of the impending flood of 1966. Their stock was saved, but their shops and Vasari's corridor, which crosses the river above the E side of the bridge, were severely damaged. It has also survived the other dangers. The oldest bridge in Florence was the only one spared in August 1944, but the retreating German army blocked access to it, mining Por S. Maria to the N and Borgo S. Jacopo to the S.

    The Ponte Vecchio was the Sarajevo of medieval Italy. At its N end, where an equestrian statue of Mars then stood, Buondelmonte dei Buondelmonti was assassinated on the Easter morning of 1215, and a smouldering personal vendetta erupted into the Guelf-Ghibelline civil wars.

    There have been shops on the Ponte Vecchio since the 13thC, occupied first by tanners, then butchers, linen merchants, greengrocers and blacksmiths. In 1593 Ferdinand I decided that these "vile arts" were inappropriate to a passage linking the two grand-ducal palaces. The shops were cleared and rented at twice the price to 41 goldsmiths and eight jewelers. The present tenants may not be able to trace their occupancy back that far, but most have been here for many generations.

    (See also *Florence/Shopping*.)

Porta Romana
Map 2E2.

Porta Romana is the southernmost of the old city gates and one of the modern city's busiest exits. Erected in 1326, the tower has been cropped, but the doors are original, as is the 14thC fresco of the Madonna. A stretch of preserved walls runs N along Viale Petrarca to Piazza T. Tasso. To the s is the old Siena road and the new road to Poggio Imperiale and Impruneta. The Viale dei Colli Alti winds eastwards from Porta Romana to Piazza F. Ferrrucci, and it is now possible to walk along the city walls as far as the *Belvedere*.

In the villa in Via Colombaia, Florence Nightingale was born in 1820.

Rucellai Palace �III ★
Via della Vigna Nuova 18. Map 4C2. Only open to special group tours.

Probably the most beautiful and certainly the most carefully considered of all Florentine palaces, Alberti's Palazzo Rucellai was the first in Florence to conform to the Classical Orders. It was built in the 1450s for Giovanni Rucellai who, after an early retirement from business, devoted himself to scholarship.

Bernardo Rossellino supervised construction, the cost of which in labor alone must have been exorbitant. Alberti's complex and subtle design is chiseled on to a flat stone surface. If you look closely you can see where the stone blocks meet across the drawn rustication.

Contemporary documents leave many crucial questions about the Rucellai unanswered. Even the attribution to Alberti, although generally accepted on stylistic grounds, is undocumented. But examination of the stone work during the most recent restoration confirms the theory that Alberti's plan suggested only the five bays on the left (as you face the palace); the left door would thus have been the central and only entrance. It was very likely Giovanni Rucellai himself who supervised the extension of the module to the right, until he was interrupted by a financial crisis caused by the loss at sea of two ships. Along the entablature, Fortune's Sail, the Rucellai heraldic device, alternates with the Medici Diamond Ring: a reminder of the political alliance of the two families.

The Rucellai Loggia, opposite the palace, was probably made for the wedding celebrations of Giovanni's son to a grand-daughter of Cosimo il Vecchio. It belongs to the 1460s, and if the design was suggested by Alberti, the execution was oddly clumsy, as you can see from the inside (the Loggia is often used for art exhibitions). This was the last of the Florentine family loggias, which became impracticable due to the rising cost of land and therefore unfashionable. It could only have been built for a person as rich and as conservative as Giovanni Rucellai, who acquired over half a dozen properties to create the site.

Behind the left flank of the palace is the little church of San Pancrazio, long since deconsecrated and under restoration. It will house a museum of sculptures by Marino Marini.

The adjacent **Rucellai Chapel ★** entered from the Via della Spada, is, at last, restored. The porter of the Palazzo Rucellai will unlock the door (tip). Alberti designed this chapel, the first barrel-vaulted building in the city, in 1467 to house Giovanni Rucellai's funerary monument, the **Aedicule of the Church of the Holy Sepulcher**. An imitation in miniature of the original antique church in Jerusalem, this aedicule is Alberti's most fascinating work, epitomizing everything he stood for as an artist. Inside the aedicule is a damaged fresco of the *Resurrection* by Baldovinetti. The wall opposite the entrance separating the chapel from the church was built in the 19thC.

Santissima Annunziata ▥ † ★
Map 3B4.

The **Via dei Servi**, which links SS. Annunziata to the Duomo, was built as a processional street between the two most important of the Florentine churches dedicated to the Virgin. It is named after the Servite Order, of which SS. Annunziata is the mother church. On the Feast of the Virgin's Nativity the Via dei Servi is lined with candy stalls and children carry paper lanterns from the Duomo to SS. Annunziata.

As you walk from the Duomo, notice among the 16thC palaces three on the left: the **Pucci** palace (entrance in Via de' Pucci), with an imposing but battered carved emblem of Leo X on the corner; the **Niccolini** palace (no. 15), built in 1550 to a design by Baccio d'Agnolo; and, on the corner of Piazza SS. Annunziata, the **Grifoni** (1557–63), one of the few brick palaces in Florence, built by Ammannati for one of Cosimo I's courtiers, and now the Riccardi Mannelli, used as the regional government headquarters.

Although Piazza SS. Annunziata is architecturally the most harmonious open space in Florence, the apparently unified design was achieved over a period of nearly two centuries. The square had assumed its present size by the 14thC, but the first attempt to regularize it was Brunelleschi's loggia of the **Innocenti Hospital** (1419–26) (**Spedale degli Innocenti**). The central arch of the church portico was built in the mid-15thC, probably by Antonio da Sangallo the Elder. Next, chronologically, came the **loggia of the Servite Confraternity** (1516–25), by Antonio da Sangallo the Younger and Baccio d'Agnolo, deliberately mimicking the Innocenti across the square. Finally, in the early 17thC, the church portico was extended into a loggia.

The equestrian **statue of Ferdinand I** in the center of the square is Giambologna's last work, finished in 1608 by his pupil P. Tacca. It is the subject of Browning's poem _The Statue and the Bust_. Also by Tacca are the two small, fantastic, poison-green **fountains** (1629).

The Spedale degli Innocenti was the first foundling hospital in the world, and Brunelleschi's **loggia ★** is the first building in Florence to apply Classical ideas to the Tuscan Romanesque style. The original loggia consists of the central nine bays. Ten of the ceramic **tondos** of swaddled babies (c.1487) are by Andrea della Robbia; the two at either end, however, are imitations.

Innocenti Gallery _(Galleria dell' Instituto degli Innocenti)_ ▥
Piazza SS. Annunziata 12 ☎ _247795. Map **5**A5_ ▧ _Open Mon, Tues, Thurs–Sat: summer 9am–7pm; winter 9am–1pm; Sun and hols 9am–2pm. Closed Wed._

This gallery on the first floor contains works by, among others, Luca della Robbia, Piero di Cosimo, and Domenico Ghirlandaio, including his _Adoration of the Magi_ (1488).

The **Church ★** of SS. Annunziata was founded in 1234 by seven aristocratic families. It became an important shrine, visited by pilgrims from all over Europe, after it was dedicated in the 14thC to a miraculous image of the Virgin Annunciate. Michelozzo, who was the brother of the Servite Prior, rebuilt the church between 1444–81.

The central door under the portico leads to Michelozzo's atrium, known as the **Chiostro dei Voti** after the life-size wax effigies the pilgrims left of themselves. By the 17thC there were some 600 of these ex-votos in the church; all have disappeared. The **frescoes** ☆ have recently been returned after restoration. Illumination is poor, so go in daytime, or use a flashlight. Right portico wall: the *Assumption* (1517) by Rosso Fiorentino; the *Visitation* (1516) by Pontormo. Right wall, far corner: the *Birth of the Virgin* (1514) by Andrea del Sarto. Nave wall: right of nave entrance, the *Arrival of the Magi* (1511) by Andrea del Sarto; left of nave entrance, *The Nativity* (1460–2) which is Baldovinetti's masterpiece, badly eroded by time and damp, but still showing one of the loveliest landscapes in Tuscan art. Left of the entrance from the portico and on the left wall: *Miracles of S. Filippo Benizzi* (1509–10), five of Andrea del Sarto's earliest frescoes.

The extravagantly stuccoed and gilded **nave** and side chapels, decorated in the 16th–19thC when SS. Annunziata was, as indeed it still is, the fashionable church of Florence, are in striking contrast to the strict harmony of the square. Immediately to the left of the nave entrance is the **tempietto** designed by Michelozzo for Piero di Cosimo to house the *Miraculous Image of the Virgin*, whose head is traditionally said to have been painted by an angel, but which has been repainted so often that it is now of no artistic importance. The *tempietto* bears an inscription which will interest students of the Florentine character that reads: 'the marble alone cost 4,000 florins.'

Many of the nave chapels contain splendid Baroque and Neo-Classical decorations. One of the best is the first on the left, the **Feroni Chapel** (1692) by G.B. Foggini. Over the altar, in an ornate, twisting frame, is the *Vision of St Julian* (c.1455) ★ by Castagno. The fresco was whitewashed 100yr after the artist's death as the result of an untrue story told by Vasari that Castagno had murdered Domenico Veneziano. In the second chapel on the left is Castagno's powerful fresco depicting the *Trinity* (1454–5) ☆ with St. Jerome between the Madonna and St Mary Cleofe; and in the chapel to the right of the presbytery, a marble *Pietà* by Bandinelli, who is buried here with his wife.

The **presbytery**, known as the Tribune or Rotonda, was begun by Michelozzo in 1451, finished by Manetti in 1477 according to advice given by Alberti, but much altered by the 18thC decorations. The chapel opposite the nave entrance was decorated by Giambologna for his own grave and those of other Flemish artists working in Florence; the frescoes are by Poccetti. In the next chapel to its left is a *Resurrection* (c.1550) by Bronzino.

The **Chiostro dei Morti** is entered from the left door under the facade portico. Over the door in the far right corner is one of Andrea del Sarto's most loved and famous works, the *Madonna del Sacco* (1525) ☆

Sant' Apollonia, Castagno Museum ▥ ★
Via XXVII Aprile 1 ☎287074. Map 3B4. Temporarily closed.
Shortly after his return from Venice in 1444, Andrea del Castagno painted his *Last Supper* ★ for the nuns of S. Apollonia. The refectory of their former convent is now a museum centered round this fresco, which is probably the best-known and most influential of all *Last Suppers*, apart from Leonardo's in Milan. The scene is set in a fantastic marbled niche. Christ has not yet revealed the mystery of the sacrament. The sculptured peasant faces of the disciples are calm. On this side of the table the brooding figure of Judas prepares us for the

announcement, "One of you shall betray me." Vasari said
Castagno looked and behaved like a Judas, and there is certainly
something sinister about much of his work.

Above the *Last Supper*, and of at least the same powerful
quality, are Castagno's three *Scenes from the Passion*, which have
tragically deteriorated. Their sinopie, uncovered when the
frescoes were detached for restoration, are displayed on the
opposite wall. Castagno's *Famous Men and Women*, painted for
the Villa Pandolfini at Legnaia and at one time hung in this
museum, are now on view in the *Uffizi*.

Santi Apostoli 🏛 †
Map **4D3**.

Charlemagne did not found SS. Apostoli, as the inscription on
the otherwise modest facade boasts, nevertheless, this beautiful
little church in the center of medieval Florence is very old.

The portal is 16thC, probably by Benedetto da Rovezzano,
but the **interior ★** apart from the 15th–16thC side chapels, is
the earliest on this side of the Arno except for the Baptistry
(*Duomo*), with which it is roughly contemporary. Vasari
confirms what will be obvious to anyone who knows the
churches of *Santo Spirito* and *San Lorenzo* when he tells us
that Brunelleschi was profoundly influenced by SS. Apostoli.
Looking at the nave and aisles from the altar end, you might
almost believe that Brunelleschi designed this interior. In the
right aisle, second altar, is Vasari's *Immaculate Conception*
(1541), one of his best and most reproduced paintings,
historically important as the most scholarly pictorial
representation of a popular belief. At the top of the left aisle is a
large terra-cotta tabernacle by Giovanni della Robbia which is
of better quality than many of his works. Next to it is Benedetto
da Rovezzano's **tomb of Oddo Altoviti** (1507), whose palace,
also by Benedetto, stands on the S side of the square.

The tiny Piazza del Limbo takes its name from the
unbaptized babies who were once buried here. To the left of the
church is a relief of the *Madonna and Child* by Benedetto da
Maiano on the flank of the Rosselli del Turco palace, the facade
of which, by Baccio d'Agnolo (1517), is in Borgo SS. Apostoli.

Santa Croce ★ 🏛 †
Map **5D4**.

"Wait then for an entirely bright morning; rise with the sun,
and go to Santa Croce, with a good opera-glass in your pocket."

If you are going to Santa Croce to study the numerous and
instructive *trecento* frescoes, you should follow Ruskin's advice.
But do leave plenty of time. Ruskin scorned the Renaissance,
but no modern tourist would want to rush in and out of the
Pazzi Chapel and miss some of the finest Renaissance sculptures
in Florence.

Santa Croce is not a particularly cheerful quarter. Before the
1966 flood, which caused terrible damage in this low-lying area,
it was densely populated with working-class families and
craftsmen's workshops. Many of these people have now moved
elsewhere and the craftsmen have been replaced by the so-called
leather factories which sell to tourists. But it is still a
neighborhood which stretches one's sense of history. This was
the center of the dyeing trade, one of the foundations of
Florentine mercantile prosperity in the 14th–16thC. One of
its main streets is still called Corso dei Tintori, and some of the
palaces were built to accommodate the dyeing vats (see *Horne*

Santa Croce

Museum). The imagination is carried back much further by three streets which trace the semicircular outline of the Roman amphitheater immediately to the w of the Piazza S. Croce.

This great Franciscan preaching church was begun in 1294, possibly by Arnolfo di Cambio, "with Giotto at his side and Dante looking on," or so Ruskin liked to imagine. The Franciscans, as he says, wanted a church for "preaching, prayer, sacrifice, burial," not for "self-glorification or town-glorification." Be that as it may, consecration was delayed by a schism in the order until the 15thC, when the Renaissance artists who worked here were evidently indifferent to Franciscan ideals of self-abnegation.

Because Michelangelo and Galileo, among other great Italians, are buried here, S. Croce can be regarded as a kind of pantheon of Italian genius. 19thC romantics found this idea irresistible and must take the blame for the hideous facade, which was paid for by an Englishman, as well as the unfortunate statue of Dante in the square and the minaret-like Gothic bell tower.

Apart from these anachronisms the square looks much as it did in the 16th and 17thC when football matches and other spectacles were staged here by the grand dukes. A disk, dated February 10, 1565 on the ground floor of the frescoed Palazzo dell' Antella (no. 21) marks the center line. The palace (1619), by Giulio Parigi, was frescoed in 20 days by 12 assistants of Giovanni da S. Giovanni. Less picturesque but architecturally more strenuous is the Serristori-Cocchi palace (no. 1, opposite the church) attributed to Baccio d'Agnolo.

During the period of puritanical hysteria induced by Savonarola, heretics were burned in this square, and book burnings continued until 1580. Earlier, in the prime years of the Medicean Republic, S. Croce was the setting for elaborate pageants in honor of Lorenzo the Magnificent's betrothal to Clarice Orsini and of Giuliano's love for Simonetta Vespucci.

The immense, barn-like **church interior** ★ (see plan) is T-shaped: a broad nave crossed at the bottom by a straight row of 12 chapels. The nave side chapels were added in 1560 by

Vasari; and the floor is paved with some 276 tombstones (14th–19thC).

The most outstanding monuments in the nave are as follows, starting with the right nave: 1. Relief carving of the *Madonna and Child* (1478) by A. Rossellino. 2. *Tomb of Michelangelo* (1570) by Vasari; there is a sad irony about this tomb made by the servant-artist to Cosimo I for the artist who always refused to work for the tyrannical duke. 3. Pentagonal marble **pulpit** (1472–6) by B. da Maiano. 4. *Monument to Vittorio Alfieri* (1810) by Canova. 5. Donatello's *Annunciation* (c.1435) ✩ in gilded *pietra serena*; the architectural surround was designed in collaboration with Michelozzo. 6. *Tomb of Leonardo Bruni* (1444) by B. Rossellino, a prototype for Florentine funerary sculpture and a direct influence on 7. Left nave: 7. *Tomb of Carlo Marsuppini* (1453) by Desiderio da Settignano. 8. 18thC *Monument to Galileo* designed by Giulio Foggini.

Chapels. **A. Castellani Chapel.** Frescoes of *Scenes from the Lives of Saints Anthony Abbot, Nicolas, John the Divine and John the Baptist* (c.1385) by A. Gaddi and pupils. **B. Baroncelli Chapel.** Frescoed (1332–8) by T. Gaddi and portraying *Scenes from the Life of Mary.* **C. Sacristy.** 16thC intarsiaed and inlaid bench chest. The beautiful *Crucifixion* on the right wall is by T. Gaddi. **D. Rinuccini Chapel.** Frescoes (c.1365) by Giovanni da Milano and the Master of the Rinuccini Chapel: right wall, *Scenes from the Life of Mary Magdalen*; and on the left wall, *Scenes from the Life of the Virgin.* Gothic wrought-iron gate (1373). **E. Novitiate Chapel** (1445) by Michelozzo, commissioned by Cosimo il Vecchio. On the altar, terra-cotta tabernacle of the *Madonna and Child with Angels and Saints* (c.1480) by Andrea della Robbia or a close follower. Galileo is buried in this chapel.

The two chapels to the right of the chancel, the Peruzzi (**F.**) and the Bardi (**G.**), were frescoed by Giotto at the height of his mature powers. An overwhelming influence on Masaccio and thus on the whole of *quattrocento* Florentine painting, they were covered with whitewash in the 18thC. Rediscovered in the 19thC they were subjected to heavy overpainting. These accretions have now been removed, and what you see is entirely by Giotto's hand. Enough is left to help you solve the puzzle but not quite enough to give instant esthetic pleasure. **F. Peruzzi Chapel** ✩ Frescoes (c.1326–30) on the right wall show *Scenes from the Life of St John the Divine*; on the left wall, *Scenes from the Life of St John the Baptist.* **G. Bardi Chapel** ✩ Ruskin compared this chapel to "a large, beautiful, colored Etruscan vase inverted over your heads like a diving-bell." Frescoes (c.1315–20) of *Scenes from the Life of St Francis.* Altarpiece on panel (c.1250–60) by the Master of the Bardi Chapel.

H. Chancel. Frescoes and stained glass (c.1380) of the *Legend of the True Cross* by A. Gaddi. The *Crucifix* over the altar is by the master of the Fogg Pietà. **I. Bardi di Vernio Chapel.** Frescoes (1335–8) show *Scenes from the Life of St Sylvester* by Maso di Banco. **J. Niccolini Chapel** (ask sacristan to open the gate). A remarkable anticipation of the 17thC Baroque style built in 1579–85 by Antonio Dossi. **K. Bardi Chapel.** The wooden **crucifix** by Donatello is supposed to be the one Brunelleschi criticized for looking like a peasant on a cross. To the right of the church is the entrance to the **cloisters**, the **Pazzi Chapel** and the **Santa Croce Museum.**

Brunelleschi planned the Pazzi Chapel around 1430. Building began in 1443, and the upper part of the facade was completed after his death. The **interior** ★ was more successful even than the *San Lorenzo* Old Sacristy, and probably sums up the modern ideal of the early Renaissance more completely than any other single monument in Florence; and there is no other place that has such a calming and restorative effect on the spirits. But it is not quite perfect. As you can see in the corners where fragmentary pilasters are awkwardly squeezed, Brunelleschi did not fully solve the structural problem he set himself here. The blue and white terra-cotta **tondos** of the *Apostles* in the chapel are by Luca della Robbia; the polychrome **tondos** of the *Evangelists* in the pendentives have been attributed to Brunelleschi.

Santa Croce Museum *(Museo Cimabue)* ☆
Piazza Santa Croce 16 ☎*244619. Map 5D4* ▦ *Open summer 9am–12:30pm, 3–6:30pm; winter 9am–12:30pm, 3–5pm. Ticket also valid for Pazzi Chapel and Cloisters.*
The most important works are in the refectory. Cimabue's *Crucifixion* ☆ is one of the most tragic victims of the 1966 flood. Donatello's St. Louis of Toulouse ☆ (1423) was originally made for *Orsanmichele*. The detached fresco of *The Last Supper* on the far wall is Taddeo Gaddi's best work. On the long walls are fragments of frescoes by Orcagna, recovered from the church where they were found beneath Vasari's altars.

The **second cloister** is entered from the far right-hand corner of the first cloister, past a splendid **portal** by Benedetto da Maiano. Finished in 1453 by a close follower of Brunelleschi, this is one of the most beautiful cloisters in Florence.

San Felice ▥
Map 4E2.
This church, in its busy little triangular piazza a few steps from the Pitti, has an attractive Renaissance facade attributed to Michelozzo. The interior is calm, spacious and much restored with a good Giottesque crucifix over the right side door.

I heard last night a little child go singing.
'Neath Casa Guidi windows, by the church,
O bella libertà, O bella!
            Elizabeth Barrett Browning, *Casa Guidi Windows*

This may have been the first center for battered wives. In the Renaissance its Dominican nuns offered refuge to women who fled from their husbands. The Brownings lived at Casa Guidi (Piazza S. Felice 8) for 15yr until Elizabeth's death in 1861. A passionate supporter of the Risorgimento, Elizabeth's existence was marred by a loathing for her neighbor, Leopold II.

Santa Felicita ▥
Map 4E3.
There has been a church on this site for nearly 2,000yr, the first being a hiding place and burial ground for early Christians. In the Renaissance the Benedictine nuns of S. Felicita ran a successful quarry on their properties behind the church, but the building was much altered in the 16thC when it was used as a private chapel by the Medici dukes. In 1736 it was thoroughly remodeled by Ferdinand Ruggieri, who did not, however, disturb the facade portico built by Vasari in 1564 to support his aerial corridor, which passes through the church on its way from the Uffizi to the Pitti. Today the oldest monument in the square is the granite column erected in 1381.

Interior. To the right of the entrance is the Brunelleschian
Capponi Chapel decorated by Pontormo 1525–8 (light
switch behind a pilaster on the left). The *Deposition* ★ over the
altar is really a meditation on the beautiful, weightless body of
the dead Christ. It is probably Pontormo's most intensely felt
and emotionally affecting masterpiece – the figure in brown on
the right may be a self-portrait. On the right wall is his
Annunciation, revealed as another masterpiece by cleaning in
the 1960s. In the pendentives of the cupola are four **tondos of
the Evangelists** (the *St Mark* is by Bronzino). The grand-ducal
tribunes are on either side of the nave W of the transepts. The
charming choir (1610–20) is by Cigoli.

Around the corner from the square in Via Guicciardini is
Palazzo Guicciardini (no. 15), birthplace of the historian
Francesco Guicciardini and still occupied by his descendants.

San Firenze ▥ †
Map **5**D5.

The facade of S. Firenze, which unites three separate earlier
buildings, is the biggest and best 18thC Baroque spectacle in
Florence. On the left side is the **facade of the church of
S. Filippo Neri** designed by Ferdinando Ruggieri in 1715. The
central and right-hand section (1772–5), formerly the church
and convent of S. Apollinare, now the Tribunal, is by Zanobi
del Rosso. Opposite is the elegant **Gondi** palace (1490–1501) by
Giuliano da Sangallo. Ring for the porter to see the courtyard.

San Frediano
Map **2**C2. *Bus 13 to Piazza T. Tasso.*

The S. Frediano gate at the SW corner of the city was erected in
1332–4, and is the one through which Charles VIII entered
Florence from the old Pisa road in 1494. Filippino Lippi
painted the gate in the background of his Nerli altarpiece in
Santo Spirito. Nearby is the 17thC church of S. Frediano in
Cestello, and on the lungarno end of its piazza is the handsome
granary made for Cosimo III.

You can climb to *Bellosguardo* from the gate in 30min.

San Gaetano ▥ †
Via Tornabuoni. Map **4**C3. *Rarely open except for
services.*

The best Baroque church facade in Florence, built by Gherardo
Silvani in 1648.

A plaque on the corner of Via de' Corsi and the Tornabuoni
commemorates the production in 1594 of the first opera *La
Dafne* by Jacopo Peri and Jacopo Corsi, the owner of the
original palace on this site.

San Lorenzo ▥ † ★
Map **4**B3.

To build their parish church the Medici hired Brunelleschi for
the first and only time. Begun in 1419 on the site of a much older
church, S. Lorenzo was built, embellished and extended by
some of the greatest artists and most skillful craftsmen of the
15th–17thC. Most of this work was initiated, supervised and
paid for by the successive members of the Medici family who
are buried here.

Seen from its busy market square, S. Lorenzo is an
impressive if not harmonious complex. The taller of the two
domes at the chancel end covers the Cappella dei Principi; the

shallower cupola completes Michelangelo's New Sacristy. The bell tower is 18thC and the unexciting statue of Giovanni delle Bande Nere (1540) is by Bandinelli. Michelangelo's model for a proposed facade, commissioned in 1516 but judged unacceptable by his Medici patrons, can be seen in the *Casa Buonarroti*.

The **interior** ★ is one of the most understatedly powerful in Italy, designed by Brunelleschi in 1420 but completed after his death by A. Manetti in 1460. The delay was caused by financial crises in the Medici banks, but it is evident that money was not stinted on the final construction. Even the *pietra serena* capitals and the arches which define the space were carved by leading sculptors of the day, including A. and M. Rossellino.

Highlights are as follows: 1. The *Marriage of the Virgin* (1523), an elegant and vivid picture by Rosso Fiorentino. 2. A fine and in its day influential **marble tabernacle** (c.1460) by Desiderio da Settignano. 3. and 4. **Bronze pulpits** by Donatello (c.1460), his last works, finished by pupils; the **Deposition panel** and **Resurrection panel** are by Donatello's own hand. 5. Bronzino's sadly faded fresco of the *Martyrdom of San Lorenzo* (1565–69). 6. Martelli Chapel. *The Annunciation* (c.1440) by Filippo Lippi, a masterpiece of perspective, clumsily restored.

The **Old Sacristy (Sagrestia Vecchia)** ★ is entered from the left transept. Brunelleschi's early masterpiece (1421–8) was completed before the church itself; Vasari says Cosimo il Vecchio was present throughout the construction. This is one of the first mathematically conceived architectural spaces of the Renaissance: a perfect cube completed by a hemispherical umbrella dome. Donatello's **sculptural decorations**, carried out in the 1430s, consist of: the four polychrome medallions illustrating *Scenes from the Life of St John the Evangelist* in the pendentives; the four polychrome **tondos of the Evangelist** in the lunettes; and the **bronze doors** flanking the apse. Donatello was responsible for the architecture of the doors as well as the bronze relief panels: the right door is the *Door of the Martyrs*; the left is known as the *Door of the Apostles* despite its 20 figures. Left of the entrance is Verrocchio's elegant *Monument to Piero and Giovanni de' Medici* (1472).

New Sacristy

1

2
3

4

5

6

Entrance to
Medici Chapels

Old Sacristy

Laurentian Library

Laurentian Library *(Biblioteca Medici-Laurenziana)* 🏛 ★
Piazza S. Lorenzo 👁 �8 *Open Mon–Sat 9am–5pm.*
Closed Sun and hols.

This library was designed by Michelangelo in 1524–34, to
house the collection of classical and humanist manuscripts
founded by Cosimo il Vecchio, later removed to Rome by
Leo X and finally returned to Florence by Clement VII who
commissioned this building.

    Vestibule. An early, dramatic, sophisticated break with the
rational, classical principles of 15thC Florentine architecture.
The staircase, which fills nearly the entire room, was left
unfinished by Michelangelo and completed in the 1550s by
Vasari and Ammannati.

    Library. The comparatively simple rectangular space is in
deliberate contrast to the vestibule. The marble intarsia floor,
designed by Tribolo, repeats the ceiling's Medici motifs of the
ram's skull and the motto 'Semper'. Among the codices is the
Medici *Virgil*.

Medici Chapels *(Cappelle Medicee)* ★
🕾213206 🚇 *Open Tues–Sat 9am–2pm, Sun and hols
9am–1pm. Closed Mon. Entrance from Piazza di Madonna
degli Aldobrandini.*

On the way to the chapels you pass through the lofty crypt
paved with tombstones of the Medici and Lorraine grand dukes.
The tomb of Cosimo il Vecchio is in a room below. A
staircase on the right leads to the **Chapel of the Princes
(Cappella dei Principi)**. Designed by Don Giovanni de' Medici
and Buontalenti and built by Nigetti from 1602, this
portentous, claustrophobic grand-ducal shrine, clad entirely in
pietradura, is really a monument to Ferdinand I who ordered it.
It was the most expensive of all Medici building projects and the
one which posterity, until recently, was to judge as being in the
worst taste. The ground plan is based on that of the Baptistry
(*Duomo*). A room in the Opificio delle Pietre dure, Via degli
Alfani 78, is devoted to the design and construction of this
chapel.

    The **New Sacristy (Sagrestia Nuova)** ★ was Michelangelo's
first realized architectural creation, begun in 1520 and left
unfinished, after interruptions, in 1534. It is an answer, half
respectful and half rebellious, to Brunelleschi's Old Sacristy.
Imitating the Old Sacristy, it makes a totally different
impression because, as Vasari tells us, Michelangelo would not
conform to the "measure, order and rule" that were the essence
of Brunelleschi's style. It was intended to be seen from the
altar.

    Leo X and Clement VII, who paid for the New Sacristy, were
less concerned to glorify the two Medici dukes entombed here
than to strengthen the authority of these dukes' bastard heirs,
and the statues of the dukes in niches over their respective
tombs are, at the least, idealized portraits, if they are portraits at
all. The melancholy mood of the sculptures made between
1524–1533 probably expresses Michelangelo's despair at the
fall of the Florentine Republic. The catenary curve of the tomb
volutes was later copied exactly by Ammannati (who did some
restorative work on the New Sacristy) in the 1550s, for his
bridge at *Santa Trinita*. Michelangelo's original design
provided for a further pair of figures at the end of each tomb.

    On the left is the **tomb of Lorenzo, Duke of Urbino**
(grandson of Lorenzo the Magnificent); the reclining figures
represent *Dawn* and *Dusk*. On the right is the **tomb of**

Giuliano, **Duke of Nemours** (Lorenzo the Magnificent's youngest son), with allegorical figures of *Day* and *Night*.

Lorenzo the Magnificent and his brother Giuliano are buried in the simple tomb opposite the altar. To confuse matters further, the Giuliano and the Lorenzo 'the Magnificent' (a common courtesy title in the 16thC) to whom Machiavelli successively dedicated *The Prince* are the dukes whose remains lie in Michelangelo's tombs and not the more famous 15thC Medici buried here in near anonymity. On this tomb is Michelangelo's deeply moving *Madonna and Child* (1521) which is flanked by *S. Cosma* by Montorsoli, and by *S. Damiano* by Raffaele da Montelupo.

In a room below, fresco drawings by Michelangelo and his pupils have recently been uncovered, and are often on display in the choir.

San Marco, Fra Angelico Museum *(Museo dell' Angelico)* ★

Piazza San Marco ☎ *210741. Map 3B4* ▨ *Open Tues–Sat 9am–2pm, Sun and hols 9am–1pm. Closed Mon.*

The **convent and cloisters** of S. Marco were Cosimo il Vecchio's greatest gift to Florence. Cosimo acquired the convent for the Dominican friars of Fiesole. The architect Michelozzo's only work of genius was transmuted by the painter Fra Angelico into a supremely noble expression of balanced Christianity: sincere, compassionate, mystic, learned.

S. Marco witnessed one of the turning points in Florence's history. By the end of the 15thC Florentines had been swung off center into a hectic, puritanical religiosity incited by Savonarola, who became Prior of S. Marco in 1491. The Medici were expelled in 1494, and Jesus Christ was proclaimed King of Florence, with Savonarola acting as political leader. In 1498 the crowds who had fervently responded to his charisma turned against him. S. Marco was besieged, and Savonarola was captured, tried and burned at the stake in the Piazza Signoria.

In 1869 the suppressed convent of S. Marco became a museum honoring Fra Angelico. Today it is a nearly complete one-man show of his *oeuvre*. Most of his greatest panel paintings have been assembled here, brought in from churches, guilds, and other galleries including the *Uffizi*, which now retains only two Angelicos.

During the 1980s new sections of the convent will be opened as a museum housing fragments salvaged from the old parts of the city demolished in the 1860s.

From the vestibule one enters Michelozzo's **Cloister of S. Antonino**. Most of the frescoes are 16thC, but some of the lunettes and the *Crucifixion with St Dominic* in the far left corner are by Angelico. To the right of the entrance is the **Ospizio dei Pellegrini** ★ which is the room where pilgrims were offered hospitality; it now houses 20 panel paintings by Angelico, well labeled as to date and provenance. The cult of Angelico as a naive painter stops here – if his spirit was still medieval, his technique was fully informed by the Early Renaissance. Some outstanding works in this room are the *Deposition* (c.1435) from S. Trinita; the *San Marco Altarpiece* (1438–43) with the Medici patron saints Cosma and Damian; the *Virgin Enthroned* (c.1433), painted for the linen drapers guild, the Linaiuoli; and the 35 *Scenes from the Life of Christ*, completed by Baldovinetti.

Across the courtyard, in the **Sala Capitolare** (the Chapter House), is Angelico's grand, mystic vision of the *Crucifixion* ★

(c.1442). Nearby in the cloister is the bell of S. Marco, the *Piagnona*, which gave the signal for the siege of the convent that led to the imprisonment of Savonarola. In the **refectory**, to the left of the stairs, is Dom. Ghirlandaio's clear, descriptive *Last Supper*, a variation on the one in the *Ognissanti* refectory.

First floor. The 44 **dormitory cells** ★ were frescoed by Angelico and assistants from 1439–45. At the top of the stairs is Angelico's justly famous *Annunciation*. If time is short, visit at least: cell 1. *Noli Me Tangere*; 3. *Annunciation*; 6. *Transfiguration*; 7. the *Crowning with Thorns*; and 9. the *Coronation of Mary*. The **library**, between cells 42 and 43, is Michelozzo's most inspired interior. This was the first public library in Europe, thanks to Cosimo il Vecchio, who donated the manuscripts. Cells 38 and 39 at the bottom of this corridor were reserved for Cosimo's retreats. Cell 11 was the prior's quarters, occupied by Savonarola, whose **portrait** by Fra Bartolommeo is in the vestibule, cell 12.

The adjacent church of S. Marco (1437–52) was built by Michelozzo, but subsequently updated by Giambologna in 1585, by P.F. Silvani in 1678 and by various 18thC decorators. In the center of the wooden ceiling is a canvas of the *Madonna in Glory* (1725) by G.A. Pucci. Poliziano and Pico della Mirandola are buried near the third altar on the left.

The administrative offices of the University of Florence, the various faculties of which are scattered all over the city, are on the E side of the square at no. 4, in the building where Cosimo I kept lions and which was later used as the grand-ducal stables.

Santa Maria Maddalena dei Pazzi † ☆
Borgo Pinti 58. Map 3C5. Open 9am–noon, 3–7pm.

Santa Maria Maddalena dei Pazzi was a Carmelite nun and member of the banking family who died in 1609 and was canonized in 1685. This church, originally built by Giuliano da Sangallo, was renamed and redesigned in her honor in 1628 by Luigi Arrigucci, who retained Giuliano's side chapels. The frescoes in the nave (1677) are by Jacopo Chiavistelli. The chancel was extended and richly decorated in the year of her canonization by P.F. Silvani, C. Ferri, P. Dandini, with two canvases by Luca Giordano. In the sacristy, off the bottom of the right aisle, is some good late Baroque stuccowork (1767).

The rest of the church complex is something of a box of surprises: frescoes by Poccetti in the Cappella del Giglio; an elegant **courtyard** (1492) by Giuliano da Sangallo, important as the first building project to carry out Alberti's instruction that arches must be supported on square pillars. But the compelling reason to visit S. Maria Maddalena dei Pazzi is in the old chapter room of the convent, where Perugino's **fresco of the Crucifixion** (1493–6) ☆ covers one wall. This lovely composition, set in a severe illusionist architectural frame, echoes the peace of the landscape bathed in early-morning light.

Nearby, at Borgo Pinti 68, is the large Panciatichi Ximenes palace, c.1499, built by Giuliano and Antonio da Sangallo as their own palace, and enlarged by Gherardo Silvani in 1620. Napoleon stayed here in June 1796.

Santa Maria Maggiore ▥ †
Via de' Cerretani. Map 4B3.

The interior is a pleasing mixture of 13thC Gothic reinterpreted by an early 20thC restoration, with 17th–18thC Baroque decoration. The side altars are by Gherardo Silvani with frescoes and canvases by Giuseppe Pinzani, Pier Dandini, Volterrano, Onorio Marinari and Vincenzo Meucci.

The prize possession of the church is in the chapel to the left of the high altar. This 13thC polyptych of the *Madonna and Child* was attributed to Andrea di Cione by Berenson, but it is now thought to be by Coppo di Marcovaldo.

Santa Maria Novella ▥ † ★
Map 4B2.

Next to the station and only five minutes from the Duomo, S.M. Novella nevertheless seems remote from the rest of Florence, as indeed it was before the final ring of walls embraced the area and the Mugnone, which once flowed here through vineyards, was diverted N of the Fortezza da Basso. The feeling that you might almost be in a different city is emphasized by the only Florentine church facade completed in the 15thC and by the high proportion of comfortable but undistinguished 19thC buildings which fill gaps left in the 16thC when the population of Florence had not yet expanded as rapidly as expected. In the 19thC S.M. Novella was known as the 'Mecca of Foreigners.' Henry James, William Dean Howells, Emerson, Longfellow and Shelley were among the literary visitors who chose to stay just a little to one side of the inspiring but noisy city.

The church of S.M. Novella was built from 1246 by the Dominicans, successful protagonists at that time of a puritanical movement similar in its aims to the 16thC Reformation, and far stricter than the doctrine propounded by the Franciscans, whose rival preaching church was begun 48yr later at *Santa Croce*. The Dominicans had taken possession in 1221 of an old church which occupied the transept of the present building, and in 1245 the piazza was opened out to receive the crowds attracted by the Dominican preacher St Peter Martyr. The new church buildings, supervised by a succession of Dominican architects, were completed by 1360. A compromise between contemporary French and native Italian styles, S.M. Novella was the first Gothic church in Italy to break away from the imported Cistercian mold.

It was in S. Maria Novella that Boccaccio described the protagonists of the *Decameron*, talking of plague, and it was the fear and consequences of the plague of 1348 which occasioned

1	Strozzi Chapel
2	Gondi Chapel
3	Filippo Strozzi Chapel
4	Sacristy
5	Rucellai Chapel
6	Spanish Chapel

Chiostro Grande

Chiostro Verde

Refectory

Santa Maria Novella

the building of many of the chapels and cloisters. But there is no hint of these gloomy associations with dogmatism and death in Alberti's brilliant rationalization of the 14thC facade. Honoring the Gothic forms of the existing facade, and retaining the lower arcade and the round window, he raised it into a mathematically organized space containable within a perfect square. The volutes, an invention much copied by later architects, conceal the nave aisles. His **facade ★** was begun in 1456. As you can see from the Rucellai device which sails across the center and from the inscription under the pediment, the patron was Giovanni Rucellai and the date of completion 1470. The two astronomical instruments were placed here in 1572.

The **interior** was updated in 1565–71 by Vasari, who deprived the nave of color and light by whitewashing frescoes and shortening the aisle windows to allow for his side chapels.

The **nave** appears longer than it is thanks to a trick of perspective played by the Gothic architects, who placed the supporting pillars at diminishing intervals. There are several distinguished monuments in the nave, but the outstanding work, halfway down on the left wall, is Masaccio's *Trinity* (c.1427) ★ with Mary and St John flanked by the donors, members of the Lenzi family. The central figures are set in an illusionist Holy Sepulchre, which may have been suggested by Brunelleschi, who designed the marble **pulpit** on the nearest pillar.

Left transept. The Strozzi Chapel occupies the raised presbytery of the original Romanesque church. The **altarpiece** (1354–7) shows *Christ giving the Keys to Peter and the Book of Knowledge to St Thomas*, by Orcagna. The frescoes (c.1351–7), by Nardo di Cione, have deteriorated: left wall, *Paradise*; altar wall, the *Last Judgement*, with Dante among the blessed; right wall, the *Inferno*. In the Sacristy is the *Crucifix* from the interior facade by Giotto. The Gondi Chapel, with striking **decorations in marble** (c.1503), by Giuliano da Sangallo, contains Brunelleschi's famous *Crucifix*, his only surviving wooden sculpture, made, according to Vasari, in answer to Donatello's *Crucifix* in *Santa Croce*, which Brunelleschi judged too crudely realistic. The chancel is decorated behind the high altar by Dom. Ghirlandaio with his most popular **frescoes** (1485–90) ★ commissioned by Giovanni Tornabuoni, Lorenzo de' Medici's uncle. Serious art historians used to dismiss this pretty narrative work as merely journalistic; Ruskin described them as not nice enough for nice people and not vulgar enough for vulgar people. But they are amongst the valuable pictorial documents we have of their period, and most modern visitors will be fascinated and charmed by them. Left wall: *Scenes from the Life of the Virgin*. Right wall: *Scenes from the Life of the Baptist*.

Right transept. The Filippo Strozzi Chapel is frescoed (c.1487–1502) by Filippino Lippi in a strange obsessive style steeped in Roman archeology and anticipating the Baroque: right wall, *Story of St Philip* ☆ and left wall, *Story of St John the Divine* ☆ Behind the altar is the **tomb of Filippo Strozzi** (1491–3) by Benedetto da Maiano. The Rucellai Chapel was raised in the 15thC. Duccio's Rucellai *Madonna*, now in the *Uffizi*, has been replaced at the altar by Nino Pisano's marble *Madonna and Child* (after 1348). In the pavement is Ghiberti's bronze **tomb of Leonardo Dati** (1425).

Cloisters (*Chiostri Monumentali*) ▥ † ★
▧ *Open Mon–Thurs, Sat 9am–2pm, Sun 8am–1pm. Closed Fri. Entrance to left of church facade.*

The **Chiostro Verde** (c.1350) is so named because of the green

tint of Uccello's **frescoes of the Old Testament**, executed in
terra verde. They are detached and usually exhibited in the
Refectory. Uccello's *Universal Deluge* (c.1445) ★ was restored
in the 1950s and again after the most recent deluge of 1966.
Tragically deteriorated, it is recognizable as his masterpiece.

The **Spanish Chapel** (c.1350) ★ was an old chapter room of
the convent, built by Jacopo Talenti, and used for worship in
the 16thC by Eleanor of Toledo's Spanish courtiers. The
monumental didactic **fresco cycle** (1365–7) by Andrea di
Firenze and assistants is a schematic depiction of the Catholic
way of life, which is determined by the scenes in the vault and
over the altar. Left wall, theology, civilization and intellectual
culture as revealed by St Thomas Aquinas; right wall, the
practical way of life, with the church militant represented by an
unrealized plan for the Duomo, the actual dome of which was of
course not finished for another 80yr. Ruskin guessed, probably
correctly, that the average tourist would spend 15min in the
Spanish Chapel, studying "its vaulted book, the most noble
piece of pictorial philosophy in Italy," whereas he had "taken
five weeks to see the quarter of this picture."

In the piazza, the large obelisks, resting on bronze tortoises,
mark the limits of the chariot race established here by Cosimo I
in 1563. At the far end is the graceful, post-Brunelleschian
Loggia di S. Paolo (1489–96), with a terra-cotta lunette over
the doorway by Andrea della Robbia. In the Via della Scala is a
perfectly preserved 17thC pharmacy (see *Florence/Shopping*).
Immediately to the NW of the piazza is the central **station**
(1935), the first functionalist terminal building in Italy.
Although admired by many, a joke made by a rival architect has
stuck to the station: "I can see the box the station came in," he
said, "but where is the station?"

San Miniato ▥ † ★
*Map 3E5. Open 8am–12:30pm, 2–6:15pm. No visitors
during services.*

The sight of S. Miniato invariably makes people smile. A small,
venerable green-and-white jewel, it stands above the city on the
highest of the hills immediately to the SE. Apart from the
Baptistry (*Duomo*) it is the oldest and most loved church in
Florence.

According to a medieval legend, S. Miniato, persecuted by
the Emperor Decius and decapitated in the amphitheater,
carried his head across the river and up the hill to this place. The
commemorative church was built in the 11thC. It was here that
the miraculous *Crucifix*, now in *Santa Trinita*, spoke to
S. Giovanni Gualberto who went on to found the reforming
Benedictine order of Vallombrosa. After the last expulsion of
the Medici in 1527 the hill was fortified by Michelangelo and
used during the siege as a key defense post against the army of
Charles V (see Vasari's fresco in the *Signoria*, Sala dei
Cinquecento). Thirty years later the fortified church which had
briefly been a symbol of Florentine love of freedom was
occupied by the soldiers of the dictator Duke Cosimo I.

The facade dates from c.1090, except for the 13thC mosaic,
restored in the 19thC when the Florentines loved S. Miniato
perhaps a little too well, and the copper eagle over the
pediment, emblem of the Guild of Calimala which administered
the church, from 1288. The crenellated **Bishop's Palace** to the
right was built in 1295 by Andrea dei Mozzi, Bishop of
Florence, as a summer residence. During the 1529 siege Baccio

d'Agnolo's squat bell tower, only just then completed, was shielded by mattresses against the Spanish cannonballs. The lovely Romanesque **interior ★** is marred only by the heavy hand of the 19thC restorer, who coated the stone column shafts with _scagliola_ and brightened the polychrome ceiling. The smaller of the Corinthian capitals are Roman. The tapestry-like strip of **pavement**, inspired by Sicilian fabrics and one of the finest of its kind in Italy, is dated 1207 in the zodiac panel.

Nave. The giant St Christopher frescoed on the right wall is by an unknown 14thC artist. At the bottom of the nave is Michelozzo's **Crucifix Chapel** (1448). The glazed terra-cotta vault is by Luca della Robbia. Off the left nave the **Cardinal of Portugal's Chapel** (1461–6) ★ is a model of collaborative Renaissance art (ask the sacristan to open the gate). Commissioned by Alfonso V of Portugal to house the tomb of his nephew Cardinal James of Lusitania, who died in Florence in 1459, this exquisite chapel was built into the side of the basilica by A. Manetti. The **cardinal's tomb** on the right wall is by A. Rossellino. On the opposite wall, above the Bishop's throne, is Baldovinetti's _Annunciation_, on panel, carefully restored. The glazed terra-cotta **vault and tondos of the Holy Ghost and four Cardinal Virtues** are by Luca della Robbia. In the lunette facing the entrance are two _Angels in Flight_, frescoed by A. and P. del Pollaiuolo.

Sacristy (to the right of the raised presbytery). Frescoes by Spinello Aretino (1385–7) represent _Scenes from the Life of St Benedict_. Presbytery. The delightful marble **pulpit** (1209) is justly famous for its carving and intarsiaed fantasy animals. The 13thC mosaic in the apse was restored by Baldovinetti. Over the altar, left, is _S. Miniato_ by Jacopo del Casentino. **Crypt**. The 36 columns are of various provenance. Frescoes in the vault show _Saints and Prophets_ by Taddeo Gaddi.

Emerging from the church you can wander for a half-hour or so among the sweet, nostalgic 19thC and early 20thC tombs in the cemetery, planned in 1839 by Niccolò Matas. The whole church complex retains examples from nearly a thousand years of funerary tradition.

San Niccolò ▥ †
Map **3**D5.

The defense **tower of S. Niccolò** in Piazza Giuseppe Poggi was erected in 1324 and has been maintained at its original height by frequent restorations. The steps behind it lead up to _Piazzale Michelangelo_. To the SW, Via Belvedere runs along the old walls and the 16thC bastion to Porta S. Giorgio and the _Belvedere_ fortress. Or you could walk W along Via S. Niccolò and Via dei Bardi, two of the best-preserved (and noisiest) medieval streets in Florence, to the _Ponte Vecchio_. The medieval road to _San Miniato_ from Porta S. Miniato is the way described by Dante in _Purgatorio XII_, (l.100). Opposite Porta S. Miniato is the church of **S. Niccolò Sopr' Arno**, with a 15thC interior made over in the 16thC. A recent restoration had emphasized the difference in taste between the two centuries by uncovering the 15thC frescoes but leaving the 16thC tabernacle frames. Sinopie of the restored frescoes are also displayed.

San Salvi † ☆
Via S. Salvi 16. ☎ _677570. Map_ **7**D5.

The work of Andrea del Sarto, Browning's "faultless painter," can sometimes seem boringly academic to modern eyes. But his masterpiece in fresco, the *Last Supper* ☆ which was commissioned in 1519 for the refectory of the S. Salvi monastery, is one of the most sumptuous visual treats in Florence. This is the perfect normative High Renaissance painting, in a near-perfect state of preservation. Its beauty saved it during the siege of Florence, when workmen, instructed to tear down any building near the city which might be used by the enemy, refused to destroy this picture.

Closed to the public after the 1966 flood, the refectory was reopened in October 1981. The monastery is now an asylum. A visit to S. Salvi could be combined with a day in *Settignano* (see *A–Z/Tuscany*). On the way from the center, notice Nervi's admirable **Stadium** (1932).

Santo Spirito 🏛 † ☆
Map 4E2.

When Florence was partitioned into four administrative sections in the 14thC, the city s of the Arno became the S. Spirito quarter. Piazza S. Spirito is still the heart of the *Oltrarno*; and it is the square connoisseurs of Florence often say they love most, the place where daily life seems least disturbed by tourists.

The most strikingly lovely of the palaces on the piazza is the **Guadagni** (1503–6) at no. 10, attributed to Baccio d'Agnolo and with a fine courtyard in the manner of Giuliano da Sangallo. In the palace next door, no. 9, is an elegant staircase leading to the Pensione Bardini.

The **church of S. Spirito** was built on the site of an earlier Augustinian monastery to a design by Brunelleschi. The foundation stone was laid in 1436 but the church was not completed until 1487, long after Brunelleschi's death. The delay was caused by financial difficulties, fire, and controversy over the interpretation of the master's design, which was fundamentally respected in the interior.

The modest voluted facade was applied in the 17thC. The slender bell tower (1503–17) is by Baccio d'Agnolo.

Brunelleschi's calm, rational **interior** ★ with its soaring forest of columns is spoiled only by the 17thC *baldacchino* in the chancel. The plan is a more subtle and complex variation on that of *San Lorenzo*. Around the perimeter are 40 semicircular chapels. Those in the transepts and apse give the clearest impression you can find in modern Florence of how 15thC religious art looked in its original context; some of the chapels have inevitably been altered, but more than enough have been left as they were to help you imagine the paintings you see in galleries back in their proper settings. Don't miss: right transept, Filippino Lippi's **Nerli altarpiece** (c.1490) ☆ and left transept, which is the most perfectly preserved part of the church, the **Corbinelli Chapel** (1492) – architecture and the sculptures by the young A. Sansovino. From the left nave, the door under the organ leads through a noble vaulted **vestibule** (1492–6), built by Cronaca to a design by Giuliano da Sangallo, into the octagonal **sacristy** (1489–92), also designed by Sangallo.

Refectory *(Cenacolo di Santo Spirito)*
Piazza S. Spirito 29 📷
This is the only part of the Gothic monastery to have survived the fire of 1471. The **frescoes**, badly damaged but of the greatest importance, were attributed by Ghiberti to Orcagna, an opinion not generally supported by modern scholarship.

Santo Stefano al Ponte ▥ †
Map **4**_D3._

The lower half of the facade and the attractive doorway are
13thC. The shoe of Buondelmonte dei Buondelmonti's horse is
supposed to have been hung here after his assassination (see
Ponte Vecchio).

The remarkable **interior** (1649–55) by Ferdinando Tacca is
unfortunately rarely open except for exhibitions. The raised
chancel is an imaginary reconstruction of a Roman theater.
Leading up to it is an extraordinary lasagna-like marble flight of
stairs (1574) by Buontalenti, formerly in Santa Trinità.

Santa Trìnita ▥ † ★
Map **4**_D2._

Piazza S. Trinita is more an intersection than a square. The
central column, a gift from the Baths of Caracalla given by Pius
IV to Cosima I in commemoration of the victory of Montemurlo
in 1537, doesn't really focus one's attention, which is pulled to
the N along **Via Tornabuoni**, the fashionable shopping street
and the widest in Florence, built on the filled-in moat of the
12thC city walls and now lined with 13th–16thC palaces.

Spanning the Arno to the S is Ammannati's **Ponte S. Trinita**
(1567–70) ★ which is the most graceful bridge in Europe.
Michelangelo advised on the design, and the curve of the
volutes is borrowed from his Medici tombs in _San Lorenzo_.
The bridge was destroyed by bombing in 1944 and rebuilt after
the war exactly as it had been before. One-sixth of the original
stone was retrieved from the Arno; the rest was supplied by the
quarries in the Boboli Gardens which were specially reopened.
The head of the _Primavera_ statue was recovered only in 1961.

On the NE corner of the square (no. 1) is the **Palazzo Bartolini
Salimbeni**, now the French Consulate. The building was
finished in 1521 just after Raphael's Pandolfini palace (see
Florence/Walk 2), which greatly influenced Baccio d'Agnolo's
design for this, his most original palace. It was the first in
central Florence to adopt the Roman tabernacle windows, and
contemporary Florentines treated it as a huge joke, pinning
notices on the facade saying that it looked more like a church.
Baccio's reply is inscribed in Latin over the door: "It is easier to
carp than to imitate." Michelangelo thought the cornice made
the palace look like a man wearing a hat too big for his body.
The palace is also known as the _Per Non Dormire_ after the
family motto inscribed over the windows. The courtyard is
decorated with elegant _sgraffiti_.

The first **church of S. Trinita** was built on this site by S.
Giovanni Gualberto, founder of the Vallombrosan Order, in
the late 11thC. The original Romanesque facade, depicted by
Dom. Ghirlandaio in the Sassetti Chapel inside the church, was
replaced by Buontalenti's uncharacteristically clumsy effort in
1594. The Gothic **interior** assumed its present appearance
beginning c.1250, when Nicola Pisano is supposed to have
begun the program of enlargement which continued
throughout the next century.

Right nave, fourth chapel. Compare Lorenzo Monaco's
pretty but heavily restored frescoes (c.1420–25) with his
altarpiece on the panel of the _Annunciation_; the predellà panels
are especially fine. The gate is early 15thC.

Right transept. In the sacristy, the **tomb of Onofrio Strozzi**
(1421), to the left of the altar, is an early example of Renaissance
funerary sculpture. The second chapel to the right of the

chancel is the **Sassetti Chapel** ✩ frescoed by Dom. Ghirlandaio
(1482–6) with *Scenes from the Life of St Francis* against a
Florentine background: the Signoria, Piazza S. Trinita, the old
Ponte S. Trinita. In the upper tier of the altar wall are portraits
of, among other contemporary Florentines, *Francesco Sassetti*,
who commissioned this chapel, *Lorenzo the Magnificent*, his
adoring protégé *Poliziano* and his sons *Piero*, *Giovanni* and
Giuliano. Over the altar is Ghirlandaio's *Adoration of the
Shepherds* (1485), set in a Tuscan landscape. *Francesco Sassetti*
and *Nera Corsi*, his wife, are portrayed on either side of the altar
and are buried in the black marble **sarcophagi**, attributed to
Giuliano da Sangallo, on the side walls.

Left transept, second chapel. On the left wall, the **tomb of
Bishop Benozzo Federighi** (1455) ✩ is considered one of Luca
della Robbia's masterworks for the intense humanity of the
crucified Christ in the central panel and the finely modeled face
of the bishop, a rare portrait by Luca. In the fifth chapel, the
wooden statue of the *Magdalen* (c.1464), by Desiderio da
Settignano and Benedetto da Maiano, invites comparison with
Donatello's more tragic figure in the Cathedral Museum (see
Duomo). In the third chapel is an *Annunciation* by Neri di
Bicci, with a sweet, inept Adam and Eve, borrowed from
Masaccio's Brancacci Chapel (see *Carmine*).

Lo Scalzo 🏛 † ✩
Via Cavour 69 ☎*484808. Map 3B4.*
The Brotherhood of St John was known as *lo Scalzo* because its
members went barefoot in obedience to the rule of poverty.

In 1511 Andrea del Sarto, then 25, began to decorate their
cloister in *terra verde* with scenes in austere *grisaille*, from the
life of John the Baptist. He worked here on and off for a period
of 12yr, developing the fresco technique which can also be
admired in color at *Santissima Annunziata* and *San Salvi*.

The earliest of the Scalzo frescoes is the *Baptism of Christ*;
the last to be painted was the *Birth of St John the Baptist*.
Notice also especially the *Visitation* (1524), *Charity* (1520),
and *Justice* (1515).

The frescoes, badly injured by damp, have been detached for
restoration and replaced in their original positions.

Science Museum *(Museo di Storia della Scienza)* 🏛
Piazza dei Giudici 1 ☎*293493. Map 5E4* ▦ ✳ *Open winter
9:30am–1pm and Mon, Wed, Fri 2–5pm, summer
9:30am–1:30pm and Mon, Fri 3:30–7pm. Closed Sun.*
The medieval Castellani palace, which now houses the Science
Museum, was at one time the seat of the Civil Tribune or
Giudici di Ruota, which gave its name to the piazza from which
one enters the museum.

For nearly three centuries after Florence had lost its artistic
supremacy, the more intelligent members of the Medici-
Lorraine grand-ducal families retained a passionate interest in
all branches of science. In 1657 an Academy of Experiment, the
Accademia del Cimento, was founded in the Pitti by Grand
Duke Ferdinand II and his brother Cardinal Leopold, both
pupils of Galileo. This is the historic nucleus of the museum,
which is very large, carefully organized and clearly labeled.
Printed guides are loaned to visitors on each floor.

Ground floor. An alchemist's laboratory; early scales, music
boxes, bicycles, fire extinguishers, and more.

First floor. Rm IV is hardly large enough for the giant

armillary sphere made in 1593 for Ferdinand I by Antonio
Santucci. The sphere demonstrates the theologically acceptable
Ptolemaic theory in defiance of the sun-centered system
evolved by Copernicus 50yr earlier. Rm V. In the case opposite
the entrance is the lens with which Galileo discovered the four
satellites of Jupiter, known as the Medici planets. Wonderfully
delicate glass instruments from the Accademia del Cimento are
displayed in the other two cases.

Second floor, opened in 1975. This floor was formerly the
headquarters of the Accademia della Crusca, the scholarly body
which sits in judgement on the purity of the Italian language. In
Rm II is the **large burning lens** made for Cosimo III by
Benedict Bregans of Dresden and later used by Sir Humphrey
Davy and Michael Faraday to accomplish the combustion of a
diamond. In Rm IV is the great lodestone (*Calamita*) given by
Galileo to Ferdinand II. Rms V–VII. Anatomical wax models;
18thC surgical implements.

Third floor. Minerals and crystals collected in the 18thC.

Signoria
Map **5**D4.

People who dislike Florence often object most to this, its main
square, with the asymmetrical fortress palace, the rows of
statues symbolizing conflicting ideologies, and dull 19thC
buildings. Lacking the gaiety and architectural unity of the
central squares of Venice or Siena, the Piazza della Signoria will
always appeal more to the historical imagination than to the
sense of pleasure. The Signoria is still the political and
commercial center of the city, as it has been for nearly seven
centuries. The Palazzo Vecchio is still the city hall, and
politicians still harangue the public from the *ringhiera*. Farmers
still talk business outside the old commercial tribunal, now the
agricultural center, in Via de' Gondi, and businessmen and
bankers make deals over lunch at Cavallino. The only
concessions to mass tourism are the postcard stalls, the high
prices at the café Rivoire and the annual historic soccer game
played in costume each year on June 24.

Embedded in the pavement of the square is a plaque marking
the place where Savonarola was hanged and then burned on
May 23, 1498. Those who honor his memory still lay flowers
here.

Palazzo della Signoria *(Palazzo Vecchio)* Ⅲ ★
Piazza Signoria ▧ *for upstairs rooms, open Mon–Fri
9am–7pm, Sun and hols 8am–1pm. Closed Sat.*

The foundation stone of the Palazzo della Signoria was laid in
1299. The design is traditionally attributed to Arnolfo di
Cambio, but the building was not finished until at least a decade
after his death. The Signoria was the highest magistracy of the
republican government established in 1293. Elected by the
guilds, the Signori served for a period of only two months
during which they lived virtually as prisoners inside the palace.
The palace, like the constitution, was designed to prevent the
government from being overtaken by extremists – subversive
activity in the streets of such a small city could be easily
searched out from the tall watchtower, where the great bell cast
in 1322 tolled danger warnings and summoned the populace to
'parliaments,' or general assemblies.

The irregular shape of the palace and the off-center position
of its tower were not, as is often thought, the result of Gothic
whim. The trapezoidal plan derives from the reluctance of the

then Guelf government to build on land previously owned by a Ghibelline family. The tower was thriftily erected on the foundations of an earlier family tower close to the church of S. Piero Scheraggio, incorporated into the *Uffizi* in the 16thC. But the original entrance, on the N flank of the palace, was originally placed symmetrically. This side, facing Via de' Gondi, was extended in the late 15thC when the Sala Consiglio Maggiore was built over the customs hall.

The w side, facing the piazza, looks very much as it did in the 14thC, except for the mezzanine windows enlarged by Michelozzo and the absence of the 14thC *ringhiera*, or tribune, which was destroyed in the early 19thC. Almost nothing, however, remains of the original interior, which was remodeled from the mid-15thC to the late 16thC according to the needs of violently shifting styles of government, from the Medici-controled republic to the revivals of true republicanism in 1494–1512 and 1527–30, to the hereditary duchy finally established in 1537.

A key date to remember when visiting the palace is 1540, when Cosimo I took the unprecedented step of moving his household from the ancestral *Medici Palace* to the Palazzo della Signoria, which was converted into a ducal palace by his court architect Battista del Tasso. Ten years later, in 1550, Cosimo was persuaded by his wife Eleanor of Toledo to change the official residence to the *Pitti*. The Signoria palace was henceforth known as the Palazzo Vecchio (the Old Palace). Vasari, who succeeded Battista as court architect in 1555, was instructed to decorate the courtyard and Sala del Consiglio in time for the wedding of Francesco de' Medici to Joanna of Austria in 1565. He labored on until his death in 1574, covering the walls of the old palace with carefully programmed frescoes glorifying the achievements, ancestors, virtues and mythological counterparts of Cosimo I. Since few modern tourists share this single-minded adoration of Cosimo I, a tour of the palace can become a dispiriting experience. A brief visit, however, should include the following sights.

The two gilded lions and Christ's emblem were placed over the **entrance** in 1528, but an inscription of the same date, inspired by Savonarola's teachings, which originally read 'Jesus Christ, King of Florence Elected by Popular Decree,' was replaced with the present words by order of Cosimo I. The **courtyard** was remodeled by Michelozzo in the middle of the

15thC. Stuccowork and frescoes of views of Austrian cities were added under Vasari for the wedding of Francesco de' Medici to Joanna of Austria in 1565. The porphyry **fountain** replaced the original well in c.1555; the original of Verrocchio's bronze putto, made in the previous century for the Medici villa at Careggi, is now upstairs in the Cancelleria.

State Apartments *(Quartieri Monumentali)* ▨
Vasari's **staircase** (1560–3) leads to the **Salone dei Cinquecento** (1495–6), known also as the Sala del Consiglio Maggiore, originally built by Cronaca to house the enlarged representative government of the penultimate republic, but later modified and decorated under Vasari's direction. It is the largest room of its kind in existence and one of the most unpleasant, not square, and lined by Vasari's frantic frescoes commemorating the Florentine victories over Pisa and Siena; the fresco program relates to Cosimo I, seen in glory on the ceiling. Some of the statues, especially Vincenzo de' Rossi's *Hercules and Diomedes*, provide welcome comic relief. But the only beautiful thing in the room is Michelangelo's *Victory* ☆ which was made for the tomb of Julius II some time between 1506–34 and presented to Cosimo I by the sculptor's nephew. Off this room is the windowless **Studiolo of Francesco I** ☆ which is a treasure-trove of late Mannerist art, built as a retreat for Cosimo's solitary, gloomy son, who kept his most precious small possessions in the cabinets, which were decorated from 1569–73 by more than 30 artists according to an allegorical system dictated by Vincenzo Borghini to Vasari. Each wall represents one of the elements, earth, air, fire and water.

From the **Quartiere di Leone X** (1556–62), rebuilt and decorated by Vasari and others, a staircase leads to the Sala degli Elementi on the second floor. The Terrazza di Saturno, to the right of the stairs, commands a wonderful view to the SE and leads on to the **private apartments of Eleanor of Toledo**. The **chapel** (1540–5) ☆ is frescoed by Bronzino.

At the end of the long Salotta di Eleanora, where the detached fresco of the *Expulsion of the Duke of Athens* (c.1343) shows the palace as it was in the 14thC, is the **Sala dei Gigli** (1476–80) ☆ by Benedetto da Maiano, one of the few beautiful rooms in the palace, with **frescoes** (1481–5) by Dom. and Dav. Ghirlandaio. The intarsiate **doors**, with carved marble surround, and the figure of the *Baptist* (1476–81) above are by B. and G. da Maiano. Off this room in the small **Cancelleria** is the original of Verrocchio's bronze **putto** (1476) from the courtyard fountain, and the famous 16thC *Portrait of Machiavelli*, attributed to Santi di Tito; also the original relief carving of *St George and the Dragon* (c.1270) from the Porta S. Giorgio.

The Sala dell' Udienza, entered from the Sala dei Gigli through the intarsiate doors, was also built by B. da Maiano; the figure of *Justice* (1476–8) over the door is by the two Maiano. The **frescoes** (1550–60) are by Cecchino Salviati at his best. Donatello's *Judith and Holofernes* (c.1456–60) ☆ which was made as a fountain for the courtyard of the Medici Palace and dragged to the Piazza della Signoria after the expulsion of the Medici in 1494 as a symbol of the new republic, was brought inside from the piazza in 1980.

Returning through the Sala dei Gigli, the stairs lead up, past the euphemistically named **Alberghettino** where Cosimo il Vecchio and Savonarola were imprisoned, to the **tower** ★ which commands what is probably the best view of all. Down this flight of stairs is the **Mezzanine**, where pictures and

sculptures left to the city in 1934 by the American Charles
Loeser (Collezione Loeser) are displayed in three rooms. The
treasures of the collection are Bronzino's *Portrait of Laura
Battiferri* ☆ who was Ammannati's poetess wife, and a marble
Angel by Tino da Camaiano.

In the piazza, the row of statues, which runs from the
northern part of the square parallel with the facade of the
palace, was deliberately aligned in the 16thC to point in
perspective diminution towards the *Uffizi*.

From N to S they are: 1. Giambologna's equestrian statue of
Cosimo I (1594). 2. Ammannati's *Neptune Fountain*
(1563–75), a reference to Cosimo's maritime victories – the
embarrassed figure of Neptune, 'Il Biancone,' the 'White
Giant,' caused a 16thC critic to coin the rhyme, "*Ammannato,
Ammannato, che bel marmo ha rovinato*" ("what beautiful
marble you have ruined"). The nymphs and satyrs, which
Ammannati came to regret as provocation of sinful thoughts
when he fell under the influence of the Counter-Reformation,
were made with the collaboration of Giambologna and other
younger artists. 3. Copy of Donatello's *Marzocco* on an elegant
15thC base; the original is in the *Bargello*. 4. Copy of
Michelangelo's *David*; the original was moved to the
Accademia in 1873. 5. Bandinelli's infelicitous *Hercules and
Cacus* (1553); Hercules was another of Cosimo's symbols.
Flanking the entrance to the palace are two marble herms by
Vincenzo de' Rossi and Bandinelli.

The **Loggia dei Lanzi** (1376–82) ★ as it has been called
since the 16thC when German halberdiers (*landsknechte*) stood
on guard here, was built for important public ceremonies by
Benci di Cione and Simone di Francesco Talenti, probably to a
design by Orcagna. Michelangelo once advised that the arcaded
module should be repeated all round the perimeter of the piazza,
a plan which would have saved the square esthetically. The
present arrangement of the statues was settled on in the 19thC.

At front, left to right: 6. Cellini's *Perseus* (1545–54) ★ the
casting of which is described in detail in his autobiography; the
originals of the relief panels and small statues round the base are
now in the *Bargello*. 7. Two lions flanking the stairs; the one
on the right-hand side is Classical, the other is a 16thC copy.
8. Giambologna's *Rape of the Sabines* (1583).

Middle row, left to right: 9. *Rape of Polyxena* (1866) by Pio
Fedi. 10. *Ajax (or Menelaus) Supporting the Body of Patroclus*,
Roman copy of a 4thC BC Greek original. 11. Giambologna's
Hercules Fighting the Centaur Nessus (1599).

Against the back wall are six Roman statues of matrons or
empresses. On the NE side of the square is the three-bay
Uguccioni palace (c.1550); the design is thought to have been
sent from Rome by Michelangelo. From the balcony, a bust of
Cosimo I looks out at the statue of himself on horseback.

Raccolta d'Arte Moderna Alberto della Ragione
Piazza Signoria 5 ▩ *Open Mon, Wed–Sat 9am–2pm, Sun
and hols 8am–1pm. Closed Tues.*
This collection of modern art, given to the city by the Genoese
Alberto della Ragione, has been installed on two floors of the
Casa di Risparmio, and provides a comprehensive overview of
the mainstream figurative, landscape and still-life traditions in
Italian painting from the 1930s to 1960s. Sculptures by Marini,
Manzù, and others; paintings by, among others, De Pisis,
Mafai, Morandi. Of local interest are the views of and from Via
S. Leonardo (see *Florence/Walk 4*) by Ottone Rosai.

Stibbert *(Museo Stibbert)*
Via Stibbert 26 ☎*475731. Map* **7***C4* ☒ ⚐ 🎨 ⚓ * Open
weekdays 9am–2pm, Sun 9am–1pm. Closed Thurs. Guided
tours on the hour.*

The Villa Stibbert is a house worthy of Citizen Kane. The
private museum Frederick Stibbert created here in the late
19thC is not quite as large as Hearst's Californian monster
mansion, but it is scarcely less amazing. Of Italian-Scottish
parentage, Stibbert was an obsessive collector of everything –
from buttons to arms and armor. The armor collection, one of
the most important in the world, is displayed on model
phalanxes which you can imagine marching against one another
through the innumerable, vast, gloomy rooms.

Nearby in the Via Bolognese is the **Villa La Pietra**, with one
of the most beautiful Italian gardens in Tuscany, re-created at
the turn of this century by an Englishman, open to guided
parties by arrangement.

Strozzi Palace 🏛 ☆
Map **4***C3* 🔲 *Open Mon, Wed, Fri 4–7pm.*

Of the 100 or so palaces built in 15thC Florence the Strozzi was
the largest. Filippo Strozzi acquired over a dozen properties to
create his site, and the building took 44yr, from 1489 to 1536.
Strozzi watched his palace being built from his small house, to
the left (facing the palace from the piazza), which he built as
temporary accommodation. The design of the Strozzi is based
on G. da Sangallo's wooden model (see Piccolo Museo), but
Cronaca, who supervised the building, made significant
alterations; and it is he who added the massive cornice, a
reproduction of an ancient Roman cornice.

The palace is faced on three sides with huge blocks of *pietra
forte*, supplied by four quarries including two in the *Boboli*.
Apart from this sheer quantity of stone and the scrupulously
Classical cornice, the exterior, which still conforms to the type
of the *Medici Palace*, was not architecturally innovative. The
fine **lamp brackets** by Niccolò Grosso on the corners flanking
the main entrance are rare surviving examples of Renaissance
ironwork. The interior is the first of the Renaissance to be made
completely symmetrical.

Piccolo Museo di Palazzo Strozzi
🔲 *Open Mon, Wed, Fri 4–7pm. It is usually possible to gain
admittance outside these hours by applying to the Vieusseux
Office.*

On the left side of Cronaca's splendid interior courtyard is the
entrance to this small museum, which explains how the Strozzi
was built, and where you can see the differences between G. da
Sangallo's original model and the actual palace.

Vieusseux Library *(Gabinetto Vieusseux)*
🔲 *Open Tues–Fri 9:15am–12:45pm, 3:15–6:45pm, Sat
9:15am–12:45pm. Closed Sun, Mon.*

At the right of the courtyard, this lending library has always
been a favorite meeting place for literary resident foreigners,
especially in pre-Risorgimento Florence when it was a center of
liberal activity. Any member of the public can borrow for a
nominal fee. About a third of the collection is in English.

The first floor rooms of the palace are used for temporary
exhibitions.

Topographical Museum   A pictorial history of the city's
growth, known as *Firenze com'era*.

Uffizi 🏛 ★

*Piazzale degli Uffizi 6 ☎218341. Map **5**D4 ▓▓ ▣ Open
Tues–Sat 9am–2pm, Sun and hols 9am–1pm. Closed
Mon. Tours of the Corridoio Tues–Sat mornings must be
booked the previous day.*

The painters of 15thC Florence trained in one another's
workshops and watched each other's progress with jealous eyes,
each sparking off the other's genius and contributing to a chain
of innovative masterpieces which is one of the wonders of
western civilization. The world's largest and finest collection
of paintings from this period is found in Rms 7–15 of the
Uffizi. First-time visitors on a very tight schedule are
advised to take the elevator straight to the picture galleries
on the second floor and explore these rooms first. But there is,
of course, a great deal more. Nearly all of some 1,700 works of
art displayed here are outstanding.

The building, which parades in solemn double file from the
Piazza della Signoria to the Arno, was designed by Vasari in
1560 as a suite of offices for Cosimo I; hence the name Uffizi,
which means offices, and the official mood of the handsome
architecture. Buontalenti carried on the project after Vasari's
death, continuing to make modifications and additions until
1586. In 1581 Francesco I had the upper loggias glazed and
made into a museum, where he could escape from state duties.

The remains of the Zecca, where the famous florin was
minted, were incorporated into the fabric of the building and
explain the absence of colonnades at the base of the w wing
where it joins the Loggia dei Lanzi. The former church,
S. Piero Scheraggio, was absorbed into the N end of the opposite
wing; the gloomy statues in niches are the work of 19thC hacks.

In 1743 the Uffizi and its contents were bequeathed to the
people of Florence by the Palatine Electress Anna Maria
Lodovica, widow of the last Medici grand duke, Gian Gastone.
The enlightened Lorraine dynasty continued to add to the
extraordinary collection assembled by the Medici over the
previous 300yr. In this century the threat of vandalism, theft
and damp has driven more and more masterpieces out of the
churches and into this relatively soulless sanctuary. Florentines
complain about the Uffizi with some justification. It is too
crowded, with an attendance of over 1.5 million people a year
(the highest of any Italian gallery), most of whom come to
photograph Botticelli's *Primavera*. The opening hours are too
short. Too many sections are subject to unannounced and
prolonged closure; and too many paintings are stored for lack of
space, a problem which has led to the State Archives being
moved to new headquarters in Piazza Beccaria.

Do remember that this is not only a picture gallery. The
superb Classical statues lining the stairs and corridors were
regarded as the chief glories of the Uffizi until hardly more than
100yr ago (nobody looked at Botticelli with much interest until
the 1880s). Shelley visited the Uffizi every day during his stay in
Florence, but took notes only on the sculptures, and Gibbon
toured the gallery 12 times before looking at a picture.

Beyond the ticket desk is a room containing the remains of
S. Piero Scheraggio and Castagno's *frescoes* ★ (c.1450) of
famous men and women.

The elevator is for the picture galleries only. Opposite, at
the end of the corridor, is a fresco of the *Annunciation* (1481) by
Botticelli, damaged but still recognizable as one of his best
works. Vasari's great staircase leads to the first floor.

Exhibitions from the **prints and drawings collection**, which is otherwise closed to the general public, are frequently held in rooms to the left and are highly recommended. The staircase carries on to the picture galleries.

East corridor. The finest of the 16thC tapestries lining the corridor are the *Months of the Year*, woven in the Medici factories, and the Flemish-made *Festivities at the Court of Catherine de' Medici and Henry III*. The collection is arranged in chronological order through the gallery's two wings. The Florentine pictures are deliberately displayed in order to illustrate the impact made by one master upon another, from Giotto through to Michelangelo and the early Mannerists.

Rm 1. Usually closed. Antique carvings.

Rm 2. Three huge **altarpieces of the Maestà ★** offer a unique opportunity to examine the roots of Florentine and Sienese painting as they were to flower over the next 200yr. On the right, Cimabue's severe and massive image (c.1280) marks the epitome of the Byzantine Middle Ages. On the left, Duccio's composition (c.1285) is similar, but notice the lighter construction of the throne, the more human relationship between Madonna and Child, and the treatment of the Madonna's hem, a virtuoso passage that anticipates the linear style of Simone Martini and Botticelli. In the center, Giotto's less-cluttered altarpiece (c.1310) achieves a new sense of realistic space by the use of *chiaroscuro*, and the placing of the angels' heads at varying angles.

Rm 3. In the second quarter of the *trecento* Duccio's successors brought Sienese Gothic painting to a peak of sophistication. In Simone Martini's *Annunciation* (1333) ★ the exquisite, poetic vision and fluttering line are in marked contrast to Giotto's measured abstraction, but the psychological and spatial realism shows his influence. The saints are by Simone's brother-in-law Lippo Memmi. Pietro Lorenzetti's altarpiece *Scenes from the Life of the Blessed Humility* (1341) is more interesting for the charming small panels than for the prosaic central figure. Ambrogio Lorenzetti's *Stories of St Nicholas of Bari* (c.1330) was painted in Florence, but the last panel, in which St Nicholas obtains miraculous supplies of grain for the starving population of Myra, is poetic and detailed in a way that Florentine painting rarely was.

Rm 4. The painters of the Florentine *trecento* worked more successfully in fresco (see *Santa Croce, Santa Maria Novella*) than on panel, and they are not especially well represented in the Uffizi. Here one can see the work of Bernardo Daddi, Taddeo Gaddi, Giottino and Orcagna.

Rms 5 and 6. In the early *quattrocento*, nearly 100yr later than Siena and the rest of Europe, Florence produced its only great Gothic painter, Lorenzo Monaco, whose *Coronation of the Virgin* (1413) dominates the room. But his *Adoration of the Magi* (c.1420) is a far more contemplative, less elaborate picture than the visiting Gentile da Fabriano's contemporary treatment of the same subject on the far wall. Gentile's fairytale extravaganza *Adoration* ✫ brings the International Gothic in this gallery to a resounding climax. Credit for the delightful *Life of the Anchorites in the Thebaid*, now attributed to Gherardo Starnina and dated c.1400–10, has in the past been given to artists as disparate as Pietro Lorenzetti, Fra Angelico and Uccello. This is by no means the naïve work it appears at first. The little figures are executed in the naturalistic manner of Giotto, and the sky, for the first time in this gallery and perhaps in the Renaissance, is blue not gold.

Rm 7. The earliest pictures in this important room are by artists whose full genius is better appreciated elsewhere in Florence. Masaccio and Masolino are represented here by a *Virgin and Child with St Anne* (1424). Fra Angelico's one-man show is in the Monastery of *San Marco*, where you can compare this *Coronation of the Virgin* (1430) with a later fresco on the same subject. There are only two other pictures by Domenico Veneziano in Florence, neither currently on view (there are only 12 in the world). This *Sacra Conversazione* (1445–8) ★ is one of the supreme achievements of the Early Renaissance master of light. Its limpid colors and precisely described architecture give it the atmosphere of a perfect silence. Domenico must have been deeply affected by the even greater genius of his pupil Piero della Francesca, whose diptych of *Federico da Montefeltro and Battista Sforza* (c.1460) ★ was painted in Urbino. The allegorical **triumphs** on the backs represent the cardinal virtues for Duke Frederico and the theological virtues for his duchess. The deep backgrounds evoke Piero's native landscape near Arezzo. Piero wrote a treatise about perspective, the new science which fascinated Paolo Uccello to the point of near insanity. This obsession is the real subject of the *Battle of San Romano* (1456) ✫ which was painted 24yr after the event and hung in a room in the Medici palace. Two flanking panels were sold in the late 18thC and are now in the Louvre and the London National Gallery. The Uffizi piece is the least impressive of the three because of its inferior condition and relatively confusing composition.

Rm 8. Filippo Lippi, a disciple of Masaccio, was much imitated in his own time. The latest and loveliest of the Uffizi Filippos is the *Madonna with Angels* (c.1465) ✫ which scholars take as evidence of Botticelli's apprenticeship to the older master. For Filippo's major achievement in Tuscany, see *Prato* (in *A–Z/Tuscany*). Filippo's Sienese contemporary Vecchietta is represented by a *Madonna Enthroned* (1457). Notice also Baldovinetti's appealing works.

Rm 9. The Pollaiuolo brothers, Antonio and Piero, were sculptors, engravers and goldsmiths as well as painters. Piero is usually judged the less talented, mainly on the evidence of these *Six Virtues* (1469), ordered by the Merchants' Tribunal. The seventh, *Strength*, was Botticelli's first public commission. The virtues do indeed seem crude and static when compared to Antonio's tiny but vividly dramatic panels of *The Feats of*

Hercules in the case between the windows. Antonio's interest in anatomy drove him to undertake human dissections. He was, above all, one of the most gifted draftsmen of the Renaissance, an innovator in the use of line to convey muscular action. In the same case are two exhilarating scenes from the grisly *Story of Judith*, by the young Botticelli when he was still under the influence of Pollaiuolo.

Rms 10–14. The great Medici Botticellis hang in this room, converted into one large area. The design of the room and the gray lighting are controversial. Botticelli was the greatest linear painter before Matisse, and the powerful melodic line and lyrical nostalgia of his art can touch the heart even of those who fail to grasp his meaning. The *Primavera* (c.1480) ★ (beautifully restored in 1983) was painted for an adolescent cousin of Lorenzo de' Medici. Until recently scholars disagreed about just what it depicts. Many now accept a revealing new gloss which relates the subject matter to the conventions of early Renaissance Italian love poetry. The central figure is the ideal woman; a man who sees her will be conquered and forever changed by Cupid's arrow. The picture 'reads' from right to left, possibly because, like Petrarch's poetry, it conveys a memory. In comes the Wind God Zephyr. At his touch, flowers grow from the lips of Chloe, the happily married nymph, who becomes Flora, goddess of spring. On the other side of the woman are her 'companion' qualities (beauty and generosity, represented by the three graces) and Mercury, god of eloquence, conciliation and reason, pointing upward to heaven.

The *Birth of Venus* (c.1485) ★ was commissioned after Botticelli's return from Rome and later hung next to the *Primavera*. The *Adoration of the Magi* (c.1475) ★ is one of a series of *Adorations* from the 1470s; others are in Washington and London. This one is of special interest because members of the Medici family appear among the adoring Magi. Lorenzo de' Medici is at the left foreground, Botticelli himself is in yellow on the extreme right. The *Man with a Medallion of Cosimo il Vecchio* (c.1475–80) may be another self-portrait. The *Madonna of the Magnificat* (c.1482) ★ is perhaps the loveliest of his religious paintings, and all the more so now that it has been cleaned; its elaborate curving design has been compared to a section cut through a rose. The *Calumny of Apelles* (c.1495–1500) is one of the few late Botticellis in the Uffizi. The frenzied, dazzlingly stylized execution reflects the political and moral earnestness that afflicted many sensitive Florentines at the end of the century under the influence of Savonarola.

Set out from the walls on a screen is a large *Adoration of the Shepherds* known as the *Portinari Altarpiece* (c.1475) ★ by the Flemish master Hugo van der Goes. Commissioned in Bruges by a Medici bank agent, Tommaso Portinari, this marvelous feat of naturalistic painting had a profound effect on all artists who saw it after its arrival in Florence in 1488. Behind it is another Flemish work, Roger van der Weyden's *Entombment of Christ* (c.1450), painted in Florence. Dom. Ghirlandaio, Filippino Lippi, Botticelli and Lorenzo di Credi, all influenced by the van der Goes, are represented in this section of the room. For Ghirlandaio and Filippino see *Santa Maria Novella* and *Santa Trinita*.

Rm 15. There is no complete or completely accepted Leonardo in the Uffizi, but no other gallery possesses such fascinating evidence of his early development. His earliest known piece of work, done when he was still in his teens working in Verrocchio's studio, is the profiled angel in the *Baptism of Christ* (begun c.1470). Vasari tells us that Verrocchio, recognizing that this angel was beyond his own very considerable capabilities, abandoned the painting. Vasari does not mention the *Annunciation* (c.1475) ✩ and its attribution has been debated by opposing teams of distinguished art historians since it was brought into the gallery in 1867. The unfinished *Adoration of the Magi* (1481) ✩ is really a drawing rather than a painting, the preparatory scaffolding Leonardo left behind when he moved to Milan in 1482. To appreciate how startlingly ahead of its time this conception was you need only to compare it with Lorenzo di Credi's small *Annunciation* (1485), a faultlessly graceful piece typical of its period. Piero di Cosimo's *Perseus Liberating Andromeda* (1515–20) and *Immaculate Conception* (c.1505–10) show this idiosyncratic artist more at home with the mythological subject. Also, Signorelli's *Crucifixion with Mary Magdalen* and the Umbrian Perugino's *Pietà*.

All Florentine work of the finest kind . . . is absolutely pure Etruscan, merely changing its subjects, and representing the Virgin instead of Athena, and Christ instead of Jupiter.

John Ruskin, *Mornings in Florence*

Rm 18. The Tribune ★ was designed in 1584 by Buontalenti as an inner temple of the arts and restored in 1970 to something like its original appearance. When Zoffany painted the Tribune in 1775 for Queen Charlotte of England, this windowless octagonal room was one of the high points of the Grand Tour. The best works of art in the gallery were displayed here, but nothing in Florence had such drawing power as the *Medici Venus* ✩ which was a Roman copy of a Praxitelean figure of the 4thC BC, brought into this inner sanctum in the 17thC by Cosimo III, who is said to have feared that she might corrupt the morals of art students in Rome. For nearly 200yr she remained a potent sex symbol for educated Europeans, inducing a cultural-erotic trance which men struggled to describe in prose and poetry. Engravings, drawings and reproductions of all sizes flooded across the Alps. Louis XIV had her copied in bronze. She was the only statue in Florence called to Paris by Napoleon. In the puritanical 19thC, a plaster cast in Philadelphia was kept under lock and key. Nathaniel Hawthorne found himself panting as he approached her along the Uffizi corridors. We cannot easily share such raptures today; but it is as well to be reminded of the vagaries of taste when in an art gallery.

Among the many fine 16thC portraits in the Tribune are Vasari's *Lorenzo de' Medici* and Pontormo's *Cosimo il Vecchio* (both posthumous); Bronzino's *Lucrezia* and *Bartolomeo Panciatichi*; and *Eleanor of Toledo with her Son Giovanni I*. Two famous charmers are Rosso Fiorentino's *Musical Angel* and Bronzino's *Don Giovanni de' Medici*.

Rm 17. Entrance (from the Tribune only) is often barred. The Room of the Hermaphrodite takes its name from a Hellenistic copy (2ndC BC) of an extraordinarily sensual bisexual figure.

Rm 19. Signorelli's *Holy Family* (c.1491) anticipates Michelangelo's *Doni Tondo* in Rm 25. By Perugino, *Madonna and Child with Saints* (1493) and the fine portrait of *Francesco delle Opere* (1494), a Florentine craftsman.

Rm 20. Dürer's *Portrait of the Artist's Father* (1490) and *Adoration of the Magi* (1504). Lucas Cranach's *Adam* and *Eve* (1528) face Dürer's *Adam* and *Eve*.

Rm 21. Venetian paintings, notably Giovanni Bellini's stupendous *Sacred Allegory* (c.1495) ★ the allegorical significance of which has never been satisfactorily explained. The attributions to Giorgione in this room are questionable.

Rm 22. Holbein's almost tactlessly faithful *Portrait of Sir Richard Southwell* (1536); Altdorfer's *Martyrdom* and *Departure of St Florian* (c.1525).

Rm 23. Two superb Mantagnas ★ the *Madonna of the Rocks* and the *Adoration of the Magi* (both c.1489); and Correggio's *Rest on the Flight into Egypt*.

South corridor. Fine views and Classical sculptures.

West corridor. This section of the gallery originally housed workshops and laboratories. The 16thC conception of 'art' embraced the crafts and sciences. Among the tapestries, note particularly the *Passion of Christ* series, woven in Florence, and the Flemish *Scenes from the Life of Jacob*.

Rm 25. The *Holy Family*, known as the *Doni Tondo* (1504) ★ is the only picture in Florence by Michelangelo apart from the drawings in the *Casa Buonarroti* and the recently discovered drawings at *San Lorenzo*. It was commissioned by Angelo Doni on the occasion of his marriage to Maddalena Strozzi during the period when the artist was in Florence working on the *David*. In opposition to Leonardo, Michelangelo held that sculpture was the supreme art, and this tondo aspires to three dimensions. The Classical past, represented by a frieze of nudes in the upper half, is linked to the new Christian era by the figure of John the Baptist. With its emphasis on gesture and deliberately shocking colors, this was a key picture for the 16thC Mannerists. The inventors of Mannerism, Pontormo (Rm 27) and Rosso Fiorentino, whose astonishing *Moses Defending the Daughters of Jethro* (1523–4) ★ hangs next to the *Doni Tondo*, were both deeply neurotic – agoraphobic, morbid and asocial and, until 50yr ago, ignored or despised by critics. Today the gratuitous violence of Rosso's *Moses* (the text from *Exodus* says nothing about all this wrenching and pounding) and its jarring, acid colors may seem very modern. In fact it was painted for a patron known for his violent temper.

Rm 26. For Andrea del Sarto see also *Pitti*, *San Salvi*, *Lo Scalzo*. *Madonna of the Harpies* (1517) ★ is a masterpiece of his early maturity. Raphael's *Virgin of the Goldfinch* (1506) shows the influence of his first contact with Florentine artists; his penetrating, scholarly portrait of the first Medici Pope *Leo X with Cardinals Giulio de' Medici and Luigi de' Rossi* (c.1519) ★ is one of his finest late works.

Rm 27. Pontormo began his career as one of Andrea del Sarto's many satellites, but by the time he painted the *Supper at Emmaus* (1525), he had discovered other models; in this case it was a woodcut by Dürer. His masterpieces are elsewhere in and near Florence: see *Santa Felicita* in *Florence*; *Carmignano*, *Galluzo*, *Pogglio a Caiano* in *A–Z/Tuscany*.

Rm 28. Titian's euphemistically entitled *Venus of Urbino* (1538) ★ is not a Venus but a pinup, one of the most intimate, alluring female nudes ever painted. Visitors to Florence have been falling in love with her since she arrived in 1631 as part of the inheritance of Vittoria delle Rovere. For Byron she was '*the* Venus.' Other fine Titians include *Flora* (c.1515), *A Knight of Malta* (c.1518), and portraits of *Eleanora* and *Francesco Maria* *della Rovere*, Duke and Duchess of Urbino (1537).

Rm 29. Parmigianino was the leading central Italian Mannerist. The striking, intricate *Virgin of the Long Neck* ✩ left unfinished at his death in 1540, is his best-known work.

Returning to the corridor via Rm 34 (Veronese and Moroni), the entrance to Vasari's **Corridoio** ★ is immediately right. Tours of it must be guided: book a day in advance. Vasari built this long covered passage for Cosimo I in 1565. It links the Uffizi to the Pitti, crossing the Arno with the Ponte Vecchio and passing through the church of Santa Felicita. The views are nearly as magnificent as the pictures, the most celebrated of which are the series of self-portraits.

Rm 35. The Umbrian master Federico Barocci's *Madonna of the People* (1575–9); Tintoretto's *Leda* (1570) and portrait of *Jacopo Sansovino* (1566) and *A Venetian Admiral*.

Rm 41. Rubens and Van Dyck.

Rm 42. The large collection of 20thC self-portraits is out of place in this fine Neo-Classical room, which has housed the 4thC Roman sculptures of *Niobe and her Children* ✩ since 1790.

Rm 43. Caravaggio's *Sacrifice of Isaac* (c.1590), *Bacchus* (c.1589), and *Medusa* (after 1590). Also, Claude Lorraine's *Seascape* (1677).

Rm 44. Three portraits by Rembrandt, including one of his greatest self-portraits, *Self-Portrait as an Old Man* (c.1664) ✩

Rm 45. 18thC French, Venetian and Spanish paintings by Nattier, Chardin, G. B. Tiepolo, Canaletto, Guardi and Goya.

At the end of this corridor are rest rooms and a pleasant bar, which opens on to a terrace over the Loggia dei Lanzi.

Exit hall (formerly Rms 34–40). The famous *Wild Boar* is a Roman copy of a 3rdC BC Hellenistic original and was the model for Pietro Tacca's *Porcellino Fountain* in the Mercato Nuovo. The exit staircase is by Buontalenti.

Zoological Museum, 'La Specola'

Via Romana 17 ☎*222451. Map 4F2* 📷 �#️ *Open Tues 9am–12:30pm, Sun 9am–noon. Anatomical rooms Sat: summer 3–6pm, winter 2–5pm.*

The Torrigiani palace which houses the Zoological Institute is known as 'La Specola,' after the astrological observatory set up here in 1775 by Grand Duke Peter Leopold.

The museum, on the second floor, is divided into two sections. The Zoological Museum consists of a collection of specimens arranged in order of organic complexity from mollusks to mammals, including hunting trophies donated by Victor Emmanuel and ending with a small selection of wax models of human and animal anatomy.

The full collection of some 600 **anatomical wax models** ✩ is displayed in the next rooms. They are among the most extraordinary objects in Florence, and remind you just how deep are the roots of the Florentine fascination with human anatomy. The Renaissance artist P. Pollaiuolo dissected corpses in order to improve his understanding of how the human body works. Here, from 1775–1814, an artist, Clemente Susini, and a physiologist, Felice Fontana, collaborated to make these tinted wax reproductions of every part of the human body. The famous *Embryonic Twins* and models of reproductive organs are in a room off Corridor 31.

Next door are the *Plague Victims* by the late 17thC Sicilian Gaetano Zumbo. The custodian will usually open these rooms on request.

Walks in Florence

Despite the irritating traffic Florence is best appreciated on foot.
The first two walks share a common plan (on opposite page). A
variation on the fourth walk might be along the recently opened
stretch of city walls between the *Belvedere* and *Porta Romana*.

Walk 1/Getting to know Florence

On your first evening in Florence, an after-dinner stroll in the
center, taking in the *Uffizi*, *Signoria* and *Duomo*, will make
you at home in the dense cluster of the city's historic nucleus.
Florence is at its best, its most beautiful, after dark when the
buses have departed and the floodlighting touches even the most
familiar monuments with fresh magic.

Start at Piazza *Santa Trinita* in order to enjoy the floodlit view
of *San Miniato* and the *Belvedere* from Ponte S. Trinita
and to admire the recently installed lighting of the **Via
Tornabuoni**. If you can resist window shopping, plunge into
medieval Florence along Via delle Terme, named for the
Roman baths which occupied this site, to the 14thC **Palazzo di
Parte Guelfa** on the left. Turn right opposite it under Chiasso
delle Misure and left into Borgo *Santi Apostoli*, crossing Por S.
Maria into Via Lambertesca, which brings you past
Buontalenti's bizarre **Porta delle Suppliche** into Piazzale degli
Uffizi. A left turn leads straight into Piazza *Signoria*. Turn right
around the N corner of the Palazzo Vecchio into Via dei Gondi
and Piazza *San Firenze*, where the towers of the *Badia* and
Bargello rise with dignity beyond the Baroque extravaganza of
the S. Firenze facade. Take the Via del Proconsolo, turning left
after *Badia* into Via Dante Alighieri. The Casa di Dante is a
19thC fiction made believable by the night lighting. Opposite is
the Castegna tower, all that remains of the earliest seat of
communal government. Turn right into Via S. Margherita, left
at the Corso and immediately right into Via dello Studio, where
you will be rewarded with one of those astonishingly sudden
views of Brunelleschi's Dome. The cathedral complex –
campanile, Baptistry, *Duomo* – reveals itself as you turn left
along its S side. Third left is Via de' Calzaiuoli which brings you
past *Orsanmichele* back into the *Signoria*.

Walk 2/A palace walk

This is a walk devoted entirely to those domestic buildings
which Italians rather grandly call palaces. It can be divided into
three separate walks if you want to go slowly and thoroughly. It
will take you, in roughly chronological order, past many of the
most important Florentine palaces built for the merchants and
bankers of the 14th–16thC.

Florentines, being the least pretentious and most ironically
humorous of Italians, will often refer in conversation to a hut as
a palazzo and a palazzo as a little house – which doesn't in the
least mean that they are not proud of their palaces. A surprising
number are still lived in by descendants of their first owners;
most are used—as flats, restaurants, shops, offices—your hotel
might be in a palace. If you are not with a large party it is always
worth ringing the bell and asking to see the courtyard; that is
the kind of independently motivated interest Florentines
respect. The palaces built in Florence during the 15thC boom
provided a model for the rest of Italy. In 15thC Tuscany there
was no significant advance on the basic Florentine type except
in *Pienza (A–Z/Tuscany)*. Nevertheless, there are certain

practical or decorative additions to Florentine palaces which
you encounter less often outside the city.

The stone benches, or *muriccioli*, which run along the base of
so many palaces were a government-imposed condition of
building permission. If you decide to rest and gossip on one of
these public benches, you will be exercising a civic right dear to
the republican hearts of Renaissance Florentines. Machiavelli
was shocked to find no *muriccioli* in Venice.

The projecting upper stories supported on brackets known as
sporti were a device to grab more living space in a crowded city.
Legislation against them generally failed.

The black-and-white decoration, or *sgraffiti*, on facades and
in courtyards originated in the 15thC and was carried on
through the 19thC. Two good 15thC examples not encountered
on this walk are the **Coverelli** palace in Via dei Coverelli and the
Lanfredini palace on Lungarno Guicciardini. The 16thC
master of *sgraffiti* was Poccetti.

I. Start in the morning at the *Davanzati*, the best-preserved
14thC merchant's house in Florence. Next, to see what had
happened to palace architecture a century later, cross the
bottom of the Tornabuoni onto Via del Parione; the first right
and an immediate left into Via del Purgatorio, brings you into
the little piazza facing Alberti's *Rucellai Palace*. Take the Via
della Vigna Nuova back to the Tornabuoni, across which you
see the *Strozzi*, later, larger and less refined than the Rucellai.
Down the Tornabuoni to Piazza *Santa Trinita*. On its NE corner
is the early 16thC **Bartolini Salimbeni**, the Roman-style palace
Florentines thought looked more like a church. Now look up
the **Via Tornabuoni** for a minute before strolling up it. The
palaces are 13th–16thC. At the top, partly closing the vista, is
the **Antinori** palace, built in the 1460s by the Boni family, who

received permission to extend their site onto public land to provide this suitably elegant finish to the Tornabuoni.

Once you have reached the Antinori, the **Cantinetta** restaurant is an ideal place to stop for lunch. Otherwise, you could have a delicious but expensive snack at **Giacosa** or **Procacci** before pressing on to the Medici Palace by way of Via Rondinelli, right into Via de' Cerretani, and left along Borgo S. Lorenzo.

II. The *Medici Palace* reopens at 3pm when the **Benozzo Gozzoli Chapel** is often less crowded than in the morning. Go around the S side of the palace and turn right at the corner of the crenellated garden wall onto **Via de' Ginori**, lined with good 13th–16thC palaces. No. 9, the **Barbolani di Montauto**, is an example of a 15thC palace modernized in the 16thC with kneeling windows and herms. Nos. 17–21, **Palazzo Taddei**, is a fine and typical early 16thC palace (1503) by Baccio d'Agnolo; Raphael lived here in 1505. After crossing Via Guelfa, Via de' Ginori becomes **Via S. Gallo**. In the 16thC this was a street of churches, monasteries and high garden walls. It has a rather forlorn atmosphere now, but in the 18thC a carriage ride to the S. Gallo gate was the fashionable evening outing. On the left, no. 25a, is the severely beautiful portal, possibly designed by Michelangelo, of the **Monastery of S. Apollonia**. Farther along Via S. Gallo on the right, no.74 is the **Pandolfini** palace (1520), designed by Raphael, who evidently thought the asymmetrical plan suitable for a large suburban site, and built by two members of the Sangallo family. The style of the palace is as Roman as the sympathies of its first owner, Giannozzo Pandolfini, Bishop of Troia, who records his gratitude to the Medici Popes for their help in acquiring the property in the inscription under the magnificent cornice. If you turn right at the corner of the Pandolfini and right again into Via Cavour, you will soon come, on the left, to no. 57, the **Casino di S. Marco** (1574), built on the site of the Medici sculpture gardens by Buontalenti in his most bizarre, satirical vein. Francesco I had his alchemical laboratories here. The Casino is now the Court of Appeals, but, more to the point, if you happen to be thirsty there is a little bar off the inner courtyard to the left.

Turn right out of the Casino, left into **Piazza S. Marco**, pausing only to admire the cathedral dome rising spectacularly on your right, and take Via Cesare Battisti into the northern corner of Piazza *Santissima Annunziata*. The rose-brick palace on the corner of Via dei Servi, a cavalier exception to the arcaded harmony of the square, is Ammannati's **Grifoni** palace. Its main entrance is on **Via dei Servi**, lined with grand-ducal palaces. Notice especially two on the right: no. 15, the **Niccolini** (1550), designed by Baccio d'Agnolo with 19thC *sgraffiti*; and on Via Pucci, the **Pucci** palace, ancestral home of the fashion designer, with a fine emblem of Leo X on this corner. Via dei Servi finishes at the *Duomo*.

III. Alternatively, on leaving the Piazza *Santissima Annunziata*, take the first left off Via dei Servi into **Via degli Alfani**. On the right is a 1930s restoration of Brunelleschi's once-important *Rotonda di S. Maria degli Agnoli*. No. 48, on the left, is the **Giugni** palace (c.1577), one of Ammannati's best buildings. The courtyard, usually open, is remarkable for the alarming use of detached Classical elements. The Tuscan order was employed as a patriotic reference to the newly unified grand-ducal Tuscany. Notice the beautiful 16thC wooden gate. Farther along, two simpler palaces on the left, nos. 34 and 32, are also by Ammannati. The green dome you see ahead belongs to the synagogue. On the next right is **Borgo Pinti**, which boasts 14th–16thC palaces. At no.26, the house with the bust of *Cosimo I* over the door, Giambologna lived and died and Pietro Tacca founded an academy.

At the bottom, as you pass under the Volta di S. Piero – bar on the left serves rough wine and good ham sandwiches – you are crossing the second circle of walls into the 12thC city. Now turn right onto **Borgo degli Albizi**, a street rich in good 16thC palaces. No.18 is the **Altoviti**, known as Palazzo dei Visacci after the herm portraits of famous Florentines. Avoid the restaurant inside. No.26 is palazzo **Matteucci Ramirez di Montalvi**, built by Ammannati for a favorite of Cosimo I whose emblem as Duke of Siena is over the door; remains of *sgraffiti* by Poccetti. No.28, the **Vitali** palace, is also by Ammannati. Opposite the Vitali, in the lobby of the cinema specialising in pornographic films, are the remains of a 15thC courtyard. On the corner of Via del Proconsolo is the **Nonfinito** palace, now housing the Institute of Anthropology, begun in 1593 by Buontalenti for Alessandro Strozzi but left unfinished. A left turn onto Via del Proconsolo will bring you into Piazza *San Firenze*, where Giuliano da Sangallo's exemplary **Gondi** palace (1490–1520) is on your right opposite the S. Firenze facade. If you are in luck and have energy enough left to ring the bell (at no. 2), you will be admitted into one of the most beautiful courtyards in Florence. You are now a minute's walk from the *Signoria* and have earned a good dinner. If you choose to dine at **Cavallino**, you will be looking out over the most famous Florentine palace of all.

Walk 3/The Oltrarno

Allow 2hr. *Maps* **4&5**

Pitti Palace

This zigzag route through the *Oltrarno* will take you to its three important churches and past many of its most interesting palace facades. A conveniently delicious beginning to the afternoon would be lunch at **Celestino**, but there are plenty of other restaurants to choose from on the Oltrarno. Start off at about 3pm, when the churches begin to reopen, from Piazza *Santa Felicita*. The Medici dukes went home to the Pitti from this church by way of Vasari's aerial corridor, but you must make do with the Via Guicciardini, where the Machiavelli family once lived opposite the Guicciardini palace (no.15).

Passing the *Pitti* on your left, turn sharp right at Piazza *San Felice* onto **Via Maggio**, so called because it was and still is the widest (*maggiore*) street on the Oltrarno. Palaces are

103

14th–17thC, but most of the earlier ones were modernized in
the grand-ducal period when Via Maggio was the best address
in Florence. No. 26 is **Bianca Cappello's house**, remodeled in
1570–4 by Buontalenti for the Venetian mistress and future
wife of Francesco I, who paid the bill. The Cappello emblem is
over the rusticated doorway; *sgraffiti* are by Poccetti. At the
bottom of Via Maggio turn left into Via S. Spirito. On the right
corner of Via dei Coverelli is **Palazzo Coverelli**, with good
restored *sgraffiti*. Turn left into Via dei Coverelli bearing left
around the apse and side of the church of *Santo Spirito*.
Imagine what the exterior would have looked like if
Brunelleschi's unique plan had been carried out; he intended
the 40 curved backs of the interior chapels to be expressed on
the outside. Crossing Piazza S. Spirito turn right at its sw corner
into Via S. Agostino. Where it crosses Via de' Serragli there is
on the right a tabernacle (1427) by Lorenzo di Bicci. Turn left
into Via de' Serragli and first right into Via dell' Ardiglione,
which soon bends to the right along the side of a pretty walled
garden; from its gate there is a picturesque view of the apse of
the *Carmine* church. This is one of those rare Florentine streets
where the bustle and noise of the city never seem to penetrate; it
might have been this peaceful when Filippo Lippi was born in
1406 at no.10. A left turn into Via S. Monaca brings you to the
church entrance. If it is now early evening, Masaccio's frescoes
might be as he intended them to be seen, lit by the setting sun.

Walk 4/To Arcetri and Pian dei Giullari

Allow 2hr. Maps **6&7**

The Tuscan countryside is only about 10min by foot from the
Ponte Vecchio. Take the narrow Costa di S. Giorgio from
behind the church of *Santa Felicità*, past the *Belvedere* and
into **Via di S. Leonardo**, the most entrancing street in the
environs of Florence, lined with old villas and walled gardens.
Jasmine, wisteria and roses clamber in season through the olives
and cypresses. On the left is the 11thC church of S. Leonardo in
Arcetri, its facade an early 20thC reconstruction. Ottone Rosai
lived at no. 49; his paintings of Via di S. Leonardo can be seen in
the Alberto della Ragione collection (*Signoria*). A plaque
marks the house on the corner of Viale Galileo where
Tchaikovsky lived in 1878, "his music nourished by the soft
hills of Tuscany." After crossing the Viale, bear left into Via V.
Vivani, left again into Via del Pian dei Giullari. As you climb,
the view to the right, overlooking the Astrophysical
Observatory, becomes more and more wild and spectacular. At
Pian dei Giullari (see *Arcetri*) you could stop for lunch or dinner
at **Omero**, or carry on walking along Via S. Margherita toward
Ponte a Ema and Antella.

Staying in Florence

Florence is a commercial city as well as a magnet for mass tourism, and it does not have enough hotels to meet the demand. It is essential, particularly from Easter through late autumn, to book rooms well in advance. The Ente Provinciale per il Turismo publishes annually a full list of hotels and *pensioni* in the city and province. If you need a hotel at the last minute, try the booking center at the station.

Cheap accommodations are much harder to find than even a few years ago. Some of the rough, reliable old *pensioni* have closed; others have been modernized with prices to match; those that remain are mostly run by older people. The distinction between *pensioni* and hotels has in any case largely broken down. Some hotels officially classed as *pensioni* do not have restaurants. Those that do have improved their food, and half-board where available can be very good value. If you are on a budget, remember that breakfast is cheaper and better at a local bar.

The modern alternatives to the old residential *pensioni* are 'residences.' These are service apartments bookable for a minimum of one week, whose standard varies greatly. One of the most attractive of the recently opened residences is **La Fonte** (*Via S. Felice a Ema 29* ☎ *(055) 224421* ▯▯), in a handsome Renaissance villa 1½km (1 mile) S of the center.

Although the general standard of cleanliness and basic efficiency in Florentine hotels is high, traffic noise is a serious problem, especially on the central Lungarni. If you are sensitive to noise it is worth sacrificing a view for a room on the garden or courtyard. Or consider staying a little way outside the center (see, for example, *Bagno a Ripoli, Fiesole, Sesto Fiorentino* and *Settignano* in the *Tuscany A–Z*). The Chianti, easily accessible from the center by car, is also well-supplied now with villas, castles, farmhouses, and even villages converted into hotels or residences. Two examples, opened since the last edition of this book: the romantic **Badia Motescalari** near *Greve* (*bookings* ☎ *(055) 959596*), a converted Romanesque abbey; and **Castel Ruggero**, near the Ugolino golf course at *Impruneta* (*bookings* ☎ *(055) 287283*), a residence where part of a farmhouse can be rented for less than the price per head of the seediest central hotel.

If you prefer to rent a reasonably priced flat in central Florence, try the agency **Florence and Abroad** (*Via S. Zanobi 58, 50129 Firenze* ☎ *(055) 490143/487004* ☉ *570093/570215*). They speak English, and will also look for villas in the Tuscan countryside.

Florence hotels, pensioni and residences
Hotels

Aprilc ▯▯	Lungarno ▮▮▮	Hermitage ▯▯
Augustus ▮▮▮	Porta Rossa ▯▯	Monna Lisa ▮▯
Baglioni ▮▮▮	Principe ▮▯	Pendini ▮▯
Balestri ▮▮▮	Regency ▮▮▮ ▭	Plaza Lucchesi ▮▮▮
Berchielli ▮▮▮	Royal ▮▮▮	Quisisana e
Continental ▮▯	Savoy ▮▮▮	Pontevecchi ▮▯
Croce di Malta ▮▮▮	Villa Belvedere ▮▮▮	Residenza ▮▯
David ▮▮▮	Villa Cora ▮▮▮ ▭	Rigatti ▮▮
De La Ville ▮▮▮	Villa Medici ▮▮▮ ▭	Silla ▮▯
Due Fontane ▮▯		Tornabuoni-Beacci ▮▮▯
Excelsior ▮▮▮	### *Pensioni*	Villa Carlotta ▮▯
Helvetia-Bristol ▮▮▯	Adria ▯▯	
Jennings-Riccioli ▮▮▯	Annalena ▮▮▮	### *Residence*
Kraft ▮▮▮	Cestelli ▯ ▭	Grand ▮▮▮
Liana ▮▯	Costantini ▯ ▭	

Adria
*Piazza Frescobaldi 4, 50125
Firenze* ☎ *(055) 215029. Map
4D2* ▭ *10 rms* ▭ *6* ⚍ ▣
Closed Aug.
Location: *Oltrarno, near Ponte S.
Trinita.* Respectably gloomy
pensione on the third floor of a
palace facing the Arno.
▱ ‡ ⋞⋟

Annalena
Via Romana 34, 50125 Firenze
☎ *(055) 222402. Map 4F2* ▭
20rms ▭ *20. Closed May* ▣ ▨
Location: *Opposite the Boboli
Gardens.* A comfortably furnished
pensione on the first floor of a 15thC
palace overlooking the largest
private garden in Florence.
▱ ⌲

Aprile
Via della Scala 6, 50123 Firenze
☎ *(055) 216237. Map 4B2* ▮▮▮
29 rms ▭ *22* ▣ ▣ ▨
Location: *Near the station.* The Via
della Scala is not the most
salubrious street in Florence, but it
has its surprises, including this
friendly, newly refurbished private
hotel in a 15thC Medici palace.
‡ ⌲ ✿ ⋎

Augustus
Piazzetta dell'Oro 5, 50123 Firenze
☎ *(055) 283054* ▣ *570110. Map
4D3* ▮▮▮ *67 rms* ▭ *67* ▤▤ ⋏ ▣
⦿ ▣ ▨
Location: *Near Ponte Vecchio.* A
modern building protected from
the hurly-burly of central Florence
by its own tiny square.
▱ ‡ ⅋ ▢ ⬚ ✿ ⋞⋟ ⋎

Baglioni
*Piazza Unità Italiana 6, 50123
Firenze* ☎ *(055) 218441*
▣ *570225. Map 4B2* ▮▮▮ *195 rms*
▭ *195* ▤▤ ⋏ ⬚ ⚍ ▣ ⦿ ▣
▨
Location: *Opposite the station.* An
enormous, efficient, well-staffed
hotel, ideal for business people.
‡ ⅋ ⌲ ⋎ *on roof* ⛆ ⋎

Balestri
Piazza Mentana 7, 50122 Firenze
☎ *(055) 214743. Map 5E4* ▮▮▮
50 rms ▭ *46* ▤▤ ⋏ ▣ ▨
Closed Dec–Feb.
Location: *On the Arno, 5min E of
Ponte Vecchio.* A 19thC hotel, for
four generations in the same family.
‡ ⅋ ⌲ ⋞⋟ ⋎

Berchielli
*Lungarno Acciaioli 14, 50123
Firenze* ☎ *(055) 264061. Map*

4D3 ▮▮▮ *80 rms* ▭ *80* ▤▤ ▣ ▣
⦿ ▣ ▨
Location: *On the Arno, near Ponte
Vecchio.* A handsome old hotel
modernized in the early 1980s.
‡ ⌲

Cestelli ▥
*Via Borgo SS. Apostoli 25, 50123
Firenze* ☎ *(055) 21413. Map 4D3*
▭ *7 rms* ▭ *2*
Location: *Near Via Tornabuoni.*
Tiny and immaculate *pensione* in
the medieval heart of the city.

Continental
*Lungarno Acciaioli 2, 50123
Firenze* ☎ *(055) 282392* ▣ *57110.
Map 4D3* ▮▮▮ *63 rms* ▭ *59* ▤▤
▣ ⦿ ▨
Location: *Near Ponte Vecchio.* An
efficient hotel in a new building
incorporating the 13thC Torre
Guelfa dei Consorti. The best
rooms are in the tower – others are
neat and functional but noisy.
‡ ⌲ ⋎ *on roof* ⋞⋟ ⋎

Costantini ▥
*Via de' Calzaiuoli 13, 50122
Firenze* ☎ *(055) 215128. Map
5C4* ▭ *17 rms* ▭ *6* ⚍ ⚍
Location: *Near the Duomo.* Basic,
clean, cheerful and central.
▱ ‡ ⋞⋟

Croce di Malta
Via della Scala 7, 50123 Firenze
☎ *(055) 282600* ▣ *570540. Map
4B2* ▮▮▮ *100 rms* ▭ *100* ▤▤ ⋏
▱ ⚍ ▣ ▨
Location: *Near the station.* The
Space Age-Renaissance decor may
not be to everyone's taste, but the
luxurious duplex apartments on the
garden are calmer and the attic
bedrooms are delightful.
‡ ⅋ ▢ ⬚ ⋎ ⇌ ⛆ ⋎

David
*Viale Michelangelo 1, 50125
Firenze* ☎ *(055) 6811696*
▣ *574553. Map 7D4* ▮▮▮ *26 rms*
▭ *18* ▤▤ ⋏ ▣ ▣ ⦿ ▣ ▨
Location: *Near the Firenze-Sud
autostrada junction.* A pleasant
private hotel in a shady garden;
nicely decorated in an unfussy
country style. Some rooms are noisy.
‡ ⌲ ✿ ⋎

De La Ville
Piazza Antinori 1, 50123 Firenze
☎ *(055) 261805/8* ▣ *570518.
Map 4C3* ▮▮▮ *75 rms* ▭ *73* ▤▤
▱ ⚍ ⚍ ▣ ⦿ ▨
Location: *N end of Via Tornabuoni.*
A modern (1961) hotel next to the
Palazzo Antinori. The building is

soundproofed and furnished with creamy, comfortable good taste.
🏠 ‡ ◻ ◿

Due Fontane
Piazza SS. Annunziata 14, 50122 Firenze ☎ *(055) 210185. bookings* ☎ *(055) 210987. Map* **5A5** ◫ *50 rms* 🛏 *50* ▦ ᴀᴇ ᴠɪꜱᴀ
A comfortable, tastefully modernized hotel facing Florence's most architecturally harmonious square.
🏠 ‡ ◻ ◿ 🎾 ⟨⟨ ♈

Excelsior
Piazza Ognissanti 3, 50123 Firenze ☎ *(055) 264201* ☏ *570022. Map* **4C1** ▥ *217 rms* 🛏 *205* ▦
🏠 ↔ ᴀᴇ ᴄʙ ◉ ◉ ᴠɪꜱᴀ
Location: 10 min w of Ponte Vecchio. The grand old hotel of Florence retains all the solid, spacious luxury of the 1920s – but not, alas, the stylish service. Red marbled pillars, wooden ceilings, polished furniture; every comfort from thick pastel carpets to enormous bathrooms. (See Il Cestello under *Restaurants*.)
‡ ⟨ ◻ ◿ ⟨⟨ ♟ ♈

Grand ▦
Piazza Ognissanti 1, 50123 Firenze ☎ *(055) 278781* ☏ *570055. Map* **4C1** ◫ *103 rms* 🛏 *103* ▦ ↔
↔ ᴀᴇ ᴄʙ ◉ ◉ ᴠɪꜱᴀ
The other old-fashioned luxury hotel, beautifully restored and reopened in 1986. All the elegance of a Swiss-run spa hotel in the 1920s; expansive spaces and luxurious bedrooms.
‡ ⟨ ◿ ⟨⟨ ♟ ♈

Helvetia-Bristol
Via del Pescioni 2, 50123 Firenze ☎ *(055) 287814. Map* **4C3** ◫ *60 rms* 🛏 *60* ↔ ᴀᴇ ◉ ᴠɪꜱᴀ
Location: Off n end of Via Tornabuoni. A genteel, late-19thC hotel facing the Strozzi palace. The same family, of Swiss origin, have run it since 1895.
‡ ◿

Hermitage
Vicolo Marzio 1, Piazza del Pesce, 50122 Firenze ☎ *(055) 287216. Map* **4D3** ◫ *29 rms* 🛏 *18* ◫
Location: near Ponte Vecchio. A comfortable, modern *pensione*. The dining-room and roof garden look out over tiled roofs onto the historic center.
🏠 ‡ ◿ 🎾 ⟱ *on roof* ⟨⟨

Jennings-Riccioli
Corso Tintori 7, 50122 Firenze ☎ *(055) 244751. Map* **5E6** ◫

55 rms 🛏 *55* ᴀᴇ ᴄʙ ◉ ◉ ᴠɪꜱᴀ
Location: On the Arno, near S. Croce. This famous, formerly seedy hotel was completely renovated in 1986. No. 21 is E.M. Forster's Room with a View.
‡ ◿

Kraft
Via Solferino 2, 50123 Firenze ☎ *(055) 284273* ☏ *571523. Map* **2C2** ▥ *67 rms* 🛏 *67* ▦ 🏠 ↔
↔ ᴀᴇ ᴄʙ ◉ ◉ ᴠɪꜱᴀ
Location: Near Le Cascine. An extremely well-managed hotel in a relatively peaceful part of the city, owned by the son of the great Swiss hotelier. Efficient more than charming. Forgettable food.
🏠 ‡ ⟨ ◿ ⟱ ⟨⟨ ≈ *on roof.*

Liana
Via Alfieri 18, 50121 Firenze ☎ *(055) 245503/4. Map* **3C5** ◫ *20 rms* 🛏 *12* ↔
Location: 15min e of Duomo. A pleasant villa in a quiet street on the edge of the center, which housed the British Embassy from 1864–70. All the immaculately clean rooms face onto the big garden, planted with mature trees.
🏠 ⟨

Lungarno
Borgo S. Jacopo 14, 50125 Firenze ☎ *(055) 264211* ☏ *570129. Map* **4D3** ▥ *71 rms* 🛏 *71* ↔ ᴀᴇ ◉ ◉ ᴠɪꜱᴀ
Location: Oltrarno, near Ponte Vecchio. A modern hotel (1968) which hangs over the Arno and, at the back, has been wrapped around the 13thC Torre Marsili. The most attractive rooms are the 14 overlooking the Arno and the 13 within the tower. The proprietor's collection of 20thC art is distributed throughout the hotel.
‡ ◻ ◿ ⟨⟨

Monna Lisa
Borgo Pinti 27, 50121 Firenze ☎ *(055) 2479751* ☏ *573300. Map* **3C5** ▥ *20 rms* 🛏 *20* ᴀᴇ ◉ ◉ ᴠɪꜱᴀ
Location: 5min e of Duomo. The Renaissance Neri Palace, part of which dates from the 14thC, retains the atmosphere of a proudly maintained private palace. Polished Tuscan brick floors and antique furniture, original vaulted wooden or frescoed ceilings, and an elegant *pietra serena* staircase. By contrast with the reception rooms, many of the bedrooms are disappointing, especially the singles, which are cramped and sometimes

overheated. Eighteen rooms overlook the pretty garden or courtyard; others are noisy.
☖ ☲ ⚓

Pendini
Via Strozzi 2, 50123 Firenze
☎(055) 211170 ☎580278. Map
4C3 ▥ 37 rms ☐ 37 ᴀᴇ ⊕ ⓒⓄ
[ᵛᴵˢᴬ]
Location: Piazza della Repubblica.
Busy, carefully managed and dead central, with big, comfortably furnished rooms.
✚ ☲

Plaza Lucchesi
*Lungarno Zecca Vecchia 38,
50122 Firenze* ☎(055) 264141
☎570302. Map **3D5** ▥ 104 rms
☐ 104 ☷ ☲ ⇌ ᴀᴇ ⊕ ⓒⓄ [ᵛᴵˢᴬ]
*Location: On the Arno, near
S. Croce.* Once a large *pensione*, this is now an efficient hotel retaining traces of its former character. The views from the front are spectacular, but so is the noise.
✚ ✓ ☐ ☲ ◁ϵ

Porta Rossa
Via Porta Rossa 19, 50123 Firenze
☎(055) 287551. Map **4D3** ▯
71 rms ☐ 71 ᴀᴇ ⊕ ⓒⓄ [ᵛᴵˢᴬ]
*Location: Off s end of Via Torna-
buoni.* The Palazzo Torrigiani was a hotel as early as the 14thC, but the present establishment dates from the 19thC. It is now faintly seedy but with a venerable charm that still appeals, especially to French and English travelers. The bedrooms are huge and will accommodate as many as six beds each – groups welcome.
✚ ☲

Principe
*Lungarno Amerigo Vespucci 34,
50123 Firenze* ☎(055) 284848.
Map **4C1** ▯ 21 rms ☐ 21 ☷
☛ ᴀᴇ ᴄв ⊕ ⓒⓄ [ᵛᴵˢᴬ]
*Location: On the Arno, near
Ognissanti.* An elegant and comfortable small hotel on a relatively quiet stretch of the Lungarno. Some bedrooms have retained old brocade wall-hangings and marble bathrooms. A loyal American clientele appreciates the efficiency and character.
☖ ✚ ☲ ◁ϵ

Quisisana e Pontevecchio
*Lungarno Archibusieri 4, 50122
Firenze* ☎(055) 216692/215046.
Map **5D4** ▥ 36 rms ☐ 36 ⇌
ᴀᴇ [ᵛᴵˢᴬ]
This is the hotel for those who are nostalgic for the sepia-tinted

city of Alinari photographs, when streetcars ran along the Lungarni and Doney was safely in the Tornabuoni. The magnificent wrought-iron elevator sets the tone, and the atmosphere of the century-old *pensione* has been preserved in all but two respects: the plumbing and the prices.
✚ ☲ ⚓ ◁ϵ

Regency ▨
*Piazza M. d'Azeglio 3, 50121
Firenze* ☎(055) 245247 ☎571058.
Map **3C5** ▥ 38 rms ☐ 38 ☷
☚ ☛ ⇌ ᴀᴇ ⊕ ⓒⓄ [ᵛᴵˢᴬ]
Location: 15min ᴇ of Duomo. This chic and comfortable small hotel in its tranquil tree-lined square might have been imported direct from Paris. The building dates from the period when Florence was capital of Italy; its mid-19thC grandeur has been enlivened with bold, sophisticated decorative schemes. The bedrooms are in dazzling but well-judged color combinations.
See **Relais le Jardin** in *Restaurants*.
☖ ✚ ⚅ ☐ ☲ ⚓

Residenza
Via Tornabuoni 8, 50123 Firenze
☎(055) 218684 ☎570215. Map
4C3 ▯ 24 rms ☐ 22
☛ *preferred* ⇌
An exceptionally charming *pensione*, on the top floors of a Renaissance palace, a miniature grand hotel offering everything from a multilingual staff (English, French and German spoken) to an excellent restaurant. The top-floor rooms, some with balconies, are nicest. Family apartments.
✚ ☲ ◁ϵ

Rigatti
*Lungarno Generale Diaz 2, 50122
Firenze* ☎(055) 213022. Map
5E4 ▯ 28 rms ☐ 15 ⇌
☛ *obligatory.*
*Location: On the Arno, between the
Uffizi and S. Croce.* A superb position on the top two floors of the Palazzo Alberti, with spacious rooms, an elegant drawing room hung with old brocade, and an outstanding view from the terrace.
✚ ☌ ⚓ *on roof* ◁ϵ

Royal
*Via delle Ruote 50–54, 50129
Firenze* ☎(055) 483287. Map
3B4 ▥ 35 rms ☐ 35 ⇌ ᴀᴇ [ᵛᴵˢᴬ]
Location: Near S. Marco. Peace and quiet in a handsome 19thC palace overlooking its own garden.
☖ ⚅ ☲ ⚓

Savoy
*Piazza della Repubblica 7, 50100
Firenze* ☎*(055) 283313* ☏*570220.*
Map **5**C4 ▥▥▥ *101 rms* ▭ *101* ▦
▭ ▭ ☲ ▣ ⊕ ⊙ ▨

*Location: In the heart of the historic
center.* The most central, if not the
most fashionable, of the grand old
Florentine hotels. Service is
efficient but rather impersonal.
☰ ⅏ ▢ ◪ ☙

Silla
Via dei Renai 5, 50125 Firenze
☎*(055) 284810.* Map **5**F5 ▥▥
32 rms ▭ *28* ▭ ▣ ▣ ⊕ ⊙
▨

*Location: Oltrarno, near Ponte alle
Grazie.* An airy, spacious *pensione*
which is especially attractive in
summer. There is a large terrace,
and the view across the Arno is
fringed by trees in the little park.
☰ ◪ ☙ ◁⊱

Tornabuoni-Beacci
Via Tornabuoni 3, 50123 Firenze
☎*(055) 212645.* Map **4**C3 ▥▥
31 rms ▭ *26* ▦ ▭ ☲ ▭ ▣
▨

Location: N end of Via Tornabuoni.
Alinari prints, faded chintzes and
rubber plants in big pots give a
dignified old-fashioned feel to this
well-known *pensione* on the top
three floors of the 14thC Palazzo
Minerbetti. Regulars include
writers, fashion buyers, actors and
ministers of state, mostly from
English-speaking countries, who
are grateful for the homey but
unintrusive atmosphere and
comfortable rooms (the good
reading lights are an unaccustomed
luxury in Florence). A roof terrace
for breakfast and drinks; meals can
be served in your rooms.
☱ ☰ ⅏ ◪ ☙ ☧

Villa Belvedere
*Via Benedetto Castelli 3, 50124
Firenze* ☎*(055) 222501.* Map **7**E4
▥▥ *27 rms* ▭ *27* ▦ ▭ ▭ ◁⊱
*Location: Poggio Imperiale, 3km
(2 miles) s.* Just the hotel for a
peaceful family vacation, in a
reconstructed Medici villa over-

looking Florence.
☱ ☰ ⅏ ◪ ☙ ☙ ◁⊱ ⊰⇌ ☇ ☧

Villa Carlotta
*Via Michele di Lando 3, 50125
Firenze* ☎*(055) 220530* ☏*573485.*
Map **2**E2 ▥▥ *27 rms* ▭ *27* ▦
▭ ▭ ☲ ▣ ▨

*Location: Near Porta Romana and
Boboli Gardens.* On a quiet street
lined with privately-owned 19thC
villas, this *pensione* has been
modernized with a rather heavy
hand but to a high standard of
comfort. The proprietress is
German, as are many of the guests.
☱ ☰ ⅏ ▢ ◪ ☙ ☧

Villa Cora ▩
*Viale Machiavelli 18, 50125
Firenze* ☎*(055) 2298451*
☏*570604.* Map **2**E3 ▥▥▥ *56 rms*
▭ *56* ▦ ▭ ☲ ▣ ▨

Location: Near Boboli Gardens. A
sumptuous Neoclassical villa in a
large private park, retaining its extrav-
agant mid-19thC Rococo features:
elaborate fireplaces, gilded stucco,
frescoed ceilings, Venetian-glass
chandeliers. It would still suit the
Princess Eugenia, who stayed here
in 1876, but today it often
caters to expensively packaged
tourists and businessmen. A car
service ferries guests into Florence—
or stroll through the Boboli
Gardens into the Pitti in 20min. A
restaurant with piano bar, the
Taverna Machiavelli, is next door.
☱ ☰ ⅏ ▢ ◪ ☙ ◁⊱ ⊰⇌ ☧

Villa Medici ▩
Via Il Prato 42, 50123 Firenze
☎*(055) 261331* ☏*570178.* Map
6D3 ▥▥▥ *108 rms* ▭ *108* ▦ ▭
☲ ▣ ⊕ ⊙

Location: Near Le Cascine. The
frontage is that of an 18thC Corsini
villa; the rest was built in 1960 in
a style that would suit James Bond.
In the immaculate apartments, all
somber chintzes and dark wood,
international businessmen and art
dealers conclude deals in private.
Most of the rooms have balconies
and overlook the gardens.
☱ ☰ ⅏ ▢ ◪ ☙ ◁⊱ ⊰⇌ ☧

Eating in Florence

Florentines are stubbornly conservative in most matters, and not
least in the way they eat. The traditional dishes, such as *crostini*,
ribollita, *bistecca* or *castagnaccio*, have their roots in the Tuscan
countryside. They are not as ubiquitous as they were, but they
are still available in Florence in the traditional surroundings:
whitewashed walls, red-tiled floors, wooden tables. Service in

such unspoiled restaurants can be brusque if not downright rude. The Florentines are said to like it that way and have nicknamed some of their favorite eating places after the rough treatment one can expect from the proprietors.

In the last decade, however, the ever-increasing pressure of mass tourism has brought certain changes. Some of the most famous of the older restaurants have dropped their standards, raised their prices, and tried, not always successfully, to cater for more 'international' palates. Some of the best of the newer restaurants (such as **Carabaccia**, **Bronzino**, **Cibrèo** or **San Zanobi**) are now deliberately located a little way out of the touristic center because their proprietors wish to avoid the notice of the kind of foreign visitor who imagines that good Tuscan cooking means spaghetti washed down with *cappuccino*.

For those tourists who prefer fast, familiar food, there are now plenty of establishments serving pizzas, hamburgers, crêpes and so on. A list of some of the more reliable fast-food restaurants can be found on page 115. Most bars serve delicious sandwiches and snacks, which can be eaten standing up. And *tavole calde*, where you serve yourself to hot food, remain very good value.

Although the price of a fine restaurant meal is no longer necessarily much cheaper than in any other major European city, there are still some unpretentious, everyday trattorias that have managed to keep their costs down. These are often very popular with the locals, but not easy for the foreigner to spot (some are not even signposted). Some suggestions are listed on page 114.

Fish, much more generally offered in Florentine restaurants than it was, is particularly fresh and well-prepared at **Cibrèo**, **Pierot**, **Silvio** and **Vittoria**. Remember, though, that fish is usually more expensive than meat and that the price quoted on the menu sometimes means 'per 100g.' Game, still standard fare in the countryside, is disappearing from the city restaurants, one notable exception being **La Maremma da Giuliano**.

Worldly gastronomes may have mixed feelings about the influence of the *nouvelle cuisine*, by now an international cliché, on traditional Tuscan cooking methods. The **Enoteca Pinchiorri** and **Da Noi**, the two most sophisticated exponents of the not-so-new French cooking, are both outstanding restaurants that could, however, just as easily be in London or New York. Other restaurants, notably **Cibrèo** and **San Zanobi**, have grafted the *nouvelle cuisine* onto the *vecchia cucina Fiorentina* to more unexpected, if less refined, effect.

Wherever you decide to eat in Florence, do not fail to do as the Florentines do and treat yourself on a fine afternoon or evening to a meal in the surrounding countryside where the cooking, the ambience and the prices have not yet been corrupted by the late 20thC. For some suggested restaurants within a 20min drive, see *Artimino*, *Bagno a Ripoli*, *Impruneta*, *Pontassieve*, *Sesto Fiorentino*, *Settignano*, and the restaurant **Zocchi** at Pratolino, near *Fiesole* (all in the *Tuscany A–Z*). The greatest rural restaurant in Tuscany is at *Montefollonico*.

Booking for all restaurants is advisable, especially for Sun lunch and in the spring and summer months. The majority close on Sun evening and in Aug.

Restaurants classified by area
Arcetri
Omero ▮▮▯

Cascine/Teatro Comunale
Baldini ▮▮▯ to ▮▮▮▮

Carabaccia ▮▯
Pierot ▮▮▮
Vittoria ▮▯ ✿

Duomo
Al Campidoglio ▢ ▢
Mosacce ▢ ▢ ❀
Ottorino ▢ ▢
Relais le Jardin ▢ ▢
Ognissanti
Il Cestello dell'Hotel
  Excelsior ▢ ▢
13 Gobbi ▢ ▢
Harry's Bar ▢ ▢
Il Profeta ▢ ▢
Sostanza ▢ ▢
*Oltrarno (Pitti, San
Spirito, Carmine)*
Cammillo ▢ ▢ to ▢ ▢
Carmine ▢ ▢ ❀
Celestino ▢ ▢
Mamma Gina ▢ ▢
Le Quattro Staggione ▢ ▢
Porta Romano
Ruggero ▢ ▢
Santa Croce
Cibrèo ▢ ▢ or ▢ ▢ ❀
Da Noi ▢ ▢
Enoteca Pinchiorri ▢ ▢

Il Fagioli ▢ ▢
La Maremma da Giuliano ▢ ▢ to
  ▢ ▢
San Marco
Bronzino ▢ ▢ to ▢ ▢
San Zanobi ▢ ▢ to ▢ ▢
San Miniato
La Loggia ▢ ▢
*Santa Trinita/Via
Tornabuoni*
Cantinetta Antinori ▢ ▢
Coco Lezzone ▢ ▢ ❀
Doney ▢ ▢
Il Latini ▢ ▢
Silvio ▢ ▢
Signoria/Uffizi
Antico Fattore ▢ ▢
Il Cavallino ▢ ▢
Da Ganino ▢ ▢
Paoli ▢ ▢
*Station/Santa Maria
Novella*
Le Fonticine ▢ ▢
Otello ▢ ▢
Sabatini ▢ ▢

Antico Fattore
Via Lambertesca 1/3 (near Uffizi)
☎ *(055) 261215. Map* **5***D4* ▢ ▢
▢ *Closed Sun, Mon (winter), Sat
(summer), Aug.*

This was once *the* Florentine
rendezvous of Italian writers and
artists. The sustaining Tuscan
peasant dishes are better than the
pastas. Tables are communal and
service slipshod.

Baldini
*Via il Prato 96 (near Teatro
Comunale)* ☎ *(055) 287663. Map*
2*C2* ▢ ▢ *to* ▢ ▢ ▢ *Closed Sat.*

A solid, capacious, conservative
restaurant of a type that is fast
disappearing from modern
Florence. Traditionalists will
respond to the gloomy rubber
plants in the window, the attentive
service, the trolleys laden with roast
meats. The *gran' pezzo* is said to
have been invented here.

Bronzino
Via delle Ruote 27 (near S. Marco)
☎ *(055) 495220. Map* 3*B4* ▢ ▢ *to*
▢ ▢ ▢ ▢ ▢ *Closed
Sun.*

A large, welcoming restaurant
currently favored by discriminating
Florentines who know that one
proprietor comes from the good old
Mamma Gina, the other from the
Excelsior's **Il Cestello**. An
ambitious menu offers interesting
variations on traditional Tuscan
dishes. Portions are
enormous.

Cammillo
*Borgo S. Jacopo 57 (Oltrarno,
near Ponte Vecchio)*
☎ *(055) 212427. Map* 4*D3* ▢ ▢ *to*
▢ ▢ ▢ ▢ ▢ ▢ ▢ *Closed Wed,
Thurs, late Dec – early Jan, Aug.*

A pleasantly bright trattoria with a
loyal American clientele and an
over-long menu.

Al Campidoglio
*Via Campidoglio 8 (near Piazza
Repubblica)* ☎ *(055) 287770.
Map* 4*C3* ▢ ▢ ▢ ▢ ▢ ▢ ▢
▢ *Closed Thurs, 3 weeks in Aug.*

A large, immaculate, old-fashioned
restaurant with a balanced menu.

Cantinetta Antinori
*Piazza Antinori 3 (N end of Via
Tornabuoni)* ☎ *(055) 292234.
Map* 4*C3* ▢ ▢ ▢ ▢ ▢ ▢ ▢
Closed Sat, Sun, Aug.

In an elegant room off the central
courtyard of the 15thC Antinori
palace, this chic, crowded
restaurant serves products from the
Antinori estates which you can take
as a quick snack at the bar or as a
build into a full dinner. Wines, oil, bread
and cheeses are all excellent.

Carabaccia
*Via Palazzuolo 190 (near Teatro
Comunale)* ☎ *(055) 214782. Map*
2*C3* ▢ ▢ *Closed Sun, Mon
lunch.*

Simple but fashionable, charming if
slightly pretentious, this restaurant
offers a limited selection of
imaginatively prepared dishes.

Carmine ✿
Piazza del Carmine 18 (Oltrarno)
☎(055) 218601. Map **2**D3–4 ☐
☐ ■ ▲ *Closed Sun, Aug.*
A rough, reliable old favorite,
especially pleasant in summer with
tables in the piazza.

Il Cavallino
Via delle Farine 6 (Piazza Signoria)
☎(055) 215818. Map **5**D4 ☐
▲ ☰ AE CB ⓪ ⓪ VISA *Closed*
Wed, Aug 1–24.
Don't be suspicious of the star
location – it might have turned
Cavallino into a tourist trap, but
hasn't. This is the sort of restaurant
Florentines treat as a second home.
Whether you dine alone with a
book or with a party of friends the
service is quick and courteous and
the food pleasant.

Celestino
Piazza S. Felìcita (Oltrarno)
☎(055) 296574. Map **4**E3 ☐
☐ ☰ AE *Closed Sun, Aug, late*
Dec.
A small, fashionable, noisy trattoria
run with polished professionalism.

Il Cestello dell'Hotel Excelsior
Piazza Ognissanti 3 ☎(055)
264201. Map **4**C1 ☐ ☐ ■ ▲
☰ ☰ AE CB ⓪ ⓪ VISA
The panorama from the roof
terrace is spectacular. Tuscan and
'international' dishes are expertly
prepared; superb pastas.

Cibrèo ✿
Via de' Macci 118 (near S. Croce)
☎(055) 677394. Map **3**D5 ☐ or
☐ ■ ▲ AE CB ⓪ VISA *Closed*
Sun, Mon, Aug to mid-Sept,
Christmas, Easter.
One of the most original and
congenial of the new generation of
restaurants, influenced but not
overwhelmed by the *nouvelle
cuisine*. Don't pass up any of the
four courses. Everything is
delicious, and the seasonal *passati di
verdura* and *sformati* offered in lieu
of pastas are outstanding, as are the
homemade desserts. You can enjoy
the same food for half the price in
the simpler surroundings of the
'*vinaria*' on the other side of the
kitchen. And around the corner,
Cibrèo Alimentari (*Via del
Verrocchio 4* ☎(055) 677298) sells
exotic delicacies to take away.

Coco Lezzone ✿
*Via Parioncino 26 (near Via
Tornabuoni)* ☎(055) 287178.
Map **4**C3 ☐ ☐ *Closed Sun,
Tues lunch, Aug.*

A white-tiled trattoria that looks
like a public rest room and is always
crammed with chic Florentines
packed elbow-to-elbow at
communal tables. The attraction is
the high quality of the
uncompromised Tuscan food,
especially the simple meat dishes.

Da Noi
Via Fiesolana 46 (near S. Croce)
☎(055) 242917. Map **3**C5 ☐
☐ ▲ ☰ *Closed Mon, Tues
lunch, Aug.*
The owners of this tiny and very
successful restaurant worked
previously at the **Enoteca
Pinchiorri**; their culinary style is a
similar blend of Italian and new
French. Book some days in advance.

Doney
Piazza Strozzi 16–19
☎(055) 212574. Map **4**C3.
For over a century Doney in the Via
Tornabuoni was the right and
proper meeting place for Anglo-
Saxon residents and Florentine
aristocrats. Its move in 1986 to
smaller premises shocked the old
guard, whose members can at least
be reassured that everything else
will remain: the grand-ducal place
settings, the grand 'continental'
food, the famous chocolates, and, of
course, afternoon tea.

Enoteca Pinchiorri
Via Ghibellina 87 (near S. Croce)
☎(055) 242757/77. Map **5**C5
☐ ☐ ■ ▲ ☰ AE *Closed
Sun, Mon lunch, Aug, Christmas.*
This restaurant, on the ground
floor of the 15thC Ciofi-Iacometti
Palace, is one of the very few
anywhere in Italy that demand to
be judged by the highest European
standards. The proprietor, Giorgio
Pinchiorri, has built up an
outstanding cellar of the finest
Italian and French wines. His
French wife is responsible for the
Franco-Italian cuisine, which is
elegant and subtle if not quite as
original as it seemed a decade ago.
There is a *menu de degustazione* of
seven courses, and if you allow the
waiter to fill your glass with the
appropriate wine for each course,
you will be able to sample the
glories of the cellar without
committing yourself to full bottles.
A restaurant for the super-rich or
expense-account business people.

Il Fagioli
Corso Tintori 47 (near S. Croce)
☎(055) 244285. Map **5**E5 ☐
☐ *Closed Sat, Sun, Aug.*

This straightforward Tuscan trattoria is a less distinguished, but more comfortable, spin-off from **Coco Lezzone**.

Le Fonticine
Via Nazionale 79 (near the station) ☎ *(055) 282106. Map 4A3* 🔟 💷 ▦ AE VISA *Closed Sat, Aug.*

The excellence of the cuisine, and especially the pasta, must be partly explained by the Emilian origins of the proprietress. Popular with visiting business executives.

Da Ganino
Piazza dei Cimatori 4 (near Piazza Signoria) ☎ *(055) 214125. Map 5C4* 🔟 💷 🚒 *Closed Sun, mid-Aug, late Dec.*

A tiny, appetizing trattoria tucked away in a miniature piazza. Serves first-class food, especially the home-made pastas and *torta di formaggio*.

13 Gobbi
Via del Porcellana 9 (off Borgognissanti) ☎ *(055) 298769. Map 4B2* 🔟 💷 AE ⊕ *Closed Sun, Mon, three weeks in Aug.*

Hungarian or Tuscan specialties accompanied by good draft beer or Chianti and gently eccentric piano music.

Harry's Bar
Lungarno Vespucci 22 (near Ognissanti) ☎ *(055) 296700. Map 4C1* ▥ 💷 ▦ AE *Closed Sun, mid Dec to mid Jan.*

Modeled on the original Harry's Bar in Venice, but with no business connection, this is a haven for English-speaking visitors. Attentive bilingual service, a good selection of American cocktails, an adequate, short menu which hardly ever changes, and the best hamburgers in town.

Il Latini
Via Palchetti 6 (behind Palazzo Rucellai) ☎ *(055) 210916. Map 4C2* 🔟 💷 *Closed Mon, Tues lunch, late July, Dec 22–Jan 6.*

Love it or hate it – and you do have to be in the mood and very hungry – this noisy, crowded restaurant with its open kitchen, communal tables and hanging hams is one of the best places to enjoy robust Tuscan country cooking.

La Loggia
Piazzale Michelangelo 1 ☎ *(055) 287032. Map 3E5* ▥ 💷 🚒 AE ⊕ VISA *Closed Wed,*

two weeks in Aug.

The spectacular views over the city from the spacious 19thC *palazzina del caffè* make this an ideal venue for a first or last meal in Florence. Also a café.

Mamma Gina
Borgo S. Jacopo 37 (Oltrarno, near Ponte Vecchio) ☎ *(055) 296009. Map 4D3* 🔟 💷 ▦ AE ⊕ VISA *Closed Sun, Aug.*

This once-famous, much-loved trattoria is nowadays better known for commercial ambition, rude service and dull food.

La Maremma da Giuliano
Via Verdi 16 (near S. Croce) ☎ *(055) 244615. Map 5D5* 🔟 to ▥ 💷 VISA *Closed Wed, Thurs, Aug.*

A justly popular, family-run trattoria offering game in season as well as other delicious specialties. Don't miss the *prosciutto di cinghiale*, hard to find elsewhere.

Mossacce ♣
Via del Proconsolo 55 (between Duomo and Bargello) ☎ *(055) 294361. Map 5C5* 💷 ▤ ▦ *Closed Sat, Sun, Aug.*

Although *mossacce* means 'discourteous,' Mossacce is always full because the meat is so excellent and such good value.

Omero
Via Pian dei Giullari 11 (Arcetri) ☎ *(055) 220053. Map 7E4* 🔟 💷 🚒 *Closed Tues, Aug.*

Such a sympathetic rustic environment in such a splendid location above the city cannot be entirely spoiled by routine, lack-luster food and service, which one encounters too often here.

Otello
Via degli Orti Oricellari 36 (near the station) ☎ *(055) 215819. Map 2C3* ▥ 💷 ▦ AE ⊕ ⊙ VISA *Closed Tues.*

A large, comfortable, dignified restaurant more appreciated by foreigners than by Florentines, who say rightly that it's not quite what it was.

Ottorino
Via delle Oche 12–16 (near Duomo) ☎ *(055) 218747. Map 5C4* 🔟 💷 ▦ AE ⊕ *Closed Sun, Aug.*

One of the city's oldest restaurants, lately moved into spacious new premises where the tastefully modernized Tuscan style of the decor is restful on a hot day and the long menu as well balanced as ever.

113

Paoli

*Via Tavolini 12 (near
Orsanmichele)* ☎ *(055) 216215.
Map* **5***C4* ■■ ▢ ■■ [AE] [◑] [◐]
[VISA] *Closed Tues.*

Inoffensive food in a spectacular
environment: imitation-Gothic
frescoes, polished mahogany
benches, wrought-iron
lampbrackets – all (apart from the
Annigoni canvas and a bust of
President Wilson) redolent of the
early 19thC when Paoli was
established in the beautiful
storerooms of a 15thC palace.

Pierot

*Piazza Taddeo Gaddi 25 (across
the Arno from the Cascine)*
☎ *(055) 702100. Map* **2***C1* ■■
▢ [AE] [◑] [◐] [VISA] *Closed Sun,
July 10–31.*

Homey, honest and very popular
fish restaurant which now also
serves classic Tuscan meat dishes.

Il Profeta

Borgognissanti 93 (Ognissanti)
☎ *(055) 212265. Map* **4***C1* ■■ ▢
■■ [AE] [VISA] *Closed Sat eve, Sun.*

A soothingly understated one-room
restaurant where the quality of the
food never seems to fall short of
excellence.

Le Quattro Stagioni

Via Maggio 61 (near the Pitti)
☎ *(055) 218906. Map* **2***D3* ■■
▢ [AE] [◑] [VISA] *Closed Sat, Sun
(summer), Sun (winter), late Aug.*

Two small rooms, usually crowded
with antique dealers and fashion
people from the Pitti Moda. The
generalized Italian food lacks real
character, but the multilingual
service is graceful.

Relais le Jardin

Piazza Massimo d'Azeglio 3
☎ *(055) 245247. Map* **3***C5* ■■
▢ ➡ ▤ ▬ [AE] [◑] [◐] [VISA]
Closed Sun.

The elegant dining room of the
Regency Hotel is a restaurant in the
grand classical style.

Ruggero

*Via Senese 89 (near Porta
Romana)* ☎ *(055) 220542.
Map* **2***E2* ■■ ▢ *Closed Tues,
Wed, July 7–Aug 7.*

This no-nonsense everyday
trattoria opposite the old horse-
watering stop on the road to Rome
is owned by a former cook at **Coco
Lezzone**. The hearty country food
makes an ideal Sunday lunch after a
walk along the city walls between
Piazzale Michelangelo and Porta
Romana. They do a good fish soup
on Fridays.

Sabatini

Via Panzani 9a (near the station)
☎ *(055) 282802. Map* **4***B3* ■■
▢ ▤ [◑] [◐] *Closed Mon,
two weeks in July.*

Sabatini is no longer the most
famous and fashionable restaurant
in Florence. But it has a pleasant
environment and often one eats
better here than some critics
suggest.

San Zanobi

Via S. Zanobi 33a (near S. Marco)
☎ *(055) 475286. Map* **3***B4* ■■ *to
■■* ▢ ▤ [AE] *Closed Sun, Aug.*

A calm, refined restaurant run by
two women who cater primarily for
the Florentine professional classes.
Inventive food, lovingly prepared.

Silvio

*Via del Parione 74 (near Via
Tornabuoni)* ☎ *(055) 214005.
Map* **4***C2* ■■ ▢ *Closed
Sun, Mon, July 20–Aug 20.*

Cozily cluttered restaurant serving
fresh fish daily, as well as the
Tuscan classics.

Sostanza

*Via del Porcellana 25 (near
Ognissanti)* ☎ *(055) 212691.
Map* **4***C2* ■■ ▢ *Closed Sat eve,
Sun, Aug.*

Known as 'il Troia,' which is
Tuscan slang for 'pigsty,' this is one
of the oldest working men's
trattorie in Florence. The prices
have gone up, but the *bistecca* is
still very good and the service still
very rude.

Vittoria ✿

*Via della Fonderia 52 (w of
S. Frediano)* ☎ *(055) 225657.
Map* **2***C2* ■■ *to* ■■ [AE] [CB] [◑]
[◐] [VISA] *Closed Wed, Aug.*

Many Florentines agree that this
very ordinary-looking trattoria is
still the best – and certainly the
cheapest – place in town to eat
fresh, simply prepared fish.
No meat.

◣Some inexpensive, traditional *trattorie*: **Angiolino** (*36 Via S. Spirito,
Oltrarno* ☎ *(055) 298976, closed Sun, Mon*); **Anita** (*Via del Parlascio 2,
S. Croce* ☎ *(055) 218698, closed Wed eve, Sun*); **Belle Donne** (*Via delle
Belle Donne 16, by the station* ☎ *(055) 262609, closed Sat evening, Sun*);

Benvenuto (*Via de' Neri 16, S. Croce* ☎ *(055) 214833, closed Wed,
Sun*); **Frizzi** (*Borgo degli Albizzi 76, Duomo-Signoria*); **La Macelleria**
(*Via S. Zanobi 97, S. Marco*); **La Maremmana** (*Via de' Macci 77,
S. Croce* ☎ *(055) 241226, closed Sun*); **L'Orologio** (*Piazza Ferruci 5,
below Piazzale Michelangelo* ☎ *(055) 6811729, closed Sun*); **Le Sorelle**
(*Via S. Niccolò 30, Oltrarno* ☎ *(055) 284422, closed Tues*).

For fast food: **La Bussola** (*Via Porta Rossa 58, off Tornabuoni*
☎ *(055) 293376*), pizzeria open all night; **La Campana** (*Borgo
S. Lorenzo 24*), pizzeria open until 2am; **Nuti** (*Borgo S. Lorenzo 38*),
huge, convenient pizzeria; **Old Bridge** (*Via de' Bardi 64, Oltrarno*
☎ *(055) 212915, closed Mon*), self-service restaurant with a terrace, on
the Arno; **Queen Victoria** (*Por S. Maria, Ponte Vecchio*), large *tavola
calda*, with garden.

Bars, cafés and ice cream shops

The bar is the nerve center of Italian daily life. If you need a
telephone, a bus ticket, a rest room or simply want to ask
directions, look for the nearest bar, which will never be far
away. In an Italian bar anyone can drink anything at any time of
day. Ordinary coffee (*caffè normale*) is a short, potent espresso;
if you like it weaker, ask for *caffè lungo*. *Macchiato* is with a dash
of milk; *correto* is laced with brandy. The coffee is almost
unfailingly excellent and a *cappuccino* with a sweet roll makes a
better and cheaper breakfast than you will find in any hotel.
Many larger bars also sell pastries, sandwiches, ice cream,
groceries, even light meals. If you sit down the price doubles.

Although open-air cafés are not characteristic of Florence,
there are four – **Paszkowski**, **Gilli**, **Donnini** and **Giubbe
Rosse** – in the unlovely but central Piazza della Repubblica.

Ice cream, as always in Italy, is light and wholesome, made
with milk and eggs in an endless variety of flavors.

Doney
Piazza Strozzi 16–19
☎ *(055) 212574. Map* **4***C3.*
In the 19th and early 20thC,
Doney in Via Tornabuoni was the
fashionable rendezvous of literary
foreigners. The young moved to
Giacosa, and Doney in 1986
moved around the corner to these
still-elegant premises.

Donnini
Piazza della Repubblica 15
☎ *(055) 211862. Map* **4***C3.
Closed Mon.*
The smallest bar in the piazza
serves the most unusual hot
sandwiches.

Giacosa
Via Tornabuoni 83
☎ *(055) 296226. Map* **4***C3.
Closed Mon.*
This is where the young elite meet
for coffee and buy their pastries,
marrons glacés and hand-made
chocolates. The *cappuccino* is the
best in town, and there are also
sandwiches and hot snacks. The
Negroni was invented here in the
1920s by Count Camillo Negroni.

Gilli
Piazza della Repubblica ☎ *(055)
296310. Map* **4***C3. Closed Tues.*
This *belle-époque* café, where an
orchestra plays old favorites in
summer, is the most attractive and
comfortable (with good rest
rooms) in Piazza della Repubblica.

La Loggia
Piazzale Michelangelo 1 ☎ *(055)
287032. Map* **3***E5. Closed Wed.*
From the 19thC *palazzina del caffè*
you can look past the 'Not-the-
Real-David' over the most famous
introductory view of the city.

Perchè Non
Via Tavolini 19 ☎ *(055) 298969.
Map* **5***C4.*
Outstanding ice creams, sorbets
and *semi-freddi* made exclusively
for Perchè Non; in summer there
are at least 30 varieties.

Procacci
Via Tornabuoni 64 ☎ *(055)
211656. Map* **4***C3. Closed Mon.*
As a treat, pamper your taste buds
with a plate of Procacci's exquisite
truffle rolls. Cold drinks only.

Rivoire
Piazza Signoria 5
☎ *(055) 214412. Map **5**D4.*
Closed Mon.
Not the exclusive tearoom it once
was, but the hot chocolate is
superb, and the view of the Palazzo
Vecchio justifies the high prices.

Robiglio
Via dei Servi 112
☎ *(055) 212784. Map **5**B5. And*
Via dei Tosinghi 11
☎ *(055) 215013. Map **5**C4. Open*
8am – midnight. Closed Mon.
A large and luscious selection of

pastries. Specialties include *Saint-
Honorés, millefeuilles,* meringues
and *torta rustica.*

Vivoli
Via Isola delle Stinche 7
☎ *(055) 292334. Map **5**D5.*
Closed Sun pm, Mon.
Don't be deceived by the humble
premises – Vivoli is one of the great
Italian ice cream makers. Some two
dozen flavors as well as open
sandwiches, pastries and coffee.
The only *gelateria* to be found in
Florence which will satisfy the true
connoisseur of ice cream.

Nightlife

Florence enjoys a livelier nightlife than many small Italian
cities, thanks partly to its large student population.

Discos and piano bars
The largest and most popular discos are **Space Electronic** (*Via
Palazzuolo* ☎ *(055) 293082*) and **Yab Yum** (*Via Sassetti 5*
☎ *(055) 282018*). Smaller discos and piano bars include: **Full
Up** (*Via della Vigna Vecchia 21* ☎ *(055) 293006*); **Jackie O'**
(*Via Erta Canina 24* ☎ *(055) 216146*); and **Oberon** (*Via Erta
Canina 12* ☎ *(055) 216516*).
    You can hear good jazz at **Bebop** (*Via dei Servi*
☎ *(055) 263004*); **La Rosa** (*Via S. Zanobi 88* ☎ *(055) 433445*);
and **Salt Peanuts** (*Piazza S. Maria Novella* ☎ *(055) 293376*).

Late-night restaurants
The best ones are **La Bussola** and **La Campana** (see
Florence/Restaurants, p115) and **Giubbe Rosse** (see
Florence/Bars, cafés and ice cream shops, p115).

Movie theaters
The **Cinema Astro** (*Piazza San Simone* ☎ *(055) 222388*) shows
English language films every evening except Mon.

Music and theater
The *Maggio Musicale*, a festival of concerts, recitals, opera and
ballet, is held in various venues throughout the city during
May – July. Information and tickets from **Teatro Comunale**.

Teatro Comunale
Corso Italia 16 ☎ *(055) 216253. Map **6**D3. Box office open Mon – Sat
9am – noon, 3 – 6pm, Sun 9am – noon.*
The main concert season is Oct – Nov, and the opera season normally
lasts from mid-Dec to mid-Jan. If you want to take a score with you to the
opera, it can be bought at **R. Mauri** (*Via del Corso* ☎ *(055) 283052*).

Teatro della Pergola
Via della Pergola 32 ☎ *(055) 262690. Map **5**B6.*
The principal legitimate theater. Plays are in performance all year round
except during the *Maggio Musicale*, when the theater is given over to
music.

Shopping

When shopping in Florence bear in mind the Florentine character, which is unique in Italy and is as remarkable a legacy of the Renaissance as any church or monument. At all social and economic levels Florentines share a profound respect for two skills: craftsmanship and business, the activities which made Florence the richest city in 15thC Europe. They are a reasoning but also reasonable people with clever hands, quick wits, laconic manners and a disdain for the cheap and showy. It is a compact, sophisticated city where good craftsmen still abound.

Shopping hours

Normally 9am – 1pm, 3:30pm – 7pm, with slight variations. Most shops close on Mon mornings, but open all day Sat, except for food stores which close on Wed. In summer some of the bigger shops close all day Sat but open Mon.

Most large shops will send your purchases abroad if you wish. Otherwise, there is a useful parcel-wrapping service near the post office in Vicolo dei Cavallari.

Where to shop

The Via Tornabuoni is the Fifth Avenue of Florence. Most of the grandest shops are in this area, near the Duomo, Piazza della Repubblica, Ognissanti, along the Lungarno, and across the Arno around Borgo San Jacopo.

How to shop

The business-like Florentines understand comparative shopping and bargaining. An aggressive manner will get you nowhere, but even in big, established shops you can try asking for a discount (*sconto* or *gentilezza*) if you buy more than one item. (See clothing sizes table on p212.)

What to buy

The best buys are anything made locally of leather, silk and straw (bags, hats and novelties). You can still buy the service of craftsmen in Florence, which is one of the few cities left in Western Europe where making and repairing of anything is done quickly and skillfully. Bookbinding, picture framing and reproduction antiques are Florentine specialties.

Antiques, auctions and reproductions

Many of the established antique shops are in Borgognissanti, Via dei Fossi and Via Maggio. Auctions are held in autumn and spring, the two leading houses being **Sotheby Parke Bernet** (*Via Gino Capponi 26* ☎ *(055) 571410*) and **Casa d'Aste Pitti** (*Via Maggio 15* ☎ *(055) 296382*). An important antiques fair is held every 2yr in the Strozzi palace.

Fallani Best
Borgognissanti 15 ☎ *(055) 214986. Map 4C1.*
The top Italian dealer in Art Nouveau and Art Deco.

Ugo Camiciotti
Via S. Spirito 9 ☎ *(055) 212137. Map 4D2.*
French Second Empire clocks and mirrors, signed and dated.

Giovanni Pratesi
Via Maggio 13 ☎ *(055) 296568. Map 4E2* `AE` `◆` `CB` `VISA`
A new and respected young dealer with a more eclectic stock of paintings, sculpture and furniture.

Florentine craftsmen are highly skilled in every branch of restoration, and many a Florentine-made reproduction has been innocently passed by experts and honest dealers.

Manetti e Masini
Via Bronzino 125
☎ (055) 700445. Map **6**D3.
Began as restorers of antique majolica, and soon found they could produce exact copies. They sell charming fabrications of 18thC plates, tureens, vases and ceramic stoves, and repair china.

Raffaello Romanelli
Lungarno Acciaioli 72–78
☎ (055) 296047 [AE] [⊙] [⊙] [VISA]
The firm has been making life-size copies of the most famous

sculptures since 1860; it will also make period fireplaces, tabletops and chess sets.

Zecchi
Via dello Studio 19
☎ (055) 211470. Map **5**C4 [AE]
[CB] [VISA]
Zecchi stocks a full range of restorers' and artists' materials, many not available elsewhere in Europe. You can buy *lapis lazuli* from Afghanistan, pure gold leaf, powdered pigments for frescoes, natural gums and resins.

Beauty
The apparently casual chic for which Florentine women are noted is not quite as natural as it looks. They pay scrupulous attention to their hair and skin.

Antica Farmacia di San Marco
Via Cavour 146
☎ (055) 210604. Map **5**B4.
This beautiful pharmacy, with its vaulted frescoed ceilings and rows of majolica jars, was founded in the 15thC by the Dominican monks of San Marco. Their specifics include an anti-hysteric, which might come in handy if you are visiting Florence in Aug. Excellent rose water and eaux de cologne.

Mario di Via Della Vigna
Via della Vigna Nuova 22
☎ (055) 294813. Map **4**C2.
Hairdressers to glamorous and busy women, including the Pitti fashion show models. The salon offers a range of beauty treatments, plus a well-stocked perfumery.

Officina Profumo-Farmaceutica di Santa Maria Novella
Via della Scala 16
☎ (055) 216276. Map **4**B2.
A perfectly preserved grand-ducal pharmacy which sells superb hand-made soaps, creams, lotions for

every skin type and a delectable *pot pourri*. Everything is made to original 17thC formulae. Service is notoriously grudging.

Profumeria Aline
Via Calzaiuoli 53
☎ (055) 215269. Map **4**C4.
The largest selection of cosmetics and perfumes in town, carrying the concessions for ranges such as Clinique and Lauder.

Profumeria Inghlese
Via Tornabuoni 97
☎ (055) 263748. Map **4**C3.
Founded by an Englishman in 1843. The mahogany shelves are well-stocked with cosmetics, soaps and perfumes, but the medicines have been moved down the Via to the Farmacia Inghlese.

Valentino
Via Tornabuoni 105
☎ (055) 212313. Map **4**C3 [AE]
[CB] [⊙] [VISA]
Long established as a favorite hairdresser of English and American visitors.

Books and prints
Florence has been catering to the needs of bookish foreigners for centuries, and foreign-language books are generally available. There are also a number of internationally renowned specialist bookstores.

Alinari
Via della Vigna Nuova 46
☎ (055) 218975. Map **4**C2. [AE]

The famous sepia photos of 19thC Florence; and one of the most complete archives of black-and-white photos of Italian art. The archive, newly installed in Palazzo Rucellai, is open Mon–Fri 11am–1pm.

BM
Borgognissanti 4
☎ *(055) 294575. Map 4C1.*
A useful shop selling books in English and Italian on Florentine culture and history, as well as maps, guidebooks, fiction and children's books.

Centro Di
Piazza dei Mozzi 1
☎ *(055) 213212. Map 5E5* ⬤
One of the most important serious art bookshops and publishers in Italy, hidden away in a basement. The fine catalogues the firm produces for major European exhibitions are on sale.

Paperback Exchange
Via Fiesolana 31
☎ *(055) 213054. Map 3C5.*
Over 10,000 English language titles in stock, mostly popular

fiction. A recycling system gives you 25–40% of the original price of your old paperbacks toward any you buy at 75% of the cover price.

Porcellino
Piazza del Mercato Nuovo 6–8
☎ *(055) 212535. Map 5D4* [AE]
⬤ [VISA]
The first self-service bookshop in Florence and the place to look for the catalogues and guides which are maddeningly not sold in museums and galleries.

Salimbeni
Via M. Palmieri 14–16
☎ *(055) 292084/298905. Map 5C5.*
One of the most reputable specialist art and antiquarian bookshops in Europe

Seeber
Via Tornabuoni 68
☎ *(055) 215697. Map 4C3* [AE]
[CB] ⬤ ⬤ [VISA]
Founded in 1865 to serve the foreign community and now one of the largest and best-known general bookshops.

Book endpapers and binding
Italy was the home of printing and all the crafts of book production. Book-binders selling hand-printed or marbled endpapers – by the sheet or applied to anything from jewel cases to desk sets – have proliferated in the last 10yr; but the prices may put their ends beyond your means.

Bottega Artigiana del Libro
Lungarno Corsini 38–40
☎ *(055) 263488. Map 4D2.* [AE]
[CB] ⬤ ⬤ [VISA]
The newest but no longer the cheapest source of endpapers.

Gianni e Figlio
Piazza Pitti 37 ☎ *(055) 212621.*
Map 4E2.

This delectable little shop opposite the Pitti, founded in 1856, is the grandfather of all the paper shops.

Il Papiro
Via Cavour 55 ☎ *(055) 215262.*
Map 5B4 [AE] [CB] ⬤ ⬤ [VISA]
Specializes in marbled papers made here. (*Branches at Piazza Duomo 24 and Via degli Alfani 12.*)

Clothes
Despite the commercial importance of the Pitti Moda shows, the creative center of Italian high fashion is still Milan. But Florentine women continue to dress, as they always have, with an impeccable chic that is never flamboyant but often striking. It is a look that depends on quality: the finest printed cotton jersey or silks, smooth gaberdines and, of course, beautiful Florentine leather accessories – these are the kind of clothes you will see in abundant, if not inexpensive, supply.

Some of the best known non-Florentine designers have outlets in and off the Via Tornabuoni, which is where you will find **Giorgio Armani**, **Yves St-Laurent**, **Roberta di Camerino**, and **Valentino**. Other fashion streets are Via de' Calzaiuoli, Via de' Cerretani, Via Roma and Via Calimala; and, across the Arno, Via Guicciardini and Borgo San Jacopo. See also *Leather* p121.

Max Mara
Via Brunelleschi 28
☎ (055) 287761. Map *4C3* AE
CB ⊕ ⊙ VISA

Some of the most efficiently stylish and wearable medium-priced day clothes and accessories in town.

Neuber
Via Strozzi 32 ☎ (055) 215763.
Map *4C3* AE
Clothing for men, women and children, all of very good quality and mostly bearing the labels of foreign houses, including Hermès, for which Neuber is the exclusive outlet. There are lots of English tweeds and cashmeres and a good selection of ties, shirts and scarves.

Principe
Via Strozzi 21/29
☎ (055) 216821. Map *4C3* AE

CB ⊕ ⊙ VISA

One of a high-class Tuscan chain selling conservative men's, women's, children's and babies' clothes at all prices.

Pucci
Via dei Pucci 6 ☎ (055) 283061.
Map *5B4* AE
The Marquese Emilio Pucci's famous designs can be bought from the atelier on the first floor of his ancestral palace. A boutique at Via Ricasoli 59.

Valditevere
Lungarno Soderini 1
☎ (055) 282707. Map *2C2* AE
⊕ ⊙ VISA
An exclusive boutique which sells reticently classical clothes that are made from its own beautiful materials.

Jewelry
Brunelleschi, Verrocchio, the Pollaiuolo brothers, Cellini, Ghiberti – some of the greatest Florentine artists trained as goldsmiths. The shops on the Ponte Vecchio have been occupied by jewelers and goldsmiths since 1593.

Gherardi
Ponte Vecchio 8
☎ (055) 287211. Map *4D3* AE
CB ⊕ ⊙ VISA
Known in Florence as the 'official coral keeper,' Gherardi's prices are about twice what you would pay in Naples, the source of most Italian coral, but the quality and design are superb. He also specializes in cultured pearls, jade, turquoise, tortoise-shell and cameos.

Manelli
Ponte Vecchio 14
☎ (055) 213759. Map *4D3* AE
CB ⊕ ⊙ VISA
The Manelli family have been dealing in semiprecious and hard stones for four generations. They can be bought loose or they will string them into a necklace in half an hour or make earrings in a week.

Melli
Ponte Vecchio 44–46
☎ (055) 211413. Map *4D3* AE
⊕ VISA
A rarified collection of antique jewelry, antique porcelains, silver and small objects d'art.

Piccini
Ponte Vecchio 23
☎ (055) 294768. Map *4D3* AE
CB ⊕ ⊙ VISA

Jewelers to the jet set, although the Concorde set may find the designs slightly dated and the prices too high-flown. They also sell antique jewelry and silver, and will re-set your heirlooms. A family firm since 1895.

Rajola
Ponte Vecchio 24
☎ (055) 215335. Map *4D3* AE
CB ⊕ ⊙ VISA
Very chic enamel work and pieces set with colored stones.

Settepassi
Ponte Vecchio 28
☎ (055) 215506. Map *4D3* AE
⊕ VISA
The oldest and one of the grandest Italian jewelers specializing in precious stones and oriental pearls set to match the incomes and tastes of the wealthiest Italian families, and to adorn crowned heads of Europe. They also sell antique and modern silver.

Tozzi
Ponte Vecchio 19
☎ (055) 283507. Map *4D3* AE
CB ⊕ ⊙ VISA
A beguiling stock of delicate objects – coral charms, gold-mesh purses, Baroque pearls – some old, some modern, some real bargains if you know your own taste.

Leather

Leather is to Florence what glass is to Venice; that is to say there is altogether too much of it, and very little of what is most prominently on display bears the slightest relation to the unrivalled workmanship of the great artisans who are still active, and whose creations are found in the shops below.

Locally produced leather goods can be up to 40 percent cheaper than abroad. If you want to see how it's done, visit the **Peruzzi** leather factory and shop (*Borgo dei Greci 8* ☎ *(055) 263039*), which is open all day.

Alessandrini
Via Vacchereccia 17
☎ *(055) 216088. Map 4C3* AE
① ⓪
The Florence outlet for the soft leather handbags manufactured by the Tuscan firm Enny.

Beltrami
Via Calzaiuoli 31
☎ *(055) 214030. Map 5C4*
AE CB ① ⓪ VISA
Successful Florentine chain selling top quality men's and women's shoes, accessories and clothes.

Bisonte
Via del Parione 11
☎ *(055) 211976. Map 4C2*
CB ① ⓪ VISA
Fashionably sporty and youthful canvas and leather bags made on the premises in good colors.

Cellerini
Via del Sole 9 ☎ *(055) 282533. Map 4C2* AE ⓪ VISA
Silvano Cellerini is the most skilled and stylish independent artisan in making leather, lizard and crocodile handbags in the city.

Ferragamo
Via Tornabuoni 16
☎ *(055) 292123. Map 4C3* AE
CB ① ⓪ VISA
Salvatore Ferragamo was the first of the internationally renowned Italian shoemakers. He started in Hollywood in 1914, and bought

this palace in the Tornabuoni in 1936. The business now has branches all over the world and makes clothes, ties and scarves as well as handbags – all in the master's stylish mold.

Gucci
Via Tornabuoni 57–59 and 73
☎ *(055) 287251. Map 4C3* AE
① ⓪ VISA
Home base for the durable and expensive leather status symbols.

Papini
Lungarno Archibusieri 10–14
☎ *(055) 213077. Map 5C4* AE
CB ① ⓪ VISA
The Papini family have been making well-crafted bags, briefcases, suitcases and solid leather boxes for 100yr. Also agents for Borbonese, Redwall, Basile.

Raspini
Via Roma 25–29
☎ *(055) 213077. Map 5C4* AE
CB ① ⓪ VISA
Raspini is one of the glamorous names in Florentine leatherware, but unlike **Ferragamo** and **Gucci** it has no outlets abroad – only licensed imitators. The shoes, bags and leather coats – all for men *and* women – are stunning. So are the clothes by top Italian designers. So are the prices, and if you are in a mousey mood you may get catty service. (*Branches at Via Martelli 5–7 and Via Por S. Maria 72.*)

Linens and lingerie

Loretta Caponi
Borgognissanti 12
☎ *(055) 213668. Map 4C1* AE
① ⓪
The dreamily girlish nightdresses hand-embroidered exclusively for Loretta Caponi are among the prettiest – and the most expensive – things you will see in Florence.

Industrie Feminile Italiane
Lungarno Corsini 34
☎ *(055) 284761. Map 4D2* AE
CB ① ⓪ VISA

Founded as a cooperative in 1901, this shop sells a vast selection of hand-embroidered table linen, sheets, towels, handkerchiefs and baby clothes. The ladies will also embroider trousseaux.

Tosco Tessile
Via del Corso ☎ *(055) 213780. Map 5C4* AE ⓪ VISA
Every kind of household linen from inexpensive towels and pillowcases in cheerful colors to exquisite sheets and table cloths.

Street markets

Mercato delle Cascine
Map 6D3. Open Tues 7am – 1pm
This weekly market in the Cascine
park is like a huge department
store laid out under the poplars
along the Arno.

Mercato Centrale
*Maps 4&5A3 – 4. Open Mon – Sat
7am – 1pm, 4 – 7:30pm.*
Immediately N of Piazza S.
Lorenzo, this impressive 19thC
cast-iron food market is the central
outlet, wholesale and retail, for
fresh meat, fish and vegetables,
and cheeses, oils and countless
other foods.

Mercato Nuovo
*Map 4D3. Open daily
9am – 5pm.*
The famous straw market, also
known as the Porcellino. As well as
straw there are leather goods,
ceramics, linens and other hand-
made goods, and – a tripe seller!

Mercato delle Piante
*Piazza della Repubblica.. Map
4C3. Open Thurs 7am – 1pm.*
A weekly flower market held under
the loggia of the central post office.

Mercato delle Pulci
*Piazza dei Ciompi. Map 3C5.
Open Tues – Sat 8am – 1pm,
3:30 – 7pm.*
The flea market of Florence sells
picturesque junk at irritatingly
jacked-up prices, but is good for
ex-votos and old postcards.

Mercato di San Lorenzo
*Maps 4&5B3 – 4. Open daily
8am – 8pm.*
The biggest and most popular of
the street markets sprawls all
around the church of S. Lorenzo
and into the adjacent streets. Best
shoe bargains in town are to be
found on the Borgo S. Lorenzo
side, where sandals and espadrilles
are half the shop price.

Textiles and trim

Florence still manufactures some of the most gorgeous
furnishing fabrics in the world. It is an industry which dates
back to the Middle Ages.

Antico Setificio Fiorentino
Via della Vigna Nuova 97
☎ *(055) 282700. Map 4C2.*
Silk furnishing fabrics – taffetas,
damasks, brocades, velvets, satins,
borders, fringes and *passementerie*
– will be made to order (minimum
30m/yds) in any color or style.
The factory across the Arno (*Via
Bartolini 4* ☎ *(055) 282700*) may
be visited by appointment –
telephone in advance.

Lisio Tessuti d'Arte
Via dei Fossi 45
☎ *(055) 212430. Map 4C2.*
This astonishing firm was founded
in 1906 by a master weaver who
was inspired to reproduce the
finest antique woven silk fabrics.
Of the many designs taken from
Old Master paintings, the
Primavera brocade is the most

popular. Lisio has made hangings
for the Sistine Chapel, costumes
for the Palio and for historic films,
and his creations are exhibited in
textile museums throughout the
world. The most elaborate designs
are produced at the rate of only a
few inches a day and prices, not
surprisingly, are high, but you
could follow the example of
Florentine women who buy just
enough for an evening skirt or
dress.

Silvi
Via dei Tavolini 5
☎ *(055) 213104. Map 5C4.*
One of the most chic of the many
Florentine trim shops, selling a
dazzling choice of braid, bindings,
passementerie, curtain ties and
fringing. Everything is made by
hand and of natural fabrics.

Toys

Bianca Benedetti
Via della Riva 20
☎ *(055) 666589. Map 5C5.*
A doll's hospital where dolls are
lovingly made whole again by
craftsmen who have cared for them
as they passed from one careless
generation to another.

Dreoni Giocattoli
Via Cavour 31 – 33
☎ *(055) 216611. Map 5A5* AE
CB ◑ ◑ VISA
Florence's largest toy shop. A
wide-ranging stock and an
especially good selection of model-
making kits.

Tuscany A – Z

The joy of Tuscany is that almost any corner of its beautiful and varied landscape is likely to harbor some natural or man-made treasure. Within this A – Z section, text and symbols describe highlight attractions. More cursory listings note additional sights and reliable but unremarkable hotels and restaurants.

Abbadia San Salvatore

*Map 9I7. 143km (89 miles) s of Florence, 75km (47 miles) s of Siena. 53021. Siena. Population: 8,232 **i** Via Mentana 97*
☎ *(0577) 778608.*
This dour little industrial town near the summit of *Monte Amiata* has grown up around the medieval abbey of San Salvatore. Skiing and climbing nearby. The medieval center is near Piazza XX Settembre.

Sights and places of interest
Abbazia di San Salvatore †
The abbey, founded in 743, became the richest and most powerful center of Benedictine feudalism in Central Italy. All that remains is the 11thC church, adapted in the late 16thC and, below, the 8thC crypt supported by 36 columns with wonderful capitals.
Borgo Medioevale (*Old Town*)
A rare and fascinating example of a Gothic-Renaissance mountain village which is almost completely intact.

≡ Near the summit of *Monte Amiata*, 14km (9 miles) w, **La Capannina** (☎ *(0577) 789713* ▢ *open July–Sept, Dec–Apr*) is a quiet skiers' hotel.

Abetone
*Map 15C4. 90km (56 miles) NW of Florence. 51021. Pistoia. Population: 859 **i** Piazza delle Piramidi Abetone*
☎ *(0573) 60001.*
In the mountains above *Pistoia* near the Tuscan-Emilian border, Abetone is one of the oldest established ski resorts in the Apennines, with the most difficult and best-equipped runs in Tuscany. There is also a short summer season for walkers and climbers. Fir trees grow in the protected **forest of Abetone**. Nearby resorts include Cutigliano and San Marcello.

≈ There are some 35 hotels which maintain an adequate but not luxurious standard. Two of the most comfortable are: **Abetone e Piramidi** (☎ *(0573) 60005* ▢); and the **Piccolo Bellavista** (☎ *(0573) 60029* ▢), both open July–Aug and Dec–Apr.

≡ Outside Abetone: **Da Bizzino** (*Via Secchio 72* ☎ *(0573) 60195* ▢▢ *closed Tues, May and Nov*) is worth the 10min drive for fresh-picked mountain mushrooms, fresh pasta and apple tart; at Cutigliano, 12km (7½ miles) to the SE, is **Da Fagiolino** (*Via Carega 1* ☎ *(0573) 68014* ▢ *closed Wed, Nov*).

Anghiari
Map 13F8. 105km (65 miles) SE of Florence, 28km (17 miles) NE of Arezzo. 52031. Pistoia. Population: 6,052.
This walled hill village in the upper Tiber valley gave its name to the battle nearby in 1440 between Florence and Milan.

Sights and places of interest
In the 18thC church of **Santa Maria delle Grazie** is a *Last Supper* (1531) by G. A. Sogliani. The Renaissance **Palazzo Taglieschi** (*Piazza Mameli 16; ring for entrance*) houses a museum of local art and customs.

123

≡**Alighiero** ✿ *(☎(0575) 788040* ▥ *closed Sat)*; **Castello di Sorci** ✿ *(Monterbene, 4km (2½ miles) on Arezzo road* ☎ *(0575) 789066* ▥ *closed Mon, hols)*, where you get five hearty, wholesome courses and as much wine as you can drink at a low fixed price.

Shopping
Busatti Tessitura *(Via Mazzini 12 ☎(0575) 788424)*. Specializes in linen, cotton, wool and hemp, since 1892.

Ansedonia
Map 8J5. 186km (115 miles) sw of Florence, 45km (28 miles) s of Grosseto. 58016. Grosseto. Population: 316.
The rocky promontory on the s coast of Tuscany was the site of the Roman city of Cosa, founded in 273 BC. Excavations have produced evidence of a large and flourishing commercial and agricultural colony, and in 1980 an important 1stC BC villa and its attendant farm buildings were uncovered nearby at Sette Finestre. Ansedonia has been developed with holiday villas.

Sights and places of interest
Ruins of Cosa
Entrance through Porta Romana.
After passing through the best-preserved of the gates, the Roman main street leads to the Forum. Nearby, a recently excavated private house and garden have been partially reconstructed; the domestic objects and decorations can be seen in the small **museum/restoration center** built by the American Academy *(▣ open Tues–Sun 9am–2:30pm)*. Above is the walled Acropolis and, at the highest point, the Capitolium, from which there are views. Below, on the beach beyond the Roman port, which has long since silted up, is the so-called **Tagliata Etrusca**, a canal cut by the Romans between their port and the Lake of Burano.

Nearby sights
Lake of Burano
Capalbio Scalo ☎ *(0564) 898829* ▣ *Open Mon–Wed, Fri during Sept–May 10am to midafternoon. Closed May–Aug.*
A bird sanctuary since 1968.

≡**Il Pescatore** *(Via della Tagliata 13 ☎(0564) 881201* ▥ *closed Tues, mid-Jan, Sept, Oct)*, near the Tagliata; **Pitorsino** *(on SS Aurelia near Orbetello Scalo ☎(0564) 862179* ▥ *to* ▥▥ *closed Wed (except July–Aug), mid-Jan to Feb)*. See also *Capalbio, Orbetello, Port'Ercole, Porto Santo Stefano*.

Arezzo ★
Map 12F7. 81km (50 miles) SE of Florence. 52100. Arezzo. Population: 92,087 i Piazza Risorgimento 116 ☎(0575) 20839.
Arezzo today is a busy, prosperous, provincial town at the center of the rich farming country of the Valdichiana and Valdarno. Its factories manufacture agricultural equipment, women's fashions, leather goods and costume jewelry; its streets buzz with new, imported motorcycles driven by stylish young Aretines with good jobs and a long, proud ancestry stretching back to the Etruscans.

Etruscan Arezzo was one of the most powerful and sophisticated cities of the federation. Later, under the Romans, it became a key stronghold thanks to its strategic location commanding all the passes of the central Apennines. Aretine craftsmen were famous throughout the Roman world for their metalwork and ceramics. As an independent republic from the late Middle Ages its sympathies were predominantly Ghibelline, and it was in the Guelf-Ghibelline Battle of Campaldino in 1289 that Arezzo suffered its first defeat by the

Guelf Florentines. The republic recovered in the early 14thC under the leadership of Bishop Guido Tarlati, when the Duomo, Palazzo del Commine, the Pieve and the church of San Domenico were built, but finally surrendered to Florence in 1384. Petrarch, Spinello Aretino, Pietro Aretino and Vasari were all born in Arezzo; and it was a leading Aretine family, the Bacci, who were responsible for what is surely one of the most inspired commissions in the history of Renaissance patronage: Piero della Francesca's frescoes in the church of San Francesco.

Events: An antique market is held in the Piazza Grande, the main square, on the first Sun of every month; the stalls do business from noon on the previous day.

The annual historic spectacle is the Joust of the Saracen (*Giostra del Saracino*), which takes place in the Piazza Grande on the first Sun of Sept.

An international choral festival in June attracts competitors from all over the world.

Sights and places of interest
Casa di Giorgio Vasari �III ☆
Via XX Settembre 55 🕾 *Open Tues–Sat 9am–2pm, Sun, hols 9am–1pm.*

Vasari lovingly supervised the building of his own house (1540–48), a delightful example of Mannerist domestic architecture. He also executed the frescoes, the most ingenuous and charming of all his creations.

Duomo †

The imposing 13th–14thC cathedral of Arezzo has an early 20thC facade, a 19thC campanile and, on the right flank, an attractive 14thC portico. The interior is illuminated by high stained-glass windows by Guillaume de Marcillat of which the finest is the *Expulsion from the Temple* at the bottom of the right aisle. The 14thC tomb of *S. Donato* in the apse is a collaborative work by Sienese, Florentine and local artists. At the bottom of the left aisle is Piero della Francesca's oddly stiff *Magdalen* (after 1466), his only surviving work in Arezzo apart from the frescoes in San Francesco. To its left is the magnificent tomb of *Bishop Guido Tarlati* (1330) by Agostino di Giovanni and Agnolo di Ventura, possibly to a design by Giotto. In the sacristy, entered from the left aisle, is a striking and strongly personal detached fresco of *St Jerome* by Bartolomeo della Gatta. The late-18thC Chapel of the Madonna of Comfort contains fine terra-cottas by the Della Robbias.

Museo Archeologico Mecenate

Via Margaritone 10 🖾 *Open Tues–Sat 9am–2pm, Sun, hols 9am–1pm.*

The loggia of the 16thC monastery which now houses the Archeological Museum is built round a curve of the 1stC BC Roman amphitheater. The famous **coralline vases** ✩ glazed according to a technique invented by Aretine craftsmen in the 1stC BC and later much copied, are in Rm. VII.

Museo Statale d'Arte Medioevale e Moderna Ⅲ

Via S. Lorentino 8 🖾 *Hours as Museo Archeologico.*

Attractively arranged on three floors of the 15thC **Bruni-Ciocchi Palace**, which has a fine courtyard possibly designed by B. Rossellino. There are important paintings by local artists, notably Margaritone d'Arezzo, Parri di Spinello, Spinello Aretino, Bartolomeo della Gatta; and, in Rms. VI–VIII, a fine **collection of majolicas** (13th–18thC).

Piazza Grande ✩

The main square of Arezzo is one of the liveliest and most architecturally heterogeneous in Tuscany. The NE side is closed by Vasari's handsome **loggia** (1573); its store-fronts retain their original stone counters. On the W is the apse of the Pieve and the extraordinary layered facade of the **Palazzetto della Fraternità dei Laici**; its ground floor is Gothic (1377), the Renaissance first floor was begun after 1434 by B. Rossellino, who made the sculptures, and the upper loggia was completed in 1460 by Giuliano and Algozzo da Settignano, who added the balustrade.

Pieve di Santa Maria Ⅲ † ✩

Corso Italia, Piazza Grande.

The rigorously ornate **facade** of this parish church is the outstanding example of Pisan-Lucchese Romanesque architecture in eastern Tuscany. The church was erected between the mid-12thC and early 14thC. Notice the fine relief carvings (1216) over the central portal. The tall campanile (1330) is the emblem of Arezzo; pierced by 40 bifore windows, it is known locally as 'the tower of 100 holes.' The nave is divided by clustered columns supporting early Gothic arches. The oldest part of the church is the raised presbytery where Pietro Lorenzetti's polyptych of the *Madonna and Saints* hung over the high altar until withdrawn in 1979.

San Domenico †

Piazza Fossombroni.

Built between 1275 and the early 1300s, San Domenico has a Romanesque portal and a Gothic campanile – which retains two of its original bells. The interior is like a giant scrapbook of fragmented frescoes (15th–16thC). Over the high altar is a moving painted *Crucifix* (1260–65) by the young Cimabue.

San Francesco Ⅲ †

The Franciscan basilica in the center of Arezzo was built in the 13th–14thC in the simple Umbrian-Tuscan style; the campanile is 15thC. In the choir is one of the major artistic masterpieces of Europe: Piero della Francesca's noble, compelling **frescoes** ✩ that were painted in the middle of his career; the subject is the *Legend of the True Cross*. The legend links man's original sin to his redemption by tracing a series of events whereby the tree from which Adam ate the forbidden fruit becomes the Cross on which Christ is crucified. Earlier painted interpretations of the story can be seen in *Santa Croce/Florence* by Agnolo Gaddi and in **San Francesco** at *Volterra* by Cenni di Francesco.

Piero's frescoes are badly decayed, especially on the W wall, and it takes time to adjust one's eyes to the complex dimensions of the scheme and the bare patches of plaster left by the latest restoration. Binoculars can be rented in the church shop. The tonality of the right wall is cooler, and the quality of the painting is higher; it was painted without assistance, probably from 1452–59, before Piero's visit to Rome. The series is thought to have been finished on the left wall after his return, with a good deal of assistance. The narrative unfolds as follows.

Right wall, apex: In the right section of the frame Adam announces his impending death; in the left section, the dead Adam is surrounded by his children and Seth plants a branch of the tree in his father's mouth. **Central band, left section**: The tree, grown so large that even Solomon cannot use it for his palace, has been made into a bridge over the River Siloam; the Queen of Sheba instinctively recognizes its sacred origins and kneels at the bridge. **Right section**: The Queen of Sheba is received by Solomon and predicts to him that a man will be nailed to the tree and the Jews will thereby be disgraced.

Right window wall, center: The beam is buried by Solomon's order; the scene deliberately prefigures the Carrying of the Cross. **Bottom**: Constantine is asleep in his tent on the eve of battle; an angel announces that he will be victorious if he fights for the sign of the Cross. **Right wall, lowest band**: The victory of Constantine over Maxentius.

Left window, middle section: Judas is tortured and reveals the whereabouts of the Cross.

Piero had the power of creating forms which immediately satisfy us by their completeness; forms which reconcile the mathematical laws of proportion with the stress and tension of growth, forms which combine the resilience of a tree trunk with the precision of a pre-dynastic jar.

Sir Kenneth Clark, *Piero della Francesca*

Left wall, central band, left section: The Empress Helena discovers the Cross; in the background a view of Arezzo represents Jerusalem. **Right section**: Judas proves the Cross by raising a man from the dead; the church in the background recalls the architectural style of Piero's friend and fellow mathematician, Alberti. **Lowest band**: 30yr after the discovery of the Cross, the Persian King Chosroes has stolen it from Jerusalem; he is defeated in battle by Heraclius, Emperor of the East. **Apex**: Heraclius returns the Cross to Jerusalem.

The other frescoes in the chapel are outside the main narrative. The most important is the *Annunciation*, on the lowest section of the left window wall, probably painted in 1466 after Piero's visit to Urbino. The prophet to the right of the window's apex is by Piero, the one on the left by an assistant. Returning to the nave, notice in the third chapel on the left the superb late 13thC *Crucifix of St Francis*, and in the second chapel the Pieroesque frescoes of the *Miracles of St Anthony of Padua* by Lorentino d'Arezzo. The glass of the rose window (1524) of the interior facade is by G. de Marcillat.

Other sights

Other points of interest in Arezzo include the Palazzo Comunale; the Fortezza Medicea, which commands splendid views; the churches of S. Maria in Gradi, SS. Annunziata, S. Agostino, and the Badia; and 1.5km (1 mile) to the s of the Piazza della Repubblica, the church of S. Maria delle Grazie, with a graceful portico by B. da Maiano. In summer it is pleasant to picnic in the Passeggio del Prato, the public gardens.

Continentale
Piazza Guido Monaco 7, 52100 Arezzo ☎ *(0575) 20251* 75 rms 75 AE ⓞ ⓞ VISA *Restaurant closed Fri, July.*
Modern, comfortable and central. The local businessmen's favorite and the most reliable kitchen in Arezzo.

Al Principe
Giovi, 8km (5 miles) to N ☎ *(0575) 362046* to Closed *Mon, Aug.*
Cool and elegant, with a garden shaded by a huge chestnut tree.

☞ ⊒Alternatives are: **Le Tastevin** (*Via de' Cenci 9* ☎ *(0575) 28304* **▮▮▯** *closed Mon, Aug*); or **Il Torrino** (*Madonna del Torrino, 8km (5 miles)* SE *on Sansepolcro road* ☎ *(0575) 357915* **▮▮▯** *to* **▮▮▮▮** *closed Tues*).

Shopping

A little shop with no name (*Piazza Grande 10*) is crammed with attractive rustic linens and woolen sweaters made locally.

Artimino

Map 15E5. 22km (14 miles) W *of Florence. 50042. Firenze. Population: 260.*

An old walled village in a wine-producing zone.

Sights and places of interest
Artimino, Villa dell' **▥▥▥** ☆

▣▣ ⊒ *Open Wed 8am–noon, 2–5pm.*

This smiling Mannerist villa, known as the 'Villa of the Hundred Chimneys,' was built by Buontalenti as a hunting lodge for Ferdinand I. The rooms are decorated with good *pietra serena* fireplaces and frescoes attributed to Poccetti and Passignano. The estate has a shop and small restaurant where its own wines are available (see *Tuscan wines*).
San Leonardo ▥▥▥ †

This well-preserved Romanesque church was allegedly founded by Countess Matilda in 1107. It was constructed with Etruscan fragments from the nearby necropolis of Pian di Rosello.

Nearby sights

There are two Etruscan tombs near Comeana, 3km (2 miles) N, where signs point to the **Tomba dei Boschetti** (7thC BC) and the monumental **Tomba di Montefortini** (*ring for custodian*).

⊒Try **Biagio Pignatta** (☎ *(055) 8718080* **▮▮▯** *closed Wed, Thurs lunch*); or **Da Delfina** (*Via della Chiesa* ☎ *(055) 8718074* **▮▮▯** *closed Mon eve, Tues, Aug*), a pleasant restaurant, specializing in game. Booking essential.

Asciano

Map 12G6. 91km (57 miles) SE *of Florence, 20km (12½ miles)* SE *of Siena. 53042. Siena. Population: 5,897.*

A walled medieval hill village in the upper Ombrone valley. The Corso Matteotti is lined with interesting old houses.

Sights and places of interest
Museo di Arte Sacra
Piazza Sant'Agata **▣▣** *Open daily 9am–noon, 2–5pm.*

Left of the Travertine Collegiata di Sant'Agata (11thC but much restored) is this notable collection of 14th–15thC Sienese School painting and sculpture. Of special interest are the **polyptych** by the young Matteo di Giovanni; *St Michael and the Dragon* by A. Lorenzetti; *Nativity of the Virgin* by the Master of the Osservanza; *Madonna* by Barna; and two graceful wooden statues of the *Annunciation* by Francesco di Valdambrino.
Museo Etrusco
Corso Matteotti **▣▣** *Open daily 9am–noon, 2–5pm.*

In the former church of S. Bernardino, this museum houses material from the Etruscan necropolis of Poggiopinci, 5km (3 miles) E of Asciano.

Bagni di Lucca

Map 15D4. 101km (63 miles) NW *of Florence, 27km (16 miles)* N *of Lucca. 55021. Lucca. Population: 7,991* **i** *Via Umberto I 101* ☎ *(0583) 87946/87245 (May–Oct).*

The healing properties of the sulfurous and saline waters at the Baths of Lucca were recognized from the 13thC, but a foreigner, Napoleon's sister Elisa Baciocchi, gave Bagni di Lucca its Empire tone. Mrs Trollope was scarcely exaggerating when she wrote "Bagni di Lucca belongs, like so much else in Italy, exclusively to foreigners;" the list of distinguished foreign literary visitors includes Montaigne, Heine, Lamartine, Shelley, Byron, Landor, the Brownings and Ouida.

A little seedy now and certainly not fashionable, Bagni di Lucca is nevertheless an inexpensive place to take the waters or merely to savor the somewhat claustrophobic atmosphere created by the mild, humid climate, the mature plane trees, and the weight of nostalgia for the vanished Victorian presence. Those who enjoy hill-climbing will share the pleasure Shelley took in scaling the steep chestnut-clad slopes.

In the Piazza del Bagno is a charming early-19thC bathhouse, now abandoned and crumbling. Just above is the **Palazzo Bonvisi**, where Shelley and Byron stayed and which Montaigne described. The **English Cemetery**, reached by a bridge over the River Lima behind the Circolo dei Forestieri, is sadly neglected.

Bridge (*Ponte a Serraglia, 3km (2 miles)* w ☎ *(0583) 97147* ▢).

Circolo dei Forestieri (*Piazza Varraud* ☎ *(0583) 86038* ▮);
Ingordo (*Via Vittorio Emanuele* ☎ *(0583) 87269* ▮ *closed Wed*).

Bagno a Ripoli
Map 12E6. 7km (4 miles) SE of Florence. 50012. Firenze. Bus no. 33. Population: 25,139.

This suburb of Florence was named after the remains of a Roman bath discovered in the 17thC. There is pretty hill country above and the 14thC church of S. Pietro a Ripoli.

Villa La Massa
50010 Candeli, Firenze ☎ *(055) 630051* ⑩ *573555* ▥ *42 rms* ▭ *42*

A 16thC villa on the Arno, now a nicely furnished and well-run hotel.

Centanni
Via Centanni 7 ☎ *(055) 630122* ▥ ▭ ▭ ▤ ▭ *Closed Sat lunch, Sun.*

In an entrancing location, especially on a hot summer evening.

Barga
Map 14D3. 111km (70 miles) NW of Florence, 37km (23 miles) N of Lucca. 55051. Lucca. Population: 10,952 i *Piazza Angelio* ☎ *(0583) 73499.*

The prettiest hill town in the Garfagnana stands above an active industrial new town.

Event: An opera festival takes place in summer.

Duomo †
The rectangular, buttermilk-colored Duomo, rebuilt from the 9thC, contains an extraordinarily well-preserved late 12thC **pulpit**, sculpted with all the serious charm of the period with scenes from the *Lives of Christ and Mary*. In the apse is a wooden statue of *St Christopher*. In the chapel to the right are attractive unglazed Robbianesque terra-cottas.

The **loggetta of the Podestà**, to the left of the Duomo, preserves a rare set of 15thC official measures.

La Pergula (☎ *(0583) 73086* ▮ *closed Fri in winter*).

Bibbiena

Map **12***E7. 59km (37 miles)* SE *of Florence, 32km (20 miles)* N *of Arezzo. 52011. Arezzo. Population: 10,716* **i** *Via Cappucci* ☎ *(0575) 93098.*

The chief town of the Casentino, the remote upper valley of the Arno enclosed by wooded mountains. The great monasteries of *Camaldoli* and *La Verna* are reached by road from Bibbiena. The 16thC Dovizi Palace stands opposite the 15thC church of San Lorenzo. Off the La Verna road is the Renaissance church of Santa Maria del Sasso, with interesting paintings inside.

♤ ≋ Amorosi Bel ♧
Via Dovizi 18, 52011 Bibbiena, Arezzo ☎ *(0575) 593046* ☐ *20 rms* ▭ *12* Ⓐ *Restaurant closed Wed; last orders 7.30pm.*
This old inn has a solemn turn-of-the-century atmosphere.

Bivigliano

Map **12***D6. 18km (11 miles)* N *of Florence. 50030. Firenze. Population: 620* **i** *Via delle Scuole 4.*

A summer resort on the W slope of Monte Senario.
High above the town is the Convent of Monte Senario, the mother house of the Servite Order, founded in the 13thC. The buildings date mostly from the late 16thC. Stupendous views of the Arno and Sieve valleys.

Nearby sight
9km (5¾ miles) s is the 15thC Servite **Convent of La Maddalena**, with frescoes by Fra Bartolommeo.

♤ Giotto Park (☎ *(055) 406608* ☐ *to* ☐☐ *closed Nov–Mar except Christmas*).

≋ In the town, **La Giulia** (*Via Roma 2* ☎ *(055) 460602* ☐ *to* ☐☐ *closed Fri*). **Dino** (*Via Faentina 329* ☎ *(055) 548932* ☐ *to* ☐☐ *closed Wed*), a cheerful country inn with rooms, 5km (3 miles) s at the Olmo intersection near La Maddalena.

Borgo San Lorenzo

Map **12***D6. 29km (18 miles)* NE *of Florence. 50032. Firenze. Population: 14,724.*

The principal center of the Mugello, this town, now an industrial center, was destroyed by an earthquake in 1919.

Nearby sights
3km (2 miles) N, approached by a fine avenue of cypresses, is the church of **S. Giovanni Maggiore**, with an 11thC campanile and, inside, a rare Romanesque intarsiaed ambo.
5.5km (3½ miles) w is **S. Piero a Sieve**, where the parish church contains a terra-cotta font in the style of Luca della Robbia; above is Buontalenti's S. Martino fortress.
7km (4 miles) SE is **Vespignano**, birthplace of Giotto. The house designated as Giotto's is N of the road. Farther along is **Vicchio**, where Fra Angelico was born and where Benvenuto Cellini took refuge from 1559–71 in the house next to the Oratory in Corso del Popolo.

≋ **Da Felicina** (*S. Piero a Sieve* ☎ *(055) 848016* ☐ *closed Sat, early Mar, mid-Sept*). Farther N are two useful restaurants near the autostrada exit at Barberino di Mugello: **La Capannina** (*Viale Don Minzoni 88, Carallino Mugello* ☎ *(055) 8420078* ☐ *closed Tues*); and **Settimo Gualtieri** (☎ *(055) 641051* ☐☐ *closed Wed*).

Camaldoli

Map **12***E7. 71km (44 miles)* SE *of Florence, 46km (28 miles)* N *of Arezzo. 52010. Arezzo. Population: 50.*

Camaldoli, mother house of a reforming Order of the Benedictines founded in the early 11thC by St Romauld, stands isolated high in the Apennines above the Casentino. Its buildings are mostly of the 17th–18thC, and of little interest apart from the 16thC **pharmacy**.

Eremo
☎ *Open 9–11am, 3:30–6pm.*

2.5km (1½ miles) above the monastery, at 1,104m (335ft), is the **eremo** (hermitage) where the medieval monks lived in absolute isolation in the midst of their magnificent **forest**. The delightful Baroque church of Il Salvatore and the 20 monastic cells, including the one occupied by St Romauld, may be visited.

There are two modest inns near the monastery, and fine walking.

≡ **Il Cedro**
Moggiona, 5km (3 miles) s on the Poppi road ☎ *(0575) 556080* ▯▯
▢ ▭ ♨ ◁≡ *Closed Mon during Oct–May.*
A serious and popular small restaurant overlooking the mountains.
Specialties: Sformati, tortelli di patate, fritti di verdure.

Capalbio
*Map **8**J6. 182km (113 miles) sw of Florence, 18km (11 miles) NE of Ansedonia. 58011. Grosseto. Population: 3,950.*
This walled medieval village is near the large **Maremma hunting reserve**, open to the public in season (*inquiries to Riserva Turistica di Caccia dell'Ente Provinciale per il Turismo, Castello Collacchioni* ☎ *(0564) 896024*). Walk around the 14thC ramparts and through the old unspoiled streets.

Restaurants
Capalbio is well endowed with attractive, aromatic restaurants which serve hunters' food, especially wild boar and roebuck cooked in unusually appetizing ways. Most light open fires in the winter and spread onto terraces in summer.

≡ **Da Maria** (*Via Comunale 3* ☎ *(0564) 896014* ▯▯ *closed Feb, Tues except July and Aug*); **La Torre** (☎ *(0564) 896070* ▯▯ *closed Thurs*); near the hunting reserve, 5km (3 miles) NW, **Al Fontanile dei Caprai** (☎ *(0564) 896216* ▯▯ *open Sat, also Sun in winter, eve in July and Aug, lunch on licensed hunting days*).

Caprese Michelangelo
*Map **13**F8. 123km (76 miles) SE of Florence, 45km (28 miles) NE of Arezzo. 52033. Arezzo. Population: 1,799.*
An agricultural hill village where Michelangelo was born on Mar 6, 1475, while his father was the Florentine magistrate (*podestà*). The magistrate's house, the Casa del Podestà, is opposite the entrance to the restored 14thC **Castello**.

♨ ≡ **Fonte della Galletta** ♣ (*6km (4 miles) to w at Alpe Faggeta* ☎ *(0575) 793925* ▯▯ *to* ▯▯ *closed Oct–Apr, restaurant closed Wed*) for game and mushrooms.

Carmignano
*Map **15**E5. 22km (14 miles) w of Florence. 50042. Firenze. Population: 7,691.*
This little town is surrounded by vineyards which produce the venerable Carmignano wines (see *Tuscan wines*).

San Michele †
In this Gothic parish church hangs Pontormo's *Visitation* ★ one of his greatest and best-known masterpieces.

≡ See *Artimino*.

Carrara

*Map **14**D2. 126km (80 miles) NW of Florence, 55km (34 miles) N of Pisa. 54033. Massa-Carrara. Population: 70,213*
i Piazza 2 Giugno 14 ☎ (0585) 70668.

To reach the Duomo in what remains of the old center of Carrara, one must penetrate a vast modern boomtown still thriving on the quarries which have yielded their famous marble for over 2,000yr and are today one of the major world sources, producing 500,000 tons a year.

Sights and places of interest
Duomo ▥ ✝ ☆

An ornate version of the Pisan-Lucchese style. The lower facade and portal date from the 12thC and the elaborately carved Gothic upper storey, with its rose window, was added in the 14thC. The simple, elegant interior contains a 14thC *Virgin Annunciate* and Gothic-style *Angel*.

Piazza Alberica boasts some fine Baroque palaces including Pietro Tacca's birthplace. In Piazza C. Battisti is the Neoclassical **Teatro degli Animosi** (1840), admired by Dickens and other 19thC travelers.
Mostra Nazionale Marmi e Macchine
Viale XX Settembre ◫ ✱ *Open Mon, Thurs, Sun 10am–1pm, Sat 10am–1pm, 4–7pm.*

A permanent exhibition demonstrating techniques of marble quarrying, cutting and carving. The **quarries** themselves, 7km (4 miles) to the E, at Colonnata and Fantiscritti, will admit visitors.

🍽**Michelangelo** (*Corso Carlo Rosselli 3* ☎ *(0585) 70861* ▮▯).

🍴**Soldaini** (*Via Mazzini 11* ☎ *(0585) 71459* ▮▮ *closed Mon, Sun eve and Aug 1–22*) is cool and pleasant; 7km (4½ miles) toward Marina di Carrara at Avenza is **Il Muraglione** (*Via Fivizzano 13* ☎ *(0585) 58771* ▮▮▮ *closed Sun*), an old country inn.

Cascina

*Map **14**E4. 75km (47 miles) SW of Florence, 17km (10 miles) SE of Pisa. 56021. Pisa. Population: 34,701.*

In this center of furniture manufacture is the 12thC **Pieve di Santa Maria**, a remarkably well-preserved example of the Pisan Romanesque style. The 14thC Oratory of San Giovanni is frescoed (1398) inside by Martino di Bartolomeo.

Nearby sights

Vicopisano, 6km (3¾ miles) to the NE, retains picturesque 14thC fortifications restored by Brunelleschi. 9km (5½ miles) to the NW is Calci, with a fine 11thC Pisan-Romanesque **Pieve**. Nearby on the Montemagno road is the **Certosa di Pisa** (◫ ▮ *open May–Oct Tues–Sat 9.30–11.30am, 3–6pm, Nov–Apr 10am–noon, 2–5pm*), a splendid complex of 17th–18thC Baroque buildings.

Castellina in Chianti

*Map **12**F6. 50km (31 miles) S of Florence, 21km (13 miles) N of Siena. 53011. Siena. Population: 2,843.*

This small town was the first seat of the medieval Chianti League and one of the original centers of the Chianti Classico winegrowing zone. The medieval **Rocca** was extended by the Florentines in 1400; Etruscan remains include the 4thC BC tomb of Montecalvario, and a well.

🍽 **Tenuta di Ricavo**
53011 Castellina in Chianti, Siena ☎ *(0577) 740221* ▮▮▮ *25 rms* ▭ *25*
🛏 ⇌ 🍴 *Closed Nov–Mar.*

Location: 4km (2½ miles) S, on San Donato road. An isolated medieval farming village transformed into an excellent Swiss-managed hotel.
⌂ ⌧ 🏊 ⚓ ⇌

❧ Villa Casalecchi
53011 Castellina in Chianti, Siena ☎ *(0577) 740240* ❑▯ *to* ▯❑▯ *14 rms*
🖭▯4 ➡ ═ 🖰 🖨 🅰🅴 🄾 🆅🅸🆂🅰 *Closed Nov–Mar.*
Location: 1km s, on Siena road. Enfolded in a pine wood in the hills.
🖼 🗺 💘 ⫷⫸ ⇶

═ La Torre
Piazza Umberto ☎ *(0577) 740236* ▯❑▯ ▭ ➥ ➡ ⬤ *Closed Fri, one week in Dec.*
A generous choice of perfected rustic dishes.

Castello
Map 6B3. 6km (3½ miles) NW of Florence. 50019. Firenze. Bus no. 14 to Careggi from Florence Duomo or station.
Here, at the base of Monte Morello, are three important Medici villas within pleasant walking distance of one another. Two more Medici villas, **Trebbio** and **Cafaggiolo**, are a short drive up the Via Bolognese (see *Route 6* in *Planning*), and *Artimino* and *Poggio a Caiano* are to the w. See *Sesto Fiorentino*.

Sights and places of interest
Villa Medicea della Petraia ▥ ☆
☎*(451208)* 🄾▯ ✗ *Open Tues–Sat 9am–2pm, Sun 9am–1pm. Closed Mon.*
The old castle, of which the adapted central tower remains, was rebuilt from c.1575–90 by Buontalenti for Cardinal Ferdinand de' Medici. In the courtyard, glassed over by Victor Emmanuel, who used it as a ballroom, is a pleasing fresco cycle by Volterrano glorifying the Medici. On the upper terrace of the garden is an elegant marble **fountain** by Tribolo dominated by Giambologna's bronze *Venus*. There is a magnificent park to the E of the villa.
Villa Medicea di Careggi ▥
Viale G. Pieraccini 🄾▯ 🄮▯ ▮ *The villa is now a nurses' home; to visit, apply to the hospital of Santa Maria Nuova in Florence.*
Careggi was one of the earliest villas used by the Medici for rest and study. The old castellated house was modified for Cosimo il Vecchio by Michelozzo, who added the loggiaed wing to the left in the 1430s. Cosimo, his son Piero and his grandson Lorenzo the Magnificent all died here. The villa was burned and looted after the expulsion of the Medici, and restored in the 16thC by Pontormo and Bronzino.
Villa Medicea di Castello ▥ ☆
🄾▯ *Garden only open daily 9am–6:30pm or sunset.*
Castello belonged to Lorenzo di Pierfrancesco de' Medici; Cosimo I was brought up here and hired Tribolo in 1537 to redesign the well-preserved **gardens** ★ which were completed in 1592 by Buontalenti, who rebuilt the villa. The **fountain** of *Hercules and Anteus*, with statues by Ammannati, was designed by Tribolo. The **grotto**, with fountains and wonderful exotic animals, is by Giambologna. The colossal bronze half-figure known as *January* in the terraced park is by Ammannati.

❧ Villa le Rondini
Via Bolognese Vecchie 224, 50139 Castello, Firenze ☎ *(055) 400081*
▯▯▯ *to* ▯❑▯ *35 rms* 🖭▭ *35* ➡ 🖰 ═ 🅰🅴 🄾 🄾 🆅🅸🆂🅰
A peaceful hotel in a 16thC villa on the hill of Monterinaldi.
🖼 🗺 💘 ⫷⫸ ⇶ ⤳

═ Lo Strettoio
Serpiolle ☎ *(055) 403044* ▯▯▯▮ ▭ ⬤ *Closed Sun, Mon, Aug.*
Honest home cooking in an old mill. Booking essential.

Castiglion Fiorentino
Map 12G7. 100km (62 miles) SE of Florence, 17km (10½ miles) s of Arezzo. 52043. Arezzo. Population: 11,164
i Corso Italia 111.
This walled market town, a major center in the Valdichiana, slopes down a hill above the Arezzo–Cortona road.

Sights and places of interest

The graceful 16thC **Loggia del Vasari** in the central Piazza del Municipio frames a fine view, and from the **castle keep** above it one can see over the Valdichiana as far as *Monte Amiata*.

Palazzo Comunale/Pinacoteca
Piazza del Municipio ☒ ▓ *Open Mon–Sat 9am–noon, Thurs, Sat also 4–6pm, Sun 10:30–11:30am.*
The most notable works in the gallery include a cheering 15thC reliquary bust of *St Ursula* as a shy, happy girl, made in the Rhineland; a 13thC Umbrian painted crucifix; and paintings by Bartolomeo della Gatta.

There are also paintings by Bartolomeo della Gatta in the **Collegiata** and, in the adjoining **Pieve**, a *Deposition* (1438) by Signorelli. The late 13thC church of **S. Francesco** possesses a *St Francis* (1280–90) by Margaritone d'Arezzo.

Nearby sights

On a hilltop 4km (2½ miles) s is the imposing 13thC **Castello di Montecchio Vesponi** (*not open to the public*), given by the Florentines to the English *condottiere* Sir John Hawkwood.

Shopping

Matteo Capitini (*Via Roma* ☎ *(0575) 65559* ▮▯ *to* ▮▮). Fine hand-made ceramics.

Castiglione della Pescaia
Map **10**/4. *162km (101 miles) s of Florence, 22km (14 miles) w of Grosseto. 58043. Grosseto. Population: 8,376*
i Piazza Garibaldi 6 ☎ *(0564) 933678.*
The main coastal resort of the Maremma is also a busy fishing village, and private and professional craft moor in the lively harbor at the mouth of the River Bruna. Above is the 14th–15thC **Rocca Aragonese** defending the original medieval village, now overgentrified. To the s stretch sand beaches.

Hotels

The hotels on the harbor are noisy and charmless. Instead try **Gli Archi** (*Via Montebello 28* ☎ *(0564) 933083* ▮▯), a modest *pensione* in the center; or, outside the village at Poggiodoro, **David** (☎ *(0564) 939030* ▮▯ *to* ▮▮).

Riva del Sole ▥
58043 Castiglione della Pescaia, Grosseto ☎ *(0564) 933625* ▮▮▮ *176 rms*
▭ *176* ▤ ☒ ▰ *AE* ⊙ *VISA Closed Oct–Mar.*
A large, modern hotel in a new resort 3km (1¾ miles) up the coast.
⌂ ❖ ঌ ☑ ⚓ ≋ ⚐ ⚘ ⚲ ♨ ⊶ ⚒

Roccamare
Loc. Roccamare, 58043 Castiglione della Pescaia, Grosseto
☎ *(0564) 941124* ▰ *500286* ▮▯ *to* ▮▮ *51 rms* ▭ *51* ▤ ☒ ⌂ ≈
AE ⊙ *OD VISA Closed Nov–May.*
A complex of bungalows, just beyond Riva del Sole.
⌂ ঌ ☑ ⚘ ≋ ⚐ ♨ ⊶

☰ **Da Romolo**
Via della Libertà 10 ☎ *(0564) 933533* ▮▯ ▱ *Closed Tues, Nov.*
The best of the fish restaurants. *Specialty: Spaghetti con frutti di mare*.

☰ Alternatives are: **Il Gambero** (*Via Ansedonia* ☎ *(0564) 937110* ▮▯); **Grottino** (*Corso Libertà* ☎ *(0564) 933970* ▱).

Certaldo
Map **11**F5. *40km (25 miles) sw of Florence, 40km (25 miles) nw of Siena. 50052. Firenze. Population: 15,899.*
Certaldo Alto, the fortified red-brick village where Boccaccio

spent much of his life and died in 1375, stands above a modern
suburb in the valley of the Elsa. The village was rebuilt in the
15thC and restored, a little too crisply, in the 19thC and again
after World War II.

Sights and places of interest
Casa del Boccaccio
Via Boccaccio 18 🔄 *Ring next door as signposted for entry.*
A postwar reconstruction of a house which possibly belonged to
Boccaccio's family.
Palazzo Pretorio
Piazzetta del Vicariato 🖼 *Open 9.00–12.30, 13.30–18.00.*
Rebuilt in the 15thC, this palace has a pretty courtyard with *quattrocento*
frescoes by P. F. Fiorentino and, in the adjacent chapel, fresco fragments
by Gozzoli and Giusto d'Andrea.
SS Michele e Jacopo †
Boccaccio's tomb was removed in 1783 by those who disapproved of his
work. The modern tomb carries his own epitaph and his portrait bust
(1503) by G. F. Rustici.

🛏 ⇌ **Il Castello** (*Via della Rena 6* 🕿 *(0571) 668250* ▮▯) is a simple
hotel with a cool brick terrace.

🛏 ⇌ **Osteria del Vicario** (*Piazzetta Vicariato* 🕿 *(0571) 668228* ▮▯
to ▮▮ *closed Wed*) has an arcaded terrace.

Chianciano Terme
*Map **9**H7. 120km (75 miles) SE of Florence, 85km (53 miles)
SE of Siena. 53042. Siena. Population: 7,294 **i** Azienda
Autonoma di Cura, Piazza Indipendenza* 🕿 *(0578) 63167.*
If you are driving from *Chiusi* you will see two Chiancianos: the
old hill town and, below it, the modern spa, one of the most
important in Italy. The curative powers of the waters have been
valued since the Roman age. There are various types of water
for internal consumption or bathing.
    A lovely rural road to the S leads to Sarteano, after 7.5km (5
miles), and Cetona, 14km (9 miles), two Etruscan villages.

🛏 There are some 200 hotels and boarding houses of all categories
during the season (April 16–Nov 15: **Capitol** (*Viale della Libertà 492*
🕿 *(0578) 64681* ▮▮▯ *to* ▮▮▮▮); **Fortuna** (*Via della Valle 76*
🕿 *(0578) 64661* ▮▮▮▮); **Macerina** (*Via Macerina 27* 🕿 *(0578) 64241* ▮▯
to ▮▮); **Michelangelo** (*Via delle Piane 146* 🕿 *(0578) 64004* ▮▮▮ *to* ▮▮▮▮);
Park (*Via Roncacci 30* 🕿 *(0578) 63603* ▮▯); **Raffaello** (*Via dei Monti*
🕿 *(0578) 64633* ▮▮▯); **Sole** (*Via della Rosa 40* 🕿 *(0578) 60194* ▮▯);
Taormina (*Via Roncacci 12* 🕿 *(0578) 63808* ▮▯).

⇌ **La Casanova**
Strada della Vittoria 10 🕿 *(0578) 60449* ▮▮▮▮ 🖵 ⇌ 🍴 🚗 ᴀᴇ 🄌 ᴠɪsᴀ
Closed Nov–Feb, Mon during Mar–May, Oct.
Set invitingly in a wooded park, this elegant restaurant offers Tuscan
cooking with inventive touches.

Chiusi
*Map **9**H7. 126km (79 miles) SE of Florence, 67km (42 miles) S
of Arezzo. 53043. Siena. Population: 9,108 **i** Via Petrarca 4
🕿 (0578) 20003.*
The Etruscan city of Camars, one of the greatest of the
lucomonies, is best known to classical scholars and readers of
Macaulay's *Horatius* for its king, Lars Porsena, who attacked
Rome in 508 BC. Today Camars lies buried around and under
the little town of Chiusi, whose street plan is that of Clusium,
the Roman military colony it became in 296 BC.

Sights and places of interest

Duomo †

Beneath the campanile of the Romanesque cathedral, constructed from building fragments of the two earlier civilizations, is a large **cistern**, possibly 1stC BC. To visit, apply to the Museo Etrusco.

Museo Nazionale Etrusco ★

One of the outstanding Etruscan museums in Italy. The material, excavated from the vast necropolis surrounding the city, notably demonstrates the influence of Greece, Mesopotamia, Egypt and Rome on this sophisticated and receptive culture. There is a superb and varied collection of cinerary urns and sarcophagi, of which the most famous is the sarcophagus depicting the battle of the Gauls with a **portrait of Lars Sentinates** on the cover. Also noteworthy are specimens of the heavy black *bucchero* ware, imitating metal, which was made only in Chiusi, and an unusually fine collection of Attic vases.

Necropoli Etrusca

🔲 📠 *Visits only with guides from the Museo Etrusco.*

The most notable Etruscan tombs are: To the N, along the Via delle Tombe Etrusche: the c.3rd–4th BC Tomba della Pellegrina, with fine sarcophagi; the 5thC BC **Tomba della Scimmia** (Monkey Tomb), which retains rare wall paintings; and the Tomba del Granduca, with cinerary urns. To the E: the 5thC BC **Tomba Bonci Casuccini**, with its original door and frescoes of games; and the 1stC BC Tomba delle Tassinaie.

❦ ═ Il Patriarca ❀

Querce al Pino, 53043 Chiusi ☎ *(0578)* 274007 ▥▮ *22 rms* ▭ *22* 🚗
🖂 ═ 𝘝𝘐𝘚𝘈 *Restaurant closed Wed.*
🏠 🖉 ⚓

The most pleasant of a cluster of hotels serving the autostrada exit.

═ 2.5km (1¼ miles) to the N, on shore of Lake Chiusi, **La Fattoria** (*with rooms* ☎ *(0578)* 21407 ▥▮ *to* ▥▮▮ *closed Mon, Jan to mid-Mar*), where tiled floors and beamed ceilings give a farmhouse atmosphere; also **Zaira** (*Via Arunte 12* ☎ *(0578)* 20260 ▥▮ *closed Mon in Winter*), a delightful restaurant in the center serving inventive food.

Colle di Val d'Elsa

Map 11F5. 49km (30 miles) s of Florence, 25km (15 miles) NW of Siena. 53034. Siena. Population: 15,618 **i** *Piazza Arnolfo di Cambio 5* ☎ *(0577) 921692.*

There is an impressive view of this two-tiered town from the *Monteriggioni* road. The upper town has conserved its medieval street plan and some fine architecture.

Colle di Val d'Elsa has been a manufacturing center of fine crystal glass from the mid-14thC. Fiercely contested between Siena and Florence in the 13thC, the town became part of the Florentine dominion in 1333. The architect and sculptor Arnolfo di Cambio was born here in 1232.

Sights and places of interest

Colle Bassa

The lower town is also known as il Piano, and its hub is the lively Piazza Arnolfo di Cambio. Nearby in Via dei Fossi is the church of **S. Agostino** with an unfinished 13thC facade and beautiful 16thC interior designed by Antonio da Sangallo the Elder.

Colle Alta ☆

The upper town and the remains of its 12thC–13thC fortifications are strung along the ridge of the hill. Notice the frescoed palace facades on Via XX Settembre and other streets. The **Porta Nuova**, leading to the Volterra road at the end of Via Gracco del Secco, is a fine piece of late 15thC military architecture, probably by Giuliano da Sangallo. The medieval village is reached by a bridge from which there are fine views; straddling the ravine is the splendid unfinished Mannerist **Palazzo Campana** (1539) by Giuliano di Baccio d'Agnolo.

The **Via del Castello** opens into the Piazza del Duomo where the

14thC Palazzo Pretorio houses the **Antiquarium Etrusco** (🔲 📷 *open Tues–Sat 10am–noon, 4–7pm*), displaying material excavated from a necropolis near Monteriggioni. Inside the Baroque **Duomo** (1619) is a bronze *Crucifix* over the high altar attributed to Giambologna and a bronze lectern by P. Tacca. The **Palazzo Vescovile** (*Via Castello 27*) houses a little **Museo d'Arte Sacra** (🔲 *open Sun summer 4–7pm, winter 3–6pm*), where ecclesiastic vestments and objects and a late 14thC Sienese school triptych are displayed in one frescoed room. In the old Palazzo dei Priori is the **Museo Civico** (🔲 *open Tues–Sun 9am–noon, 2–5pm*), with pictures by R. Manetti, P. F. Fiorentino and others; under a loggetta are frescoes by S. Ferri of *David and Goliath* and *Judith and Holofernes*. Toward the bottom of Via Castello, no. 63 is the early 13thC **tower-house of Arnolfo di Cambio**.

≡ La Vecchia Cartiera
Via Oberdan 5–9 ☎ *(0577) 921107* 🍽 📖 💺 🍴 🚗 🛏 ⏢ 💵 📷
💳 *Closed Sun eve, Mon, July.*
A popular restaurant in an old paper mill. *Specialty:* Game.

Collodi

*Map **15**D4. 63km (39 miles)* NW *of Florence, 17km (10 miles)* NE *of Lucca. 51014. Pistoia. Population: 2,233.*
Just to the W of *Pescia* is the picturesque village where Carlo Lorenzini, author of *Pinocchio*, spent his youth and gained his pen name, Carlo Collodi.

Sights and places of interest

Parco di Pinocchio
🔲 ✱ *Open daily 8am to sunset.*
Games, statues and pavilions on the theme of Pinocchio and his creator.

Villa Garzoni Gardens ☆
🔲 *Open daily summer 8am–1pm, 2:30pm to sunset; winter 9am–noon.*
This sparkling beautiful and well-preserved garden, which flows downhill from the *castello*, was laid out in the mid-1600s by the Garzoni family. The villa assumed its present form in the late 18thC.

≡ Gambero Rosso (*Via S. Gennaro 2* ☎ *(0572) 429364* 🍽 *to* 🍽
closed Tues, mid-Nov), dull but convenient. See also *Pescia*.

Cortona ☆

*Map **13**G8. 102km (63 miles)* SE *of Florence, 32km (20 miles)* SE *of Arezzo. 52044. Arezzo. Population: 22,561* i *Piazza Signorelli 10* ☎ *(0575) 603056.*
The mythical founder of Cortona was Corythus, father of Dardanus, which suggests that Cortona was older than Troy; and certainly the town was already long established when it was occupied by the Etruscans in the 8th–7thC BC. The Romans took over in the 4thC BC; and in 217 BC the main Roman army was destroyed nearby at Lake Trasimeno by the Carthaginian general Hannibal. The commune which emerged from the Dark Ages in the 12thC was brutally sacked by Arezzo in 1258, recovered in the 14thC under the steadying rule of the Casali lords, and was eventually sold to Florence in 1411. The new association with Florence and the arrival of Fra Angelico, who spent some 10yr in the monastery then attached to San Domenico, freed the art of Cortona from the archaizing domination of Siena. In the second half of the 15thC Cortona produced its own great native painter, Luca Signorelli, whose work can be seen in the Diocesan Museum and the church of San Nicolò. The painters Pietro da Cortona and the Futurist Gino Severini were also natives of Cortona.

Modern Cortona, the principal town of the Valdichiana, is a serious place inhabited by farmers and bookish foreigners.

The brown sandstone buildings of the old town are scattered down the steep upper slope of Monte Sant'Egidio and wrapped in medieval walls which incorporate large sections built by the Etruscans. The main street, Via Nazionale, known locally as Ruga Piana because it is the only level street in the town, leads from Piazza Garibaldi to the medieval nucleus of Cortona, Piazza Repubblica – the first bar on the left of Via Nazionale as you leave Piazza Garibaldi serves fine ice cream.

Events: Market day is Sat. There is an annual antique fair from Aug 25 – Sept 25.

Sights and places of interest

Leave time to explore some of its atmospheric old streets: Vie Benedetti, Maffei, Guelfa, Roma, Dardano, and Berretini.

Museo dell'Accademia Etrusca ⅢⅢ
Palazzo Pretorio, Piazza Signorelli 🔄 *Open Tues – Sun 10am – 1pm, 4 – 7pm.*

The Palazzo Pretorio, which houses the Etruscan Academy, was built in the 13thC and was later the residence of the Casali rulers; it was extended in the 17thC. In the main hall is the centerpiece, the famous but repulsive **Etruscan Lamp ★** (5thC BC), the largest and most elaborate Etruscan object of its kind. Small Etruscan objects are displayed in the glass cases, and among the pictures are the entrancing Greco-Roman painting on slate of the *Muse Polyhymnia* and a very fine Pietro da Cortona *Madonna and Saints*. The following rooms are filled with an intriguing, badly-labeled miscellany of Egyptian objects, porcelains, a good coin collection and, at the end, a small room devoted to Gino Severini.

Museo Diocesano ⅢⅢ
Piazza Trento Trieste 🔄 *Open daily summer 9am – 1pm, 3 – 6:30pm, winter 9am – 1pm, 3 – 5pm.*

This important museum is opposite the Duomo in a former church which was modified and partly frescoed by Vasari. Its rather gloomy atmosphere is lit up with the glowing spirituality of Fra Angelico's *Annunciation ★* (1433); the predella is unusually fine, especially the episode of the *Meeting at the Golden Gate*. The other Angelico, a triptych of the *Madonna and Child with Saints*, also has a superb predella depicting *Scenes from the Life of St Dominic*. Most notable among a number of Signorellis are his *Deposition* and *Communion of the Apostles*. Other highlights are the Sassetta *Madonna and Saints*; P. Lorenzetti's *Crucifix* and *Madonna and Angels*; and the Roman **sarcophagus decorated with Amazons and Centaurs**, admired by Brunelleschi and Donatello.

At the far end of Via Dardano is the **Porta Colonia**, the best-preserved section of Etruscan wall, which commands a wonderful view.

Other sights

The most charming of the churches is **San Domenico**, and behind it are public gardens where one may walk and enjoy fine views of the plain below. The **Sanctuary of St Margaret**, farther along Via S. Margherita, is an ugly 19thC church which conserves the beautiful Gothic **tomb of St Margaret**, by Angelo and Francesco di Pietro. From there it is a short climb to the **Fortezza Medicea**, commanding another magnificent view.

Nearby sights
Madonna del Calcinaio ⅢⅢ † ★
3km (2 miles) s, off Camucia road 🔄 *For entry ask custodian, who lives in adjacent farmhouse.*

A masterpiece of church architecture, designed (1485 – 1513) by the military engineer Francesco di Giorgio, and notable for the springing energy of the interior space, organized so that the crossing is lighted at all times of day by the round windows above. Vasari's answer, the church of **Santa Maria Nuova** (1554), is above the town.

There are four **Etruscan tombs** in the vicinity. Those at Sodo, to the NW towards Arezzo, and at Camucia, to the S towards Lake Trasimeno, are under huge mounds of earth known as *meloni*, and date from the 7th–6thC BC. The two near the Madonna del Calicinaio, the Grotta di Tanella and the Tanella Angora, may date from the 4thC BC.

3.5km (2 miles) to the NE, in a lovely location, is the **Convent Le Celle**, founded by St Francis between 1211–21; one may visit St Francis' cell and the little 16thC church.

☞ Gugliemesca ✿
Villa Gugliemesca, 52044 Cortona ☎ *(0575) 603365* ▥ *26 rms* ▭ *26*
▰ ▱ ⇌ AE ◉ CB VISA *Closed Nov–Mar.*
Location: 10km (6 miles) to N, on road for Città di Castello. This delightful, unpretentious hotel is perched in a wood on Monte Sant'Egidio.

☞ L'Oasi
Via Contesse 1, 52044 Cortona ☎ *(0575) 603188* ▥ *36 rms* ▭ *36* ▰
▱ ⇌ *Closed Nov–Mar.*
Location: Just outside walls to the S. L'Oasi retains the hushed atmosphere of the former convent in which it is housed. It is a clean, somber hotel.
▱ ⚘ ⚘ ⚘

☞ San Michele
Via Guelfa 15 (0575) 604348 ▥ *36 rms*
Recently opened in an old building in the center.

⇌ Local dishes are served in the cool, intimate, brick-vaulted rooms of **La Loggetta** (*Piazza Pescheria* ☎ *(0575) 603777* ▰ *closed Mon, Jan*); **Tonino** (*Piazza Garibaldi 1* ☎ *(0575) 603100* ▰ *closed Tues, Nov*) is a noisy restaurant known for its antipasti.

Elba ★
Map **10***/2–3. Province: Livorno. Getting there: By ferry, from Piombino, 1hr by car ferry, 30min hovercraft – ferries run frequently throughout the day, booking advisable in July–Aug from Livorno, daily boat takes 3hr direct to Portoferraio or 5hr with stops at islands of Gorgona and Capraia; by air, in summer, flights from Pisa. Getting around: By bus, the service is run by ACIT; by car, main car rental agencies are Avis, Arrighi (travel agents), Porto Azzurro* ☎ *(0565) 95000, Maggiore, Tessi (travel agents), Portoferraio* ☎ *(0565) 92386. Population: 28,429* **i** *Calata Italia 26, Portoferraio* ☎ *(0565) 92671.*

Elba is the largest of the Tuscan islands, at 27km (17 miles) long and 18km (11 miles) across at its widest, E end, with an extremely irregular coastal perimeter measuring nearly 150km (93 miles). The highest point is the summit of the granite Monte Capanne (1,018m; 3,340ft.) which dominates the wild western lobe of the island. Around the rest of the coast majestic cliffs alternate with inviting sandy bays backed by evergreens.

The iron ore of Elba has been mined for at least 3,000yr. The Greek name for the island was Aethalia (Soot Island) and the Etruscans transported the iron ore in great quantities to the mainland for smelting at *Piombino*; the main port was named Portoferraio (Port Iron) in the 8thC.

The more recent history of Elba was affected by two of the great modern imperialists: Duke Cosimo I of Florence and Napoleon. In 1548 Cosimo built and fortified Portoferraio, and called it Cosmopolis. His ostensible purpose was to police the pirate-infested Tyrrhenian Sea; his more compelling motive was to gain a stronghold against the forces of Spain and France. In the end he was obliged to share control of the island with the Spanish, who built their own fortress at Porto Azzurro.

In 1814 the Congress of Vienna ceded Elba to Napoleon as his

dominion in exile. He spent nine restless months here,
reforming the administration of the island, furnishing his two
villas, and plotting his escape, which took place on Feb 26, 1815.

The island can offer vacationers facilities for sailing,
waterskiing, spearfishing, tennis, golf and riding.

Hotels and restaurants on Elba

The standards of the 140 hotels on the island are extremely
variable. Many hotels insist on half-board, which is a pity,
because their kitchens can rarely cope with the fresh fish which
is the great gastronomic treat of Elba. Nearly every species of
Mediterranean fish is caught in the clear waters; which you
order will determine the price of the meal. All the local wines are
excellent, with a distinctive flavor from minerals in the soil.

A–Z of towns

Capoliveri

*Map 10I3. 5km (3½ miles) sw of Porto Azzurro. Population:
2,397.*

An isolated mining, fishing and wine-producing village on the
SE lobe of the island below the iron mountain of Monte
Calamita. Stunning views to the w.

≡ **Il Chiasso** (☎ *(0565) 968709* ▮▮ *closed Tues*).

Lacona

Map 10I3. 14km (9 miles) s of Portoferraio. Population: 200.
A quiet swimming resort on the s coast at the head of the long
promontory which Napoleon made into his hunting estate.

☞ **Capo Sud**
Lacona, 57037 Portoferraio, Isola d'Elba ☎ *(0565) 964021* ▮▢ *to* ▮▮▮
39 rms ▱ *39* ➡ ▱ ≡ ⊡ *Closed Oct–Apr.*
A quiet and comfortable group of cottages.
⌂ ▱ ⚓ ⚓ ⟨⟨ ⇗ ✂

Marciana

*Map 10I2. 27km (17 miles) w of Portoferraio. Population:
2,272.*
This wine-producing village on the slope of Monte Capanne is
dominated by the ruined castle of the Appiano, the hereditary
rulers of Elba in the Middle Ages. The **Antiquarium** (▨ *open
Thurs–Tues 10am–noon, 4–7:30pm, closed Wed; apply to
custodian in Via della Fonte*) displays pre-historic, Etruscan and
Roman material.

The **summit of Monte Capanne** ☆ is reached by funicular
(▮▮ ✳ *open daily 10am–noon, 2:30–6pm*) in 30 min or by mule
in about 2½hr. A 40min drive to the NW is the sanctuary of the
Madonna del Monte, where Napoleon stayed in 1814.

≡ **Publius** (*at Poggio* ☎ *(0565) 99208* ▮▮▮ *closed Oct–Easter*).

Marciana Marina

*Map 10I2. 20km (12½ miles) w of Portoferraio. Population:
1,907.*
A relatively unspoiled fishing village in a lovely open position.

☞ **Gabbiano Azzurro**
57033 Marciana Marina, Isola d'Elba ☎ *(0565) 99226* ▮▢ *39 rms*
▱ *39* ▤▤ ▱ ⟨AE⟩ ⟨VISA⟩
Modern, straightforward, friendly. No dining-room.

≡≡ **Rendez-Vous da Marcello**
Piazza della Vittoria ☎ *(0565) 99251* ▥ ▭ ◁∈ *Closed Wed in winter.*
Popular fish restaurant on the harbor.

Marina di Campo
*Map **10**/2. 17km (10½ miles) sw of Portoferraio. Population: 1,732.*
This fishing village and beach resort commands a wide arc of sand on the Gulf of Campo on the S coast.

≈☞ **Lo Scirrocco**
Loc. Fetovaia Casa 19, 57034 Campo nell'Elba ☎ *(0565) 987060* ▮▯
16 rms ▭ *16* ⌂ ⌂ ≡≡
Location: 9km (6 miles) w at Fetovaia. A handsomely decorated and comfortable private hotel overlooking a pleasant, isolated sand beach.
⌂ ≉ ⊠ ⊁ ⚓ ◁∈ ☞ ●

≈☞ An alternative is **Galli** (☎ *(0565) 987965* ▮▯ *closed Oct–Apr*).

≡≡ **Bologna**
Via Firenze 27 ☎ *(0565) 97105* ▮▯ ▭ AE CD VISA *Closed Tues except summer.*
A big, cheerful fish restaurant in an old boat house.

≡≡ **Da Gianni**
2.5km (1½ miles) N at La Pila Airport ☎ *(0565) 976965* ▮▯ *to* ▥ ▭
▰ *Closed Fri (except July–Aug) and Nov–Mar.*
A small, welcoming restaurant. ***Specialty:*** *Risotto di mare al forno.*

Porto Azzurro
*Map **10**/3. 15km (9 miles) se of Portoferraio. Population: 2,960.*
The center of the Spanish protectorate in the 16th–17thC, Porto Azzurro is still a charming sight from the Narengo side of the Gulf of Mola, although the harborfront has been spoiled by timid development. To the N is the massive Fortezza di Portolongone, built by the Spanish in 1603; soon afterward they built the nearby sanctuary of the **Madonna di Monserrato**, which still stands 1.5km (1 mile) to the N of the town.

Portoferraio
*Map **10**/3. Population: 11,135* ℹ️ *Calata Italia 26*
☎ *(0565) 92671.*
The busy main town of Elba is magnificently located on a promontory which shelters its fine harbor. The old port is guarded by two fortresses built by Cosimo I in 1548, the large **Forte del Falcone** and the picturesque **Forte della Stella**.

Sights and places of interest
Palazzina Napoleonica dei Mulini ☆
▨ *Ticket also good for Villa Napoleonica. Open Tues–Sat 9am–1:30pm, Sun, hols 9am–12:30pm.*
Napoleon created his residence in exile from two old windmills above the city near the Forte della Stella. The furnishings for this delightful little palace were commandeered from his sister Elisa's house at Piombino; the plate and library were brought from Fontainebleau.
Villa Napoleonica di San Martino ☆
6km (4 miles) to w, on Marciana road ▨ *ticket also good for Palazzina Mulini. Open Tues–Sat 9am–1:30pm, Sun, hols 12:30pm.*
Even in exile, an emperor must have a country estate; Napoleon filled this modest villa with personal symbols.
   The long Neoclassical **Pinacoteca Foresiana** (1851), nearby, houses a large collection of 16th–19thC art.

⚑ Hermitage
La Biodola, 5703 Portoferraio ☎ *(0565) 969932* 🕾 *500219 (summer 211116 (winter)* ▦ *100 rms* 🛏 *100* ▦ ⇌ 🏠 AE *Closed Nov–Apr*

Location: 10km (6 miles) SW at La Biodola. Discreetly set into a hillside overlooking a beautiful bay. **La Biodola** (☎ *(0565) 969966* ▯) is under the same management.
🏠 🗺 ▢ 🌙 ⚴ ⧫ ⇌ 🐾 ✌ ❀ ☻ ▼ ●

⚑ Picchiae Residence
57037 Portoferraio ☎ *(0565) 966072* ▦ *95 rms* 🛏 *95* 🚗 🏠 ⇌ AE ⧫ *Closed Oct–Apr.*

Location: 8km (5 miles) S of Portoferraio, off Porto Azzurro road. A modern, peaceful hotel offering marvelous views.
🏠 ⚴ ⧫ ⇌ 🐾 ⚘

⇌A restaurant in the town with pleasant outdoor tables is: **La Ferrigna** (*Piazza Repubblica* ☎ *(0565) 92129* ▯ *closed Tues, Dec, Jan*).

Procchio
*Map **10**|2. 10km (6 miles) SW of Portoferraio. Population: 532.*
One of the chief sand-beach resorts on the N coast.

⚑ Desirée
Lido di Spartaia, 57030 Procchio ☎ *(0565) 907502/3* 🕾 *590649* ▯ *to* ▦ *69 rms* 🛏 *12* 🚗 ⇌ 🏠 AE ⧫ VISA *Closed Nov–Apr.*
A modern and anonymous but efficiently managed hotel.
🗺 ⚴ 🌙 ⧫ ⇌ 🐾 🐾 🐟 ❀

⚑ ⇌ Golfo
57030 Procchio ☎ *(0565) 907565* 🕾 *590690* ▯ *to* ▦ *75 rms* 🛏 *75* 🚗 ▦ 🏠 AE ⧫ VISA *Closed Nov–Apr.*
A large, modern hotel in a pine wood with an especially attractive beach, and an unusually good restaurant.
⧫ ⇌ 🐾 🐾 🐟 ▼

Rio Marina
*Map **10**|3. 20km (12 miles) E of Portoferraio. Population: 2,420.*
This is the principal mining town of Elba, and on the third floor of the Palazzo Comunale is an interesting little **mineral museum** (🖃 *open Apr–Sept Mon–Sat 9am–noon, 3–6pm, Sun 9am–noon*). The **iron mines** may be visited on Sat in summer by appointment (☎ *(0565) 962001*).

Excursions
Island of Capraia
Boats depart from Portoferraio daily in summer, Mon and Wed in winter; the journey takes 2–3hr each way.

⚑ ⇌ **Il Saracino** (☎ *(0565) 905018* ▯ *closed Oct–Mar*).

Island of Montecristo
Hotels and travel agents will arrange party bookings to visit the deserted island now designated as a nature reserve.

Empoli
*Map **15**E5. 33km (20 miles) W of Florence. 50053. Firenze. Population: 45,802* **i** *Piazza Farinata degli Uberti* ☎ *(0571) 76115.*
The vast and unlovely sprawl around Empoli, an important center of glass manufacture, disguises exceptional works of art.

The painters Pontormo and Jacopo Chimenti, called Empoli, were born here. The modern composer Ferrucio Busoni was also a native of the area. There is a festival of Busoni's works in the autumn.

Sights and places of interest
Collegiata ⅢⅡ †
At the historic center of Empoli is the church which marks the western limit of the influence of Florentine Romanesque; the lower section of the facade dates from 1093. The upper part is a post-World War II reconstruction of F. Ruggieri's late-18thC 'rationalization.'
Museo della Collegiata ☆
Piazzetta San Giovanni, to the right of the Collegiata 🖼 *Open Tues – Sun 10am – noon.*

The museum incorporates the Baptistry of the Collegiata.

Ground Floor: A 15thC stone emblem shows the original appearance of the Collegiata facade; there is also a School-of-Donatello baptismal font, and a 16thC English brass lectern.

First floor: **Rm.** 5 contains Bicci di Lorenzo's *St Nicholas of Tolentino defends Empoli from the Black Death* (1445), interesting for the view of early 15thC Empoli. In **Rm.** 6: Lorenzo Monaco's *Madonna Enthroned with Saints* (1404); Bicci di Lorenzo's *Madonna Enthroned with Saints* (1423); two works by Pontormo, *St John the Evangelist* and *St Michael Archangel*; and a tabernacle of *St Sebastian*, sculpted by A. Rossellino and painted by Francesco Botticini. In **Rm.** 7 are two free-standing sculptures of the *Madonna Annunciate* and the *Angel Gabriel* (1447) by B. Rossellino; a *Madonna and Child*, usually attributed to the young Filippo Lippi; a tabernacle of the *Holy Sacrament* (1484) by Francesco and Raffaello Botticini. Two more images of the Madonna in this room are the relief sculptures by Tino da Camaiano (early 14thC) and by Mino da Fiesole (c.1465–70). **Rm.** 8: *Pietà* and other detached frescoes (c.1425) by Masolino, from the church of Santo Stefano; and frescoes of *St Andrew* and *John the Baptist*, rare works by Gherardo Starnina. **Rm.** 9: Terra-cottas from the Della Robbia workshop.

In the 14thC church of **Santo Stefano** in Via S. Stefano there is a *Madonna and Child* (1424) and other frescoes by Masolino.

Fiesole ☆
*Map **12**E6. 8km (5 miles) NE of Florence. 50014, Firenze. Population. 14,788. Getting there: No. 7 bus from Florence* **i** *Piazza Mino da Fiesole 45* ☎ *(055) 598720.*

When Florence was a mere cluster of buildings on the Arno, Fiesole, on its conical hill overlooking the valleys of the Arno and the Mugnone, was one of the chief cities of Etruria. Some scholars place the Etruscan settlement as early as the 8thC BC, although the town is not recorded until 225 BC. Faesulae was an important Roman military colony from 80 BC and later the capital city of Roman Etruria. In 1125 Florence sacked and superseded its mother city. *Pietra serena*, the cool gray stone employed so effectively by Florentine architects, comes from the nearby quarries of Monte Ceceri.

Fiesole is slightly cooler than Florence in summer, although the difference is often wishfully exaggerated.

Event: The *Estate Fiesolana*, a festival of concerts and films, takes place in the Roman Theater in July – Aug.

Sights and places of interest
The main square, on the site of the Roman forum, is the **Piazza Mino da Fiesole**.
Duomo †
The exterior of the Duomo (San Romolo), enlarged in the 13thC, was made dreary by a 19thC restoration. The **Cappella Salutati**, to the right of the choir, contains two fine works by Mino da Fiesole: the **tomb of Bishop Salutati**, and an altar front of the *Madonna and Saints*.

Museo Bandini
Via Dupré ☎ *(055) 59061* ▨ *Open Tues–Sun Mar–Apr, Oct 10am–12:30pm, 2:30–6pm; Nov–Feb 9:30am–12:30pm, 2–5pm; May–Sept 10am–noon, 3–7pm.*

A miscellany of furniture, majolica, Renaissance pictures and Etruscan fragments.

San Francesco †
Above the public gardens is this 14thC church enlarged in the 15thC but now nearly ruined by ill-considered restoration in the early 20thC. The cloisters are charming, and there are magnificent views.

Below S. Francesco is the ancient basilica of **S. Alessandro**, on the site of the Roman temple of Bacchus. The wonderful marble columns dividing the interior space are Roman.

Teatro Romano ▥ ☆
Via Marini ☎ *(055) 59477* ▨ *Hours as Museo Bandini.*

Atmosphere and views as well as the Roman theater (c.80 BC), which has a capacity of 3,000; it was rediscovered in 1809 and excavated in 1873. To the right are the baths, discovered in 1891, and to the left the Roman-Etruscan temple, first fully revealed in 1918. Behind is a stretch of **Etruscan wall**.

Nearby sights
Badia Fiesolana ▥ † ★
Ask at porter's lodge for entry.

300m NW of San Domenico, this was the cathedral of Fiesole until the 11thC. Cosimo il Vecchio commissioned an unknown architect to rebuild this church in the mid-15thC. The unfinished facade (1464) incorporates the little green and white Romanesque facade of the earlier church. The superb cruciform **interior** is one of the glories of Renaissance architecture.

San Domenico ▥ † ☆
In this hamlet, 1.5km (1 mile) sw of Fiesole, is the monastery of S. Domenico, built for Dominican monks in the early 15thC. Fra Angelico took religious orders here and was prior from 1449–52. The church portico and campanile were added in the 17thC by Matteo Nigetti, and the **interior** remodeled in the late 15th–early 16thC, when the elegant stone arches to the nave chapels, some by Giuliano da Sangallo, were added. Over the first altar on the left is the fascinating **altarpiece** by Fra Angelico (c.1428), with its background repainted by Lorenzo di Credi (c.1501), recently cleaned.

In the convent, to the right of the church portico (*ring for admission*), the Chapter House has a fresco of the *Crucifixion* by Fra Angelico. His fresco of the *Madonna and Child*, now damaged, was in the church.

Villa Medici
Just to the w of the center of Fiesole. Not open to the public.

This was one of the first pleasure villas of the Renaissance, probably built for Cosimo il Vecchio by Michelozzo.

☜ Villa San Michele ▥
Via Doccia 4, 50014 Fiesole ☎ *(055) 59451* ☎*570643* ▥ *28 rms* ▨ *28* ☞ ▤ ☞ ☞ *AE* ⊕ *◑* *VISA* *Closed mid-Nov to Feb.*

In a 14thC villa enlarged in the 15thC by Santi di Tito, the hotel is furnished like a private villa, with four-poster beds, old oak wardrobes and original fireplaces.

⌂ ‡ ⛭ ⌷ ▱ ⚡ ⚓ ⚜ ≈ ⛵

☜ At San Domenico: **Bencistà** (☎ *(055) 59163* ▯ *to* ▥) *closed Nov–Mar*) is a comfortable old villa, as is **Villa San Girolamo** (☎*(055) 59321* ▯), run by Irish sisters.

☰ Unpretentious favorites in the center are: **Mario** (☎ *(055) 59143, closed Tues*); **Pizzeria Etrusca** (☎*(055) 5998838* ▯), both in Piazza Mino da Fiesole; nearby, **La Romagnola** (*Via Gramsci 43* ☎ *(055)59258* ▯ *closed Mon*); at San Domenico, **Le Lance** (*Via Mantellini 2b* ☎ *(055) 599090, closed Mon, Jan*) is a superior pizzeria with a terrace. At Pratolino, **Zocchi** (☎ *(055) 409202* ▥ *closed Mon*) is a big, sunny restaurant offering a huge array of antipasti and meat from the charcoal grill. See also *Bivigliano, Settignano*.

Forte dei Marmi

Map **14**D2. *104km (65 miles)* w *of Florence, 34km (21 miles)*
NW *of Lucca. 55042. Lucca. Population: 10,193* **i** *Piazza
Marconi* ☎ *(0584) 80091.*

Forte dei Marmi is the quiet, discreet upper-class resort of the
Versilia laid out in near rows among the pine wood and used
mainly by Italians. The fort (1788) stands in the central piazza.

Hotels

If you have not booked a hotel, you will find a good selection of
all categories in Viale Morin.

Augustus
Viale Morin 169, 55042 Forte dei Marmi, Lucca ☎ *(0584) 80202*
🕾*590673* **IIII** *to* **IIII** *81 rms* 🛏 *81* 🍴 🚗 🛥 ⇌ AE ⊕ ⓒ VISA
Closed Oct to mid-May.
A modern hotel near the beach.
🏠 ‡ 🕯 🔲 🖊 ⚓ 🔌 ⇌ 🐾 🎾 ⛵ ➤ 🎯 ⊙

Hermitage
Via Cesare Battisti ☎ *(0584) 80022* 🕾*590673* **IIII** *65 rms* 🛏 *65* 🍴 🚗
🚗 ⇌ AE ⊕ ⓒ VISA *Closed Oct–May.*
A luxury hotel noteworthy for its unusually good restaurant, **Il Pozzetto**.
🏠 ‡ 🕯 🔲 🖊 ⚓ 🔌 ⇌ 🐾 🎾 ⛵ ➤ 🎯 ⊙

Tirreno
Viale Morin 7, 55042 Forte dei Marmi, Lucca ☎ *(0584) 83333* **IIII**
59 rms 🛏 *59* 🚗 ⇌ AE ⊕ *Closed Oct–Easter.*
An attractive second-category hotel in an old villa.
🖊 🔌 🚗

Also: **Astoria Garden** (*Via Leonardo da Vinci 10* ☎ *(0584) 80754* **IIII**
closed Nov–Mar); **Bell'Ombra** (*Viale Morin* ☎ *(0584) 82225* ▢ *closed
Nov–Mar*), a decent, cheerful *pensione*; **Raffaelli Park** (*Via Mazzini 37*
☎ *(0584) 81494* **IIII**

⇌ La Barca
Viale Italico 3 ☎ *(0584) 89323* **IIII** ▭ 🍴 🚗 ◁ AE ⊕ ⓒ VISA
Closed Mon eve, Tues, Nov.
Overlooking the beach, one of the most pleasant fish restaurants.

⇌ Also: **Bagno Bruno** (*Via Arenile 22* ☎ *(0584) 89972* **IIII** *closed Mon*);
Cervo Bianco (*Via Risorgimento 9* ☎ *(0584) 89640* **IIII** *closed Wed, Nov*).

Gaiole in Chianti

Map **12**F6. *69km (43 miles)* SE *of Florence, 28km (17 miles)*
NE *of Siena. 53013. Siena. Population: 2,627.*

The medieval lord of this market town in the Chianti Classico
zone was one of the founders of the original Chianti league. On a
hill to the E, which can be climbed in 15min on foot, is the
medieval village of **Barbischio**. The fortified **Fattoria Meleto**
stands in the midst of its vineyards 2.5km (1½ miles) to the S.

⚲ ⇌ Castello di Spaltenna 🏛
Just above Gaiole to the W ☎ *(0577) 749483* **IIII** *7 rms* 🛏 *7* ▭ ⇌
🚗 ◁ AE *Closed Mon, Tues lunch, Nov–March.*
Austere but comfortable rooms and good traditional Tuscan cooking in
the monastery of the 13thC Pieve di Spaltenna.

⇌ Badia a Coltibuono 🏛
Coltibuono, 5km (3 miles) to NE ☎ *(0577) 749424* **IIII** ▭ ⇌ 🍴 🚗
◁ AE ⊕ ⓒ VISA *Closed Mon, early Nov to mid-Dec.*
The 11thC ex-monastery buildings (which include a Romanesque
church) are now part of an active wine estate, where wine and oil are on sale.

Galluzzo (Certosa del) 🏛 † ☆

*Map **6**E3. 6km (4 miles) s of Florence ☎ (055) 2049226. Bus no. 36 or 37 from Florence* 🅿 *✗ Open daily summer 9am–noon, 3–6pm; winter 9am–noon, 2.30–5pm.*

The monastery which stands impressively above the Via Cassia was founded by the Florentine Niccolò Acciaiuoli in 1342. The **Pinacoteca** is housed in the Gothic Palazzo degli Studi; the dominating works are Pontormo's damaged **lunettes of the Passion cycle** (1522–25), detached from the *chiostro grande*. They were painted while he was living in the monastery during a plague in Florence and, although deeply influenced by Dürer, are striking examples of the Mannerist style Pontormo helped to invent. There are also paintings by Mariotto di Nardo, Dürer and Ridolfo del Ghirlandaio. The church of **S. Lorenzo**, in its large 16thC courtyard, has a high *pietra serena* facade (1556). The interior is divided into two sections: the Monks' Choir (with good 16thC stalls) and the Lay Brethren's Choir. A staircase leads to the subterranean chapels where members of the Acciaiuoli family are buried. The superb **tomb slab of Cardinal Agnolo II Acciaiuoli** was attributed to Donatello by Ruskin and others, but is now thought to be 16thC. Notice also especially the Gothic **monument to N. Acciaiuoli**.

The monastic complex includes the *parlatorio*, with 16thC stained glass; the *sala capitolo*, with a frescoed *Crucifixion* by Mariotti Albertinelli; the *chiostro grande*, embellished with 66 terra-cotta medallions of *Saints and Prophets* by Andrea and Giovanni della Robbia. Off the *chiostro grande* are the cells. The pharmacy sells liqueurs distilled in the monastery.

Gargonza

*Map **12**G7. 80km (50 miles) SE of Florence, 28km (17 miles) sw of Arezzo. 52048. Arezzo.*

The 13thC houses in this tiny fortified village, where Dante took refuge after learning of his exile from Florence, can be rented by the week or, out of season, by the night. Gargonza is freely open to visitors, complete and unspoiled within its walls.

🏠 ⚞ Castello di Gargonza

Info and bookings: Count Roberto Guicciardini, Castello di Gargonza, 52048 Monte San Savino, Arezzo ☎ (0575) 847021 or (055) 296151 🆔571466 **Ⅲ** *to* **Ⅲ** *40 rms in 20 houses* 🛏 *in each house* ▤▤ ⟷ 🆑 ⟻ *Closed Jan.*

The interiors have been attractively modernized, and the high position, surrounded by woodland, is open to cooling breezes and extensive views of the Valdichiana. The restaurant, **Il Castello** (☎ *(0575) 847065* **Ⅲ** *closed Mon*), just outside the walls, offers plain Tuscan cooking.

🏠▨ ⚐ ≪ ⌖ ➤ ☞ 🛆

Giglio

*Map **8**K4. 14km (9 miles) SE of Monte Argentario. Getting there: By boat, 1hr from Porto Santo Stefano. 58013. Grosseto. Population: 1,706* i *Via Umberto 1, Giglio Porto* ☎ *(0564) 809265.*

The second largest island in the Tuscan archipelago, Giglio is wilder, poorer and much smaller than *Elba*, being only 8.5km (5 miles) long and 5km (3 miles) across at its widest. The three centers – Giglio Porto, Giglio Castello, a hilltop town, whose maze of steep traffic-free streets is surrounded by anti-pirate walls, and Campese – are linked by a hair-raising bus service. Campese is the main sand-beach resort and there are other sand beaches at Cala dell'Arenella and Cala delle Cannelle.

☞ The **Arenella** (☎ *(0564) 809340* ▯▯ *to* ▮▮▮) is quiet and adequately comfortable; in Giglio Porto is the bright, clean and modest **Il Saraceno** (☎ *(0564) 809006* ▮▯).

🍽In Giglio Porto: **Il Doria** (*Via Thaon de Revel* ☎ *(0564) 809000* ▯▯ *closed Oct to Easter*); **Da Ruggero** (*Via Umberto 1* ☎ *(0564) 809253* ▮▯ *closed Oct to Easter*); at Giglio Castello, open in the evenings only, is **La Galera** (*Via della Casa Matta* ☎ *(0564) 806106* ▮▯).

Greve

Map **12***F6. 27km (17 miles) s of Florence, 40km (25 miles) N of Siena. 50022. Firenze. Population: 10,232.*

The main market town of the Chianti is graced with a delightful asymmetrical central square, Piazza Matteotti, lined with porticoed 17thC buildings.

    Events: Market day is Sat, and a wine fair is held in Sept.

☞ **Villa le Barone**
Via San Leolino 19, 50020 Panzano in Chianti, Firenze ☎ *(055) 852215* ▮▮▮▮ *25 rms* 🛏 *25* 🚗 🍽 🏠 AE *Closed Nov–Mar.*
An exceptionally attractive country villa in an isolated position.
🏠 🎿 ⚓ 🏔

🍽 The calm, pleasant **Giovanni da Verrazzano** (*Piazza Matteotti* ☎ *(055) 853189* ▮▮▯ *closed Sun eve, Mon*), with some rooms. Outside the town, **Trattoria Cappelli** (*s on the SS222* ☎ *(055) 852014* ▮▮▯ *closed Mon*) is part of the Montagliari wine estate, serves good chianina beef.

🍽 **Omero** ✿
Passo dei Pecorai, 5km (3 miles) to N ☎ *(055) 850716* ▭ ▭ ▬
🍴 *Closed Wed, Aug.*
A classic family restaurant. **Specialties:** *Homemade pastas and desserts.*

Grosseto

Map **8***I5. 141 km (87 miles) s of Florence, 73km (45 miles) s of Siena. 58100. Grosseto. Population: 69,301* 🛈 *Viale Mongerosa 206* ☎ *(0564) 22534.*

Grosseto is the principal city of the Tuscan Maremma, the coastal plain where the natives regard themselves as a special and separate breed of Tuscans, toughened by centuries of hardship and proud of their land's recently restored fertility.

    In the period of the great Etruscan cities which flourished here, the area to the NE of Grosseto was a navigable gulf. By the Middle Ages it was a freshwater lake, which eventually subsided into malaria-infested swampland.

    The history of the Maremma after the fall of the Roman Empire was that of a battlefield contested by Florence, Siena, the Papal States and pirates from the Barbary Coast. When it became part of the Sienese territories in the late Middle Ages it was scantily populated; and in the mid-18thC, two centuries after the Florentine conquest of Siena, the area was nearly deserted. The first effective efforts to reclaim the land and rid the Maremma of malaria were initiated by the Lorraine grand duke Leopold II in 1828, but it was not until the early years of this century that significant progress was made. In 1943–44, Grosseto was the victim of severe bombing raids. The early 1950s saw a systematic program of agricultural incentives and repopulation, and since then the population of Grosseto has grown by more than five times.

    It is against this violent background that Grosseto today must be seen. Its spirit is that of a modern city which has not quite discovered its own character.

Sights and places of interest

The main square is Piazza Rosselli, just to the N of Porta Nuova. What remains of the original urban nucleus is contained within an impressive hexagon of bastioned **brick walls** built by the 16thC Medici. Traffic is prohibited in the center.

Duomo †

Originally built in 1294–1302, but the imitation Romanesque facade dates from 1845; inside is a 15thC font and, in the left transept, an *Assumption* by Matteo di Giovanni.

Museo Archeologico e d'Arte della Maremma ☆

Piazza Baccarini 3 🕿 *(0564) 27290* 👁 *Open Mon, Tues, Thurs–Sat 9:30–12:30pm, 4:30–7pm, Sun, hols 9:30–12:30pm. Closed Wed.*

The collection is displayed chronologically beginning with prehistory and ending with 13th–17thC paintings on the second floor.

The ground floor is largely devoted to material excavated from *Roselle.* On the first floor is a topographical explanation of the Etruscan Maremma and material from the sites. On the second floor are 13th-17thC Sienese pictures of which the most noteworthy are Sassetta's *Madonna of the Cherries* and Pietro di Domenico's *Pietà.*

San Francesco †

Piazza della Independenza.

Over the high altar of this 13thC Gothic church is a *Crucifixion*, an early work by Duccio.

🍴 Near the museum is the sensible, modest **La Maremma** (*Via Fulceri P. dei Calboli 5* 🕿 *(0564) 21177* 🔳 *closed Tues*); near the station, **Enoteca Ombrone** (*Viale Matteotti 63–73* 🕿 *(0564) 22585* 🍴 *closed Sat eve, Sun, early July, early Jan*) has an extensive cellar. Outside the town, **La Casareccia**, to the N on the road to *Roselle* at Poggione (*Via Senese 202* 🕿 *(0564) 451470* 🔳 *to* 🍴 *closed Wed, Aug*) is a friendly little restaurant with high gastronomic standards.

Impruneta

*Map **12**E6. 14km (9 miles) s of Florence. 50023. Firenze. Population: 14,884.*

This large agricultural village is located on a plateau overlooking the Greve and Ema valleys.

Event: The lively agricultural fair of St Luke in mid-Oct.

Sights and places of interest

Santa Maria dell'Impruneta 🏛 †

The fine porticoed facade which overlooks the main square was added in 1634; the tall bell tower is 13thC. The design of the handsome **aedicules** (1456) flanking the entrance to the polygonal presbytery is attributed to Michelozzo, and they are embellished with terra-cotta decorations by Luca della Robbia. To the right of the church are two pretty cloisters.

🍴 **Bellavista**

Via della Croce 2 🕿 *(055) 2011083* 🍴 🔳 ▭ 🍴 *Closed Thurs, Nov.*

This unpretentious, cozy, small-town restaurant specializes in traditional Florentine cooking.

🍴 **I Tre Pini**, 6km (4 miles) N at Pozzolatico (🕿 *(055) 208065* 🍴 *closed Mon, mid-Aug*) is pleasant in summer.

Istia d'Ombrone

*Map **11**I5. 140 km (87 miles) s of Florence, 7km (4⅜ miles) NE of Grosseto. 58040. Grosseto. Population: 1,405.*

A medieval village with one of the best restaurants of the Tuscan Maremma.

Nearby sights

13km (8 miles) to the SE, taking the road for Scansano, an unpaved road near Pancole leads to the **Castello Sergardi di Montepo**, a romantic fortified 16thC castle.

≈ **Terzo Cerchio** ✿
Piazza del Castello 1 ☎ *(0564) 409235* ▥ ▬ ▆ ⬭ AE VISA
Closed Mon, Nov.
It was in the third circle (*terzo cerchio*) of hell that Dante observed the fate of gluttons, and if this outstanding restaurant has a fault it is the temptation to commit gluttony. You choose from a succession of courses brought to your table. The unlabeled Scansano wine is excellent.

La Verna
Map 13E8. 75km (47 miles) SE of Florence, 58km (36 miles) N of Arezzo. 52010. Arezzo.

Monastery †
This monastery, reached by a beautiful twisting road of 26km (16 miles) from *Bibbiena*, was founded in 1214 by St Francis, who received the stigmata here on Sept 14, 1224. The chief artistic attractions are the Andrea della Robbia terra-cottas in the churches, of which the loveliest are the *Annunciation* and *Adoration of the Child* in the Chiesa Maggiore.
   Above the monastery is a magnificent **forest** of old beeches and firs.

Livorno
Map 10F3. 116km (72 miles) w of Florence, 19km (12 miles) s of Pisa. 57100. Livorno. Population: 177,101
i Piazza Cavour ☎ *(0586) 33111; at the port, Palazzo Dogana* ☎ *(0586) 25320.*
The major commercial port of Tuscany and still one of the greatest in the Mediterranean, Livorno was the creation of the Medici grand dukes – their most ambitious and successful project. The transformation of the medieval fishing village into a port which would more than compensate for the silted-up port of Pisa was initiated by Cosimo I in 1571. Six years later, the new 'ideal city' of Livorno designed by Buontalenti was founded. In 1593 Ferdinand I declared Livorno an open city, guaranteeing tax exemptions, free trade with all international ports, and freedom of worship for all religions; and in 1621 that remarkable Englishman, Robert Dudley, the marine engineer in the service of the grand dukes, completed the extension of the harbor with his great Medicean *mole* (harbor wall).
   By 1600 Livorno had a population of 5,000, enlivened, then as now, by a substantial Jewish community. 18thC foreign visitors found it a charming as well as prosperous city with many fine contemporary palaces. These disappeared along with the charm and the historic center during the bombardment of 1943.
   The old English name Leghorn, from the early Italian Legorno, is rarely used today except, of course, to describe the type of straw hat first made here in the 19thC.

Sights and places of interest
The old pentagonal center envisaged by Buontalenti is bisected by its main street, Via Grande, which links the huge harbor complex with the Piazza Repubblica. The city is guarded by two fortresses: the Fortezza Nuova (1590) above Piazza Repubblica, and the Fortezza Vecchia (1534), designed by Antonio da Sangallo the Younger, in the harbor.
Monument to Ferdinand I (*'Quattro Mori'* or *'Four Moors'*)
Piazza Micheli.
Facing the old harbor, this esthetically controversial monument consists of a statue of *Ferdinand I* (1595) wearing the order of St Stephen by G. Bandini and the **four bronze Moors** added by P. Tacca in 1626. Some admire these straining Michelangeloesque figures; others would say that they combine ineptitude with unfeeling virtuosity. The diarist John Evelyn, who was of the first opinion, described the scene he

149

witnessed in this piazza in 1644 when Livorno was the chief slave port of the northern Mediterranean: "Here. . . . is such a concourse of slaves, Turcs, Moors and other nations, that the number and confusion is prodigious; some buying, others selling, others drinking, others playing, some working, others sleeping, fighting, singing, weeping, all nearly naked, and miserably chained." The **English Cemetery** (*Via Verdi 63*) was the first Protestant cemetery in Italy. Tobias Smollett lies here.

Museo Civico G. Fattori
Villa Fabbricotti 🖼 *Open Tues – Sat 10am – 1pm, Thurs, Sat also 5 – 8pm in summer, 4 – 7pm in winter.*

☛ The **Gran Duca** (*Piazza Micheli 16* ☎ *(0586) 32024* ▥) faces the harbor.

▤ **La Banditella da Cappa** (*Via Diego Angioletti 3* ☎ *(0586) 501246* ▥ *closed Sun, Aug*); **Oscar** (*Via O. Franchini 78* ☎ *(0586) 501258* ▥ 🖵 🍽 *closed Mon, early Sept, late Dec*) and **A1** 77 (*Via Mondolfi 77* ☎ *(0586) 502038* ▥ *closed Sun, mid-Oct to mid-Nov*), are the best fish restaurants, all at Ardenza, a pretty beach, immediately s of Livorno.

▤ Also: **Antico Moro** (*Via di Franco 59* ☎ *(0586) 34659* ▯ *closed Wed, Aug*); **La Barcarola** (*Viale Carducci 63* ☎ *(0586) 402367* ▥ *closed Sun, Aug*); **Da Norma** (*Via Provinciale Pisana 60* ☎ *(0586) 401032* ▥ *closed Sun, late Aug*); **La Parmigiana** (*Piazza Luigi Orlando* ☎ *(0586) 807180* ▯ *closed Sun*), near the harbor.

Lucca ★

Map 14E3. 74km (46 miles) w of Florence, 22km (14 miles) NE of Pisa. 55100. Lucca. Population: 91,814 **i** *Via Vittorio Veneto 40* ☎ *(0583) 46915.*

Alone of all the Tuscan city-states, Lucca resisted the thrust of Florentine imperialism and remained independent of united Tuscany until the 19thC. The town is still a separate and special place, its narrow medieval streets, red-brick palaces and tower houses and elaborate Romanesque churches encircled by the best-preserved 16th – 17thC walls in Italy.

A Roman colony from 180 BC, capital city of Tuscany under the medieval Lombard and Frankish emperors, and a free commune from 1119, Lucca emerged in the early 14thC as the second richest city in Tuscany. Under the forceful leadership of the merchant-soldier Castruccio Castracani, Lucca became a serious threat to Florence; but Castracani's death in 1328 left the government divided and open for short periods to subjection by its enemies.

In 1369 Lucca was granted a charter of independence by the Emperor Charles IV. Representative governments alternated with periods of signorial rule until the mid-16thC when the oligarchy closed ranks against the populace. Thus protected from internal opposition the Republic fortified itself against the threat of Cosimo I's pan-Tuscan policies with its new ring of walls and retained its autonomy until 1799. Napoleon gave Lucca to his sister Elisa Baciocchi as a principate in 1805; in 1817 it passed as a duchy to Maria Louisa de Bourbon; and in 1847, Lucca was finally absorbed into the Tuscan grand duchy.

The Romanesque churches of the Tuscan silk town are in the Pisan style, richly embroidered with polychrome marble insets and relief carvings executed for the most part by visiting Lombard and Pisan sculptors. Another, later visitor, Jacopo della Quercia, carved a number of works for Lucca including his early masterpiece, the tomb of *Ilaria del Carretto* in the Duomo. The most talented local sculptor, hardly represented outside his native city, was Matteo Civitali, active in the 15thC.

In the 16th–18thC the Lucchese nobility built grand summer retreats in the cool hills to the NE. These villas (see *Excursions*) are among the most exhilarating examples of Mannerist and Baroque architecture in Tuscany. The Anglicized gardens of many of the villas testify to Lucca's long-standing special relationship with Britain.

Events: The birthplace of Luigi Boccherini and Giacomo Puccini is still musically active. In spring and early summer there is a festival of sacred music performed in the churches. Concerts of contemporary and classical music are held throughout the *Estate Musicale* from July to Sept, and in Aug a festival of music and theater takes place in the Villa at Marlia.

The feast of the Holy Cross is celebrated on the previous evening with a procession from S. Frediano to the Duomo.

An itinerant antique market comes to Piazza San Martino on the second Sun of each month.

Sights and places of interest

Piazza Napoleone is the main square. The Neoclassical monument to *Maria Louisa de Bourbon* in the center is by L. Bartolini. The Palazzo della Provincia (begun 1578) on the W side is based on designs by Ammannati; its early 19thC interior is by L. Nottolini.

A delightful walk can be taken along the tree-shaded path on the 4.2km (3 miles) ring of **ramparts**. Be sure also to see **Via Guinigi** and **Via Fillungo**, well-preserved medieval streets.

Duomo ▥ † ★

Erected in the 11th–13thC, the cathedral's asymmetrical facade (1204) is largely the work of Guidetto da Como. Under the portico are fine relief carvings (begun 1233) by a Lombard master. The interior was Gothicized in the 14th–15thC. Four of Puccini's ancestors served here as organists and choir-masters.

In the left transept is Jacopo della Quercia's **tomb of Ilaria del Carretto** ★ (c.1406), his earliest surviving masterpiece and the first sculptural creation of the Renaissance to use Roman decorative motifs. The statue of *St John the Evangelist* nearby is also by Jacopo. In the adjoining chapel is an exceptionally fine panel of the *Madonna with Sts Stephen and John the Baptist* by Fra Bartolommeo. In the left nave is the **tempietto** (1484) by Matteo Civitali which houses the Volto Santo, the 11thC effigy of Christ carried through the city in procession on Holy Cross eve. Other works in the Duomo by Civitali include the pulpit (1498) in the right nave, and, in the right transept, two angels (1477) and the monumental S. Regalo altarpiece.

Museo Nazionale ▥

Villa Guinigi ▨ *Open Tues–Sat 9am–2pm, Sun, hols 9am–1pm.*
The Villa Guinigi was built in 1418 for Paolo Guinigi, political leader of Lucca from 1400–30.

Ground floor: Etruscan and Roman pieces excavated locally; works by Lucchese sculptors of the 8th–15thC, including M. Civitali.

First floor: 13th–19thC paintings, intarsia work, furniture and textiles. One of the painted crosses in Rm. XI is signed by Berlinghieri. In Rm. XIV are two altarpieces by Fra Bartolommeo.

Pinacoteca Nazionale ▥

Palazzo Mansi, Via Galli Tassi 43 ▨ *Open Tues–Sat 9am–2pm, Sun, hols 9am–1pm.*
This collection of Renaissance to 19thC pictures from the Medici collection was given to Lucca by Leopold II. The 17thC palace retains much of its elaborate furniture.

San Frediano ▥ † ★

Erected from 1112–47 on the site of a 6thC basilica. The mosaic of the *Ascension* on the facade, possibly by Berlinghieri, was heavily restored in the 19thC. Inside, the 12thC font at the top of the right nave is decorated with relief carvings of the story of *Moses*, the *Good Shepherd* and the *Apostles*. In the Trenta Chapel at the bottom of the left aisle are reliefs by

Jacopo della Quercia and assistants, notably a Gothic polyptych
altarpiece (1422) with a superb predella.

Across the Via Fillungo the oval outline of the Roman amphitheater is
traced by medieval houses forming the intensely picturesque **Piazza
Anfiteatro** ☆ Via Cesare Battisti, which twists s towards S. Michele in
Foro, is flanked by 17th–18thC palaces.

San Michele in Foro Ⅲ † ☆
A few steps to the N of Piazza Napoleone, Piazza San Michele occupies
the site of the Roman forum. On the corner of Via Vittorio Veneto is the
Renaissance **Palazzo Pretorio**, designed by M. Civitali, altered in the
16thC.

Begun in 1143, the church of S. Michele is a typical example of
Pisan-Lucchese architecture. The high white marble facade belongs to
the 13thC and the Lucchese tradition of rich decoration; the apse is in the
Pisan style, possibly by Diotisalvi. Inside is a *Madonna and Child* by
Andrea della Robbia and, in the left transept, a panel painting of *Four
Saints* by Filippo Lippi.

Among other notable churches in Lucca are S. Giovanni, S. Maria
Forisportam, S. Giulia and S. Alessandro.

ᐅ Napoleon
Viale Europa 1 ☎ *(0583) 53141* ▥▥ *63 rms* ▤ *63* ▦ ▭ ▱ ▰ ⇌
Location: Outside the walls to the sw. Thoughtfully modernized behind
the earlier villa facade.
‡ ☐ ▱ ⚓ ⚓

⇌ Two excellent restaurants within the walls are **Buca di
Sant'Antonio** (*Via della Cervia 3* ☎ *(0583) 55881* ▯ *closed Sun eve,
Mon, late July*), where regional specialties are served, and the simpler **Da
Giulio in Pelleria** (*Via San Tommaso 29* ☎ *(0583) 55948* ▯ *closed
Sun, Mon in Aug, Christmas*). In the countryside nearby are **Solferino**
(*San Macario in Piano* ☎ *(0583) 59118* ▯ *to* ▯▯ *closed Tues eve, Wed,
Aug*), which has one of the most ambitious kitchens in rural Tuscany; and the
charming **Vipore** (*Pieve Santo Stefano* ☎ *(0583) 59247* ▯▯ *closed
Mon, Tues lunch, 10 days in Jan*).

See also *Excursions* below.

Shopping
Many gourmets consider the olive oil of Lucca to be the best
produced in Italy – be careful that you are buying real Lucca oil.
Ice cream parlor
Gelateria Veneta di Arnoldo (*Via Vittorio Veneto 74*
☎ *(0583) 47037*) serves the best ice cream in town.

Excursions
1. Villas outside Lucca ★
Head N from Lucca on the *Abetone* road, along the E bank of
the River Serchio. After 16km (10 miles) is the 11th–12thC
Pieve di Brancoli.

Then make for Marlia, near Fraga.
Villa Imperiale Ⅲ
Marlia ▨ ▦ *Open July–Oct Tues, Thurs, Sun 9am–noon, 3–6pm;
Nov–June Tues–Sat 9am–noon, 3–6pm.*
The most famous and imposing of the villas near Lucca, adapted and
redecorated in First Empire style when it was the summer residence of
Elisa Baciocchi. Magnificent 17thC park.

Take the road for Segromigno Monte.
Villa Mansi Ⅲ
3km (1½ miles) E *of Marlia* ▨ ▱ *Open daily 10am–12:30pm,
3–6pm.*
A late-16thC villa transformed in the early 18thC with a charming facade
and good Baroque furnishings and pictures on the first floor. A tavern
attached to the villa serves produce from the estate.

Take the road for Camigliano.

Villa Torrigiani 🏛
1.5km (1 mile) s of Segromigno 🚾 *Open daily Easter to Nov
9am–1pm, 2–6pm; park always open in daylight.*
Built in the 16thC, with a spectacular Mannerist facade. The 17thC park
was Anglicized in the 19thC except for the sunken garden and the
ingenious surprise fountains.

〓 La Mora
Via Sesto Moriano 104 ☎ *(0583) 57109* 🍽 🖵 🍴 〓 🚗 🚙 〈€ AE
CB ① CD VISA *Closed Wed eve, Thurs.*
Near Ponte a Moriano, 9km (6 miles) from Lucca. The shop sells wines
and olive oil. **Specialties:** *Antipasti, tacconi, Gran Faro.*

2. Santa Maria del Giudice 8km (5 miles) sw of Lucca
Two Romanesque churches in the Pisan-Lucchese style: **San
Giovanni Battista**, and **Santa Maria Assunta**.

〓 Da Peppino is large, modern, popular (☎ *(0583) 379482* 🍽 to 🍽🍽
closed Mon, Aug).

Massa
*Map **14**D2. 115km (71 miles) NW of Florence, 45km (28
miles) NW of Pisa. 54100. Massa–Carrara. Population:
65,814.*
A booming, untidy frontier town at the mouth of the Frigido
valley below the foothills of the Apuan Alps, Massa did not
become part of Tuscany until 1859, and it is still the least
'Tuscan' of Tuscan provincial capitals.

Piazza Aranci, the old center, is dominated by the startling
17thC Palazzo Cybo Malaspina, which encloses an attractive
loggiaed courtyard (1665) by G.F. Bergamini. The Duomo has
a modern facade and a Baroque interior.

Above the town is the medieval **Rocca** (🚾 *open Tues–Sat
9am–noon, 4–7pm*) and a Renaissance palace which was the
residence of the 16thC Malaspina dukes.

Massa Marittima
*Map **10**H4. 132km (79 miles) sw of Florence, 64km (40 miles)
sw of Siena. 58024. Grosseto. Population: 10,297 **i**
(summer only) Palazzo Comunale ☎ (0566) 902296.*
The mineral-rich territory of Massa Marittima was mined by
the Etruscans and Romans; the copper and silver mines were
the economic base of the independent republic which was
constitutionally established in 1225 and flourished proudly
until it was conquered by Siena in 1335. The Duomo, one of the
most beautiful and richly decorated churches in Tuscany, was
erected during the period of communal independence; and the
first miners' code in Europe was drawn up in the city in 1310.

Event: The *Balestra del Girofalco*, a crossbow competition
with a mechanical falcon as target, takes place in medieval
costume on May 20 and second Sun in Aug.

Sights and places of interest
The town is in two distinct parts: the Romanesque lower town
or Città Vecchia is linked by Via Moncini to the Gothic upper
town or Città Nuova, built after the Sienese conquest.

The center of the old town is Piazza Garibaldi.

Duomo 🏛 † ★
This lovely cathedral in the Pisan Romanesque-Gothic style was
completed between 1287–1304. The **relief carvings** over the portal

depict five episodes in the life of San Cerbone, patron saint of the cathedral, with the beguiling beasts that helped him. The campanile rising from the arcaded left flank was largely reconstructed in the 1920s.

At the top of the right aisle is the font, where St Bernardino was baptized in 1380, with relief carvings (1267) by Giraldo da Como and a 15thC tabernacle rising from its center. In the chapel to the left of the high altar is a panel painting of the *Madonna della Grazie* (c.1316), closely influenced by Duccio's *Maestà* in *Siena*.

Ask the sacristan to unlock the access door to the subterranean chapels. In the polygonal undercroft is the exquisite **Arca di San Cerbone** (1324), San Cerbone's tomb, by the Sienese sculptor Coro da Gregorio in a painterly style influenced by illuminated manuscripts.

Opposite the Duomo is the **Palazzo Comunale**, the town hall created from a complex of 14th–15thC tower houses.

Museo/Palazzo del Podestà ▥

🖸 *Open summer Tues–Sun 10:30am–12:30pm, 4–7pm.*
The magistrate's palace, c.1230, now houses a small archeological collection and Sienese pictures; outstanding is A. Lorenzetti's *Maestà*.

Upper town (*Città Nuova*)

The upper town is guarded by the huge **Fortezza dei Senesi**, built by the Sienese after their conquest of Massa Marittima in 1334. Its center is Piazza Matteotti, from where the Corso Diaz leads to the Gothic church of S. Agostino (1299–1313), which possesses interesting 16th–17thC pictures by Empoli, Pacchiarotti, Lorenzo Lippi and others.

Nearby sights

Museum of Mining (Museo della Miniera) in Viale Martiri di Niccioleta (🖸 *hours as museum in Palazzo del Podestà*).

━━ **Roma** (*Via Norma Parenti 17–19* ☎ *(0566)* 902644 ▢ *closed Wed*).

Montalcino

*Map **8**H6. 109km (67 miles) s of Florence, 41km (25 miles) s of Siena. 53024. Siena. Population: 5,702* **i** *Via Mazzini 41* ☎ *(0577) 848242.*

Montalcino stands on an olive-clad hill above the Ombrone and Asso valleys. The site was inhabited by the Etruscans and Romans, and in the early Middle Ages belonged to the Benedictine abbey of **Sant'Antimo** (see opposite). A period of communal independence came to an end in 1260 when the town was subjected to Sienese rule after the battle of Montaperti. Montalcino provided sanctuary for Sienese aristocratic Republicans who fled their besieged city in 1555. Sienese gratitude is still expressed twice a year when the standard the procession which precedes the Palio.

Brunello di Montalcino is one of the great Italian wines.

Sights and places of interest

Piazza del Popolo is the main square; the **Palazzo Comunale** with its high tower dates from the 13th–14thC; the imposing loggia was added in the 14th–15thC. Above, in Piazza Garibaldi, is the church of **Sant'Egidio** built by the Sienese in 1325. Over the first altar on the left notice the wooden *Crucifixion* (15thC) framed by 16thC inlaid wooden doors.

The **Rocca** which dominates the town was built by the Sienese in 1361 and was one of the most crucial defense posts of the Republic. Inside is an *enoteca* of local wines.

Museo Civico e Diocesano

Via di Ricasoli 29 🖸 *Open daily summer 10am–noon, 4–6pm; winter 10am–noon, 3–5pm.*
Below the Rocca, this museum houses 14th–15thC Sienese pictures; ecclesiastic objects including a 12thC illuminated bible; 15thC

polychrome wooden statues; and a separate archeological collection.

In Piazza Cavour is the former pharmacy of the Hospital of Santa Maria, frescoed by V. Tamagni.

Nearby sights
Sant'Antimo ▥ † ★
Near Castelnuovo Abate, 8km (5 miles) to s. Apply for entry to custodian at Via del Centro 12, Castelnuovo Abate.
This radiantly lovely Romanesque church, set in a gentle golden valley, is built of travertine with architectonic decorations in alabaster and translucent onyx quarried locally. It dates mostly from the early 12thC. The monastery was founded, according to tradition, by Charlemagne early in the 9thC. The doorway on the left flank, adorned with geometric carvings in the Lombard style, and the crypt survive from the earlier building. The beautiful **interior** is embellished with fine capitals. There are frescoed apartments off the clerestory.

≈ ⇌ The best of the restaurants in the center of the town is **Il Giglio** (*Via S. Saloni 49* ☎ *(0577) 848167* ▯ *closed Mon, late Feb*).

⇌ **Taverna dei Barbi**
2km (1¼ miles) s of Montalcino, off the Sant'Antimo road
☎ *(0577) 848277* ▥ ▯ 🍽 🏠 ⇌ ≪ ◖ *Closed Wed.*
Superb Brunello wines with a limited selection of plain Tuscan food.

Monte Amiata
Map 8H6.
The isolated conical peak of this extinct volcano 1,738m (5,702ft.) high is visible from Siena and in much of its art.

"Surely here, if anywhere in the world," wrote the Sienese Pope Pius II in his *Commentaries*, "sweet shade and silvery springs and green grass and smiling meadows allure poets." The upper slopes are equipped for skiing and climbing.

The summit is most easily reached from *Abbadia San Salvatore*, the most populous center. Other, more picturesque villages, are Arcidosso, Bagnone, Castel del Piano, Piancastagnaio and Santa Fiora.

Montecatini Terme
Map 15D4. 49km (30 miles) NW of Florence, 49km (30 miles) NE of Pisa. 51016. Pistoia. Population: 21,764 i *Viale Verdi 66* ☎ *(0572) 70109. The season is Apr–Oct.*
One of the most famous and fashionable spas in Europe, Montecatini Terme was laid out in the early 20thC around a stately park. The warm saline waters are recommended for liver ailments and skin problems. The café of the **Stabilimento Tettuccio** is the main meeting place.

From Viale A. Diaz, a funicular railway ascends to the beautifully located old town, Montecatini Alto. To the N there is lovely walking country in the Valdinievole.

Nearby sight
8km (5 miles) s at Ponte Buggianese is the church frescoed by the modern painter Pietro Annigoni.

≈ Montecatini has some 500 hotels, mainly clustered around the **Parco delle Terme**; most open only during the season. The best-known luxury hotel is the **Grand Hotel e la Pace** (*Via della Torretta 1* ☎ *(0572) 75801* ▥▥ *closed Nov–Mar*).

⇌ A very classy restaurant in the center is the **Enoteca da Giovanni** (*Via Garibaldi 25* ☎ *(0572) 71695* ▥ ▱ ◉ *closed Mon, late Jan*). In the old town above is the highly recommended ≈ ⇌ **Vittoria** (*Viale della Libertà 2* ☎ *(0572) 79271* ▯ *closed Nov–Mar*).

Montefollonico

Map 12H7. 112km (70 miles) SE of Florence, 60km (37 miles) SE of Siena. 53040. Siena. Population: 820.

A walled hill village overlooking the valleys of the Orcia and Chiana. There is also an unpaved road from *Montepulciano* which can be walked in 45min.

⇶ La Chiusa

☎*(0577) 669668* ▥ ▢ ⊟ ⇌ ⫷ AE ◉ *Closed Tues, Jan–Mar.*

Like so many of the greatest Italian restaurants, La Chiusa specializes in local produce prepared according to the most refined culinary traditions of the area. Before embarking on the feast you would be wise to discuss the menu and top price with the enthusiastic young proprietors.

Monte Oliveto Maggiore

Map 8J6. 104km (65 miles) SE of Florence, 36km (22 miles) SE of Siena. 53020. Siena.

The abbey †

▣ *Open daily 9am–12:45pm, 3–7pm.*

Magnificently located above the barren clay hills near *Siena*, the red-brick buildings of this abbey date from the 14th–18thC; their institutional appearance is the result of a 19thC restoration.

The **chiostro grande** is decorated with important but heavily restored and overpainted frescoes of *Scenes from the Life of St Benedict*. Nine are by Signorelli (1497–98), the rest by Sodoma (from 1505). In the church the intarsiaed **choir stalls** (1503–05) by Giovanni da Verona are exceptionally sophisticated exercises in perspective.

⇶ **La Torre** (☎*(0577) 707022, closed Tues* ▢).

Montepulciano ☆

Map 12H7. 119km (74 miles) SE of Florence, 65km (40 miles) SE of Siena. 53045. Siena. Population: 14,297 i Via Cavour 15 ☎*(0578) 77049.*

Like *Pienza*, 14 km (9 miles) to the W, Montepulciano is neither town nor village, but a miniature Renaissance city. See these two little hill cities one after another and you will have captured the essence of the 15thC urban ideal as realized by some of the most distinguished Italian architects of the period. From the 12thC, Montepulciano modeled itself on Florence and Siena, its political masters. Its fortifications were rebuilt when Montepulciano fell to the Sienese in 1495–1511.

Agnolo Ambrogini, the leading humanist poet and scholar of the 15thC and tutor to Lorenzo de' Medici's children, was born in Montepulciano and called himself Poliziano after the medieval Latin name of his birthplace, Mons Politianus. The Jesuit Cardinal Robert Bellarmine was largely responsible for the flourish of Baroque architecture which followed.

Vino Nobile di Montepulciano is a redoubtable Tuscan wine.

Event: An annual music festival, the *Cantiere Internazionale d'Arte*, takes place here in early Aug. Founded in 1975 and run by a distinguished international committee, it emphasises community involvement in performances of 20thC music.

Sights and places of interest

Follow the Corso from Porta al Prato to the far end of the town and loop back along its western edge.

The Corso

Via Gracciano nel Corso: The Corso is lined with good Renaissance palaces. No. 99, Palazzo Avignonesi, is attributed to Vignola; no. 72, the Cocconi, is attributed to Antonio da Sangallo the Elder. The lower story of no. 81, the Palazzo Bucelli, is faced with a mosaic of Etruscan and Roman tombs and cinerary urns. On the right is Michelozzo's delightful, Gothic-Renaissance church of **Sant'Agostino**; the lovely terra-cotta relief over the portal of the *Madonna and Child with Sts John the Baptist and Augustine* is also by Michelozzo.

Via di Voltaia nel Corso: The palace on the left, the Cervini, no. 21, with graduated rustication and a breaking-wave frieze, was designed by Antonio da Sangallo the Elder but not completed. Farther along on the left is the church of Gesù, which has a charming curved Baroque interior.

The last stretch of the Corso, **Via dell'Opio**, leads to the Via del Poliziano past no. 5, the house where Poliziano was born in 1454, to the Gothic church of S. Maria dei Servi, which has a Baroque interior.

The highest point of Montepulciano is its center, the wide and splendidly various **Piazza Grande**.

Duomo †

Designed by Ippolito Scalza and built on the site of the earlier parish church from 1592–1630, the Duomo contains a superb altarpiece of the *Assumption* (1401), possibly Taddeo di Bartolo's best work. Michelozzo's **Tomb of Bartolomeo Aragazzi**, dismantled in the 17thC, is now displayed in fragments placed to the left of the entrance, on the first two pillars of the nave, on either side of the altar and elsewhere. Notice also, in the right nave, the 15thC Sienese school polychrome *Annunciation*.

The **Palazzo Comunale**, next to the Duomo, was begun in the late 14thC, but its facade is later, possibly designed by Michelozzo. Opposite are the Tarugi (no. 3) and Contucci (no. 6) palaces by Antonio da Sangallo the Elder.

Museo Civico 🏛

Via Ricci 11 📧 *Open Tues–Sun 9.00–13.00, 17.00–18.00.*

The Gothic Neri-Orselli Palace houses 13thC–17thC paintings, terra-cottas and 15thC illuminated choir books.

Nearby sight

San Biagio 🏛 † ★

Situated just outside the town to the sw, this church (1518–45) is the masterpiece of Antonio da Sangallo the Elder. The densely classicizing interior, all in the same pale-honey travertine, is weighted with loyalty to the architectural principles of Bramante. The **Canon's House** and **well-head** were also designed by Sangallo but completed posthumously.

🛏 � Il Marzocco

Piazza Savonarola 🕿 *(0578) 757262* ▯ *18 rms* 🛏 *13* 🍴 � AE ℗ VISA

Conveniently located inside the walls, this small hotel-restaurant offers clean, cozy rooms and good, simply prepared food. ♥

� Fattoria Pulcino

Strada per Chianciano 37 🕿 *(0578) 757905* ▯ 🍴 ➼ 🚗 ➤ ◁Ɛ *Closed mid-Feb.*

2.5km (1½ miles) from Montepulciano on the Chianciano road, this heartily informal country restaurant serves meats grilled over cured wood and eaten at long communal tables. Local wines, oil and cheeses as well as wholesome snacks can be bought from the **Osteria Porta di Bacco** (🕿 *(0578) 757907, at the same address*).

See also *Montefollonico*.

Monteriggioni

*Map **11**F5. 55km (34 miles) s of Florence, 15km (9 miles) nw of Siena. 53035. Siena. Population: 6,573.*

A complete medieval village encircled by 13thC walls built by the Sienese against the Florentines: Dante compared the 14 towers to giants (*Inferno, XXXI*).

Nearby sight

Abbadia Isola †

Less than 3km (1¾ miles) sw, this tiny village conserves a Romanesque church in the Lombard style from the 11thC Cistercian abbey of

S. Salvatore. The church possesses an altarpiece (1471) by Sano di Pietro; a fresco of the *Madonna and Child with Saints* by Taddeo di Bartolo; an early 15thC font; and an Etruscan-Roman cinerary urn. In the priest's house is a *Madonna and Child*, possibly by Duccio.

⌂ ≡ Casalta
Strove, 53035 Monteriggioni, Siena ☎ (0577) 50701 ▯ *10 rms* ▭ *10*
◕ ▭ ≡ VISA *Closed Nov–Mar. Restaurant closed Wed.*
A well-managed hotel and restaurant serving above-average Tuscan food, 6km (4 miles) sw past Abbadia Isola.
⌂ ◁

≡ Il Pozzo
Piazza Roma 2 ☎ (0577) 304127 ▯▯ ▭ AE ◉ *Closed Sun eve, Mon, Aug.*
An elegant and efficient country restaurant.

Monte San Savino
*Map **12**G7. 86km (53 miles) SE of Florence, 22km (14 miles) sw of Arezzo. 52048. Arezzo. Population: 7,565.*
An agricultural hill village, birthplace of the sculptor Andrea Sansovino. The main street is the Corso Sangallo, lined with fine palaces and churches. The little church of Santa Chiara in Piazza Gamurrini contains terra cottas by Sansovino and other sculptors. Sansovino is thought to have designed the handsome **Loggia dei Mercanti** farther along the Corso. The **Palazzo Comunale** opposite is by Ant. da Sangallo the Elder.

⌂ Sangallo (*Piazza Vittorio Veneto ☎ (0575) 843010* ▯▯).

≡ Good restaurants at Lucignano, 6km (4 miles) s, include **La Rocca**, **La Tavernetta** and **Da Totò**.

⌂ ≡ See also *Gargonza*.

Monti dell'Uccellina, Parco Naturale della Maremma ☆
*Map **11**I-J5. 157km (98 miles) s of Florence, 17km (10 miles) s of Grosseto. Entrance at Alberese ☎ (0564) 407098* ▨ 🛈 *on foot ✳ Open Wed, Sat, Sun, hols.*
The extremely varied ecological balance of the coastal terrain is protected in the Maremma Nature Reserve. Demonstrations of cattle roping are sometimes given by the local *butteri* (cowboys).

≡ **Tonale**, an isolated farmhouse at Podere Tonale near Alberese (☎ (0564) 407027 ▯ *closed Thurs*). See also *Talamone*.

Orbetello
*Map **8**J5. 183km (113 miles) s of Florence, 43km (27 miles) s of Grosseto. 58015. Grosseto. Population: 14,749* 🛈 *Corso Italia 121 ☎ (0564) 867389.*
The capital of the Spanish Garrison States, the *Presidii*, from 1557 retains something of the atmosphere (and the faces) of a Spanish colonial town. The fortifications on the mainland side were initiated by the Sienese and extended by the Spanish.
    The **Duomo** (1376) has a pretty Gothic facade decorated in the Sienese style. In the first chapel on the right is a rare pre-Romanesque marble **altar front**.
    The **Orbetello Oasis**, a sanctuary for migrating birds, is nearby. For information ☎ (0564) 860239.

Presidi (*Via Mura di Levante* ☎ *(0564) 867601* ▮▯ *to* ▮▮▯) is a sensible, friendly hotel on the lagoon.

Osteria del Lupacante (*Corso Italia 103* ☎ *(0564) 867618* ▮▮▯ *closed Wed, Jan*) has a large terrace and the most interesting food. Also pleasant are **Il Cantuccio** (*Via Mentana 7* ☎ *(0564) 867587* ▮▮▯ *closed Mon, Nov*), and **Egisto** (*Corso Italia 190* ☎ *(0564) 867469* ▮▮▯ *closed Mon, Dec*).

Two restaurants 7km (4½ miles) NE on the Via Aurelia near Orbetello Scalo, both with rooms, are: **Il Cacciatore** (☎ *(0564) 862020* ▯ *closed Wed*); and **La Ruota** (☎ *(0564) 862137* ▮▮▯ *closed Thurs*). See also *Ansedonia*, *Port'Ercole*, *Porto Santo Stefano*.

Pescia
*Map **15**D4. 61km (38 miles) NW of Florence, 19km (12 miles) NE of Lucca. 51017. Pistoia. Population: 18,979.*

This horticultural and papermaking center in the Valdinievole is renowned for its carnations and asparagus. The town has been divided into five districts or *quinti* since the 13thC. The civic centre, Piazza Mazzini, is on the right bank of the River Pescia; the religious center, Piazza del Duomo, on the left bank.

Sights and places of interest
Piazza Mazzini
The long, narrow square is a lively architectural farrago of 14th–19thC houses, closed at the S end by the 15thC **Oratory of the Madonna di Piè di Piazza**, possibly designed by Brunelleschi's adopted son Buggiano, and at the N end by the 13th–14thC Palazzo dei Viacri.

In the nearby Piazza S. Stefano is the **Museo Civico** (▭ *open Mon, Wed, Fri 4–7pm*) with Tuscan paintings of the 14th–16thC.
Duomo †
The Baroque Duomo (1693) has a late 19thC facade and a sturdy Romanesque-Gothic campanile. Inside are the Renaissance **Turini Chapel** by G. di Baccio d'Agnolo, and the remains of a 13thC ambo.
San Francesco †
Via Battisti.

The restored interior of this Gothic church contains a rare Romanesque painting by Bonaventura Berlinghieri of *St Francis* (1235), executed only 9yr after the death of the saint. The Brunelleschian **Orlandi-Cardini Chapel** (1451) may have been designed by Buggiano.

Also in Via Battisti is the 11th–14thC Oratory of Sant' Antonio containing a moving wooden group of the *Deposition*.

The huge steel and glass flower market, the **Nuovo Mercato dei Fiori**, occupies a site of 48,000sq.yd. on the road to Chiesina Uzzanese.

Nearby sights
3km (1¾ miles) to the E of Pescia is the beautifully located village of Uzzano, and 12km (7 miles) to the N is the isolated **Pieve di Castelvecchio** (11th–12thC), the area's best Romanesque church.

See also *Collodi*.

Cecco ❀
Viale Forti 84 ☎ *(0572) 477955* ▮▮▯ ▭ ⮡ ⮌ ⮎ 🆑 *Closed Mon, mid-Nov to early July.*

Pleasant service and exceptional food. In Apr and May try the local *asparagi giganti*. **Specialties:** *Pastas, pollastrino al mattone*.

Pienza★
*Map **9**H7. 120km (75 miles) S of Florence, 52km (33 miles) S of Siena. 53026. Siena. Population: 2,622 **i** Vicolo della Canonica 1* ☎ *(0578) 74558.*

Few men have left such a vivid and complete picture of their period as did Enea Silvio Piccolomini, born in 1405 of an impoverished branch of a noble Sienese family, Pope as Pius II from 1458–64, in his candid autobiography, the *Commentaries*.

Pienza, the Utopian city with which he glorified his humble birthplace, Corsignano, is the first modern example of considered town planning. This joyous little Renaissance new town is a celebration of the bracing winds of change that blew from every direction through the culture of 15thC Italy. It is a meeting ground of the Gothic and Renaissance styles, of the German church architecture Pius had seen on his travels and the strict Classical principles laid down by Alberti, of Florentine and Sienese art, of the Tuscan countryside and the sophisticated urbanity of the Tuscan quattrocento spirit.

As soon as Pius was elected Pope he commissioned Bernardo Rossellino to rebuild Corsignano. Work began in 1459. Three years later the piazza and street grid were complete and the new city was renamed Pienza by Papal bull. Pius left instructions that his cathedral, "the finest in all Italy," should never be altered in the smallest detail. The remote location of Pienza has ensured that his order was carried out.

Sights and places of interest

The central **Piazza Pio II** is like an open-air room looking S through the two window spaces on either side of the cathedral, which is flanked by the Palazzo Piccolomini on the right and the Palazzo Vescovile (Bishop's Palace) on the left. The N side is closed by the Palazzo Comunale and a wing of the Ammannati Palace, built by one of Pius' cardinals. The beautifully carved wellhead (1462) was designed by Rossellino.

Cattedrale ⅢⅢ †

The travertine facade follows Alberti's Classical principles of organization. On the pediment is the papal coat of arms. The interior was inspired by the German *Hallenkirchen* Pius admired.

He specially commissioned the **paintings** by illustrious Sienese artists: Giovanni di Paolo, Matteo di Giovanni, Vecchietta and Sano di Pietro. The Classical frames and the decorative carvings elsewhere in the church were executed by Sienese craftsmen. The Gothic **canons' stalls** (1462) in the central chapel are magnificent. In the crypt, below the apse, is a **baptismal font** by Rossellino.

Museo della Cattedrale

▧ *Open daily Nov−Feb 10am−1pm, 2−4pm; Mar−Oct 10am−1pm, 3−6pm.*

In the Canon's House. Sienese paintings, Flemish tapestries, illuminated choir-books and ecclesiastical vestments including, most notably, the **cope** embroidered for Pius II in England.

Palazzo Piccolomini ⅢⅢ

Piazza Pio II ▧ *First floor open daily 10am−12:30pm, 3−6pm; ring bell for admission.*

The papal residence is a rougher version of Alberti's and Rossellino's *Rucellai Palace, Florence*, with one important addition, the three-tiered loggia on the S side. The elegant courtyard gives access to the hanging gardens below the palace.

Palazzo Vescovile

Pius acquired for Rodrigo Borgia, the future Pope Alexander VI, the old Gothic Palazzo Pretorio, which Borgia adapted and later gave to the city.

Pieve di Corsignano †

Below the town, 1km (⅔ mile) from the Porta al Ciglio. Pius II was baptized in the rough stone font which remains in this endearing little Romanesque church which now stands alone in a sloping olive grove.

═◀ **Il Prato**

Piazza Dante 25 ☎ *(0578) 748601* ▯ *Closed Wed, July.*

Excellent antipasti − and don't fail to sample the vin santo.
   See also *Montalcino*, *Montefollonico* and *Montepulciano*.

Shopping

The **Bottega Verde** (*Corso Rossellino 38*) sells wine and herbs.

Pietrasanta

*Map **14**D3. 104km (64 miles) NW of Florence, 35km (22 miles) N of Pisa. 55045. Lucca. Population: 25,722 **i** Via Donizetti 14, Tonfano ☎ (0584) 20332.*

The main town of the Versilia and center of marble working is 3.5km (2 miles) inland from its coastal resort Marina di Pietrasanta. The imposing 13th–14thC Duomo is much restored.

Event: An exhibition of marble work by local artisans is held July–Sept in the Consorzio Artigiani.

≡ **Il Gatto Nero** (*Piazza Carducci 32* ☎ *(0584) 70135* ▥ *closed Mon, Oct*) is a family-run restaurant with personality; **Wagener,** 3.5km (2 miles) E at Valdicastello Carducci (☎ *(0584) 772018* ▢ *closed Thurs*) offers homey food in an old marble workshop. See also *Forte dei Marmi*.

Pisa ★

*Map **14**E3. 91km (56 miles) W of Florence, 3km (2 miles) N of Galileo Galilei international airport at S. Giusto. 56100. Pisa. Population: 103,849 **i** Piazza del Duomo ☎ (050) 23535.*

The golden age of Pisa was the 12thC, when the Duomo was completed and the Baptistry and Campanile were begun. Pisa had enjoyed a modest maritime economy even during the Dark Ages, thanks to its natural harbor at the mouth of the Arno, and was favored by successive emperors who needed the support of its strong navy. In 1162 Emperor Federico Barbarossa granted the commune control of a large coastal territory stretching to the N and S beyond the modern Tuscan borders.

The Duomo, a mix of the Italian and Oriental styles familiar to Pisan sailor merchants, was widely copied and infused

Tuscan Romanesque architecture with new vigor. In sculpture, too, Pisa led the way, producing in Nicola and Giovanni Pisano the first great modern figure sculptors.

After the destruction of its fleet by the Genoese at the battle of Meloria in 1284, the communal government, distracted by internal conflict, neglected the shallow harbor, which began gradually to silt up. The city fell to Florence in 1406, the port in 1421. There was one final bid for independence in 1495 when Pisa, under the protection of Charles VIII, revolted, not to be retaken until 1509.

The Florentines paid special attention to the welfare of their prize conquest, which remained commercially active even after the harbor had finally silted up in the 16thC. The University, which is today one of the most respected in Italy, was revived in 1472 by Lorenzo de' Medici, who temporarily forbade Florentines to study elsewhere, and in 1561 Cosimo I made Pisa headquarters of his new Crusading Order of St Stephen.

Pisa's most illustrious son was Galileo, who taught at the University (which has had a strong science faculty ever since). In the 19thC when Walter Savage Landor, Shelley, Byron and later the Brownings all made their homes in Pisa for short periods, the city was a brooding backwater shrouded in the mists of its Maremma where the rich grazing lands had once been a source of its republican prosperity. Elizabeth Barrett Browning found it "very beautiful and full of repose"; but to Shelley's more feverish imagination Pisa sometimes seemed "a desolation of a city, which was the cradle, and is now the grave of an extinguished people." In the last years of World War II some of Pisa's greatest monuments were severely damaged.

Events: The annual *Regatta di San Ranieri*, a race among the city's four historic quarters, is held on the evening of June 17.

The *Gioco del Ponte*, a mock battle in 16thC costume between residents of the Mezzogiorno (s of the Arno) and Tramontana (N of the Arno), takes place on June 28.

Concerts are given in the Palazzo dei Cavalieri, Dec-May.

Sights and places of interest

The center of the modern city is Piazza Garibaldi. Immediately to its s is the **Ponte di Mezzo**, the city's oldest bridge, which gives the best view of the elegant palaces lining the Arno.

Campo dei Miracoli *(Piazza del Duomo)* ★

▣ *Open daily 9am–1pm, 3pm to sunset.*

The buildings of Pisa's religious center are placed on their emerald lawn like carved ivory pieces in a great ecclesiastical game. The complex is enclosed on the w and N sides by sections of the 13thC city walls.

Baptistry IIII ✝ ★

▣ *Open daily 9am–1pm, 3pm to sunset.*

Begun in 1152 by Diotisalvi, carried forward from 1260–84 by Nicola and Giovanni Pisano, the Baptistry was completed by its Gothic dome in the 14thC. Of the four beautiful portals notice especially the one facing the Duomo. The *Madonna* in the lunette is a copy of Giovanni Pisano's original now in the Museo Nazionale. Inside, to the left of Guido da Como's octagonal **baptismal font** (1246), is Nicola Pisano's **pulpit** ★ (1260); the style of his relief carvings was affected by the Roman sarcophaghi which in the 13thC were used as the tombs of Christian Pisans buried around the Duomo; this pulpit marks the first appearance in Italy of Classical Gothic sculpture. The panels illustrate the *Nativity*, *Epiphany*, *Presentation at the Temple*, *Crucifixion* and *Last Judgement*. The statues around the walls, by Nicola and Giovanni Pisano, were originally on the exterior of the Baptistry.

Campanile IIII ✝ ★

▣ *Open daily 9am to sunset.*

The circular bell tower of Pisa is perhaps even more famous for leaning 4.5m (15ft) out of line than for its architectural elegance. Begun in 1173, its foundations were tilted by a settling of the soil when the third story was half built. After a pause of 100yr the tower was completed in the mid-14thC. It is, of course, from this tower that Galileo is supposed to have dropped the three metal balls of different masses which disproved Aristotle's theories about the acceleration of falling bodies. A spiral staircase of 294 steps leads to the top.

Camposanto *(Cemetery)* ✿

📷 *Open daily 9am to sunset.*

Legend has it that earth for the cemetery of Pisa was brought in shiploads from the Holy Land early in the 13thC. This sacred ground was enclosed by a rectangular building begun in 1277 and completed in the 15thC. The walls of the interior portico were frescoed by leading Italian artists including Taddeo Gaddi, Spinello Aretino and Benozzo Gozzoli. Over the centuries, a precious collection of antique sarcophaghi was assembled here. What could be salvaged from wartime damage has been painstakingly pieced together; but the ghostly frescoes speak more eloquently through their sinopias, now in the **Museo delle Sinopie**.

The most interesting works are in the N section. In the N portico are the remains of Gozzoli's popular *Grape Harvest* and *Drunkenness of Noah*; and, among other fine sarcophaghi, the 2ndC AD sarcophagus depicting *Phaedra and Hyppolitus* which affected the style of Nicola Pisano's Baptistry pulpit. Off the portico, to the left of the Cappella Ammannati, is the **Salone degli Affreschi**, where the greatest of the Camposanto frescoes, detached and restored, are hung. The most famous is the *Triumph of Death* (*Trionfo della Morte*) by an unknown late-14thC master, which inspired Liszt's *Totentanz*, hence the bust of the composer near the entrance. Among the sculptures are Giovanni Pisano's *Madonna and Child*, and five statues from Tino da Camaiano's *Tomb of the Emperor Henry VII* in the Duomo.

Duomo ⅢⅢ † ★

Open daily 7:45am–1pm, 3pm to sunset.

The most influential Romanesque building in Tuscany and the first to be dressed in black and white horizontal stripes, the Duomo was begun in 1064 by Buscheto; its tiered facade was added in the 12thC by Rainaldo. Entrance is normally by the Porta di San Ranieri on the s transept; the crudely energetic and touching bronze doors (1180) by Bonanno represent *Scenes from the Life of Christ*.

The grandly proportioned interior consists of a nave with double aisles crossed by unusually deep transepts. The interior was heavily restored in the early 16thC after a devastating fire. At the bottom of the left side of the nave is Giovanni Pisano's **pulpit** ★ (1302–10). It bears an inscription suggesting that this extremely complex work caused the artist considerable worry. The result was one of the most personal and dramatic sculptural masterpieces of its own or indeed any time. The relief panels divided by figures of prophets and saints, depict scenes from the New Testament beginning with the *Birth of the Baptist*, facing the column. The sequence continues with the *Annunciation, Visitation, Nativity, Adoration of the Magi, Presentation at the Temple, Flight into Egypt, Slaughter of the Innocents, Kiss of Judas* and *Passion, Crucifixion, The Elect,* and *The Damned*.

In the E corner of the right transept is a reconstruction of Tino da Camaiano's **tomb of Emperor Henry VII**, commissioned when the sculptor was made Head of Works of the Cathedral in 1315. On the balustrade flanking the entrance to the presbytery are two **bronze angels** by Giambologna, who also made the *Crucifix* over the high altar. On the right as one enters the presbytery is Andrea del Sarto's charming *St Agnes*. More paintings by Andrea hang below the choral galleries. The 13thC mosaics of the *Redeemer in Glory* in the vault of the apse were completed with the head of *St John the Evangelist* by Cimabue in 1302. Below hang good canvases by Beccafumi.

Museo delle Sinopie ✿

☎ *(050) 22531* 📷 *Open 10am–1pm, 3–5pm.*

Opposite the s side of the piazza, in the Ospedale Nuovo della Misericordia, this fascinating display of preparatory drawings, revealed by the detachment of the Camposanto frescoes, is a unique opportunity to study the technique of some of the leading artists of the 13th–15thC. They include the *Triumph of Death* and Gozzoli's *Scenes from the Old Testament* and *Annunciation*.

Museo Nazionale di San Matteo ★

Lungarno Mediceo ☎ *(050) 23750* 🚾 *Open Mon–Sat 9am–2pm, Sun, hols 9am–1pm.*

Behind the church of San Matteo on the Lungarno Mediceo, a former convent, once used as a prison, now houses a superb collection of Pisan sculpture and 12th–15thC Tuscan pictures. Among the many outstanding pieces, notice especially: **figures from the exteriors of the Duomo and Baptistry** by Giovanni Pisano; the *Madonna of the Milk* by Andrea Pisano, formerly in Santa Maria della Spina; two *Crucifixes* by Giunta Pisano; the *Madonna and Child* and *Scenes from the Childhood of Christ* by the Master of San Martino; Simone Martini's polyptych of the *Madonna and Child with Saints*; Masaccio's *San Paolo*, part of a polyptych (of which the other sections are now scattered or lost) that was the master's first major work.

Nearby on the Lungarno Mediceo is the Toscanelli palace where Byron lived in 1821–22.

Piazza dei Cavalieri ☆

Five minutes' walk from the Duomo is the central square of medieval Pisa, rebuilt in the 16thC by Vasari as headquarters of the Knights of the Order of St Stephen. The **Palazzo dei Cavalieri** (1562) is decorated with splendid and fantastic *sgraffiti* incorporating the busts of six Medici grand dukes.

To its right is the church of **S. Stefano dei Cavalieri** (1569), also designed by Vasari but with a later facade. The **Palazzo dell'Orologio**, on the N of the square, was adapted in 1607; it stands on the site of the tower where Count Ugolino della Gherardesca and his male heirs were starved to death by their political rivals in 1288; this episode, grimly described by Dante in *Inferno, XXXIII*, inspired Shelley's poem *The Tower of Famine*.

Santa Maria della Spina ⅢⅢ † ★

Lungarno Gambacorti. Open daily 8am–noon.

Named after a thorn from Christ's crown brought from the Holy Land by a Pisan merchant, this beautiful church was the swan song of the Pisan Gothic style. The last of the great Pisan churches and perhaps the loveliest, it assumed its present size in the 1320s. The building originally stood closer to the Arno; in 1871 it was moved, stone by stone, to its present drier site.

Other sights

Other Pisan churches well worth visiting are S. Caterina, S. Francesco, S. Michele in Borgo, S. Paolo a Ripa d'Arno, S. Nicola, S. Sepolcro, S. Zeno, S. Frediano.

⌬ Dei Cavalieri

Piazza della Stazione 2 ☎ *(050) 43290* ☎ *590663* ⅢⅢ *102 rms* ▭ *102*
🔲 🔲 🔲 ⇌ AE ◐ ⓪ VISA

Conveniently located near the station and air terminal, this well-managed modern hotel has an elegant and tranquil restaurant.
♨ ☞ ♨

⌬ Ariston

Via Maffi 42 ☎ *(050) 24255* ▭ *33 rms.*

A basic hotel near the Duomo.

⌁ Sergio

Lungarno Pacinotti 1 ☎ *(050) 48245* ⅢⅢ *to* ⅢⅢ ▭ 🍴 ⇌ 🔲 AE CB
◐ ⓪ VISA *Closed Sun, Mon lunch, Jan, one week in July.*

The fashionable restaurant of Pisa and the most reliable cuisine. Service is attentive and practiced.

⌁ Other good restaurants are: **Buzzino** (*Via Carlo Cammeo 44* ☎ *(050) 27013* ⅢⅢ *closed Tues, two weeks in Nov*), with imaginative variations on regional cuisine, although regular clients get the best advice and fastest service; **Lo Schiaccianoci** (*Via Vespucci 104* ☎ *(050) 21024* ⅢⅢ *closed Mon, Aug, early Jan*); **Vecchi Macelli** (*Via Volturno 49* ☎ *(050) 20424* ⅢⅢ *closed Wed, Sun lunch, Aug, Christmas*); **Del Violino** (*Via La Tinta 33* ☎ *(050) 22524* ⅢⅢ *closed Sat lunch, also Mon in July and Aug*).

See also *Excursions* opposite.

Excursions
1. S. Piero a Grado †
6km (4 miles) sw of Pisa is a Romanesque basilica (*open daily 9am – 6pm*) of the mid-11thC built on the site where St Peter is thought to have landed on his way from Antioch to Rome.

≈ There is a good choice of fish restaurants on the coast near S. Piero. At Marina di Pisa, try **L'Arsella** (*Via Padre Agostino* ☎ *(050) 36615* ▯ *to* ▮▮▯ *closed Tues eve, Wed, Jan*), or **Janett** (*Via Maiorca 34* ☎ *(050) 36521* ▮▮▯ *closed Mon*). At Tirrenia, **Belvedere** (*Largo Belvedere* ☎ *(050) 37673* ▯ *to* ▮▮▮▮ *closed Mon*).

---

2. Tenuta di San Rossore
6km (4 miles) w of Pisa is a protected littoral wood of oaks and pines (*open Sun, hols 9am – sunset*), formerly a royal estate, between the mouths of the Arno and the Serchio.

≈ North of the Serchio, at Migliarino, is the excellent family restaurant **Ugo** (*Via Aurelia 342* ☎ *(050) 804455* ▮▮▯ *closed Mon, Tues eve, late July*).

Pistoia ★
Map 15D5. 37km (23 miles) nw of Florence. 51100. Pistoia. Population: 94,637 **i** *Via XXVII Aprile 13* ☎ *(0573) 21622.*

In 63 BC the Roman revolutionary Catiline was cornered by Roman legions near Pistoia; facing defeat he plunged through the enemy ranks to his death. Dante considered the Pistoiesi to be even more dangerous than Catiline; and certainly their past is deeply scarred by factional conspiracy and violence. It was in Pistoia, as Dante recounts in the *Inferno, XXIV*, that the fierce political contest between Blacks and Whites originated.

For at least 200yr after the commune had surrendered to Florence in 1329 its citizens retained their reputation for rude manners and rough justice. Machiavelli described them as "brought up to slaughter and war"; and when the first pistols were made in Germany in the 16thC, they were named after the vicious little daggers worn by Pistoiesi and known as *pistolese*. Today Pistoia is a peaceful provincial capital surrounded by the orchards and nursery gardens which are the basis of its economy. Its main attraction for tourists is the wealth of Romanesque sculpture, especially the three pulpits in S. Bartolommeo, S. Giovanni Fuorcivitas, and S. Andrea, which, if seen in that order, will enable one to follow the first 'renaissance' of Tuscan sculpture as it evolved from 1250 – 1300.

Sights and places of interest
The early 14thC walls, still partly intact, were later strengthened with bastions by the Medici. But the main historic monuments of the town lie within the earlier walls, the outline of which is traced in part by Corso Gramsci.
Duomo ⏣ †
The marble porch, which gives the cathedral the appearance of crouching ready to pounce, was added in the mid-14thC to the 12th – 13thC Pisan-style facade. The terra-cottas (1505) over the central portal and in the vault above are by Andrea della Robbia. The interior walls are decorated with fragments of 13th – 14thC frescoes uncovered during a recent restoration. At the top of the right aisle is the 14thC **tomb of Cino da Pistoia**, who was Dante's friend. In the Cappella di San Jacopo, off the right aisle, is the extraordinary silver **St James Altar**, one of the supreme examples of the Italian goldsmiths' art and crowded with many endearing details. It was created from 1287 – 1456 by a succession of Tuscan sculptors including Brunelleschi, who made the two **figures**

165

on the left side. In the chapel to the left of the high altar is a *Madonna and Saints* (1485) by Lorenzo di Credi, possibly begun by Verrocchio; also the bust of *Archbishop Donato de' Medici* by A. Rossellino or Verrocchio.

Baptistry †
Opposite the cathedral is the tall, hexagonal Gothic Baptistry (1338–1359), by Cellino de Nese to a design by Andrea Pisano. The interior is bare except for the original font, rediscovered during a recent restoration, and the shameful commercial art exhibitions which are, incredibly, permitted to take place here from time to time.

Palazzo del Comune ▥
▧ *Open Tues – Sat 9:30am – 12:30pm, Sun, hols, 10am – 1pm.*
The town hall, a very fine example of Gothic civic architecture, was founded in 1294 by the enlightened Florentine governor Giano della Bella but building was delayed by political upheavals and not completed until 1355. Over the central door and on the corners are the crests of Medici Popes. The aerial corridor from the Sala Maggiore to the Duomo was added in 1637. The **Marino Marini Center** (the sculptor was born in Pistoia in 1901) is off the courtyard; among the works on display are portraits of *Thomas Mann*, *Henry Miller* and *Chagall*. The **Museo Civico**, opened in 1981, occupies rooms on the first and second floors.

Palazzo del Podestà
This 14thC building is still the city's tribunal. To the left of the entrance is the old court, complete with judge's seat, table of justice and bench of the accused.

Ospedale del Ceppo ▥
Piazza Giovanni XII. Not open to the public.
The startling frieze over the porch of the hospital looks at first glance like the work of a Russian social realist. It was executed in the early 16thC by members of Andrea della Robbia's workshop and illustrates the *Seven Works of Mercy*, a fascinating picture of poverty and illness in the 16thC. The lovely Verrocchiesque tondi over the columns are probably by Andrea himself. The hospital is still in use.

Sant'Andrea ▥ †
The 12thC church has an enchanting but unfinished facade. The reliefs (1166) of the *Journey and Adoration of the Magi* over the central portal are by the brothers Gruamonte and Adeodato. The blonde, barnlike interior is dominated by the city's outstanding work of art, the **pulpit ★** (1298–1301) by Giovanni Pisano. This pulpit was finished a year before Giovanni started work on the pulpit of the **Duomo** in *Pisa*. These carvings are so intensely dynamic that one can scarcely believe they were created two centuries before the age of Michelangelo. Their subject is the *Life of Christ* and the *Last Judgment*. Opposite the pulpit is a wooden *Crucifix* also by Giovanni, in a fine 15thC tabernacle frame.

San Bartolomeo in Pantano †
Piazza S. Bartolomeo. Hours very irregular.
This 12thC church contains a reconstructed **pulpit** (1250) by Guido da Como.

San Giovanni Fuorcivitas †
Via Francesco Crispi.
The name refers to the original 8thC church which stood outside the city walls. The building was erected from the mid-12th to 14thC and restored after damage during World War II. The entrance is by the decoratively vivid but scarred N flank. Inside, the **holy water stoup** in the center is notable for the four busts of cardinals by the young Giovanni Pisano. On the right wall is the **pulpit** (1270) by Gugliemo da Pisa, a follower of Nicola Pisano; the reliefs illustrate *Scenes from the New Testament*. On the left wall are the glazed terra-cotta figures of the *Visitation*, a moving work attributed to Luca or Andrea della Robbia. To the left of the altar is a large polyptych (1353–55) by Taddeo Gaddi.

Zoo *(Giardino Zoologico)*
Via Pieve a Celle 160 ☎ *(0573) 571280* ▧ ▣ ✦ *Open daily 9am to sunset.*
The new and attractively planned zoo is 4km (2½ miles) sw of Pistoia.

Other sights
Visitors with leisure should also look at the churches of S. Francesco; S. Domenico; S. Paolo; S. Maria delle Grazie, designed by Michelozzo; and the Cappella Tau, decorated with 14th–15thC frescoes.

☎Arcobaleno
Via Valdi e Collina 37, Sanmommè, 51020 Pistoia ☎ *(0573) 470030*
▮▯ *25 rms* ▭ *25* ⚊ ⚌ 🏠 *summer* ⬤ *Closed 10 Jan–10 Feb.*
Location: 15km (9 miles) to N at Sanmommè. A vacation hotel in the
mountains popular with children for the sports facilities and disco.
⌂ ▱ 🜨 ⟨⟨ ≈ ℅ 🜚 ●

☎Residence il Covento
Via S. Quirico 33, 51100 Pistoia ☎ *(0573) 452651* ▮▮ *24 rms* ▭ *24*
⚊ ⌂ ⚌ AE VISA
Location: 5km to NE near Ponte Nuovo. A peaceful retreat in an 18thC
ex-convent overlooking Pistoia.
⌂ ▱ 🜞 🜨 ⟨⟨

⚌ In the center is the unfussy and comfortable **Chiavi d'Oro** (*Via
Pacini 19* ☎ *(0573) 30226* ▯ *closed Tues, late Aug*). Just outside are:
Checco (*Via Dalmazio 454* ☎ *(0573) 22135* ▮▮ *closed Wed, Aug*); and
Rafanelli (*Via S. Agostino 47* ☎ *(0573) 532046* ▮▮ *closed Sun eve, Mon,
early Aug*).

⚌ Osteria del Contadino
Via Provinciale Pratese 58, Agliana ☎ *(0574) 71450* ▮▮ ▯ ▰ ⚊
Closed Mon, Aug.
This rustic, friendly country place, halfway between Pistoia and Prato,
prepares Tuscan home cooking with a daily set menu.

⚌ Signorino
Via Bolognese 207 ☎ *(0573) 475028* ▮▮ ▯ ▰ ⚌ 🛆 ⟨⟨ AE
Closed Mon, Oct–July, mid-Jan.
A cheerful and popular country restaurant 10km (6 miles) N of Pistoia
with a good cold table as well as hearty regional specialties.

Pitigliano
*Map 9J7. 218km (134 miles) s of Florence, 74km (46 miles)
SE of Grosseto. 58017. Grosseto. Population: 4,443.*
Pitigliano from a distance is one of the most amazing sights in
Tuscany. Carved out of a rock escarpment above a natural moat
formed by three deep ravines, this was the seat of the Roman
Orsini barons when they took control of the area in 1293. It
retains the dour, impressive stamp of a warlord's headquarters,
remarkably intact, charmless but fascinating.

The main square, Piazza della Repubblica, is dominated by
the 14th–15thC **Palazzo Orsini**, modified in the 16thC by
Giuliano da Sangallo. The strongly atmospheric medieval *borgo*
straddles the escarpment beyond the Duomo.

⚌ **Guastini** (*Piazza Petruccioli 4* ☎ *(0564) 616065* ▯ *closed Fri, late
June*).

Poggibonsi
*Map 11F5. 41km (25 miles) s of Florence, 33km (20 miles) NW
of Siena. 53036. Siena. Population: 25,784.*
A commercial and industrial center (wine and furniture).

Nearby sights
2km (1¼ miles) s is the 13thC Gothic church of San Lucchese, rebuilt after
World War II, containing frescoes by Bartolo di Fredi.

8km (5 miles) SE on the Siena road is the fortified medieval hamlet of
Staggia, where the museum (🔲 *apply at sacristan's house*) attached to the
parish church possesses a panel of the *Communion of the Magdalen* by A.
del Pollaiuolo.

☎ ⚌ **Alcide** (*Viale Marconi 67a* ☎ *(0577) 937501* ▯ *closed Wed,
July*).

Poggio a Caiano
Map **15***E5. 17km (10 miles) w of Florence. 50046. Firenze.*
Population: 5,892.

Villa Medicea di Poggio a Caiano ▥ ★
▨ *Gardens only open 8:30am to sunset.*
The most innovative and influential of all Medici country houses, built
for Lorenzo de' Medici from 1480–85, and the only important surviving
building for which he was personally responsible. The architect was
Giuliano da Sangallo, who adapted the antique Roman villa type to the
requirements of Renaissance country life.

The arcaded ground floor provides a balcony for the *piano nobile*. The
central loggia with its Robbianesque terra-cotta frieze was probably
added in the 16thC. The curved staircases were added in the 17thC.

The traditional central courtyard is replaced by a two-story-high
salone frescoed by Andrea del Sarto (until 1512), Franciabigio (until
1520), Pontormo (until 1532) and completed by A. Allori (1582). The
Classical subjects refer to events in Medici history. The highpoint is
Pontormo's fresco in the lunette of the right wall of *Vertumnus and
Pomona* (1521), an idyllic and graceful picture of a Tuscan summer's day
and a masterpiece of design.

🚅 See *Artimino*.

Pontassieve
Map **16***E6. 18km (11 miles) ε of Florence. 50065. Firenze.*
Population: 19,752.
A commercial wine town. The Wed market is good for shoes.

🏰 Castello di Sanmezzano
50067 Leccio-Rignano Sull'Arno, Firenze 🕿 *(055) 867911* 🖅 *573078*
▥▥▥ *15 rms* ▤ *15* 🛏 🚗 🚅 AE 💳 VISA
Location: Near the Incisa autostrada exit from Florence. A 17thC castle
stupendously decorated in 19thC Moorish style.
⌂ ♨ ▭ ▨ 🏊 ⚓ 🎿 ⛷ 🎣

🚅 **Il Girarrosto** ❁ (*Via Garibaldi 27* 🕿 *(055) 8302048* ▥▥ 🗔 ▅ 🍴
🚗 💳 *closed Mon, July*). **Specialty:** Game.

Pontremoli
Map **14***B2. 164km (102 miles) nw of Florence, 53km (33
miles) nw of Massa. 54027. Massa-Carrara. Population:
10,335* **i** *in the Municipio* 🕿 *(0187) 831180.*
The principal town of the Lunigiana, named after the Etruscan
city of Luni (which is now in Liguria).

A 19thC Neoclassical facade has been added to the Baroque
cathedral. The town boasts a pretty oval Rococo church, the
Madonna del Ponte (1738).

Other sights
In the **Castello** on the hill of Piagnaro is a museum (▧ *open Tues–Sun
9am–noon, 2–5pm summer, 4–7pm winter*) exhibiting the strange,
totemic *stela* statues and other pre-Etruscan material discovered in the
area.

1.5km (1 mile) to the se of the center, the church of SS Annunziata has
a fine 16thC interior with a marble *tempietto* (1527) attributed to Jacopo
Sansovino.

🏰 **Golf** (*Via Pineta* 🕿 *(0187) 831573* ▥▥).

🚅 **Da Bussè** (*Piazza Duomo 9* 🕿 *(0187) 831144* ▥ *closed Fri, early
July*), an old-fashioned rustic trattoria. At Azzelato the restaurant of the
Hotel Falco delle Apuane (🕿 *(0187) 835003* ▥ *to* ▥▥ *closed Nov*) is
pleasant and popular.

Poppi
Map 12E7. 53km (33 miles) SE of Florence, 38km (24 miles) N of Arezzo. 52014. Arezzo. Population: 5,790.
Poppi is the starting point for the beautiful drive to *Camaldoli*. It is worth pausing here to admire the arcaded old streets.

Sights and places of interest
Palazzo Pretorio ▥
Piazza Grande ▣ Open Mon–Sat 9am–2pm.
Originally the castle of the Guidi lords, the palace was rebuilt in 1274 and extended in 1291. Its resemblance to the *Palazzo Signoria, Florence* suggests that Arnolfo di Cambio may have had a hand in the design.
Primo Parco Zoo
☎ *(0575) 58602* ▰▰ � ⚹ *Open daily 8am to sunset.*
Just outside the town, in a ravishing setting, this is the first zoo in Europe to be devoted exclusively to European animals.

Populonia
Map 10H3. 149km (93 miles) SW of Florence, 89km (55 miles) NW of Grosseto. 57020. Livorno. Population: 122.
The only Etruscan town built on a coastal site, Populonia was inhabited from the 9thC BC and in the 7thC BC became a rich industrial city – the blast furnace of the ancient world. Iron ore imported from *Elba* was smelted here in such quantities that the necropolis was buried in slag and the beaches are still streaked with black. The inhabitants may have been the first Etruscans to mint coins, in the 5thC BC. Populonia fell under the influence of Rome in the 3rdC BC, and by the 4thC AD was nearly empty.

The village is dominated by its restored medieval **rocca**. A privately owned **Etruscan museum** on the main street (*apply to custodian at no. 11*) houses an interesting collection of small, sacred and domestic objects from the necropolis.

Necropolis ✩
3km (2 miles) E of village ▣ ▰ tours roughly on the hour. Open daily 9am–noon, 4–8pm summer, 9am–noon, 2–6pm winter.
This complex comprises tombs of the 9th–3rdC BC.

Port'Ercole
Map 8J5. 190km (118 miles) S of Florence, 50km (31 miles) S of Grosseto. 58018. Grosseto. Population: 3,400.
A fashionable sailing resort on the E coast of Monte Argentario which has attracted a faithful English summer colony. The Etruscans gave it the name of Port of Hercules. The three fortresses which guard it testify to its strategic importance; there is nowhere else except Malta where one can see Renaissance principles of fortification so well defined.

Sights and places of interest
Forte Filippo ▥
▰▰ ▰ *Tours on Wed.*
The best demonstration of late-Renaissance fortification in the Mediterranean. Mathematically and technically flawless, it is in an excellent state of preservation. Now converted into private apartments.
Forte Stella ▥
South of the harbour, this now abandoned hexagonal fort on a four-sided bastion base was built by the Spanish in the 17thC.
Rocca Spagnola ▥
▣ *Open Apr–Dec 20 10am–1pm, 4pm to sunset; Dec 21–Mar 10am–1:30pm, 3:30pm to sunset. Permission necessary from mayor's office (easily obtained).*
The Rocca Spagnola is the original nucleus of the medieval fortress, refined and extended in the 15th–16thC, which dominates the historic

center of the town, Piazza Santa Barbara. It forms a complete village.

On the Tombolo di Feniglia is a protected pine forest and a sandy beach where Caravaggio died in 1610.

Don Pedro
Via Panoramica 7, 58018 Port'Ercole, Grosseto ☎*(0564) 833914* **❚❚❐**
44 rms ▭ *44* ▦▦ ▦ ◪ ▭ *Closed Nov–Easter.*
The most attractive and best managed medium-price hotel in the area.
♠ ▨ ◪ ◪

Il Pellicano ⚑
Cala dei Sanli, 58018 Port'Ercole, Grosseto ☎*(0564) 833801*
⊛*500131* **❚❚❚❚** *34 rms* ▭ *34* ▦▦ ▭ ▭ ▭ ⒶⒺ ⒸⒷ ◉ *VISA* *Closed Jan to mid-Mar.*
Location: 3km (2 miles) N toward Porto Santo Stefano. Luxurious American country house decor and isolated position.
▨ ▨ ⚓ ✦ ⚘ ⚑ ⚗ ⚒ ◉

 ══**La Lampara** (*Lungomare Andrea Doria* ☎*(0564) 833024* **❚❚❐** *closed Tues in winter and Dec–Feb*) is a simple, long-established restaurant on the sea front.

There is a better choice of restaurants at *Porto Santo Stefano*.

Excursion
The island of Giannutri
23km (14 miles) to the s, the island is reached from Port'Ercole. Near Cala Maestra is a 1stC AD Roman villa. Good spear-fishing in the clear waters of the Cala dei Grottoni.

Porto Santo Stefano
Map **8***J5. 193km (121 miles) s of Florence, 53km (33 miles) s of Siena. 58019. Grosseto. Population: 10,100* **i** *Corso Umberto 55a* ☎*(0564) 814208.*
This active fishing port on the N coast of Monte Argentario retains some of its charm. Boats depart frequently for *Giglio*.

Torre di Cala Piccola ⚑
58019 Porto Santo Stefano, Grosseto ☎*(0564) 825133* **❚❚❐** *56 rms*
▭ *56* ◪ ══ *summer* ⒶⒺ ◉ *VISA* *Closed Oct–Mar.*
Location: 8km (5 miles) w. The main luxury hotel on the Argentario coast.
▱ ▨ ⚘ ⚓ ⚓ ⚑

 ══**Armando** (*Via Marconi 1/3* ☎*(0564) 812586* **❚❚❚❚** *closed Wed, Nov*) is a fish restaurant in the town. Others, all beautifully located a little way outside are: **La Fontanina**, (*S. Pietro* ☎*(0564) 812029* **❚❐** *to* **❚❚❐** *closed Wed, Jan*), above the town and with a vine-covered terrace; **La Formica** (*on the beach at Pozzarello* ☎*(0564) 814205* **❚❐** *closed Wed, Oct or Nov*); **Nellumbo** (*Via Panoramica delle Cannelle* ☎*(0564) 814685* **❚❚❚❚** *closed Mon in winter*; **Orlando** (*Via Breschi 3* ☎*(0564) 812788* **❚❐** *to* **❚❚❐** *closed Thurs, Nov–Jan*), an intimate restaurant with a terrace just above the harbor.

Prato ★
Map **15***D5. 19km (11 miles) NW of Florence. 50047. Firenze. Population: 156,955* **i** *Via L. Muzzi 51* ☎*(0574) 35141.*
Florentines say that if you listen closely in Prato late at night when the textile factories are closed you will hear a whirring: it is the sound of the inhabitants spinning in their back parlors. 75% of the manufactured wool exported from Italy comes from Prato, and most of it is produced by small, privately owned

firms. Its population has doubled in 30yr and is now the fourth largest and possibly the most affluent in Central Italy. Florentines also call Prato the tail that tries to wag the dog.

The first cloth mills on the banks of the Bisenzio were in operation in 1108, half a century earlier than the first in Florence. But the prosperous city which grew up around a meadow (*prato*) was no more successful than most Tuscan communes at self-government. Unable to control its political factions, Prato placed itself under the protection of the Anjou rulers of Naples in 1313. In 1351, the Queen of Naples sold her rights to the city to Florence for 17,500 florins. The commercial fortunes of Prato were given an enormous boost later in the 14thC by the business operations of Francesco di Marco Datini, subject of Iris Origo's admirable biography, *The Merchant of Prato*. But although Prato enjoyed a greater economic and political autonomy than many Florentine-dominated cities, it rebelled on several occasions; and in the 16thC Florence punished it by rationing its permitted production of wool.

Apart from its distinctive green-and-white striped churches, there are two artistic masterpieces, both by Florentines, which compel a visit to Prato: Filippo Lippi's frescoes in the Duomo and Giuliano da Sangallo's church Santa Maria delle Carceri.

Events: The Metastasio Theater in Via Benedetto Cairoli is the home of an enterprising experimental company which plays from Oct–Apr. In spring and summer, concerts are given in the Metastasio and in the Castello.

The *Ostensione del Sacro Cingolo*, which is the ceremonial display of the Virgin's Holy Girdle from the external pulpit of the Duomo, takes place on May 1, Easter Day, Aug 15, Sept 8, and Dec 25.

Sights and places of interest
The old town sits within a partly intact hexagon of 13thC walls on the SW bank of the River Bisenzio.

Castello dell'Imperatore
▣ *Open Mon, Tues, Thurs–Sat 9am–noon, 4–7pm.*
For a good orienting view walk around the battlements of this castle, built in the 13thC for the Emperor Frederick II.

Opposite the Castello is **Santa Maria delle Carceri** (see over).

Duomo 🏛 ✝ ★
The striped facade was applied to the Romanesque building in 1384–1457. The glazed terra-cotta lunette of the *Madonna with Sts Stephen and Lawrence* (1489) over the portal is by Andrea della Robbia. Projecting from the right corner is the covered **pulpit of the Holy Girdle** (1428–38) by Donatello and Michelozzo. The originals of Donatello's carvings of *Dancing Putti* have been removed to the Cathedral Museum.

The sturdy green and blonde interior conserves remarkable works of art, but the nave is bare except for the pulpit (1473) by Mino da Fiesole and A. Rossellino. Left of the entrance is the **chapel of the Holy Girdle** (1385–95); the legend of the Holy Girdle is illustrated by Agnolo Gaddi's frescoes (1392–95). The Holy Girdle was brought from the Holy Land to Prato in the 12thC, and its story is still popular in Tuscany. Over the altar is a *Madonna and Child* (c.1317) by Giovanni Pisano. Behind the high altar of the cathedral, in the choir, are Filippo Lippi's frescoes ★ (1452–66) of the martyrdom of *St John the Baptist*, on the right wall, and of *St Stephen*, on the left (a coin-operated light switch is on the left of the last chapel in the left transept). Filippo labored over these frescoes for 14yr during which he was tried for fraud and fathered a child by the nun Lucrezia (who may be the model for the dancing Salome). They are the considered masterpieces of his troubled maturity, and yet they glow with a clear-eyed vivacity and apparently spontaneous grace which make them among the most immediately pleasing of Renaissance paintings.

The chapel to the right of the altar is frescoed with scenes from the *Lives of the Virgin and of St Stephen*, begun by Paolo Uccello or a disciple and completed, still in the early 15thC, in a strange quasi-Mannerist style by Andrea di Giusto. In the right transept is a tabernacle of the *Madonna of the Olive* (1480) by all three Maiano brothers; also a panel painting of the *Death of St Jerome* by Filippo Lippi.

Museo dell'Opera del Duomo (*Cathedral Museum*)
🔳 *Open Mon, Wed–Sat 9am–12:30pm, 3–6:30pm, Sun, hols 9:30am–12.30pm. Closed Tues.*

In the Bishop's Palace to the left of the Duomo. The main attractions are Donatello's reliefs of *Dancing Putti* from the exterior pulpit, but they are less good than the miniature frieze of dancing putti on the exquisite **reliquary of the Holy Girdle** (1446) by Maso di Bartolomeo.

Galleria Comunale
Piazza Comune 🔳 *Open Tues–Sat 9am–7pm, Sun, hols 9am–noon.*

The gallery occupies three floors of the 13th–14thC Palazzo Pretorio. The large collection includes minor 14th–15thC altarpieces in good condition, two panels by Filippo Lippi, Neapolitan fruit paintings, and plaster models by L. Bartolini.

Santa Maria delle Carceri 🏛 † ★
Giuliano da Sangallo's harmoniously proportioned cruciform interior, begun 1485, is a masterpiece of Italian Renaissance architecture, a perfect restatement of Brunelleschi's principles. The blue and white terra-cotta decorations and medallions are by Andrea Della Robbia.

Other sights

Palazzo Datini in Via Rinaldesca, which Francesco di Marco Datini had built for himself in the late 14th–early 15thC; Datini's tomb is in the nearby church of **San Francesco**; the late 14thC frescoes in the chapter room off the cloister include a picture of *St Matthew as a Money Changer*, a rare, but in Prato appropriate, genre subject.

🍽 **Il Piraña**
Via Valentini 110 ☎ *(0574) 25746* 💷 ⬜ ▦ AE CD *Closed Sat, Aug.*
Do not be deterred by the location of this restaurant, which is 10mins' drive from the center opposite a string of factories. Even the Florentines will tell you that this is now one of the best fish restaurants in Italy, although the decor is an excessively fussy attempt to be ultra-modern.

🍽 Restaurants in the center include **Baghino** (*Via dell'Accademia 9* ☎ *(0574) 27920* 💷 *closed Sun, Mon, lunch during Aug*), and **Tonio** (*Piazza Mercatale 161* ☎ *(0574) 21266* 💷 *closed Sun, Mon, Aug, early Jan*), which has good pictures on the walls, a small varied menu and a loyal business clientele.

Punta Ala

Map **10**/*5. 150km (93 miles) sw of Florence, 40km (25 miles) w of Grosseto. 58040. Grosseto. Population: 190.*

This luxurious resort on a headland overlooking the island of *Elba* was founded in 1960. It offers golf, sailing, riding, polo, tennis, sand beaches and is near the Etruscan sites.

Hotels

Alleluja
58040 Punta Ala, Grosseto ☎ *(0564) 922050* 📺 *500449* 💷 *43 rms*
🛏 *43* ▦ 🅿 🛄 🍽 AE CD *Closed Feb.*
The most attractive of the hotels, which preserves something of the mood of the old Tuscan farmhouse, the nucleus of the original estate.
🏠 ‡ ⚲ 🗄 🖤 ⚓ ⇌ ⚱ ℘ ∫ 🔌 ⊸ ⵙ ●

Cala del Porto
Via del Porto, 58040 Punta Ala, Grosseto ☎ *(0564) 922455* 📺 *590624*
💷 *46 rms* 🛏 *46* ▦ 🅿 🛄 ⇌ AE CD CD *Closed Oct–Apr.*
Comfortably appointed hotel overlooking the sea.
🏠 ♿ 🗄 🖤 ⚲ ⚓ ⇌ ℘ ∫ 🔌 ⊸ ⵙ ●

Gallia Palace Hotel 🏨
Via delle Sughere, 58040 Punta Ala, Grosseto ☎ *(0564) 922022/3/4/5*
📠 *590454* 🛏 *98 rms* 🍽 *98* 🏢 ⚓ 🅿 ⇌ 🅰🅴 *Closed Oct–May.*

The modern luxury hotel of Punta Ala is an architecturally impersonal
building set in a splendid garden. Good service.
🛁 ‡ 🔥 🗄 📷 ⚓ 🌊 ⇌ 🐎 ♫ ✔ ⛴ 🚣 ♟

⇌ Restaurants on the port include a reasonable self-service. See also
Castiglione della Pescaia and *Tirli*.

Radda in Chianti

*Map **12**F6. 58km (36 miles) s of Florence, 34km (21 miles) N
of Siena. 53017. Siena. Population: 1,588.*

A little hill village which became headquarters of the Chianti
League in 1415. The medieval street plan and sections of the
fortifications survive. 3km (1¾ miles) N is **Volpaia**, the prettiest
of the small medieval Chianti villages.

⇌ **Petroio** (☎ *(0577) 738094* □ *closed Thurs*) for good pasta and
superb roast chicken.

Roselle

*Map **11**I5. 131km (81 miles) s of Florence, 10km (6 miles) NE
of Grosseto. Grosseto.*

Etruscan Roselle, like *Vetulonia*, was an island dominating the
waters of the gulf which then filled part of the Grosseto
Maremma. Excavations have revealed layers of civilization
stretching back to the Neolithic age. The Etruscan city, one of
the federation of 12, was taken over by Rome early in the
3rdC BC. Portable material uncovered is now in *Grosseto*.

The **ruins** ☆ (🅴 *hours unrestricted*) are in a remarkably
complete state of conservation, surrounded by a nearly intact
ring of Etruscan- and Roman-built walls. Remains of the
Roman city include the forum, a stretch of paved street,
basilicas, villas, amphitheater and baths. Etruscan remains
include rare artisans' cottages of the 7th–6thC BC.

⇌ See *Istia d'Ombrone* and *Grosseto*.

San Casciano in Val di Pesa

*Map **15**E5. 17km (10½ miles) s of Florence. 50026. Firenze.
Population: 14,522.*

A busy agricultural-industrial town graced by the church of the
Misericordia which possesses several fine Sienese paintings,
including a *Crucifixion* on panel by Simone Martini.

Nearby sights

3km (1¾ miles) to the N is the one-street hamlet of **Sant'Andrea in
Percussina**, where Machiavelli spent 15yr in exile from Florence during
which he wrote his six great works, including *The Prince*. His house is
privately owned but sometimes open to the public.

⇌ **Nello** ♣
Via IV Novembre 64 ☎ *(055) 820163* 🍽 *Closed Wed eve, Thurs, July.*
Substantial country cooking, including game in season.

⇌ **La Tenda Rossa**
Piazza Monumento 9/14, Cerbaia Val di Pesa ☎ *(055) 826132* 🍽 □
⇌ 🅰🅴 *Closed Wed, Thurs lunch, three weeks from Aug–Sept.*

This outstanding trattoria, 6km (4 miles) to the N, excels in pastas.

San Galgano ⅏ † ★

*Map 11G5. 101km (63 miles) sw of Florence, 33km (20 miles)
sw of Siena.*

The ruined church of San Galgano is one of the most moving
sights in Tuscany. Although meadow grass now grows in the
roofless nave, the magnificence of the once-powerful Cistercian
foundation is still apparent. Built between 1218–80, the church
introduced French Gothic architecture to Tuscany.

On a hill above is the little Romanesque church of **San
Galgano**, with the 14thC chapel frescoed by A. Lorenzetti.

San Gimignano ★

*Map 11F5. 55km (34 miles) sw of Florence, 38km (24 miles)
nw of Siena. 53037. Siena. Population: 7,501 i Piazza del
Duomo ☎(0577) 940008; Via San Giovanni 125
☎(0577) 940809.*

San Gimignano '*delle belle torri*' (of the beautiful towers) is the
best-preserved medieval town in Tuscany. Its defense system
once involved more than 70 towers, of which 13 survive.
Warring factions dropped rocks and burning tar on their
enemies from these towers, which were also important status
symbols. Height meant prestige for medieval Tuscan
noblemen, as for 20thC American tycoons; and from a distance
San Gimignano bears an eerie resemblance to a tipsy, miniature
New York.

Most Italian cities looked very like San Gimignano in the
12th–13thC. The skyline of medieval Siena bristled with over
50 such towers, and that of Florence with over 100. E.M.
Forster's early novel, *Where Angels Fear to Tread*, is set in San
Gimignano, which he calls "Monteriano".

The narrative painter Benozzo Gozzoli was born here. His
charming frescoes in the Collegiata and the church of San
Agostino are not great art, but are easy to enjoy.

Events: Colorful masked processions take place on the first
and last Sun of the carnival period before Lent.

Operas are performed in summer in Piazza del Duomo.

Sights and places of interest

Porta San Giovanni (1262), the finest of the town gates, is the
main entrance; there is a car park nearby. The town is in any
case best toured on foot.

There are marvelous views from the 13thC town **walls** and
from the **Rocca**, built by the Florentines in 1353.

Piazza della Cisterna
The main square is actually triangular, and retains at its center the
original 13thC cistern. The buildings are 13th–14thC, of which the
finest is the 14thC Palazzo Tortoli (no. 7), in the Sienese style.

Piazza del Duomo
The monumental buildings and seven towers of the Piazza del Duomo
are all pre-1400. On the w of the square is the Collegiata. The Palazzo del
Popolo is on the s side and the Palazzo del Podestà on the e.

Collegiata †
The Romanesque facade of the Collegiata was enlarged by Giuliano da
Maiano in the 15thC, but has been often restored since. The interior is
notable for its 14th–15thC frescoes. On the interior facade the frescoes
include the *Martyrdom of St Sebastian* (1465) by Gozzoli; polychrome
statues of the *Annunciation* (1421) by Jacopo della Quercia. On the right
wall are *New Testament Scenes* (c.mid-14thC) by Barna da Siena,
completed by Giovanni d'Asciano.

Off the right nave is the **Cappella di Santa Fina** ★ – 1468 (🎟 *ticket
also good for Pal. del Popolo, hours as Pal. del Podestà*), one of the high
points of Renaissance architecture, built by Giuliano da Maiano with an

altar by Benedetto da Maiano. The beautiful frescoes (1475) by Domenico Ghirlandaio and assistants depict two *Scenes from the Life of Santa Fina*; according to the legend, wallflowers sprang from the towers on the day she died.

In the presbytery, the ciborium over the high altar is by B. da Maiano. The choir stalls in the apse are by Antonio da Colle. On the left nave wall are frescoes of the *Old Testament* (c.1367) by Bartolo di Fredi, and in the 14thC Baptistry loggia, off the left nave, is a fresco of the *Annunciation* by Domenico Ghirlandaio.

Palazzo del Podestà ▥▥▥
🔊 *Open Apr–Oct Tues–Sun 9:30am–12:30pm, 3:30–6:30pm; Nov–Mar Tues–Sun 10am–1pm, 2:30–5:30pm. Closed Mon.*
On the E side of the square, this 13thC building was enlarged in the 14thC. Its imposing Torre dell Ragnosa at 51m (167ft) was meant to set the maximum legal height for towers, but tower-building rivalry continued.

Palazzo del Popolo
Piazza del Duomo 🔊 *ticket also good for Cappella di Santa Fina in Collegiata. Hours as Pal. del Podestà.*
On the S side of the square, this building houses the Pinacoteca Civica, and offers a spectacular view from the top of its tower, the **Torre Grossa**. Inside, on the first floor, the Sala di Dante, so called because the poet spoke here in 1300 in favor of an alliance with Florence, contains an important *Maestà* (1317) by Lippo Memmo. The **Pinacoteca**, on the next floor, has a beguiling collection of 13th–15thC Sienese and Florentine paintings.

Sant' Agostino †
A Romanesque-Gothic church (1290–98) of impressive simplicity. In the Cappella di S. Bartolo, right of the main entrance, is a marble altar (1494) by B. da Maiano. Over the high altar, the *Coronation of the Virgin* (1483) is a major work by Piero del Pollaiuolo. In the choir Gozzoli's *Life Story of St Augustine* has 17 frescoed scenes (1464). In the left nave is Gozzoli's *St Sebastian* (1464).

Via San Matteo
The main street has travertine paving and medieval buildings, especially the Romanesque church of San Bartolo and the *casa-torre* Pesciolini at no. 32.

Other sights
Of the many more Romanesque churches within the walls, the most interesting is San Jacopo, at the NE corner.

Outside the walls, 4.5km (3 miles) from Porta San Matteo, is the Romanesque **Pieve di Cellole** (1237).

🏩 ⇌ **Bel Soggiorno**
Via San Giovanni 91, 53037 San Gimignano, Siena 🕾 *(0577) 940375*
▥▥ *27 rms* 🛏 *27* 🔲 🍴 *Restaurant closed Mon.*
Wonderful views of the town from this 13thC house.
⇕ 🖾 🥾 ◁€

🏩 ⇌ **La Cisterna**
Piazza della Cisterna 23, 53037 San Gimignano, Siena
🕾 *(0577) 940328* ▥▥ *46 rms* 🛏 *46* 🔲 ⇌ 🍴 AE ⊕ ⑩ VISA
Huge rooms in a 13thC palace with an Edwardian atmosphere. The restaurant, **Le Terrazze** (▥▥ *closed Tues, Wed lunch*), offers splendid views from spacious rooms with low ceilings with exposed beams.
🔲 ⇕ 🕭 🖾 ◁€ 🍷

🏩 ⇌ **Le Renaie e Leonetto**
6km (4 miles) N *at Pancole* 🕾 *(0577) 955044* ▥ *26 rms* AE ⊕ VISA
Closed early Nov, restaurant closed Tues.
A pleasant country inn.
🔲 🥾 ⇌

🏩 **Pescille**
4.5km (3 miles) S *near San Donato* 🕾 *(0577) 940186* 🔲 *32 rms* 🚗
Closed Jan, Feb.
A modest, peaceful hotel.
🔲 🖾 🥾 ◁€ ⇌ ⁑

San Giovanni Valdarno
*Map **11**F6. 45km (28 miles) SE of Florence, 37km (23 miles) W of Arezzo. 52027. Arezzo. Population: 19,908.*

The birthplace of the painters Masaccio and Giovanni da San Giovanni is now the chief industrial town of the Valdarno.

See also *Pontassieve*.

2km (1½ miles) to the S, in the church of the convent of Montecarlo, is one of Fra Angelico's masterpieces, an *Annunciation* (c.1440), with a fine predella. 13km (8 miles) to the NE, near Loro Ciuffenna, is the tiny farming hamlet of Gropina. Its Romanesque church, **S. Pietro**, has unusual capitals and primitive carvings on its pulpit.

5km (3 miles) SE is Montevarchi where a market is held on Thurs.

San Miniato
*Map **15**E4. 44km (27 miles) W of Florence, 39km (24 miles) E of Pisa. 56027. Pisa. Population: 24,701.*

Medieval San Miniato was the seat of the Lombard Imperial Vicariate in Tuscany and therefore known as S. Miniato al Tedesco ('of the German'). The fortifications, of which only two towers remain, were rebuilt in 1240 by Frederick II.

Sights and places of interest
The 13thC **Duomo** has been rebuilt and restored many times and its pompous interior decorations are 18th–19thC. Its bell-tower, the **Torre di Matilde**, predates the Duomo and was built as a defense tower.

The **Museo Diocesano** (🖼 *open Tues–Sun summer 9am–noon, 4–7pm; winter 9am–noon, 2:30–5pm*), to the left of the Duomo, retains sacred art from the region including works by Filippo Lippi, Neri di Bicci, Fra Bartolommeo, Empoli and Verrocchio.

A short, stiff climb from the Prato del Duomo brings one to the tower which is the last surviving reminder of Frederick II's **Rocca**, a reconstruction of the original which was destroyed during World War II. On a clear day the view embraces the whole of the Arno plain. Below the Prato del Duomo is **Piazza della Repubblica**, the most picturesque in the town. The Seminario retains 14thC storefronts and 17thC *sgraffiti*.

🛏 🍽 **Miravalle** (*Piazza Castello 3* 🕿 (*0571*) *418075* 🏧).

San Quirico d'Orcia
*Map **8**H6. 111km (64 miles) SE of Florence, 43km (29 miles) SE of Siena. 53027. Siena. Population: 2,231 **i** Piazza Liberta 2* 🕿 (*0577*) *43252.*

A village overlooking the Orcia and Asso valleys.

Collegiata †
The Romanesque-Gothic Collegiata has three magnificent **portals**: on the facade (1080); on the right flank (late 13thC), adorned with lions and caryatids by a follower of Giovanni Pisano; and at the head of the right transept (1298). Inside is an unusually fine triptych by Sano di Pietro and good choir stalls (1502) by Antonio Barili.

Nearby sights
San Giovanni d'Asso, 15km (9 miles) N, dominated by its 12thC Castello; and **Castiglione d'Orcia**, 5km (3 miles) S, hometown of the artist Vecchietta, which is near the atmospheric medieval village of **Rocca d'Orcia**. 6km (4 miles) SE is the little spa town of **Bagno Vignoni**, now rather run down.

🛏 🍽 **Posta-Marcucci** 🌸
53027 Bagno Vignoni, Siena 🕿 (*0577*) *887112* 🏧 *48 rms* 🛏 *43* �
🄥🄸🄻🅂🄰

Location: 6km (4 miles) S, off the Via Cassia. Its thermal baths, used by St Catherine of Siena and Lorenzo the Magnificent, make this simple but comfortable hotel a restful place to take the waters.

🄴🄰🄻🄱🅆🅈

Sansepolcro

Map **13***F8. 114km (71 miles) SE of Florence, 39km (24 miles)
NE of Arezzo. 52037. Arezzo. Population: 15,695.*
In this somewhat mournful town close to the Umbrian border
Piero della Francesca was born after 1420 and spent the last
14yr of his life writing his treatises on *Perspective* and the *Five
Regular Bodies*. It was probably in the early 1460s that he
executed his masterpiece, the *Resurrection*, in his native town.

Museo Civico
Via Aggiunti 65 🔲 *Open daily 9:30am–1pm, 2:30–6pm.*
Piero's hypnotic *Resurrection* ★ has been called the greatest picture in
the world. Sir Kenneth Clark describes the spell it casts.

"Before Piero's Risen Christ we are suddenly conscious of values for
which no rational statement is adequate; we are struck with a feeling of
awe, older and less reasonable than that inspired by the Blessed
Angelico. This country god, who rises in the gray light while humanity is
asleep, has been worshipped ever since man first knew that the seed is not
dead in the winter earth, but will force its way upward through an iron
crust. Later He will become a god of rejoicing, but His first emergence is
painful and involuntary. He seems to be part of the dream which lies so
heavily on the sleeping soldiers . . . ."

Opposite is Piero's early polyptych, the *Madonna della Misericordia* ★
(1446–c.1458). Like the *Madonna del Parto* at **Monterchi** (see below),
this Madonna of Mercy is both a pretty, young peasant girl and icy
goddess, whose state of spiritual detachment has been likened to that
evoked by Buddhist and African sculpture. The whole polyptych is in
uneven condition and other sections were painted by assistants. Also by
Piero are the frescoes of *St Julian* and *St Louis of Toulouse*.

Notable among the other works in the museum are a processional flag
representing the *Crucifixion* by Signorelli; Pontormo's *St Quentin*; and
battered but fine 15thC choir stalls which demonstrate the influence of
Piero on perspective intarsia work.

Other sights
In the Romanesque-Gothic **Duomo,** paintings include two panels by
Matteo di Giovanni, part of a polyptych of which the central panel, the
Baptism of Christ by Piero, was purchased for the London National
Gallery in 1861 – for £241 (about $1200).

The church of **San Francesco** retains it Gothic high altar (1304) for
which Sassetta painted his *St Francis* altarpiece, an early influence on
Piero, now scattered, parts being in London and Paris.

In the 16thC church of **San Lorenzo** is a dramatic *Deposition*
(c.1528–30) by Rosso Fiorentino.

🍽 �. **Il Fiorentino** (*Via L. Pacioli 60* ☎ *(0575) 74233* 📖 *restaurant
closed Fri*). English and French spoken. See also *Anghiari*.

Excursion
17km (11 miles) s of Sansepolcro, in the tiny cemetery chapel on
the edge of the village of **Monterchi**, is another masterpiece by
Piero, the *Madonna del Parto* ★ (📷 *custodian always on duty*).
Pointing proudly to her pregnant womb, she is revealed to us by
two triumphant angels, reverse images of the same cartoon.

Saturnia
Map **9***K7. 215km (134 miles) s of Florence, 57km (35 miles)
SE of Grosseto. 58050. Grosseto. Population: 631.*
The Etruscan town on this site was called Aurinia. The Romans
named it Saturnia because they believed it had been founded by
Jupiter's father. The walls built by the Sienese in the 15thC
incorporate Etruscan and Roman sections.

The Etruscan necropolis lies to the N of the walls, the most
interesting tombs being in the Puntone area.

The spa of **Terme di Saturnia**, where sulfurous water springs at a constant temperture of 99°F (37°C), is 3km (2 miles) to the s.

The road N to *Monte Amiata* passes through a beautiful, sparsely populated landscape dotted with medieval castles and villages.

☞ Terme di Saturnia
Strada della Follonata, 58050 Saturnia, Grosseto ☎ *(0564) 601061*
🅿️ *500172* 🏨 *104 rms* 🛏 *104* 🖩 ▬ 🚗 🆎 ⊙ 🆚
A serious first-class spa hotel offering a wide range of treatments.
🏠 ✇ 🕭 ⬚ 🖼 ⚓ ≈ ℘ 🏋 🏌

≡ Da Michele
In the main square ☎ *(0564) 601074* ▮▮▯ *Closed Tues except summer.*
This excellent restaurant is one of the most popular in the Maremma. Be sure to book.

☞ ≡ Laudomia
9km (6 miles) s at Podori di Montemerano ☎ *(0564) 620062* ▮▮▯ ⌂
▬ 🚗 🆎 🆚 *Closed Thurs, June.*
A welcoming traditional rustic hotel and restaurant.

Scarperia
*Map **16**D6. 30km (19 miles) N of Florence. 50038. Firenze. Population: 5,190.*

An industrial and crafts center (furniture, wrought iron, knives, copper) in the Mugello with a fine Palazzo Pretorio of 1306 and, in the church opposite, a tondo of the *Madonna and Child* by B. da Maiano. **Event:** International motorcycle rallies take place at the autodrome on Sun.

Nearby sights
The road to the N climbs through the mountain **pass of Scarperia** at 882m (2,920ft), the 'little Switzerland' of the Mugello, known as '*il Giogo*,' which links the Mugello to the Santerno Valley.

3.5km (2 miles) NE of Scarperia is the village of **Sant' Agata**, with a strikingly unusual Romanesque **pieve**.

≡ The homey, delightful **Molunuccio** (☎ *(055) 8406952* ▮▮ *closed Mon)*, 2km (1¼ miles) beyond Sant'Agata at Molinuccio, has a trout pond.

Shopping
Coltelleria Artigiana Giglio (*Via dell'Oche 48* ☎ *(055) 846148* ▮▯); knives of all kinds at low prices.

Sesto Fiorentino
*Map **6**B2–3. 9km (6 miles) NW of Florence. 50019. Firenze. Bus 28 from Florence station. Population: 44,458.*

An important center of the porcelain and ceramics industry. In the central square, Piazza Ginori, is the 15thC Palazzo Pretorio.
Museo delle Porcellane di Doccia
Via Pratese 🚌 *Open Tues–Sat 9:30am–1pm, 3:30–6pm.*
In a park along the Via Pratese, this modern museum (1965) exhibits a superb collection of 18th–20thC porcelains from the Doccia factory founded in 1737 by Carlo Ginori.

Nearby sight
To the E of Sesto is **Quinto**, where the imposing 7thC BC Etruscan **tomba della Montagnola** is in the Via Fratelli Rosselli (custodian at no. 95).

☞ Villa Villoresi
Via delle Torri 63, 50019 Sesto Fiorentino, Firenze ☎ *(055) 4489032*
▮▮▮ *28 rms* 🛏 *28* 🚗 🖩 ▬ ⊙
A beautifully maintained 14thC villa.
🏠 🖼 ⚓ ◁€ ≈

🏨 ≈ **Motelagip** (*Campo Bisenzio* ☎ *(055) 440081* ▮▯ *to* ▮▮).

≋ **Giuseppe Alessi**
Via Bolognese 11, Montorsoli ☎ *(055) 401059* ▮▮▮ ▭ ≈ ↝ 🆅🆂🅰
Dinner only. Closed Sun, Tues, Aug.
This is a restaurant for serious eaters only. You must book a table 3–4
months in advance. The proprietor is a scholar of Renaissance cooking,
and his great dishes are carefully researched historic re-creations made
with the best ingredients still to be found in the Tuscan countryside.

≋ **La Terrazza** (☎ *(055) 8879078* ▮▯ *to* ▮▮▮ *closed Sun, Mon, Aug*) is
in the Castello of Calenzano; **Vecciolino** (*Via Colli Alti* ☎ *(055) 448194*
▮▯ *closed Tues*).

Settignano
*Map **7**D5. 8km (5 miles) E of Florence. Bus 10 from Piazza
San Marco, Florence. 50135. Firenze. Population: 1,563.*
A Florentine suburb in the Fiesolan Hills graced by cypresses,
olive groves and fine old villas. Renaissance sculptors who were
born or made their home for a time in the area near the *pietra
serena* quarries of Monte Ceceri include Desiderio, the
Rossellino brothers, the Maiano brothers, Benedetto da
Rovezzano, and Michelangelo. Boccaccio set the *Decameron* in
these hills, and D'Annunzio lived here during his love affair
with Eleanora Duse in the Villa Capponcina.

One of the many foreign literary residents was Walter Savage
Landor, author of *Imaginary Conversations*, who lived in the
15thC Villa Gherardesca in the 1820s; another was the art
historian Bernard Berenson, whose **Villa I Tatti** (☎*603251,
open by appointment Tues, Thurs, pm*), is now run by Harvard
University as a center for Renaissance Studies. The English
attachment to this countryside reached a peak late in the 19thC
when Queen Victoria visited the Castle of **Vincigliata** (see
below). The gushing sensibilities of English esthetes were
satirized by Anatole France in his novel *Le Lys Rouge*.

See also *Fiesole*.

Sights and places of interest
Approaching from central Florence, the Via G. D'Annunzio leads past
Nervi's concrete **Stadium** in the Campo di Marte to Ponte a Mensola
where the church of **S. Martino a Mensola** (*ring for entrance*) has an
elegant *quattrocento* interior with a triptych by Taddeo Gaddi. The Via
D'Annunzio then climbs to the village of Settignano. There is a good view
of Florence from Piazza Desiderio and, in the 16thC church of the
Assunta, a pulpit designed by Buontalenti, and a Della Robbia *Madonna*.

1km (⅔ mile) SE is the **Villa Gamberaia** which has one of the great
Italian gardens (*rarely open to the public*).

To the NE is Montebeni, Berenson's favorite walking country and still
unexpectedly rural. A left turn off the Montebeni road leads to the Castle
of **Vincigliata**, Victorianized in 1855 by John Temple Leader.

🏨 The **Villa Linda** (*Poggio Gherardo 5* ☎ *(055) 603913* ▭) is a
simple *pensione* run by Benedictine nuns.

≋ **Le Cave**
Via delle Cave 16, Maiano ☎*(055) 59133* ▮▮▮ ▭ ▮▮▮ ◁≪ 🅰🅴 ⊕ ⓒⓓ
↝ ↝ *Closed Thurs, Sun eve, Aug.*
An old *bottega* which once served the quarry workers. The food is not
above ordinary and the interior is noisy; but the location is magical.

≋ **Osvaldo**
Via G. D'Annunzio 51 ☎ *(055) 602168* ▮▮▮ ▭ ↝ *Closed Tues eve,
Wed, Aug.*
A favorite with fellows of **I Tatti**.

Siena ★

Map **11**G6. 68km (42 miles) s of Florence. 53100. Siena.
Population: 64,251 **i** Piazza del Campo 55
☎ _(0577) 280551; Via di Città 5_ ☎ _(0577) 47051._

Soft Siena, City of the Virgin, stands on her pedestal of three
hills, vain of her beauty, absorbed in her past. She is the other
half of Tuscany, feminine counterpart to the hardheaded
masculinity of Florence. According to a persistent legend,
Siena was founded by Senius, son of Remus; hence the wolf,
one of the city's most prominent emblems. But the earliest
certain knowledge we have of Siena, apart from evidence of an
Etruscan settlement, is of the Roman colony Saena Julia.

During the early Middle Ages Siena enjoyed a privileged
relationship with the Hohenstaufen emperors; and as a free
republic from the early 12thC she attained a precocious pre-
eminence in banking and trade, and became the leading
Ghibelline center in Tuscany and the natural rival of Guelf
Florence. Although the defeat of Florence at the Battle of
Montaperti in 1260 is still celebrated in Siena as a glorious
event, it was less significant than the Florentine victory 9yr later
at Colle di Val d'Elsa. Then Siena joined the Guelf alliance and
from 1287 was governed as an oligarchy by a Council of Nine
'Good Men' chosen from the middle classes. The Republic
flourished under the balanced, methodical rule of the Nine; the
late 13th to early 14thC was an age of stability, prosperity and
artistic achievement. But the turmoil and discontent following
famines and the Black Death of 1348 led to the overthrow in
1355 of the Nine by the nobles assisted by the working class.

There is nothing in the world quite like Siena; it is a medieval
city that might be likened to a rare beast, with heart, arteries,
tail, paws and teeth. Only the skeleton is left, intact, and it is
enough to astound us.

Bernard Berenson

Spiritually Siena was guided through the turbulent post-
plague years by two remarkable religious reformers, later
canonized as St Catherine of Siena (1347–80) and St
Bernardino of Siena (1380–1444). Politically, the next two
centuries were marked by fruitless wars, voluntary submission
to foreign control – Charles IV from 1355, Gian Galeazzo
Visconti from 1399, Charles V in 1530 – and periods of unstable
independence when the power of nobility became increasingly
stronger.

In 1552 the city rebelled against the Spanish occupation, and
2yr later the combined forces of Charles V and Duke Cosimo I
of Florence advanced on Siena and laid seige for 18 months
during which the population was halved and the countryside
devastated. In 1557 Charles sold the city outright to Cosimo,
and in 1559 Siena and her territories were officially annexed to
the Tuscan grand duchy by the Peace of Cateau-Cambrésis.

As the unwilling bride of Florence, Siena was treated as a
second-class member of the Tuscan empire. No public banks
were permitted to operate until 1622; the wool industry
collapsed in the mid-17thC and by the mid-18thC most Sienese
noble families were deeply in debt. "Cracking, peeling, fading,
crumbling, rotting," Henry James wrote of the city in 1909.

And yet, visitors to Siena in the late 20thC will find more here
than art to admire and even envy. It seems that the ideal of the
Common Good, practised by the Nine and revealed to posterity

in Ambrogio Lorenzetti's famous frescoes in the Palazzo Pubblico, may not have been forgotten.

Sienese art

Siena is a Gothic city. Its greatest buildings – the Duomo and Palazzo Pubblico – and best-known pictures – Duccio's *Maestà*, Simone Martini's *Maestà* and Ambrogio Lorenzetti's *Good and Bad Government* – were created in the late 13thC–14thC. In the 15thC the Sienese by and large ignored the Florentine Renaissance. They continued to build ogival palaces and even their major painters, Giovanni di Paolo and Sassetta, made decorative, two-dimensional pictures on gold backgrounds. It was not until the 16thC that Renaissance painting arrived with Sodoma and Domenico Beccafumi, the greatest Sienese Mannerist.

Most important works of art were commissioned by the government or religious bodies, powerful, conservative groups who knew exactly what they wanted as to style and subject matter. Over half the pictures commissioned between 1350–1550 were of the Virgin, Queen of Siena; and collaborative projects were more common than in Florence.

Sienese sculpture advanced earlier and further than its sister arts, thanks partly to the influence of Giovanni Pisano, whose figures for the facade of the Duomo are among the most important examples of Gothic sculpture in Italy. The greatest native Sienese sculptor, Jacopo della Quercia, effected the transition to the Renaissance; his principal works in the city are the Fonte Gaia and the Baptistry font.

Events: The *Palio*, the bare-backed horse race around the Campo on July 2 and Aug 16, is the central event of the Sienese calendar and the focal point of every Sienese citizen's life. It is one of the strangest and most magnificent public spectacles there are: a mixture of pomp, licensed violence and corruption, skill, courage, luck, history, and fantasy. Ten of the city's 17 *contrade* (wards) are chosen by lot to participate in the race, which is preceded by a spectacular procession. The *palio*, or banner, is the prize. The second and more important *Palio* on Aug 16 is in honor of the Assumption of the Virgin. Tickets are extremely expensive, but the rehearsals on the previous days can be viewed for a more reasonable price from a seat at one of the restaurants in the Campo.

Master classes and a festival of concerts are held in July and Aug under the auspices of the Accademia Musicale Chigiana, 82 Via di Città ☎(0577) 46152.

A weekly market is held on Wed morning.

Sights and places of interest

Siena is built on three landlocked hills which form the most westerly spur of the Chiana mountains. Since the early 13thC the city has been divided into three districts, or *terzi*: Città, San Martino and Camollia. The essential civic unit is the *contrada*, or ward, of which there are 17. Their fantastic names (Caterpillar, Eagle, Dragon, etc.) derive from allegorical carts paraded at the Palio. Every Sienese is a member of the *contrada* in which he is born and remains loyal to it for life.

The old city is surrounded by 7km (4⅔ miles) of intact walls, entered through eight gates. The main streets are the Via di Città, Banchi di Sotto and Banchi di Sopra, which meet just above the Campo, the hub of the city, at the **Croce del Travaglio**, a good starting point for a tour of the city.

Traffic is excluded from the center; convenient parking lots are near S. Domenico, the Stadium and the Lizza.

Campo ★

The central square of Siena, one of the most magical public spaces in Europe, lies at the confluence of the three hills on which the city is built. Its sloping, semicircular shape often elicits comparisons: to a fan, or shell, or amphitheater. For the Sienese it is a cloak – the cloak of the Madonna spread out to protect her favored city. The perimeter of the cloak is trimmed with lacy palaces of which the most striking is the curved **Sansedoni**, originally a group of 13 palaces extended in the 14thC and restructured in the early 18thC.

The brick paving is divided into nine sections symbolizing the government of the Nine Good Men, who were responsible for the systematic development of the Campo from the late 13thC. At the center of the curve is a reproduction of Jacopo della Quercia's Fonte Gaia, the original of which is now in the **Palazzo Pubblico**.

Palazzo Pubblico ▥ ★

The structure of the most graceful Gothic civic building in Tuscany reflects that of the communal government for which it was erected from 1297–1342. The wings (raised by one story in 1681) were occupied respectively by the Podestà, responsible for justice, and the Nine, responsible for administration, and separated by the central body housing the Biccherna, or treasury, and the General Council. The black and white communal shield, the *balzana*, decorates all the openings of the facade. From the left corner, the bell tower (1325–48), known as the *Mangia* after the nickname ('wastrel') of its first bell-ringer, leaps – in William Dean Howell's vivid words – "like a rocket into the starlit air." The **Cappella di Piazza** at the base of the Mangia was built from 1352–76 and modified in 1468. To its right is the entrance to the Cortile del Podestà, which gives access to the sections of the palace open to the public. For a stunning view climb the 503 steps to the top of the Mangia.

Museo Civico ★

First floor 🖼 *Open Apr–Sept Mon–Sat 8:30am–7:30pm; Oct–Mar 8:30am–7pm, Sun, hols 8:30am–1pm.*

Sala del Risorgimento: The six frescoes, by the best late 19thC-Sienese artists, relate episodes from the life of Victor Emmanuel II. **Sala di Balia:** The only room in the palace decorated by non-Sienese artists. The frescoes (1407) by Spinello Aretino and Pari di Spinello depict the life of the Sienese Pope Alexander III. **Sala dei Cardinali:** Sculptures by followers of Jacopo della Quercia. **Sala del Concistro:** Portal by B. Rossellino, frescoes by Beccafumi of the *Political Virtues* (1529–36).

Antechapel: Frescoes (1414) by Taddeo di Bartolo. The huge *St Christopher* symbolizes the duty of the commune to care for the weak. **Chapel:** The elegant iron gate (1437) may have been designed by Jacopo della Quercia. The Gothic **choir stalls** (1428) illustrate the Nicene Creed. Frescoes of *Scenes from the Life of the Virgin* (1407) by Taddeo di Bartolo. Over the altar, the *Sacred Family with St Leonard* by Sodoma.

Sala del Mappamondo: The room where the city council met. The painted map after which the room was named no longer exists, but a recent restoration has revealed the existence of yet another 14thC fresco beneath the equestrian portrait of *Guidoriccio da Fogliano* ★ until recently assumed to be by Simone Martini. Originally part of a cycle running round three walls of the room and illustrating the castles conquered by Siena after 1314, this fresco records the victory over the nobles of Montemassi and Sassoferrato. On the opposite wall is the *Maestà* ★ (1315) signed "Siena had me painted by the hand of Simone [Martini]." The Virgin is represented by the Queen of Heaven and Siena.

Sala della Pace: Sienese dedication to law and order received its most complete and vivid pictorial expression with Ambrogio Lorenzetti's *Allegory of Good and Bad Government* ★ (1338–40), painted for the council chamber as a reminder of the Augustinian and Thomist teachings that justice and common good are the first aims of good government. On the wall opposite the windows, *Good Government* is represented by a king wearing the colors of the *balzana* and surrounded by symbolic virtues and attributes. On the right wall, we see the *Effects of Good Government in the City and Country*. For all its didactic intricacy, this picture may still be enjoyed in the spirit as St Bernardino described it in the 15thC: "I see merchants buying and selling, I see dancing, the houses being repaired, the workers busy in the vineyards or sowing the fields. . . ." On the left wall is the ruined fresco of *Bad Government and its Effects*.

Sala dei Pilastri: Sienese pictures of the 14th–15thC, including Neroccio di Bartolommeo's diptych of *St Bernardino*. **Loggia:** The remains of Jacopo della Quercia's carvings for the **Fonte Gaia** ★ (1409–19). The fountain commemorated the appearance of water in the Campo.

Chigi-Saracini Palace 🏛
Via di Città 89 🚉 🚊 *Visits on request* ☎ *(0577) 46152.*

Built in the 14thC for one of the great Sienese banking families, this lovely stone and brick palace now houses the distinguished Accademia Musicale Chigiana, who hold some of their summer concerts here (see events opposite) and a collection of 14th–17thC Tuscan paintings.

Across the Via di Città, at no. 126, is the **Palazzo Piccolomini delle Papesse** (1460–95), built for Pius II's sister, probably by B. Rossellino, in the Florentine Renaissance style.

Duomo 🏛 † ★

The cathedral of Santa Maria dell'Assunta was the most expensive and carefully considered building project of Siena's golden age. Its construction, which occupied nearly two centuries, was in the beginning supervised by committees of Sienese citizens, and there was no Sienese artist or craftsman of any distinction who did not work at some time on the cathedral. Long after the structure was completed in the late 14thC, they continued to embellish the interior. The result is perhaps less satisfying as a work of architecture than for its individual components.

The site chosen for the building, which began in the late 12thC, was the Castelvecchio, the earliest inhabited part of the city. The basic structure was complete in 1215, the hexagonal cupola in 1264, and the facade was begun in 1284. In 1339 an extraordinary and hopelessly ambitious decision was made: Siena would build a new and greater cathedral, rivaling those of Florence and Orvieto, for which the old cathedral would serve as transept. This unwieldy and, as it turned out, prohibitively expensive scheme was abandoned after the 1348 plague, and the old cathedral was finally completed in 1382.

The skeletal remains of the new cathedral (**Duomo Nuovo**), now housing the Cathedral Museum (**see over**), stand to the right of the Duomo, behind Buontalenti's Palazzo della Prefettura. Opposite the

Duomo is the **Hospital of Santa Maria della Scala** Ⅲ (open daily *9am–noon*), the most important institution in medieval and Renaissance Siena after the Duomo and Palazzo Pubblico. The building, which dates from late 13th to 14thC, is still in use as a hospital; in the Sala d'Infermeria modern patients are surrounded by frescoes illustrating the care of the sick in the Renaissance. Over the high altar of the adjoining church of **Santa Maria della Scala**, rebuilt in 1466, is Vecchietta's superb bronze *Risen Christ* (1476). To the left of the Duomo is the early 18thC imitation-Gothic Palazzo Arcivescovile (Archbishop's Palace), with Ambrogio Lorenzetti's enchanting, naturalistic *Madonna Lactans*.

The polychrome marble **facade of the Duomo** is best studied from the far right corner of the square. The lower section (1284–96), the first building project in Tuscany to reflect the Gothic influence of *San Galgano*, was designed by Giovanni Pisano. The statues are copies of the originals, by Giovanni or assistants, now in the Cathedral Museum (see opposite). The central bronze door dates from 1958, and the gabled upper section in the high Gothic style was begun in 1376; the mosaics are 19thC. From the right transept rises the Romanesque **campanile** (1313).

The **interior** is most immediately striking for the giddy optical effect of the black and white stripes. The **floor** ★ is paved in marble with 56 designs produced by over 40 leading Sienese artists, executed by craftsmen in *sgraffiti* or intarsia, a remarkable collaborative work carried out between 1369–1547. Notice especially Beccafumi's *Old Testament Scenes* between the cupola and high altar.

Libreria Piccolomini ★
Off the left nave Open daily *9am–7pm*.
The most brilliantly decorative room in Tuscany, this was built in the 1490s by Francesco Todeschini Piccolomini (Pope Pius III). The vividly charming frescoes (1502–05) by Pinturicchio depict ten *Scenes from the Life of Pius II*. In the center of the room is the beautiful and influential *Three Graces*, a 3rdC Roman copy of a Hellenistic statue. Fine illuminated choir books are displayed on late 15thC benches.

To the w of the library is the great **Piccolomini Altar** (1503), designed by Andrea Bregno. The statues of *Sts Peter and Pius* and *Sts Gregory and Paul* are by the young Michelangelo.

Left transept: The **chapel of St John the Baptist** (1481–98) is entered through an elegant marble portal. Frescoes include Pinturicchio's two portraits of *Alberto Arighieri*, in youth and old age. The vigorous bronze statue of the *Baptist* (1457) is by Donatello; that of *St Catherine of Alexandria* (1487) is by Neroccio. The **pulpit** ★ (1266–68) is by Nicola Pisano, assisted by his son Giovanni and pupils including Arnolfo di Cambio; 6yr later than the great **Baptistry** pulpit at *Pisa*, this work is freer and more innovatory. The seven panels, separated by figures of prophets and angels, depict *Scenes from the Life of Christ*. The staircase was added by Riccio in 1570.

The **Chapel of St Ansano** contains a **monument to Cardinal Petroni** (1317–18) by Tino di Camaino and, in the pavement, the slab **tomb of Bishop Giovanni Pecci** by Donatello.

Presbytery: The **high altar** (1532) by Peruzzi bears a huge **ciborium** (1462–72) by Vecchietta. The two higher flanking *Angels* (1489) are by Giovanni di Stefano, those placed lower down (1499) by Francesco di Giorgio Martini. Eight serenely beautiful **candelabra-angels** (1548–50) on the nave pilasters are by Beccafumi, perhaps his masterpieces as a sculptor. In the apse are 51 finely carved **choir stalls** (14th–16thC). The **window** above (1288) is one of the earliest examples of Italian stained glass, made from cartoons by Duccio.

Right transept: The **Chigi chapel** (1661) was built for the morbidly pious Fabio Chigi, Pope as Alexander VII, to designs by Bernini. *St Jerome* and the *Magdalen* in niches on the entrance wall are by Bernini. The *Madonna del Voto* over the altar is by Guido da Siena or a follower.
Baptistry ★
Reached by a steep flight of steps to the right of the Duomo. Facing its own Piazza San Giovanni, the Baptistry is situated beneath the apse of the cathedral. The impressive Gothic **facade** (1317–82) is incomplete in the upper section. The **interior** was designed by Camaino and Tino di Camaino and frescoed by, among others, Vecchietta. At its center is Jacopo della Quercia's hexagonal marble **font** ★ (1411–30), a masterpiece of artistic collaboration in the Gothic-Renaissance style. Two of the statues around the basin, *Faith* and *Hope*, are by Donatello.

The six gilded bronze relief panels include Jacopo della Quercia's powerful *Zacharias expelled from the Temple*, Ghiberti's *Baptism of Christ* and Donatello's *Herod's Feast*.

To the E of the Baptistry is the **Palazzo del Magnifico** (1504–08), designed by G. Cozzarelli for Pandolfo Petrucci, autocratic political leader of Siena from 1487–1524. The beautifully wrought bronzes on the handsome facade have been replaced by copies.

Museo dell'Opera del Duomo (*Cathedral Museum*) ★
In right aisle of the Duomo Nuovo ☒ *Open daily 9am–7pm.*
Ground floor: Among the carvings from the cathedral facade, the **ten figures** ★ (1284–96) by Giovanni Pisano are among the most important Gothic sculptures in Italy. In the center is a bas-relief of the *Madonna and Child with St Anthony Abbot and Cardinal Antonio Casini*, a late work by Jacopo della Quercia.

First floor: Sala di Duccio. Duccio's *Maestà* ★ (1308–11), the inaugural work of the great period of Sienese painting, was carried to the Duomo when complete in a magnificent candlelit procession while the bells of Siena pealed the Gloria and the citizens offered prayers and alms to the poor. It stood over the high altar of the cathedral until removed to a side chapel in 1505. Originally painted on both sides, the panel was split and dismantled in the 18thC. The *Madonna Enthroned* now faces the 26 *Scenes from the Passion*. On the left wall are 19 **panels from the predella and upper section** (others are in London, Washington and New York).

On the right wall are P. Lorenzetti's triptych of the *Nativity of the Virgin* (1342) and a *Madonna and Child* (1283) by the young Duccio.

Sala del Tesoro: The finest treasures are Giovanni Pisano's tiny wooden *Crucifix* and F. da Valdambrino's busts of saints.

Second floor: Sala della Madonna degli Occhi Grossi. The room is named after the 13thC panel of a large-eyed *Madonna* in the center. The outstanding picture is Simone Martini's *Blessed Agostino Novello with Four of his Miracles* ★ (c.1330), formerly in Sant' Agostino. **Sala dei Conversari:** Works by Matteo di Giovanni, Beccafumi, Pomarancio and Luca Giordano. From the next room one may climb to the rim of the Duomo Nuovo for spectacular views.

The **Cripta delle Statue** (*hours as museum*) is entered from the steps leading to the Baptistry. It contains statues from the Duomo and fresco fragments (1270–80), the earliest known Sienese wall paintings.

Fonte Branda
The most famous and one of the oldest of the many Sienese wells.
Fontegiusta †
Via Fontegiusta, off Via Camollia.
The church of the Madonna of Fontegiusta was built in 1482–84 in gratitude for a Sienese victory over the Florentines. The elegant portico was added in 1489. The unusual square interior contains 16thC Sienese paintings and a large tabernacle by Marrina.

Via Camollia ends at the **Porta Camollia** (1604), the most northerly of the Sienese gates opening onto the Florence road. The famous Sienese welcome *Cor magis tibi Sena pandit* (Siena opens wide its heart to you) was inscribed when the gate was rebuilt in honor of a visit by Ferdinand I.

Forte di Santa Barbara
Built in 1560 by Duke Cosimo I, this fort now houses the Enoteca Italica Permanente (see *Tuscan wines*). The views from the ramparts are best at sunset. To the NE is the **Lizza**, the triangular public park of Siena.

Loggia della Mercanzia
Erected in 1428–44 where the three principal streets of Siena meet above the Campo, and now housing the Provincial Tourist Board. The statues of saints are by Vecchietta and A. Federighi. The upper story is 17thC.

Piccolomini Palace ▥ ☆
Via Banchi di Sotto ☉ *Open Mon–Fri 9:30am–1pm,*
Sat 9am–12:30pm.
The palace, begun in 1469, was very likely designed by B. Rossellino. It resembles his *Rucellai Palace, Florence* and **Piccolimini Palace** at *Pienza*. With the nearby **Logge del Papa** (1462), designed by A. Federighi, this constitutes the most important Renaissance building complex in Siena. The palace houses the State Archives; among the documents on view are the **covers of the registers of Biccherna**, the treasury, illuminated by leading Sienese artists from 1258–1659.

The 16thC ex-monastery opposite the palace is the seat of the University of Siena. Via San Vigilio leads to the picturesque medieval

buildings of the **Corte del Castellare degli Ugurgieri**.
Pinacoteca Nazionale ⅢⅢ ★
Via San Pietro 29 🔁 *Open Tues–Sun 8:45am–1:45pm.*
The outstanding collection of 12th–early 17thC Sienese pictures is
housed in the graceful early 15thC Gothic **Palazzo Buonsignori**. The
display is arranged chronologically beginning on the second floor. The
following is an introductory tour of some of the major works.

Rm. I: Altar frontal of *The Redeemer* with symbols of the Evangelists
and scenes from the Passion (1215), the earliest dated Sienese painting.
Rm. II: Works by Guido da Siena (13thC) the first of the great Sienese
masters. Rms. III–IV: Duccio, especially the finely executed but
damaged *Madonna dei Francescani*. Rm. VI: Simone Martini's *Madonna
and Child*. Rms. VII–VIII: The *Two Views*, attributed to A. Lorenzetti,
are the earliest known examples of pure landscape painting in pre-
Renaissance European art. Also by A. Lorenzetti: *Madonna with Saints
and Angels* and *Annunciation* (1344). P. Lorenzetti: *Madonna and Child*
(1328–29), originally in the center of an altarpiece of which the superb
Stories of the Carmelite Order formed the predella. *Birth of the Virgin*
(c.1380–90) by Paolo di Giovanni Fei.

Rm. XIII: Giovanni di Paolo's *Last Judgment* and *Madonna of
Humility*; Sassetta's *Last Supper* and *St Anthony Abbot*. Rm. XIV:
Neroccio's *Madonna and Saints* (c.1475); Francesco di Giorgio's
Annunciation and *Nativity*. Rm. XVIII: Sano di Pietro's *The Virgin
Commending the City of Siena to Pope Calixtus II* (1456); Francesco di
Giorgio's *Coronation of the Virgin*.

First floor. Rm. XXIII: Pinturicchio's *Holy Family with the Young St
John*. Rms. XXX–XXXII: Sodoma's *Nativity*, *Scourging of Christ*
(c.1511–14), *Deposition*. Rm. XXXIII: Beccafumi's *St Catherine
Receiving the Stigmata* (c.1515) and *Birth of the Virgin* (1543).
Rm. XXXVII: Beccafumi's *Descent into Hell* (c.1530–35). Sodoma's
Descent into Hell and *Gethsemene* (c.1525).
Salimbeni Palace ⅢⅢ
This beautiful 14thC palace is the headquarters of the Sienese-owned
Monte dei Paschi bank. On the right side of Piazza Salimbeni is the
Renaissance **Spanocchi Palace** (1470) by G. da Maiano, and on the left
the 16thC Tantucci Palace.
Sant'Agostino †
The 13thC building, remade in the 18thC, retains important paintings,
notably Perugino's *Crucifixion* (1506), A. Lorenzetti's *Madonna and
Saints*, Matteo di Giovanni's *Slaughter of the Innocents* (1482) and, over
the high altar, Sodoma's *Epiphany*.
Santa Caterina (*Santuario Cateriniano*) †
A complex of chapels created in and around the house of Catherine
Benincasa, the eloquent mystic who was canonized in 1461. **The Oratory
of St Catherine** (1465–74), facing Via S. Caterina, was built by the
contrada of Fontebranda, whose symbol, the goose, adorns the facade.
Inside is a wooden statue of *St Catherine* (1474) by Neroccio and five
frescoed *Angels* by Sodoma. The Oratorio della Camera is built over St
Catherine's cell. The Baroque Oratorio del Crocifisso contains the 13thC
Crucifix before which the saint received the stigmata at Pisa in 1375. The
Oratorio Superiore has a ceiling by Riccio, and a 17thC tiled floor.
San Domenico †
The stark red-brick Dominican preaching church crowns the hill above
Fontebranda. The present building, incorporating the original early-
13thC church, dates from the 14th–15thC. The campanile was
completed in 1340. The only authentic portrait of *St Catherine*, who
assumed the Dominican habit in this church, is that by her friend Andrea
Vanni, in a chapel at the w end. In the Chapel of St Catherine, off the
right side, are Sodoma's frescoes of *Episodes from the Life of St Catherine*
(1526). The *Ciborium* and two *Angels* (1475) are by B. da Maiano.
San Francesco †
As in Florence, the Franciscan preaching church stands across the city
from that built by the Dominicans. An earlier church on this site was
begun immediately after the death of St Francis. The present building
(1326–1475) was altered after a fire in the 17thC and again in the late
19thC. The Neo-Gothic facade was applied in 1913. In the N transept are
detached frescoes (1331) by P. Lorenzetti of the *Crucifixion* and by A.
Lorenzetti of *St Louis of Anjou before Pope Boniface VII* and the
Martyrdom of the Franciscans.

On the s side of the piazza is the **Oratorio di San Bernardino** (*custodian at no. 19*). This oratory was built in the 15thC on the site where the Franciscan St Bernardino had preached. The upper chapel is elegantly decorated with 15thC stuccowork, carvings and frescoes by Sodoma, G. del Pacchia and Beccafumi. The Via del Comune descends to the 14thC **Porta Ovile**.

Santa Maria dei Servi †
Piazza Alessandro Manzoni

The building dates from the 13th–15thC; the interior naves and aisles were reworked in 1471–1528. Most important of the Sienese school pictures are: right aisle, Coppo di Marcovaldo's *Madonna* (1261); right transept, P. Lorenzetti's fresco of *The Slaughter of the Innocents*; left transept, Lippo Memmi's *Madonna*.

Nearby is the imposing **Porta Romana** (1327), from which the Via Cassia leads to Rome.

Santo Spirito †
Via dei Pispini

The brick Church of the Holy Spirit dates from 1498. The portal is attributed to Peruzzi and the cupola (1508) to Cozzarelli. Inside are works by Sodoma, Cozzarelli and Beccafumi. At the end of Via dei Pispini is the 14thC **Porta Pispini**, with the remains of a fresco of the *Nativity* (1531) by Sodoma.

Tolomei Palace ▥
11 Via Banchi di Sopra

The oldest private palace in Siena, now occupied by the Florentine Savings Bank, was built in 1208, and altered in c.1267.

Other sights outside the city walls

Diavoli Palace ▥

Just beyond Porta Camollia in Via Fiorentina is a medieval building, rebuilt in 1460 by A. Federighi. This palace is one of the first and most original pieces of Sienese Renaissance architecture.

Osservanza ▥ †

2.5km (1½ miles) from Porta Ovile, beyond the railway crossing, is the most interesting church in the environs of Siena, founded by St Bernardino in 1423 and rebuilt after damage in World War II to the original designs (1474–90) of Giacomo Cozzarelli. It contains a terracotta group of the *Annunciation* by Andrea della Robbia and, in the sacristy, a large *Pietà* by Cozzarelli.

Hotels

Certosa di Maggiano ▥
Via Certosa 82, 53100 Siena
☎ *(0577) 288180* ⊕*574221* ▮▮▮▮
14 rms including 9 suites ▭ *14*
▤ ▬ ▥ ⤨ AE ⊕ VISA *Closed Nov–Feb.*

Location: E *of Porta Romana off the Arezzo/Rome road.* An exceptionally civilized hotel around the cloister and church of a 14thC monastery. The restaurant is now open to non-residents.
⌂ ▢ ▱ ⋓ ⁓

Park Hotel ▥
Via Marciano 16, 53100 Siena
☎ *(0577) 44803* ⊕*571005* ▮▮▮▮
69 rms ▭ *69* ▤ ▬ ▥ ⤨ AE
CB ⊕ ⊕ VISA

Location: 2km (1¼ miles) to NW. *A slick, modernized 15thC suburban villa. Standards have improved since it was taken over by the Ciga chain, but the service still doesn't live up to the luxurious accommodation.* Good restaurant.
⌂ ⍖ ▢ ▱ ⁂ ⋓ ⁓ ⚓

Palazzo Ravizza
Pian dei Mantellini 34, 53100 Siena ☎ *(0577) 280462* ▮▯ *to* ▮▮▯
28 rms ▭ *20* ▬ ▥ ⤨ AE ⊕
⊕ VISA

Location: 5min walk from the Duomo and Campo. *This attractive first-class* pensione, *run by the same family for nearly 200yr in a 17thC villa, has kept its old-fashioned character better than most.*
⍖ ⅗ ▱ ⋓ ⟨⟨

Villa Scacciapensieri
Via di Scacciapensieri, 53100 Siena ☎ *(0577) 41411/41442* ▮▮▯
to ▮▮▯ *30 rms* ▭ *30* ▬ ▬
⤨ AE ⊕ ⊕ VISA *Closed Nov to mid-Mar.*

Location: 3km (2 miles) to N. *A big, comfortable country villa set in a large garden with wonderful views of Siena. The generous breakfasts are a rare treat in Tuscany.*
⌂ ⍖ ⅗ ▱ ⋓ ⟨⟨ ⁓ ⁂

Restaurants

To dine in the Campo on a starlit evening is one of life's most magical experiences, but there isn't much to choose between the two restaurants: **Il Campo** (☎ _(0577) 280725, closed Tues_) and **Mangia** (☎ _(0577) 281121, closed Mon_).

Away from the Campo – and the tourists – the culinary standards are somewhat higher: **Le Campane** ((_Via della Campane 6_ ☎ _(0577) 284035_ ▯▯ _closed Sun, part of Nov_); **Da Guido** (_Vicolo Pettinaio 7_ ☎ _(0577) 280042_ ▯▯ _to_ ▮▮ _closed Mon, July_); **Le Logge** (_Via del Porrione 33_ ☎ _(0577) 48013_ ▯▯ _closed Sun, June_); **Al Marsili**)_Via del Castoria 3_ ☎ _(0577) 47154_ ▯▯ _to_ ▮▮ _closed Mon_); **Nello La Taverna** (_Via del Porrione 28_ ☎ _(0577) 289043_ ▯▯ _closed Sun eve, Mon, Feb_); **Tullio ai Tre Christi** (_Vicolo Provenzano 1_ ☎ _(0577) 280608_ ▯▯ _to_ ▮▮ _closed Mon, Feb_).

La Taverna ✿
Via del Sergente 5, Vagliagli
☎_(0577) 322532_ ▯▯ ▭ ➤ ➪
▣ ▥ _Closed Mon._

This is a warm, cheerful tavern in a small hill town N of Siena. **_Specialties:_** _Homemade pastas._

Taverna Il Colombaio
SS 222, Querciagrossa, 2km N of Siena ☎ _(0577) 51144_ ▯▯ ▭ ▬
▬ ➪ ➪ ▥ _Closed Mon, Jan._

The old inn serves its own ham and wine from the Villa Colombaio estate of the Ugurgieri family.

Vecchio Maniero
Via Stretta 5, Sovicille
☎ _(0577) 314340_ ▯▯ ▭
▤ ▣ ▥ _Closed Mon._

In an ancient manor house in the medieval village of Sovicille, 7km (4 miles) w of Siena. **_Specialties:_** _Pastas, funghi porcini, game._

Sinalunga
Map **_12_**_G7. 103km (64 miles) SE of Florence, 45km (28 miles) SE of Siena. 53048._

Hill town in the heart of the Valdichiana near the entrance to the autostrada A1.

▱ Delle Grotte ✿
Viale Matteotti 35 ☎_(0577) 630269_ ▭ ▮ ➪ ➪ ▣ ▣ ▣ ▥
Closed Wed.

▱ Locanda dell'Amorosa
2km (1¼ miles) s ☎ _(0577) 679497_ ▮▮ ▭ ▮ ➤ ➪ ▣ ▣ ▥
Closed Mon eve, Tues, Jan–Feb.

An unusually elegant restaurant, with comfortable rooms, in the converted brick stables of a wine-growing estate.
Specialties: _Filetto di cinghiale, zuppa ribollita, fracosta al Chianti._

Sovana
Map **_8_**_I6. 226km (141 miles) s of Florence, 82km (51 miles) SE of Grosseto. 58010. Grosseto._

A solitary, semi-abandoned village with Etruscan-Roman foundations on a plateau 8km (5 miles) NW of _Pitigliano_. The **Rocca** was built by the Aldobrandeschi lords in the 13thC. The main street is flanked by medieval houses. At one end is the 13thC **Palazzo Pretorio**, modified in the 15thC, and the Romanesque church of **Santa Maria** which contains a c.8th–9thC **ciborium**, a rare example of pre-Romanesque sculpture. At the far end is the splendid and dramatically situated Romanesque **Duomo**.

The **Etruscan necropolis** ☆ is in cool birch woods 1.5km (1 mile) below the town. (_A guide can be found at the Taverna Etrusca. Allow a minimum of 1hr._) The architectonic tomb fronts are carved from the rock face of the gorge with burial grottoes beneath. The most sophisticated is the 2ndC BC Tomba Ildebranda in the form of a temple facade.

≈ **Taverna Etrusca** ♣ *(Piazza Pretorio* ☎ *(0564) 616183, closed Mon, two to three weeks in June–July).*

Stia

*Map **12**E7. 49km (30 miles) E of Florence. 52017. Arezzo. Population: 3,023.*

At the head of the Casentino just below **Monte Falterona**, where the Arno has its source. Its central Piazza Tanucci is a piece of first-class town planning, and the Romanesque church preserves a *Madonna and Child* (1437) by A. della Robbia and an *Annunciation* (1414) by Bicci di Lorenzo.

Nearby sights

In the late Middle Ages Stia was closely surrounded by the castles of the Guidi lords who ruled the upper Casentino and with whom the exiled Dante took refuge. The noblest of the ruined castles is the **Castello di Romena** (☒ 🚺 *open daily 9am–noon, 3–7pm),* 3km (2 miles) S. Nearby, on a parallel road, is the 10th–12thC **Pieve di Romena** *(custodian in house next door),* the finest Romanesque church in the Casentino but over-restored. A magnificent 4hr walk N from Stia will take one to the summit of Monte Falterone via the source of the Arno.

≈ **Loris** ♣ (☎ *(0575) 58680* ☐ *closed Tues)* is 2km (1 mile) N at Papiano Alto.

Talamone

*Map **8**J5. 164km (102 miles) S of Florence, 24km (15 miles) S of Grosseto. 58010. Grosseto. Population: 485 i See Porto Santo Stefano.*

A fishing village and tourist harbor on a headland S of *Monti dell'Uccelina* overlooking Monte Argentario. The Sienese purchased Talamone from the Abbey of San Salvatore in 1303; their intention to make it into a port rivaling Pisa and Genoa was derided by Dante *(Purgatorio, XIII).* It became part of the Spanish Garrison States in 1556.

😺 **Corte dei Butteri** 🏨
58010 Fonte Blanda, Grosseto ☎ *(0564) 885547* 📶 *87 rms* 🛏 *87* 🎴 🔲 🔳 ≈ *Closed mid-Oct to Apr.*
Location: Fonte Blanda, 4km (2½ miles) NE. A modern luxury hotel.
🏠 🏋 🔥 🖼 🏊 ⛷ 🎾 🎿 🦆

😺 On the promontory is the **Capo d'Uomo** (☎ *(0564) 887077* 📶 *closed Oct–Mar).*

≈ Restaurants in the center are more reasonably priced than those on the Argentario but are rather self-consciously geared to tourists. The two favorites are: **La Buca** (☎ *(0564) 887067* 📶 *closed Mon, Jan–June);* and **Da Flavia** (☎ *(0564) 887091* 📶 *closed Tues except summer, Dec–Mar).* For more genuine food of the region try **Il Bracconiere**, 3km (2 miles) NE at Fonte Blanda ☎ *(0564) 885523* 📶 *closed Tues).*

Tirli

*Map **11**I5. 26km (16 miles) NE of Grosseto. 58040. Grosseto. Population: 597.*

≈ **Tana del Cinghiale** (☎ *(0564) 945810* 🔲 *to* 📶 *closed Wed, Jan),* a remote restaurant and hunting lodge (with rooms) in the hills specializing in wild boar.

Torre del Lago Puccini
*Map **14**E3. 95km (59 miles) w of Florence, 16km (10 miles) N of Pisa. 55048. Lucca. Population: 5,450.*

Just to the E of the dull little village of Torre del Lago Puccini is **Lake Massaciuccoli**, the largest of the few lakes in Tuscany. The opera composer Giacomo Puccini, who settled here in 1891, once described this place as his "supreme joy, paradise, Eden, the Empyrean, turris eburnea, vas spiritualis, kingdom." He built himself a house on the shore of the lake, where he lived until shortly before his death in 1924.

Event: A festival of Puccini operas is held in early Aug. News and reservations: Segreteria del Festival Pucciniano, Piazza Puccini, 55048 Torre del Lago, Lucca ☎(0584) 342006.

Villa Puccini ☆
▩ *𝕗 Open daily summer 9am–noon, 3–7pm; winter 9am–noon, 2–5pm.*

The villa is preserved as it was in Puccini's lifetime, and he is buried here in a mausoleum built, appropriately, between his piano and his gunroom. The house is a shrine as well as a vivid testimony to this likeable genius.

⊨ Next to the villa are **Butterfly-da Franco** (☎ *(0584) 341024* ▨ *closed Thurs, Nov*) with rooms; **Da Cecco** (☎ *(0584) 341022* ▨ *closed Mon, early July, two weeks in Nov–Dec*).

The food is more interesting at **Calimero** (*Viale Europa* ☎ *(0584) 340264* ▨ *closed Oct–Easter*).

Vallombrosa
*Map **12**E6. 33km (20 miles) SE of Florence. 50060. Firenze.*
In the NE Pratomagno Hills, reached by beautiful twisting roads, is the monastery of Vallombrosa, the mother house of the order founded in the early 11thC by the Florentine religious reformer San Giovanni Gualberto.

Monastery ▥ †
▣ *Open daily 9am–noon, 3–7pm.*

The imposing monastery, like a finely designed symmetrical castle, has a facade (1635–40) by G. Silvani. The campanile is 13thC, and the tower 15thC; the church itself is mainly 17thC. A plaque records that Milton stayed here in 1638. All around is a magnificent **forest**.

Nearby sights
9km (6 miles) above, near the summit of **Monte Secchietta** at 1,449m (4,216ft), is fine walking country, also equipped for skiing. **Saltino**, a modern summer and winter sports resort, is 2km (1¼ miles) w, and **Consuma**, another holiday resort, is 10km (6 miles) NE.

⌂ Vallombrosa
50060 Saltino, Firenze ☎ *(055) 862012* ▨ *80 rms* ▭ *80* ⌂ ⊨ ᴀᴇ ᴄʙ ⊙ ⊚ ᴠɪsᴀ *Closed Sept–Jun.*
Location: Montemignaio, 1km (⅗ mile) to w. A comfortable wooded summer retreat.
⌂ ⇵ ⊡ ⚲ ⊰

⊨ **Sbaragli**, at Montemignaio (☎ *(055) 8306500* ▨ *closed Tues*) with rooms.

Vetulonia
*Map **11**I5. 141km (87 miles) SW of Florence, 29km (18 miles) NW of Grosseto. 58040. Grosseto. Population: 615.*
Vetulonia is the most enigmatic of the great Etruscan city-states. Like *Roselle*, Etruscan Vetulonia was a maritime city situated on an island rising from the navigable waters of the gulf which then filled part of the Grosseto plain. Its culture

flourished from the 8th–6thC BC and then seems to have died out with mysterious suddenness. The Roman symbol of power, the fasces, was borrowed from archaic Vetulonia.

Sights and places of interest
Museo Archeologico
🔊 *Open Tues–Sun summer 9am–noon, 4–7pm; winter 9am–noon, 3–6pm.*
This small, interesting museum occupies the site of the acropolis at the entrance to the village. Above are remains of the **walls** (6thC BC) built of huge polygonal blocks of stone and commanding a magnificent view.
Necropolis ☆
3km (1¾ miles) to NE 🔊 🗲 *inquire about tours at museum.*
The most important tombs are the **tumulo della Pietrera**, domed in the manner of Mycenaean tombs, and, 400m (¼ mile) below, the **tumulo del Diavolino**; both probably late 7thC BC.

≡ *See Tirli.*

Viareggio
Map 14D3. 97km (60 miles) w of Florence, 27km (17 miles) w of Lucca. 55049. Lucca. Population: 59,460 ℹ *Viale Carducci 10* ☎ *(0584) 42233; summer only, RR station, Piazza Dante* ☎ *(0584) 46382.*
The capital of the Versilia Riviera is one of the oldest seaside resorts in Italy. The climate is healthy and mild in winter, but the atmosphere today is that of a tough, citified seaside strip masking a sleazy but more congenial port area. Stately Liberty buildings and palm-fringed avenues were laid out at the turn of the century in strict parallel roads where the medieval King's Highway (Via Regia) once ran through the pine woods. The fine-sand beach is over 100m (325ft) wide and divided into well-equipped and expensive bathing establishments. The harbor is lively with fishing and tourist boats.

To the N, Viareggio merges with the modern and less expensive Lido di Camaiore. To the s, a protected pine forest stretches as far as *Torre del Lago* and there are free beaches.

The monument to Shelley in Piazza Shelley records that the poet's body was washed up on the beach in 1822.

Event: Viareggio Carnival, the most elaborate in Tuscany, takes place throughout the month before Lent. Festivities include processions of allegorical floats, masked balls, fireworks, and a soccer tournament.

📾 Astor
Viale Carducci 54, 55049 Viareggio, Lucca ☎ *(0584) 50301*
📞*624031* 🕮 *68 rms* ▭ *68* ≣
▱ ▱ ⟺ ▱ AE ⊕ ⊙ VISA
This ultra-modern luxury hotel is part of the SINA chain. Service apartments available
♨ ⟁ ▭ ✍ ✈ ⟨⟨ ⇌ ☎ ➤
⛱

📾 Palace
Via Flavio Gioia 2, 55049 Viareggio, Lucca ☎ *(0584) 46134*
78 rms ▭ *78* ⟺ ▱ ≡ AE ⊕
⊙ VISA
An attractive first-class hotel decorated in red, white and gold Second Empire style.
✍ ☎ ⛱

📾 Principe di Piemonte
Piazza Puccini 1, 55049 Viareggio, Lucca ☎ *(0584) 50122* ▥▥▥
123 rms ▭ *103* ≣ *partial* ▱
▱ ⟺ AE ⊕ ⊙ *Closed Oct–Apr.*
A spacious turn-of-the-century grand hotel decorated in sugared-almond colors with polished mahogany and fresh flowers.
✍ ⟨⟨ ⇌ ☎ ⛱

≡ Buonamico
Via Sant'Andrea 27
☎ *(0584) 43038* ▥▥▥ ▭ ➤
Closed Mon, Nov.
A small, dark restaurant on a side street near the fishing port. Next door is a tiny fish shop where you may choose what you want for your dinner. Book.

191

⇌ Il Patriarca
Viale Carducci 79
☎ *(0584) 53126* ▥ ▭ ▰ ◱
▦ ◂ AE CB ⊕ CD VISA *Closed*
Wed, mid-Sept to mid-June.
One of the super-smart restaurants
of the Versilia. Good soups,
risottos, *baccalà*.

⇌ Romano
Via Mazzini 122
☎ *(0584) 31382* ▥ ▭ ▰ ◱
Closed Wed, Nov–Dec.

Skillfully inventive variations on
the fresh fish motif. Ask advice.

⇌ Also recommended: Fedi da
Gianfranco (*Via Verdi 111*
☎ *(0584) 48519* ▥ *closed Tues,*
four weeks in Sept–Oct); **Foscolo**
(*Via Ugo Foscolo 79* ☎ *(0584) 44220*
▥ *closed Tues*); **Gusmano** (*Via*
Regia 58 ☎ *(0584) 31233* ▥ *closed*
Tues, Nov); **Montecatini** (*Viale*
Manin 8 ☎ *(0584) 42129* ▥ *closed*
Mon, early Dec).

Vinci

Map **15***E5. 43km (27 miles) w of Florence. 55009. Firenze.*
Population: 13,577.
Leonardo's birthplace is on Monte Albano, N of *Empoli*.

Museo Vinciano
▦ *Open Mon–Sat 9:30am–noon, 3–6pm, Sun, hols, 10am–noon,*
3–6:30pm.
The town has dedicated rooms in its restored 13thC *castello* to a small
museum about its famous son, displaying models made from his designs.

Nearby sights
3km (2 miles) N at **Anchiano** is the farmhouse where Leonardo may
have spent his childhood, in a ravishing setting amidst olive groves.
    The drive N over Monte Albano to *Pistoia* is spectacularly beautiful.

Volterra ★

Map **10***F4. 81km (50 miles) sw of Florence, 57km (35 miles)*
w of Siena. 56048. Pisa. Population: 14,911 **i** *Via G. Turazza*
2 ☎ *(0588) 86150.*
Volterra was the northernmost and one of the most powerful of
the federated Etruscan city-states. Its name was Velathri, it was
three times the size of the present town, and it controlled a
territory stretching from Pisa to Populonia and from the sea
inland as far as the Pesa valley. 522m (1,712ft) above sea-level
and protected by 7km (4⅜ miles) of walls which were in places
12m (39ft) high, it became a prosperous Roman municipality in
the 4thC BC, but supported Marius against Sulla in the civil war
and was conquered by the latter in 82–80 BC.
    During the Middle Ages, Volterra's struggle against the
ecclesiastic lords for communal independence was bitter and
protracted but, in the 13thC, successful. Although taken under
the 'protection' of Florence from the mid-14thC the Republic of
Volterra remained technically independent until 1470. This
was the year when Lorenzo de' Medici, desperate to safeguard
the crucial Florentine rights to alum mining in Volterra's
territory, hired the Duke of Urbino to invade the city. The
brutality of the siege remained one of the few blots on Lorenzo's
diplomatic career; one of his would-be assassins in the Pazzi
Conspiracy 8yr later was a Volterran.
    Lorenzo built a new fortress, known as the Fortezza Nuova
or *'Il Maschio'* (now a prison) and fortified the old 14thC tower,
the Fortezza Vecchia or *'La Femmina.'* The city waited in the
shadow of these loathed symbols of foreign domination until the
final and futile rebellion of 1530, which was quickly subdued by
the Florentine general Federigo Ferrucci.
    Many travelers have remarked on the uncanny atmosphere of
Volterra, where a chill wind can spring up from nowhere on the

the balmiest summer day, and where the hill on which the town stands has sheered off, forming the cliffs, the *Balze*, to the NE, and carrying parts of the Etruscan city with them. D. H. Lawrence saw the city "that gets all the wind and sees all the world" as "a sort of inland island, still curiously isolated, and grim." It is certainly very much its own place. Unlike its neighbor and traditional enemy *San Gimignano*, Volterra does not primp for tourists. The inhabitants are courteous, but there is about them an air of brooding energy which can prompt the fancy, especially when the wind is high, that Volterra is still waiting, and for something more important than tourists. Meanwhile, the town is economically if not politically independent. The quarrying and carving of alabaster are the chief occupations.

Sights and places of interest
The medieval city is contained within 13thC walls. The views, on a clear day, extend to the mountains below *Carrara*, to Corsica and inland *Monte Amiata* and the Casentino.

The parking lot nearest the Piazza dei Priori, the main square, is in Piazza Martiri della Libertà, the S entrance to the town. The following itineraries assume a day's visit, half devoted to the medieval town and half to the remains of the Etruscan city and to visiting the *Balze*.

Duomo ⅢⅢ †
The simple facade is 12thC, adapted to the Pisan style in the 13thC. The interior, altered in the 16thC, has an attractive painted wooden ceiling. In the right transept is a polychrome wooden *Deposition* (1228), an unusual larger-than-life-size folk-Romanesque scene made by Pisan sculptors, more religious theater than art. Over the high altar is Mino da Fiesole's exquisite **ciborium** (1471) flanked by his two charming *Angels* resting on 12thC twisted columns. In the left aisle is the **pulpit**, remade from 12thC carvings, and an *Annunciation* (1497) by Albertinelli.

In the chapel off the entrance to the nave are two niches containing 15thC polychrome terra-cotta groups by Zacchi Zaccaria of the *Epiphany* (right) and *Nativity* (left). The background to the *Nativity*, a delightful panoramic fresco of the *Magi*, is by Gozzoli.

Inside the 13thC **Baptistry** is a **baptismal font** (1502) by A. Sansovino.

Museo di Arte Sacra
Via Roma ☎ *(0588) 86192* ☒ *Open Mon–Wed, Fri–Sun 10am–1pm, 3–6pm. Closed Thurs.*
A display of architectural fragments, sculptures, reliquaries and paintings, next to the Duomo. Notice particularly Andrea della Robbia's bust of *St Linus*, the silver bust of *St Octavian* by A. Pollaiuolo, and a gilded bronze *Crucifix* by Giambologna.

Museo Etrusco Guarnacci ★
Via Don Minzoni 15 ☎ *(0588) 86347* ☒ *Open daily 9am–1pm, 2:30–5:30pm.*
This is one of the largest and most important Etruscan collections outside Florence and Rome. There are some 600 cinerary urns in tufa, alabaster or terra-cotta, dating from the 6th–1stC BC. For D. H. Lawrence these urns were like "an open book of life"; for scholars they are like a book about Etruscan beliefs about the afterlife. They are arranged according to subject matter of the carvings. In Rm. 24 on the first floor is the tiny Giacometti-like *Ombra della Sera* and other Etruscan bronze votives.

Piazza dei Priori
The central square retains its character thanks partly to some modern imitations of the medieval architecture. The **Palazzo Pretorio**, on the NE side, is a 13thC complex but much restored; its crenellated tower, adapted in the early 16thC, is known as the *'porcellino'* (piglet).

Palazzo dei Priori/Galleria Pittorica ⅢⅢ
Piazza dei Priori ☎ *(0588) 86025* ☒ *Open Mon, Wed–Sat 10am–1pm, Sun, hols 10am–1pm, 3–6pm.*
The town hall (1208–54) is the oldest civic building in Tuscany; on the lower facade are the terra-cotta emblems of the 15th–16thC Florentine

commissioners. In the **Galleria Pittorica** on the second floor is a
collection of 14th–17thC Florentine and Sienese pictures by, among
others, D. Ghirlandaio and Signorelli; but the museum is worth visiting
if only for Rosso Fiorentino's vivid, whirling *Deposition* ☆ (1521).
Climb the tower for stunning views.

Quadrivio dei Buomparenti
The intersection of Via Roma with Via Ricciarelli and Buomparenti is the
most picturesque corner of the medieval town. The 13thC tower-houses
of the Buomparenti are remarkably intact.

San Francesco †
The **Cappella della Croce di Giorno** is entirely covered with frescoes of
the *Legend of the True Cross* (1410) by Cenni di Francesco Cenni.

⌂ Nazionale
Via dei Marchesi 2, 56048 Volterra, Pisa ☎ *(0588) 86284* ☐ *34 rms*
▭ *34* ☎ ⌦
"The hotel is simple and somewhat rough, but quite friendly, pleasant in
its haphazard way." D.H. Lawrence's description of 1927 still fits.
▥

▤ **Da Beppino** (*Via delle Prigioni 15/19* ☎ *(0588) 86051* ▮ *closed
Wed, Nov*) is the locals' favorite, which also serves the best food. **Etruria**
(*Piazza dei Priori 8* ☎ *(0588) 86064* ▮ *closed Thurs, Nov*) is on the main
square; another simple, reliable restaurant is **Porcellino** (*Canto delle
Prigioni* ☎ *(0588) 86392* ▮ *closed Tues, Oct and Mar*).

Shopping
There are dozens of shops selling objects made of alabaster. The
central outlet and information center is the **Cooperativa Artieri
Alabastro** (*Piazza dei Priori 2* ☎ *(0588) 87590*).

Walks
Walk 1/Etruscan and Roman Volterra
Just to the w of Piazza Martiri della Libertà is the **Arco Etrusco**,
the s entrance to the Etruscan city. The uprights and bases on
the inner side are Etruscan; the archivolt was rebuilt by the
Romans who reincorporated the three Etruscan heads. Via
Porto dell'Arco lies on the cardinal axis of the Etruscan-Roman
city, which continues with Via Matteotti, lined with medieval
tower-houses, and into Via Guarnacci, the site of part of the
Roman Forum. Turn left into Via Lungo le Mura del
Mandorlo, which overlooks the **Roman Theater** (1stC BC) and
Baths (3rdC BC). Beyond the Porta Fiorentina, the pretty Via
Diana leads to the Porta Diana, the N Etruscan gate of which
only fragments survive. Beyond is the site of the **Necropoli del
Portone**. The empty underground tombs are mostly
unmarked, but some, in the middle of a farm, are signposted
Ipogei dei Marmini.

Walk 2/To the Balze
Start at the church of San Francesco; the *Balze* are 2km (1¼
miles) by foot from Porta S. Francesco. Taking Borgo S.
Stefano, turn left under Vicolo della Penera, then make a sharp
right behind the handrails and you will find a path running
along the base of the stretch of the **Etruscan walls** known as the
Mura Etrusche di S. Chiara, which in summer are festooned
with flowering capers, to the **Balze**, the cliffs formed by
repeated landslides. The views to the w are superb, and on a
peaceful summer midday when the scent of broom is sweet and
strong, one may wonder at Augustus Hare's description of the
Balze as "an arid and ghastly desert." But if you go just before
sunset you could share his vertiginous apprehension "that the
flowery surface on which you are standing may be hurled into
destruction tomorrow."

Biographies

A personal selection of major 13th–17thC Tuscan artists.

Alberti, Leon Battista (1404–72)
Influential Renaissance architect, theoretician and scholar.

Ammannati, Bartolomeo (1511–92)
Florentine sculptor and architect influenced by **Michelangelo**.

Andrea del Sarto (1486–1531)
'Flawless painter' of the early Florentine High Renaissance.

Angelico, Fra Giovanni (active c.1418–55)
Dominican monk and Renaissance painter.

Arnolfo di Cambio (before 1245–c.1302)
Gothic architect and sculptor, a pupil of **Nicola Pisano**.

Baccio d'Agnolo (1462–1543)
Florentine Renaissance architect and woodcarver. His son,
Giuliano (1491–1555) was a fine Mannerist architect.

Baldovinetti, Alesso (c.1426–99)
Florentine Renaissance painter and mosaicist.

Bartolommeo della Porta, Fra (1472/5–1517)
A leading painter of the Florentine High Renaissance.

Beccafumi, Domenico (c.1486–1551)
The outstanding Sienese Mannerist painter and sculptor.

Botticelli, Sandro (1445–1510)
The greatest linear painter of the Florentine Renaissance.

Bronzino (Agnolo Allori) (1503–72)
Florentine Mannerist painter, a polished portraitist.

Brunelleschi, Filippo (1377–1446)
The creator of Florentine Renaissance architecture.

Buontalenti, Bernardo (1531–1608)
Florentine Mannerist architect to the Medici grand dukes.

Castagno, Andrea del (active c.1442–died 1457)
Renaissance painter strongly influenced by **Donatello**.

Cellini, Benvenuto (1500–71)
Florentine sculptor, goldsmith and autobiographer.

Cimabue, Giovanni (c.1240–?1302)
Florentine painter and mosaicist who may have taught **Giotto**.

Civitali, Matteo (1436–1501)
The most important Renaissance sculptor of Lucca.

Cronaca (Simone del Pollaiuolo) (1457–1508)
Florentine architect and stonemason.

Daddi, Bernardo (c.1290–c.1348)
Florentine painter influenced by Giotto and the **Lorenzetti**.

Della Robbia, Luca (1400–82)
One of the greatest Florentine Renaissance sculptors; the
inventor of a method of applying vitreous glazes to terra-cotta.
His nephew **Andrea** (1424–1525) and sons **Giovanni**
(1464–after 1529) and **Girolamo** (1488–1556) continued the
family workshop.

Desiderio da Settignano (1428–64)
Renaissance sculptor of delicate reliefs and portrait busts.

Donatello (1386–1466)
The greatest Italian sculptor of the early Renaissance.

Duccio di Buoninsegna (documented from 1278, died 1318/19)
The greatest and most influential of early Sienese painters.

Ferri, Ciro (1620/34–89)
Baroque painter, **Pietro da Cortona's** most important pupil.

Francesco di Giorgio Martini (1439–1502)
Sienese architect, military engineer, sculptor and painter.

Gaddi, Agnolo (active c.1370–died 1396)
Florentine painter, son of **Taddeo**.

Biographies

Gaddi, Taddeo (active c.1325–died 1366)
Giotto's most important disciple.
Ghiberti, Lorenzo (1378–1455)
Florentine early Renaissance bronze sculptor.
Ghirlandaio, Domenico (1449–94)
Florentine Renaissance painter, a teacher of **Michelangelo**,
and master of a large studio run with his brother **Davide**
(1452–1525) and son **Ridolfo** (1483–1561).
Giambologna (Jean Boulogne) (1524–1608)
Flemish-born court sculptor to the Medici.
Giotto di Bondone (1267/77–1337)
The first great innovatory genius of Florentine painting.
Giovanni da San Giovanni (1592–1636)
Tuscan Baroque painter of frescoes in Florence and Rome.
Giovanni di Paolo (1403–82/3)
A leading 15thC Sienese painter working in 14thC style.
Gozzoli, Benozzo (c.1421–97)
Florentine narrative painter, a pupil of **Angelico**.
Guido da Siena (active mid-13thC)
Founder of the Sienese school of painting.
Leonardo da Vinci (1452–1519)
One of the greatest figures in the history of Western art, with an
apparently limitless power and range of intellect. Engineer,
anatomist, sculptor, architect and creator, with **Michelangelo**
and Raphael, of the High Renaissance style of painting.
Lippi, Filippino (1457–1504)
Son of Filippo and distinguished quasi-Mannerist painter.
Lippi, Fra Filippo (active c.1432–died 1469)
Florentine Renaissance painter; disciple of **Masaccio**.
*Lorenzetti, Ambrogio (active 1319–47) and Pietro (active
1320–45)*
The Sienese Lorenzetti brothers worked in a style which
synthesized the prevailing Florentine and Sienese schools.
Maiano, Benedetto da (1442–97)
Florentine Renaissance sculptor especially of fine reliefs. His
brother **Giuliano** (1432–90) was an architect.
Margaritone d'Arezzo (active mid-13thC)
One of the earliest Italian painters to sign his work.
Martini, Simone (active c.1315–died 1344)
The leading Sienese exponent of International Gothic painting.
Masaccio (1401–c.1428)
The great founder of Florentine Renaissance painting.
Michelangelo Buonarroti (1475–1564)
Painter, architect, poet and sculptor of deeply expressive
human figures.
Michelozzo di Bartolomeo (1396–1472)
Cosimo de' Medici's favorite architect.
Mino da Fiesole (1429–84)
Florentine Renaissance sculptor in marble.
Nanni di Banco (c.1384–1421)
Late Gothic–early Renaissance Florentine sculptor.
Orcagna, Andrea (Andrea di Cione) (active c.1343–died 1368)
The greatest mid-14thC Florentine painter, sculptor and
architect.
Piero della Francesca (1410/20–92)
One of the outstanding Tuscan painters and theorists.
Piero di Cosimo (1462–1521)
Idiosyncratic Florentine painter of mythological subjects.
Pietro da Cortona (1596–1669)
Painter and architect: a founder of Roman High Baroque.

Pisano, Andrea (c.1290–1348)
Sculptor known for the bronze s doors of Florence Baptistry.
Pisano, Giovanni (c.1245–c.1315) *and* **Nicola** (c.1223–c.1284)
Nicola and his son Giovanni created modern figure sculpture.
Poccetti, Bernardino (before 1548–1612)
Florentine painter, the leading master of *sgraffiti*.
Pollaiuolo, Antonio (c.1432–98) *and* **Piero** (c.1441–96)
Florentine painters, sculptors, engravers and goldsmiths.
Antonio, one of the great draftsmen of the Renaissance, is
considered the more talented of the brothers.
Pontormo, Jacopo Carucci (1494–1556)
Deeply religious painter and one of the creators of Mannerism.
Quercia, Jacopo della (1374–1438)
The greatest Sienese sculptor of the early Renaissance.
Rossellino, Antonio (1427–79) *and* **Bernardo** (1409–64)
Brothers whose sculpture exemplifies the 'sweet style' of the
Florentine Renaissance. **Bernardo** worked also as an architect.
Rosso Fiorentino (1495–1540)
A founder of Mannerism; important religious painter.
Salviati, Francesco (or Cecchino) (1510–63)
Florentine Mannerist painter and friend of **Vasari**.
Sangallo
Florentine family of architects. **Giuliano** (c.1443–1516), a
follower of **Brunelleschi**, was Lorenzo the Magnificent's
favorite architect. His brother **Antonio the Elder**
(c.1453–1534) introduced the Roman High Renaissance style
to provincial Tuscany. Both were military architects as was
their nephew **Antonio the Younger** (1483–1546).
Sansovino, Andrea (c.1460–1529)
High Renaissance sculptor in terra-cotta and marble.
Sansovino, Jacopo (1486–1570)
Andrea's pupil and namesake and city architect of Venice.
Sassetta (Stefano di Giovanni) (c.1423–50)
The most important early 15thC Sienese painter.
Signorelli, Luca (c.1441/50–1523)
Tuscan painter; an influence on **Michelangelo**.
Silvani, Gherardo (1579–1675)
One of the best High Baroque architects outside Rome.
Sodoma (1477–1549)
Interpreter to Siena of **Leonardo's** style of painting.
Spinello Aretino (active 1373–died 1410/11)
Narrative painter in the style of **Giotto**.
Starnina, Gherardo (c.1354–before 1413)
Florentine painter, a modest anticipator of **Uccello**.
Tacca, Pietro (1577–1640)
Sculptor to the Medici grand dukes after **Giambologna**.
Tino di Camaino (c.1285–1337)
Sienese sculptor who also worked in Pisa, Florence and Naples.
Tribolo (1500–50)
Florentine sculptor and designer of gardens.
Uccello, Paolo (1387–1475)
Florentine Renaissance painter famous as a perspectivist.
Vasari, Giorgio (1511–74)
Architect, painter and author of the first history of art.
Vecchietta (1412–80)
Sienese sculptor, painter and architect.
Verrocchio, Andrea del (1435–88)
Painter, goldsmith and the leading bronze sculptor of his day.
Volterrano (1611–89)
Tuscan Baroque painter influenced by **Pietro da Cortona**.

Tuscan wines

Wine has been an element of Tuscan life for ages. We know that the Etruscans made wine three millennia ago. The Romans followed suit, and though vine cultivation lapsed during the Dark Ages, wine was back in prominence through the Renaissance, flourishing as nutrient of body and soul and as a source of inspiration for who knows how many works of art or grandiose ideas.

Tuscans in their time have contributed notably to the development of wine making as art and science, to techniques of bottling and shipping wine and establishing the rituals that have grown around its service and consumption. Today more than 100,000 Tuscans are involved in the production and sale of wine, the mainstay of the region's agricultural economy.

I believe that there is much happiness in people who are born where good wines are found.

Leonardo da Vinci

Tuscany's hills, with their range of temperate micro-climates, are especially renowned for red wines, which have a similarly broad range of character. Chianti, Italy's most abundant wine of controlled name and origin, classified DOC (*Denominazione di Origine Controllata*), is grown in seven delimited zones covering much of the region, from N of Florence to S of Chiusi and from Pisa inland to Arezzo. It is usually served in the famous rounded flask, but some of the best Chianti, labeled *riserva*, is aged for several years in wood and then put into straight Bordeaux-style bottles.

Strictly outside the Chianti, Brunello di Montalcino, from S of Siena, is among the world's most prized and expensive wines when at its best. This and Vino Nobile di Montepulciano, from SE of Siena, are the two Tuscan wines among the four designated for Italy's highest classification, the government guaranteed DOCG.

All Tuscan DOC red wines are based on the versatile Sangiovese grape, sometimes used alone (as in Brunello and Morellino di Scansano), sometimes mixed with other varieties (as in Carmignano, Chianti, Elba Rosso, Montescudaio Rosso, Parrina Rosso, Rosso delle Colline Lucchesi and Vino Nobile). Not all the fine reds are DOC, however: Tignanello, Monte Antico, Rosso di Cercatoia and Le Pergole Torte are but a few of the Sangiovese-based wines sold under individual names. There is also a trend to introduce foreign vines, such as Cabernet and Merlot. Sassicaia, a Cabernet Sauvignon produced since 1968 from near Livorno, is considered by some to be Tuscany's finest modern wine.

Tuscan whites have gained stature as new wine making methods have improved quality. Among DOC whites, Vernaccia di San Gimignano, from the vine of that name, and Montecarlo, which mixes the native Trebbiano with French varieties, stand out. The other DOC whites are gradually reaching markets beyond the region.

Among a great many unclassified whites produced in Chianti zones, two names are emerging to prominence: Galestro, a light wine produced only by large-scale wineries with the most modern equipment; and Bianco della Lega, made in traditional ways by individual estates in Chianti Classico. Almost every Tuscan vineyard, large or small, makes a special white, though style and quality vary markedly. The introduction of outside grape varieties, such as the Pinots, Chardonnay, Riesling, Traminer and Tocai Friulano, have added fruitiness and fragrance to the rather bland native Trebbiano, which is planted to excess in Tuscany.

Among sweet dessert or aperitif wines, Vin Santo, made from semi-dried grapes and well aged in small sealed barrels, is beloved by Tuscans, but, alas, production is painstaking and there is little of this true 'holy wine' to be found. Another lightly sweet white, Moscadello di Montalcino, is coming back into favor after a long decline, and is appreciated for its refreshingly light Muscat aroma. There are, as well, a great many curiosities, experiments, and esoteric wines to be found here and there around the region.

Everywhere local wine of the latest vintage is served by the flask as the natural accompaniment to the local food. Perhaps because Tuscans take so intuitively to wine, the idea of formal wine tourism has never been exploited. Still, even the most spontaneous sort of wine tour can be rewarding. The authorities of a wine zone, or even an individual estate (*fattoria*), sometimes offer the added attraction of an *enoteca*, or wine library, where the wines can be bought. For those who like to combine the enjoyment of art and history with the pleasures of food and wine, few regions offer such exciting possibilities. All major wine zones are within easy reach of Florence.

Chianti Classico

For all the violent history that transpired in this buffer zone between Florence and Siena, Chianti Classico, the most important of the seven Chianti zones, is today one of the most peacefully handsome of all places where wine is made. Follow the Via Chiantigiana (SS222) s from Florence through Strada, Greve, Panzano and Castellina to Siena, through wooded hills where vines and olive groves, cypresses and pines surround medieval castles, villas and stone farmhouses. The complete Chiantigiana route includes a detour through the domain of the original Chianti League, founded in the 13thC by the feudal barons of Castellina, Gaiole and Radda. This can be extended to take in the Castello di Brolio near San Regolo, where modern Chianti was 'invented' in the last century by Baron Bettino Ricasoli, and the villages of Castagnoli, Villa a Sesta, San Gusme, Castelnuovo Berardenga and Vagliagli.

Most Chianti Classico estates welcome visitors, though to assure a reception it would be wise to arrange a tour with the Chianti Classico *consorzio* (*Via de' Serragli 146 in Florence* ☎ *(055) 229351/2/3*). Two of the most historically important estates, Castello di Brolio (☎ *(055) 263681*) and Marchesi Antinori (☎ *(055) 282202/3*), are not in the *consorzio*, but both welcome visitors by appointment. Antinori's wines are served at the Cantinetta Antinori in the center of Florence (see *Florence/Restaurants*).

A complete selection of Chianti Classico is sold at the Enoteca del Gallo Nero in Greve, the hub of Chianti and the setting of an annual wine fair in early Sept. Other stores with a good selection include the Bottega del Chianti Classico at Greve, the Enoteca del Chianti Classico at Panzano and the Bottega del Chianti Classico at Castellina. Several estates have a *trattoria* or *osteria* on the premises, and noteworthy examples include: the Trattoria di Montagliari near Panzano; the Badia a Coltibuono near Gaiole; the Taverna del Solimano of the Fortilizio Il

Colombaio estate near Quercegrossa; and the Tavernetta Serristori 'Albergaccio' (where Niccolò Machiavelli spent much of his exile from Florence) at S. Andrea in Percussina.

Siena/Montalcino/Montepulciano/San Gimignano

Siena is sometimes called the capital of Italian wine, partly because it is the center of Tuscany's most important production zones and also because the **Enoteca Italica Permanente**, the public national wine library, is located in its Medici fortress. Though the *enoteca* is open only by appointment (☎ *(0577) 288497*), select wines can be tasted at a bar which is open daily. The city makes a convenient headquarters for traveling oenophiles – in Siena's province are the original sector of Chianti Classico, the Chianti Colli Senesi zone, the vineyards of the exceptional Brunello di Montalcino and Vino Nobile di Montepulciano, and the superb white Vernaccia di San Gimignano.

Montalcino, a hill town 45km (28 miles) S of Siena, is the home of the fabled red Brunello and the even older but currently less renowned Moscadello di Montalcino. The Medici fortress in the center of town houses a museum of Brunello. Outside Montalcino, visits to one of the leading producers and what ranks as Italy's most famous wine estate, Il Greppo of Biondi-Santi, can be made by appointment (☎ *(0577) 47136*), and the Fattoria dei Barbi has an *osteria* on the estate, where its several wines are served with good country food (☎ *(0577) 848087*). Other wine estates which welcome visitors are: Casale del Bosco, Castiglion del Bosco, Col d'Orcia, Poggio alle Mura, and the immense new conglomeration Poggio d'Oro of Villa Banfi.

The lovely Renaissance town of Montepulciano, 37km (23 miles) farther E, is surrounded by the vineyards of Vino Nobile, known for centuries as 'King of Wines.' Visits can be arranged to the Cantine Contucci (☎ *(0578) 77006*), and the Vecchia Cantina cooperative (☎ *(0578) 77692/3*). In nearby Pienza, the Enoteca Regionale of Sandro Morriconi sells good wines from the area.

San Gimignano, with its many towers jutting over a landscape of vines and olives, may be the most charming of all Tuscan wine towns. Many producers of the vigorous white Vernaccia sell bottles in individual shops in the town. Vineyards open to visitors include the following: Fattoria di Cusona, Raccianello, and Pietrafitta. The Ponte a Rondolino vineyard serves its Vernaccia at its own trattoria situated outside the town.

Florence/Rufina/Carmignano

Florence is itself a wine town, center of the Colli Fiorentini Chianti zone and headquarters of many important Tuscan wineries. Outstanding arrays of Italian wine are available at the Enoteca Nazionale of Giorgio Pinchiorri (*Via Ghibellina 87* ☎ *(055) 263653*), and the Enoteca Internazionale De Rham (*Piazza SS Annunziata 4* ☎ *(055) 298849*).

Rufina, a small DOC zone 20km (13 miles) E of Florence, makes some of the finest Chianti. Within its limits are some of Tuscany's best-known wine houses: Ruffino and Melini at Pontassieve; the Pomino and Nipozzano estates of Marchesi de' Frescobaldi; and Spalletti, in the villa of Poggio Reale, designed by Michelangelo, at Rufina. All welcome visitors.

Carmignano, a zone some 25km (16 miles) W of Florence,

produces very little of a red wine that insiders consider Tuscany's most consistently impressive DOC. There are only about a dozen producers, and their wine can be sold as Carmignano only if approved by experts in a rigorous annual blind tasting. Carmignano's wines are displayed at a small *enoteca* in the center of town. The Fattoria di Artimino, in the Medici villa of the 'Hundred Chimneys,' is open to visitors, and serves its wines in its own restaurant.

Other itineraries

The Chianti Putto *consorzio* (*Lungarno Corsini 4, Florence* ☎ *(055) 270168*) can help arrange visits to estates in the other six Chianti zones: Colli Aretini, Colli Fiorentini, Colline Pisane, Colli Senesi, Montalbano and Rufina.

Nearly every center of interest to tourists has a wine area nearby. Pisa has Bianco di San Torpe to the SE. Lucca has two DOC zones, Rosso delle Colline Lucchesi, to the N, and Montecarlo, a white wine produced around the village of that name. From farther E, near Montecatini Terme, comes Bianco della Valdinievole. In Arezzo province, the broad Chiana valley between Cortona and Montepulciano is the home of Bianco Vergine della Valdichiana.

The Tuscan coastal strip also produces good wines. Not far from Viareggio and the Tuscan Riviera is the new DOC zone of Candia dei Colli, with red, white and Vin Santo, and the island of Elba, with red and white DOC wines and a sweet red Aleatico di Portoferraio, which Napoleon supposedly liked. In the Maremma hills of Grosseto province there are three DOCs: Morellino di Scansano, Bianco di Pitigliano and, adjacent to the Argentario peninsula, Parrina.

Vintage chart

The chart gives a general idea of recent vintages for five wines. As a general rule, Vernaccia di San Gimignano should be drunk young (1–3yr). Regular Chianti should be drunk from 1–5yr, *riserva* from 5–10yr, or from good vintages even older. Carmignano and Vino Nobile di Montepulciano age similarly to Chianti *riserva*. Brunello di Montalcino needs at least 6yr to mature; from great vintages it can last for decades.

	1974	1975	1976	1977	1978	1979	1980	1981	1982	1983	1984	1985
Brunello di Montalcino	○	●	○	●	●	●	●	◑	●	●	○	○
Carmignano	◑	●	○	●	●	●	○	◑	●	●	◑	◑
Chianti	◑	●	○	●	●	●	○	◑	●	●	◑	◑
Vino Nobile di Montepulciano	◑	●	○	●	●	●	○	◑	◑	●	◑	◑
Vernaccia di San Gimignano						●	●	◑	◑	●	◑	◑

Key: ● above average to outstanding   ◑ average   ○ acceptable

Sports, leisure, ideas for children

There is plenty to do in Tuscany besides sightseeing, as families traveling with small children may be relieved to learn, and foreigners can usually buy temporary membership in private sports clubs and organizations.

Bicycling

Bicycles and tandems can easily be rented by the hour or week. *Federazione Ciclistica Italiana*, P. Stazione 2, 50123 Firenze ☎(055) 283926, is the organization for serious cyclists.

Camping

A list of campsites and booking forms is obtainable from the *Centro Internazionale di Prenotazioni Campeggio*, Casella Postale 649, I-50100, Firenze. The *Touring Club Italiano* runs camping sites equipped with tents and restaurants. Information from *TCI*, Corso Italia 10, 20122 Milano.

Mountain huts can be rented from the *Club Alpino Italiano*, Via Ugo Foscolo 3, 20121 Milano ☎(02) 802554.

Fishing

The clear waters off the rocky southern coast are excellent for snorkelling, and spearfishing is allowed anywhere except in harbors. Oxygen bottles for aqualungs are available in the main resorts. For fishing in most lakes and rivers, an inexpensive license is required, as is membership in the *Federazione Italiana della Pesca Sportiva*, Via De' Neri 6, 50122 Firenze ☎(055) 214073.

Gardens

Many great Tuscan gardens are still privately owned, but those not normally open to the public can occasionally be visited. Lists of gardens are published by local tourist offices.

Golf

18-hole courses open all year are at: *Ugolino*, Strada Chiantigiana 3, 50023 Impruneta ☎(055) 2051009; and at *Punta Ala* ☎(0564) 922121.

Horse racing and trotting

There are two racecourses in the Cascine in Florence, with trotting races in summer and racing in winter. There are also racecourses at San Rossore, Montecatini and Punta Ala, and trotting races near Follonica.

Hunting

A hunting reserve is open to foreigners near Capalbio.

Italian

Since the purest Italian is spoken in Tuscany, it is an ideal place to learn the language. Most of the schools will help enrolled students find accommodations.

British Institute Palazzo Lanfredini, Lungarno Guicciardini 9, 50123 Firenze ☎(055) 284031

Centro Linguistico Italiano Dante Alighieri PO Box 194, Via de' Bardi 12, 50125 Firenze ☎(055) 284955

The University of Siena's *Scuola Lingua e Cultura per Stranieri*, Banchi di Sotto 55 ☎(0577) 280695, organizes summer courses for foreigners in Siena; and the University of Pisa offers two three-week summer courses in Viareggio. Information from *Corsi per Stranieri*, Istituto di Glottologia dell'Università, Via S. Maria SC, 56100 Pisa ☎(050) 24773.

Music

Florence is one of the musical capitals of Italy; and the *Accademia Musicale Chigiana* at Siena is among the most distinguished Italian music academies. Lucca and Prato are musically active too, and there are summer festivals at Barga, Batignano, Cortona, Gargonza, Montepulciano, S. Gimignano and Torre del Lago Puccini.

Nature parks and reserves

Some of the reserves can be entered only with permission, usually obtainable from the communal government offices nearest the site. The Maremma is well-supplied: see *Ansedonia*, Monte Argentario and, especially, *Monti dell'Uccellina*. Other reserves are at Bolgheri, Cavriglia, Migliarino (near Pisa), Montecristo and Orechiella (Garfagnana). See also *Zoos* below.

Riding

Riding is popular in Tuscany. The *Associazione Nazionale per il Turismo Equestre* organizes trekking holidays. Information is available from the *Federazione Italiana Sport Equestri*, Via Paoletti 54, 50134 Firenze ☎ (055) 480039.

Sailing

There are tourist harbors at Cala Galera, Castiglione della Pescaia, Elba, Giannutri, Giglio, Port'Ercole, Punta Ala, Talamone and Viareggio. Report to the *Capitaneria di Porto* (Harbor Master).

Federazione Italiana Vela   Cas post 49, 54036 Marina di Carrara ☎ (0585) 57323, for information

Federazione Italiana Motonautica   Via Goldora 16, 55044 Marina de Pietrasanta ☎ (0584) 20963, for all boats

A useful guidebook is *The Tyrrhenian Sea* by H.M. Denham (John Murray).

Skiing

The best skiing is in the Apennines, at Abetone, Cutigliano and S. Marcello Pistoiese. Nearer to Florence, in the Pratomagno hills, there are winter sports facilities at Consuma, Stia and Vallombrosa. Monte Amiata has some 20km (12 miles) of piste; its principle resort is Abbadia S. Salvatore.

Information from the *Federazione Italiana Sports Invernali*, Viale Matteotti 15, 50121 Firenze ☎ (055) 576987.

Swimming

Beaches vary from superb to squalid. The best sandy beaches are shown in the orientation map in *Planning*. Below Livorno and on Elba the coast is mostly rocky with small sandy bays. Although there are some free beaches, those which provide facilities are fairly expensive. Most inland towns have well-maintained public pools: in Florence, the *Piscine Bellariva*, Lungarno Colombo; *Piscine Costoli*, Viale Paoli; *Piscine Pavoniere*, Viale degli Olmi; and at the *Circolo del Tennis*, Via Visarno 1, a private club in the Cascine open to foreigners.

Tennis

Public courts and tennis clubs are widespread; the best in Florence are in the Cascine at Viale Visarno 1.

Walking

All Tuscan cities and villages are best seen on foot. Near Florence there is pleasant country walking in the Fiesolan hills and around Arcetri. There are marked trails through the protected forests at Abetone, Camaldoli, La Verna and Vallombrosa. Maps showing footpaths are obtainable from *Istituto Geografico Militare*, Viale Strozzi 14, Firenze. Information about mountain walking from *Club Alpino Italiano*, Via Proconsolo 10, 50123 Firenze ☎ (055) 216580.

Zoos

There are zoos at Pistoia, Poppi, at Tirrenia near Pisa, and a small one in Florence.

A guide to Italian

This glossary covers the basic language needs of the traveler: for for pronunciation, essential vocabulary and simple conversation, finding accommodations, visiting the bank, shopping and using public transport or a car. There is also a special menu decoder, explaining all the most common descriptions of food terms.

Pronunciation

Most Italian words are pronounced exactly as they are written, with each syllable clearly enunciated. Some letters change their individual sounds, however, when grouped together, as shown below. Double consonants, such as in cappello, are strongly pronounced. The letter 'r' is rolled. Stress in Italian nearly always falls on the penultimate syllable. An accent is used when the stress is final (e.g. with città, caffè), but accentuation in any word is always strong.

Vowels

a	as the <u>a</u> in f<u>a</u>ther; e.g. and<u>a</u>re
e	as the <u>e</u> in p<u>e</u>t; e.g. p<u>e</u>zzo, or as the <u>a</u> in m<u>a</u>y; e.g. part<u>e</u>
i	as the <u>i</u> in mach<u>i</u>ne; e.g. pr<u>i</u>mo, or, when followed by another vowel, as the <u>y</u> in <u>y</u>ou; e.g. p<u>i</u>ù, p<u>i</u>ove
o	as the <u>o</u> in p<u>o</u>t; e.g. n<u>o</u>tte, or as in v<u>o</u>te; e.g. R<u>o</u>mà
u	as the <u>u</u> in pr<u>u</u>ne; e.g. <u>u</u>scita, or, when followed by another vowel, as the letter <u>w</u>; e.g. <u>u</u>omo, g<u>u</u>ida

Consonants/letter groups

c,g	before e,i	soft, as the <u>ch</u> in <u>ch</u>urch and the <u>g</u> in <u>ag</u>ent; e.g. ba<u>c</u>io, <u>G</u>ino
c,g	before a,o,u	hard, as the <u>k</u> in <u>k</u>ing and the <u>g</u> in <u>g</u>et; e.g. <u>c</u>amera, <u>c</u>osa, <u>g</u>atto, <u>g</u>uida
ch,gh	before e,i	hard, as the c or the g above; e.g. <u>ch</u>iesa, al<u>gh</u>erghi
cc	before e,i	soft, as the <u>ch</u> in <u>ch</u>urch; e.g. fa<u>cc</u>io, salsi<u>cc</u>e
gg	before e,i	soft, as the <u>dg</u> in do<u>dg</u>e; e.g. o<u>gg</u>etto, o<u>gg</u>i
gli		as the <u>ll</u> in mi<u>ll</u>ion; e.g. fi<u>gli</u>o
gn		pronounced nasally, as the <u>n</u> in <u>n</u>ew; e.g. ba<u>gn</u>o
qu		as in s<u>qu</u>are; e.g. <u>qu</u>esto
s	between vowels	soft, as the <u>z</u> in ga<u>z</u>e; e.g. ri<u>s</u>o, ca<u>s</u>a
sc	before e,i	as the <u>sh</u> in <u>sh</u>ift; e.g. <u>sc</u>ena, <u>sc</u>iopero
z		as the <u>ts</u> in ca<u>ts</u>; e.g. gra<u>z</u>ie, or as the <u>ds</u> in bir<u>ds</u>; e.g. me<u>zz</u>o

N.B. Gender

Gender has been indicated, where necessary, when not apparent from the regular masculine (-o, pl. -i) and feminine (-a, pl. -e) endings.

Reference words

Monday	lunedì	Friday	venerdì
Tuesday	martedì	Saturday	sabato
Wednesday	mercoledì	Sunday	domenica
Thursday	giovedì		

January	gennaio	July	luglio
February	febbraio	August	agosto
March	marzo	September	settembre
April	aprile	October	ottobre
May	maggio	November	novembre
June	giugno	December	dicembre

1	uno	11	undici	21	ventuno
2	due	12	dodici	22	ventidue
3	tre	13	tredici	30	trenta
4	quattro	14	quattordici	40	quaranta
5	cinque	15	quindici	50	cinquanta
6	sei	16	sedici	60	sessanta
7	sette	17	diciassette	70	settanta
8	otto	18	diciotto	80	ottanta
9	nove	19	diciannove	90	novanta
10	dieci	20	venti	100	cento

First	primo, -a	Quarter–past	.... e un quarto
Second	secondo, -a		
Third	terzo, -a	Half–past	.... e mezzo
Fourth	quarto, -a	Quarter to	.... meno un quarto
One o'clock	l'una		
Six o'clock	le sei		

Mr	signor(e)	Ladies	signore, donne
Mrs	signora	Men/gentlemen	signori, uomini
Miss	signorina		

Basic communication

Yes	sì	Hot	caldo, -a
No	no	Cold	freddo, -a
Please	per favore/per piacere	Good	buono, -a
Thank you	grazie	Bad	cattivo, -a
I'm very sorry	mi dispiace molto/mi scusi	Beautiful	bello, -a
Excuse me	senta! (to attract attention), permesso! (on bus, train, etc.), mi scusi	Well	bene
		Badly	male
		With	con
Not at all/you're welcome	prego	And	e, ed
Hello	ciao (familiar), pronto (on telephone)	But	ma
		Very	molto
		All	tutto, -a
Good morning	buon giorno	Open	aperto
Good afternoon	buona sera	Closed	chiuso
Good evening	buona sera	Entrance	entrata
Good night	buona notte	Exit	uscita
Goodbye	ciao (familiar), arrivederci, addio (final or familiar)	Free	libero
		On the left	a sinistra
		On the right	a destra
Morning	mattino	Straight on	diritto
Afternoon	pomeriggio	Near	vicino
Evening	sera	Far	lontano
Night	notte (f)	Up	su
Yesterday	ieri	Down	giù
Today	oggi	Early	presto
Tomorrow	domani	Late	tardi
Next week	la settimana prossima	Quickly	presto
Last week	la settimana scorsa	Pleased to meet you.	Molto lieto/piacere.
.... days ago	.... giorni fa		
Month	mese (m)	How are you?	Come sta?
Year	anno	Very well, thank you.	Benissimo, grazie.
Here	qui		
There	lì	Do you speak English?	Parla inglese?
Big	grande		
Small	piccolo, -a	I don't understand.	Non capisco.

205

Words and phrases

I don't know. Non lo so.
Please explain. Può spiegare per favore.
Please speak more slowly. Parli più lentamente per favore.
My name is . . . . Mi chiamo . . .
I am American/English. Sono inglese/americano, -a.
Where is/are . . . . ? Dov'è/dove si trova/dove sono . . . . ?
Is there a . . . . ? C'è un, una . . . . ?
What? Cosa?

When? Quando?
How much? Quanto?
That's too much. È troppo caro.
Expensive caro
Cheap a buon mercato
I would like . . . . Vorrei . . . .
Do you have . . . . ? Avete . . . . ?
Just a minute. Un momento.
That's fine/OK. Va bene/benissimo/OK
What time is it? Che ore sono?
I don't feel well. Non mi sento bene/sto male.

Accommodations

Making a reservation by letter

> *Dear Sir/Madam,*
> *Egregio Signore/Signora,*
> *I would like to reserve one double room (with bathroom) –*
> *Vorrei prenotare una camera doppia (con bagno) –*
> *– a twin-bedded room, and one single room (with shower)*
> *– una camera con due letti, e una camera singola (con doccia)*
> *for 7 nights from 12 August. We would like bed and breakfast/half board/full board*
> *per 7 notti dal 12 agosto. Vorremmo una camera con colazione/mezza pensione/pensione completa*
> *and would prefer rooms with a sea view.*
> *e possibilmente camere con vista sul mare.*
> *Please send me details of your terms with the confirmation.*
> *Sarei lieto di ricevere dettagli del prezzo e la conferma.*
> *Yours sincerely,*
> *Cordiali saluti,*

Arriving at the hotel
I have a reservation. My name is . . . .
Ho già prenotato. Sono il signor/la signora . . . .
A quiet room with bath/shower/toilet/wash basin
Una camera tranquilla con bagno/doccia/WC/lavandino
. . . . overlooking the sea/park/street/the back.
. . . . con vista sul mare/sul parco/sulla strada/sul retro.
Does the price include breakfast/tax/service?
E' tutto compreso – colazione/tasse/servizio?
This room is too large/small/cold/hot/noisy.
Questa camera è troppo grande/piccola/fredda/calda/rumorosa.
That's too expensive. Have you anything cheaper?
Costa troppo. Avete qualcosa meno caro?

Floor/story piano
Dining room/restaurant sala da pranzo/ristorante (m)
Manager direttore, -trice
Porter portiere
Have you got a room? Avete una camera?
What time is breakfast/dinner? A che ora è la prima colazione/la cena?
Is there a laundry service? C'è il servizio lavanderia?
What time does the hotel close? A che ora chiude l'albergo?
Will I need a key? Avrò bisogno della chiave?
Is there a night porter? C'è un portiere di notte?
I'll be leaving tomorrow morning. Parto domani mattina.
Please give me a call at . . . . Mi può chiamare alle . . . .
Come in! Avanti!

Shopping La Spesa

Where is the nearest/a good . . . . ? Dov'è il più vicino/la più vicina . . . ? Dov'è un buon/una buona . . . . ?
Can you help me/show me . . . . ? Mi può aiutare/Può mostrarmi . . . . ?
I'm just looking. Sto soltanto guardando.
Do you accept credit cards/travelers cheques? Accettate carte di credito/travelers cheques?

Can you deliver to ....? Può consegnare a ....?
I'll take it. Lo prendo.
I'll leave it. Lo lascio.
Can I have it tax-free for export? Posso averlo senza tasse per l'esportazione?
This is faulty. Can I have a replacement/refund? C'è difetto. Me lo potrebbe cambiare/rimborsare?
I don't want to spend more than .... Non voglio spendere più di ....
Can I have a stamp for ....? Vorrei un francobollo per ....

Shops

Antique shop negozio di antiquariato
Art gallery galleria d'arte
Bakery panificio, forno
Bank banca
Beauty salon istituto di bellezza
Bookshop libreria
Butcher macelleria
Clothes shop negozio di abbigliamento, di confezioni
Dairy latteria
Delicatessen salumeria, pizzicheria
Fish store pescheria
Florist fioraio
Greengrocer ortolano, erbivendolo, fruttivendolo
Grocer drogheria
Haberdasher merciaio
Hairdresser parrucchiere, -a

Jeweler gioielleria
Market mercato
Newsstand giornalaio, edicola
Optician ottico
Pastry shop pasticceria
Perfumery profumeria
Pharmacy farmacia
Photographic shop negozio fotografico
Post office ufficio postale
Shoe shop negozio di calzature
Stationer cartoleria
Supermarket supermercato
Tailor sarto
Tobacconist tabaccheria (also sells stamps)
Tourist office ente del turismo
Toy shop negozio di giocattoli
Travel agent agenzia di viaggio

At the bank

I would like to change some dollars/pounds/travelers cheques
Vorrei cambiare delle sterline/dei dollari/dei travellers cheques
What is the exchange rate?
Com'è il cambio?
Can you cash a personal check?
Può cambiare un assegno?
Can I obtain cash with this credit card?
Posso avere soldi in contanti con questa carta di credito?
Do you need to see my passport?
Ha bisogno del mio passaporto?

Some useful goods

Antiseptic cream crema antisettica
Aspirin aspirina
Bandages fasciature
Cotton cotone idrofilo
Diarrhea/upset-stomach pills pillole anti-coliche
Indigestion tablets pillole per l'indigestione
Insect repellant insettifugo
Laxative lassativo
Sanitary napkins assorbenti igienici
Shampoo shampoo

Shaving cream crema da barba
Soap sapone (m)
Sticking plaster cerotto
Sunburn cream crema antisolare
Sunglasses occhiali da sole
Suntan cream/oil crema/olio solare
Tampons tamponi
Tissues fazzoletti di carta
Toothbrush spazzolino da denti
Toothpaste dentifricio
Travel sickness pills pillole contro il mal di viaggio

Bra reggiseno
Coat cappotto
Dress vestito
Jacket giacca
Pants mutande
Pullover maglione (m)

Shirt camicia
Shoes scarpe
Skirt gonna
Stockings/tights calze/collants
Swimsuit costume da bagno (m)
Trousers pantaloni

Film pellicola
Letter lettera
Money order vaglia

Postcard cartolina
Stamp francobollo
Telegram telegramma (m)

Words and phrases

Driving

Service station   stazione di rifornimento (f), distributore (m)
Fill it up.   Faccia il pieno, per favore.
Give me . . . . lire worth.   Mi dia . . . . lire.
I would like . . . . liters of gasoline.   Vorrei . . . . litri di benzina.
Can you check the . . . . ?   Può controllare . . . . ?
There is something wrong with the . . . .   C'e un difetto nel/nella . . . .

Accelerator acceleratore (m)		Lights fanali, fari, luci	
Axle l'asse (m)		Oil olio	
Battery batteria		Spares i pezzi di ricambio	
Brakes freni		Sparking plugs le candele	
Exhaust lo scarico, scappamento		Tires gomme	
Fan belt la cinghia del ventilatore		Water acqua	
Gear box la scatola del cambio		Windshield parabrezza (m)	

My car won't start.   La mia macchina non s'accende.
My car has broken down/I have a flat tire.   La macchina è guasta/la gomma è forata.
The engine is overheating.   Il motore si scalda.
How long will it take to repair?   Quanto tempo ci vorrà per la riparazione?
I need it as soon as possible.   Ne ho bisogno il più presto possibile.

Car rental

Where can I rent a car?   Dove posso noleggiare una macchina?
Is full/comprehensive insurance included?   E' completamente assicurata?
Is it insured for another driver?   E' assicurata per un altro guidatore?
Does the price include mileage?   Il kilometraggio è compreso?
Unlimited mileage   kilometraggio illimitato
Deposit   deposito
By what time must I return it?   A che ora devo consegnarla?
Can I return it to another depot?   Posso riportarla ad un altro deposito?
Is the gas tank full?   E' il serbatoio pieno?

Road signs

Accendere le luci in galleria lights on in tunnel	Divieto di sosta no stopping
Autostrada highway	Lavori in corso road repairs ahead
Caduta di massi falling stones	Passaggio a livello level crossing
Casello tollgate	Pedaggio toll road
Dare la precedenza give way	Raccordo anulare beltway
Divieto di accesso, senso vietato no entry	Rallentare slow down
Divieto di parcheggio no parking	Senso unico one-way street
Divieto di sorpasso no overtaking	Tangenziale bypass
	Tenersi in corsia keep in lane
	Uscita autocarri exit (for trucks)

Other methods of transport

Aircraft aeroplano		Train treno	
Airport aeroporto		Ticket biglietto	
Bus autobus (m)		Ticket office biglietteria	
Bus stop fermata		Single andata	
Coach corriera		Round trip andata e ritorno	
Ferry/boat traghetto		Half fare metà prezzo	
Ferry port porto		First/second/economy prima classe/seconda classe/turistico	
Hovercraft aliscafo			
Station stazione (f)		Sleeper/couchette cuccetta	

When is the next . . . . for . . . . ?   Quando parte il prossimo . . . . per . . . . ?
What time does it arrive?   A che ora arriva?
What time does the last . . . . for . . . . leave?   Quando parte l'ultimo . . . . per . . . . ?
Which platform/pier/gate?   Quale binario/molo/uscita?
Is this the . . . . for . . . . ?   E'questo il . . . . per . . . . ?
Is it direct? Where does it stop?   E' diretto? Dove si ferma?
Do I need to change anywhere?   Devo cambiare?
Please tell me where to get off.   Mi può dire dove devo scendere.
Take me to . . . .   Mi vuol portare a . . . .
Is there a buffet car?   C'è un vagone ristorante?

Food and drink

Have you a table for . . . . ?   Avete un tavolo per . . . . ?
I want to reserve a table for . . . . at . . . .   Vorrei prenotare un tavolo
per . . . . alle . . . .
A quiet table.   Un tavolo tranquillo.
A table near the window.   Un tavolo vicino alla finestra.
Could we have another table?   Potremmo spostarci?
I did not order this.   Non ho ordinato questo.
Breakfast/lunch/dinner   prima colazione/pranzo/cena
Bring me another . . . .   Un altro . . . . per favore.
The bill please.   Il conto per favore.
Is service included?   Il servizio è incluso?

Hot caldo	Sweet dolce, amabile
Cold freddo	Salt sale (m)
Glass bicchiere (m)	Pepper pepe (m)
Bottle bottiglia	Oil olio
Half-bottle mezza bottiglia	Vinegar aceto
Beer/lager (draft) birra (alla spina)	Mustard senape (f)
	Bread pane (m)
Fruit juice succo di frutta	Butter burro
Mineral water acqua minerale	Cheese formaggio
Orangeade/lemonade aranciata/limonata	Milk latte (m)
	Coffee caffè (m)
Carbonated/noncarbonated gassata/non gassata	Tea tè (m)
	Chocolate cioccolato
Red wine vino rosso, vino nero	Sugar zucchero
White wine vino bianco	Steak bistecca
Rosé wine vino rosé	well-done ben cotto
Vintage di annata	medium medio
Dry secco	rare al sangue

Menu decoder

Abbacchio baby lamb	Branzino sea bass
Acciughe anchovies	Bresaola dried salt beef
Acqua cotta thick bread and vegetable soup with egg	Brodetto fish soup
	Brodo consommé
Affettati sliced cold meats	Bruschetta garlic bread
Affumicato smoked	Burrida fish stew
Aglio garlic	Burro (al) (cooked in) butter
Agnello lamb	Busecca tripe soup
Agnolotti pasta envelopes	Cacciagione game
Agro sour	Cacciucco fish stew
Albicocche apricots	Calamaretti baby squid
Amaro bitter	Calamari squid
Ananas pineapple	Calzone half-moon-shaped pizza
Anatra/anitra duck	Cannelloni stuffed pasta tubes
Anguilla eel	Capitone large conger eel
Animelle sweetbreads	Cappelletti stuffed pasta hats
Antipasto hors d'oeuvre	Cappe sante scallops
Aragosta *langouste*, lobster	Capperi capers
Arancia orange	Carciofi alla giudia artichokes fried in oil and lemon juice
Aringa herring	
Arrosto roast meat	Carne meat
Arselle baby clams	Carote carrots
Asparagi asparagus	Carpa carp
Astaco river crayfish, lobster	Carpaccio raw lean beef fillet
Baccalà dried salt cod	Carrello (al) from the trolley
Basilico basil	Casa (della) of the restaurant
Bianchetti whitebait	Casalingo, -a homemade
Bianco plain, boiled	Castagnaccio chestnut cake
Bietola Swiss chard	Castagne chestnuts
Biscottini di Prato small, hard almond biscuits	Castrato mutton
	Cavolfiore cauliflower
Bistecca alla fiorentina grilled T-bone steak	Cavolini di Bruxelles sprouts
	Cavolo cabbage
Bollito misto boiled meats	Ceche young eels
Brace (alla) charcoal-grilled	Ceci chick peas
Braciola chop	Cèfalo gray mullet

Words and phrases

Cenci   fried pastry twists
Cervella   brains
Cervo   venison
Cetriolo   cucumber
Cicoria   chicory
Ciliege   cherries
Cima   cold stuffed veal
Cinghiale   wild boar
Cipolle   onions
Cocomero   watermelon
Coda di bue   oxtail
Coniglio   rabbit
Contorno   vegetable side dish
Controfiletto   sirloin steak
Coppa   cooked pressed neck of pork or an ice cream sundae
Cosciotto di agnello   leg of lamb
Costata di bue   entrecôte steak
Costolette   cutlets
Cotto   cooked
Cozze   mussels
Crema   custard, cream soup
Crespolini   savory pancakes
Crostacei   shellfish
Crostini   small savory toasts
Crudo   raw
Dentice   species of fish like sea bream
Diavola (alla)   in a spicy sauce
Dolci   desserts, sweets
Espresso   small black coffee
Fagiano   pheasant
Fagioli all'uccelletto   beans with tomatoes and garlic
Fagiolini   French beans
Faraona   guinea hen
Farcito   stuffed
Fatto in casa   homemade
Fave   fava beans
Fegatini   chicken livers
Fegato   liver
Ferri (ai)   grilled
Fesa di vitello   leg of veal
Fettina   slice
Fettuccine   thin flat pasta
Fettunta   garlic bread
Fichi   figs
Filetto   fillet
Finocchio   fennel
Finocchiona   fennel-flavored salami
Focaccia   dimpled savory bread
Formaggio   cheese
Forno (al)   cooked in the oven
Fragole   strawberries
Fresco   fresh
Frittata   omelet
Frittelle   fritters
Fritto   fried
Frutta   fruit
Frutti di mare   shellfish
Funghi   mushrooms
Gamberetti   shrimps
Gamberi   big prawns
Gelato   ice cream
Giorno (del)   of the day
Girarrosto (al)   spit-roasted

Girello   rump of beef
Gnocchi   small pasta dumplings
Grana   Parmesan cheese
Granchio   crab
Granita   water ice
Gran'pezzo   roast sirloin of young beef
Graticola (alla)   grilled
Griglia (alla)   grilled
Indivia   endive
Insalata   salad
Involtini   skewered veal and ham
Lamponi   raspberries
Lampreda   lamprey
Lasagne   baked flat pasta
Lenticchie   lentils
Lepre   hare
Lesso   boiled (meat)
Limone   lemon
Lingua di bue   ox tongue
Lombata. -ina   loin, loin chop
Lonza   cured fillet of pork
Luccio   pike
Lumache   snails
Macedonia di frutta   fruit salad
Magro   lean
Maiale   pork
Mandorle   almonds
Manzo   beef
Marmellata   jam
Medaglioni   rounds of meat
Mela   apple
Melagrana   pomegranate
Melanzane   eggplants
Melone   melon
Merlano   whiting
Merluzzo   cod
Miele   honey
Minestra   soup
Minestrone   vegetable soup
Misto   mixed
Mostarda   pickle
Muscolo alla fiorentina   beef casserole with beans
Nasello   hake
Naturale (al)   plain
Nocciole   hazelnuts
Noce di vitello   veal top round
Noci   nuts
Nodino di vitello   veal chop
Nostrale, nostrano   local
Oca   goose
Orata   gilthead bream
Osso buco   veal knuckle
Ostriche   oysters
Paglia e fieno   green and white tagliatelle
Paillard   thin grilled steak
Palombo   dogfish
Panforte di Siena   hard cake with honey, fruit and almonds
Panino imbottito   roll
Panna   cream
Panzanella   salad of soaked bread and fresh vegetables
Pappa al pomodoro   thick tomato-and-bread soup
Pappardelle   long flat pasta
Passato   purée

210

Pasta e fagioli   bean-and-pasta soup
Pasticcio   layered pasta pie
Pasto   meal
Patate   potatoes
Pecorino   hard ewe's-milk cheese
Penne all'arrabbiata   short pasta tubes with a fiery sauce
Peperoni   sweet peppers
Pera   pear
Pernice   partridge
Pesca   peach
Pesce   fish
Pesce persico   perch
Pesce San Pietro   John Dory
Pesce spada   swordfish
Pesciolini   small fry
Pesto   green basil sauce
Petto di pollo   chicken breast
Pezzo   piece
Piacere   according to taste
Piatto del giorno   today's dish
Piccante   spicy, piquant
Piccata   thin scallop
Piccione   pigeon
Pinzimonio   oily vegetable dip
Piselli   peas
Polenta   corn pudding
Pollame   poultry
Pollo   chicken
Polpette   meat balls
Polpettone   meat loaf
Polpo   octopus
Pomodoro   tomato
Pompelmo   grapefruit
Porchetta   roast suckling pig
Prezzemolo   parsley
Primizie   spring vegetables
Prosciutto   ham
Prugne   plums
Quaglie   quails
Radicchio   red bitter lettuce
Ragù   meat-and-tomato sauce
Rane   frogs
Ravanelli   radishes
Ravioli   stuffed pasta squares
Razza   skate
Ribollita   thick vegetable soup
Ricci   sea urchins
Ricciarelli   almond biscuits
Ricotta   cheese – similar to cottage cheese
Rigatoni   ridged pasta tubes
Ripieno   stuffed
Risi e bisi   pea-and-rice soup
Riso   rice
Risotto   savory rice dish
Rognoni   kidneys
Rombo liscio   brill
Rombo maggiore   turbot
Rosmarino   rosemary
Rospo (coda di)   tail of angler fish
Salsa (verde)   (green) sauce
Salsiccia   sausage
Saltimbocca alla romana   veal scallops with ham and sage
Salvia   sage
Sarde   sardines

Scaloppine   scallops
Scampi   Dublin bay prawns
Scelta (a)   of your choice
Schiacciata alla fiorentina   vanilla sponge cake
Scottadito   grilled lamb cutlets
Selvaggina   game, venison
Semifreddo   frozen dessert
Semplice   plain
Seppie   cuttlefish
Sgombro   mackerel
Sogliola   sole
Sottaceti   pickled vegetables
Spaghetti
    all'amatriciana   spaghetti with bacon, tomatoes
    alla bolognese   with ragù
    alla carbonara   with bacon, eggs
    alla napoletana   with tomato
Spezzatino   meat stew
Spiedini   skewers, kebabs
Spiedo (allo)   on the spit
Spigola   sea bass
Spinaci   spinach
Squadro   monkfish
Stagionato   hung, well-aged
Stagione (di)   in season
Stracciatella   clear egg soup
Stracotto   beef in red wine
Stufato   braised, stew(ed)
Sugo   sauce
Suppli   rice croquettes
Susina   plum
Tacchino   turkey
Tagliatelle   thin flat pasta
Tartufi   truffles
Tegame (al)   fried or baked
Telline   cockles
Timballo   savory pasta pie
Tinca   tench
Tonno   tuna
Tordi   thrushes
Torta   flan, tart
Tortellini   small stuffed pasta
Tost   toasted sandwich
Totano   squid
Tramezzino   sandwich
Trancia   slice
Trenette   flat, thinnish pasta
Trifolato   fried in garlic
Triglia   red mullet
Trippa   tripe
Trota   trout
Uccelletti   grilled beef on skewers
Umido (in)   stewed
Uova   eggs
Uva   grapes
Verdure   green vegetables
Vitello   veal
Vongole   clams
Zabaglione   egg-yolks-and-Marsala whip
Zucca   marrow
Zuccotto   ice cream liqueur cake
Zuppa   soup
Zuppa inglese   trifle

211

Glossary of art and architecture

Aedicule Niche framed by columns

Ambo Early form of pulpit

Architrave A supporting beam above a column

Archivolt Continuous moulding around a door or window

Atrium Central room or court of pre-Christian house; forecourt of early Christian church

Baldacchino Canopy, usually over altar, throne, etc.

Basilica Rectangular Roman civic hall; early Christian church of similar structure

Bottega An artist's workshop

Campanile Bell tower

Camposanto Cemetery

Caryatid Carved female figure used as column

Chiaroscuro (Heightened) light and shade effects in painting

Ciborium Altar canopy; casket for the Host

Crossing Space in church at intersection of chancel, nave and transepts

Diptych Work of art on two hinged panels

Ex-voto Work of art offered in fulfilment of a vow

Fresco Technique of painting onto wet plaster on a wall

Herm Sculpted male nude or bust on tapered pillar

Intarsia Inlay of wood

Loggia Gallery or balcony open on at least one side

Lunette Semicircular surface or panel, often painted or carved

Misericord Ledge or bracket projecting from pew or stall

Ogival Of a double-curved line, both concave and convex

Piano nobile Main floor of house, usually raised

Pieta Representation of the Virgin lamenting over the dead Christ

Pietradura Mosaic of semiprecious stone

Predella One or more small paintings attached to the bottom of an altarpiece

Putto The plump, naked child, often winged, in works of art

Scagliola Plaster-work polished to resemble marble

Sgraffiti Designs scratched into glaze to reveal base colour

Sinopia Preparatory drawing made beneath a fresco

Stucco Light, reinforced plaster

Tondo Circular painting or sculpture

Transept Transverse arms of a cruciform church

Tribune Raised area of gallery in a church; the apse in a basilica

Triptych Work of art on three hinged panels

Clothing sizes

When shops give clothing sizes in centimeters, use the following conversion scale to determine the correct size

12 *in*	16	20	24	28	32	36	40	44	48
30 *cm*	40	50	60	70	80	90	100	110	120

When standardized codes are used, although these may be found to vary considerably, the following provides a useful guide.

Women's clothing sizes

UK/US sizes	8/6	10/8	12/10	14/12	16/14	18/16
Italian sizes	36	38	40	42	44	46
Bust *in/cm*	31/80	32/81	34/86	36/91	38/97	40/102

Men's clothing sizes

European code (suits)	44	46	48	50	52	54	56
Chest *in/cm*	34/86	36/91	38/97	40/102	42/107	44/112	46/117
Collar *in/cm*	13½/34	14/36	14½/37	15/38	15½/39	16/41	16½/42
Waist *in/cm*	28/71	30/76	32/81	34/86	36/91	38/97	40/102
Inside leg *in/cm*	28/71	29/74	30/76	31/79	32/81	33/84	34/86

Men's and women's shoe sizes

UK/US sizes	3/4½	4/5½	5/6½	6/7½	7/8½	8/9½	9/10½	10/11½	11/12½
European	36	37	38	39	40	41	42	43	44

Index and gazetteer

The Florence index contains only items particular to Florence, arranged by category. Other categories, such as artists' names, are in the general index, as are all places outside Florence. Sights or places of interest are indexed individually in the general index, rather than under the town or city where they are found, because entries in the text are themselves arranged alphabetically by town. Hotels, restaurants, etc. are not indexed because they too are easily located within A–Z entries.

Page numbers in bold indicate the main entry.

Florence index

Florence gazetteer

Museums

Anthropological, **47**, Map 5C5

Antica Casa Fiorentina, **54**, Map 4D3

Archeological, **47–8**, Map 3B–C5

Argenti, 65, **67**, Map 4F2

Bardini, 49, Map 5F5

Bargello, 45, **49–51**, 52, 63, Map 5C–D5

Botanical, 52, Map 3B4

Casa Buonarroti, **61**, 77, 98, Map 5C5

Castagno, **71–2**, Map 3B4

Cathedral, 55, 56, **57–8**, Map 5C5

Coach, 68, Map 4F2

Davanzati, **54**, Map 4D3

"Firenze com'era", 58, 64, Map 5C5

Fra Angelico, **79–80**, Map 3B4

Horne, **59**, Map 5D5

Michelangelo, **61**, 77, 98, Map 5C5

Opera del Duomo, 55, 56, **57–8**, 87, Map 5C5

Opificio delle Pietredure, 78, Map 5A5

Pitti, **67**, Map 4F2

Porcelain, 52, Map 4F3

S. Croce, 63, 75, Map 5D6

S. Marco, **79–80**, Map 3B4

Science, **87–8**, Map 5E4

La Specola, 99, Map 4F2

Stibbert, **92**, Map 7C4

Strozzi, 92, Map 2C3

Topographical, **58**, 64, Map 5C5

Zoological, **99**, Map 4F2

Palaces

Altoviti, 103

Antella, 73

Antinori, 101, Map 4C3

Arte della Lana, 63

Barbolani di Montauto, 102

Bartolini-Salimbeni, 86, 101

Castellani, 87

Corsi, Map 4C3

Corsini, 54, Map 4C2

Coverelli, 101

Davanzati, **54**, 101, Map 4D3

Giugni, 102

Gondi, 76, 89, 103, Map 5D4

Grifoni, 70, 102

Guadagni, 59, 85, Map 4E2

Guicciardini, 76, Map 4D2

Horne (Corsi), 59, 73, Map 4C3

Lanfredini, 101

Matteucci Ramirez di Montalvo, 103

Medici Riccardi, 24, **60–1**, 64, 89, 90, 95, 102, Map 5B4

Niccolini, 70, 102

Nonfinito, 47, 103

Oddo Altoviti, 72

Pandolfini, 86, 102

Parte Guelfa, 100, Map 4D3

Pitti, 52, 60, 62, **64–8**, 75, 89, 99, Map 4F2

Podestà, 50

Pucci, 70, 102, Map 5B4

Riccardi Manelli, 70

Rosselli del Turco, 72

Rucellai, 24, **69**, 101, 160, 185, Map 4C2

Serristori-Cocchi, 73, Map 5F6

Signoria, 23, 51, 60, 64, 83, 87, **88–91**, Map 5D4

Strozzi, 92, 101, Map 4C3

Taddei, 102

Torrigiani, 99, Map 5E4

Uguccioni, 89, 91

Vecchio, *see* Signoria

Vitali, 103

Refectories

Ognissanti, 62, 80

S. Apollonia, 71, 72

S. Salvi, 84, 85, 87, 98

S. Spirito, 85

Towers

Castegna, 100

Gallo, 47, 64

Montauto, 51

S. Niccolò, 64, 84

Petraia, 64

Signoria, 49, 88, 89, 90

Villas

Bellosguardo, 51

Belvedere al Saracino, 51

La Gallina, 47

Il Gioiello, 47

Ombrellino, 51

La Pietra, 92

Stibbert, **92**

Florence gazetteer of street names

A

Lung. Acciaioli, Map 2D3

V.d. Acqua, Map 5D5

V.d. Agli, Map 4C3

V.d. Agnolo, Map 2C–D5

V. S. Agostino, Map 4E1

Borgo d. Albizi, Map 4D5

V. Aleardo Aleardi, Map 2D2

V.d. Alfani, 78, Map 4A–B5

V.d. Alloro, Map 4B3

Lung. Amerigo Vespucci, Map 3C1–2

V.d. Amorino, Map 4B3

V.d. Anguillara, Map 5D5

V.d. Anselmi, Map 4C3

V. Antonio Gramsci, Map 3C6

Arcetri, 47, 164, Map 7E4

Lung. Archibusieri, Map 4D3–4

V.d. Ardiglione, 104, Map 2D2

V.d. Ariento, Map 4A3

Arno, 53, 62, 64, 68, 85, 86, 93, 99

V. Arte d. Lana, 63, Map 4D3

V.d. Artisti, Map 2B5–6

V.d. Avelli, Map 4B2

B

V.d. Banchi, Map 4B2–3

V. Barbadori, Map 4E3

V.d. Bardi, 84, Map 5E4

V.d. Bartolomeo, Map 3A5

V.d. Bellosguardo, Map 2D1–2

V. Belfiore, Map 2B2

V. Belle Donne, Map 4B2–3

Bellosguardo, 51, 76, Map 6F3

V.d. Belvedere, Map 3E4

V.d. Benci, 59, Map 5D–E5

V. Benedetta, Map 4B1

V. Benedetto Marcello, Map 2B1

V.d. Bentaccordi, Map 5D5

V. Bolognese, 92, Map 7C4

Borgognissanti, Map 4C1

V.d. Brache, Map 5D5

Pza. Brunelleschi, Map 4C3

V.d. Brunelleschi, Map 4C3

V. Bufalini, Map 55

V.d. Burella, Map 5D5

C

V.d. Caldaie, Map 4E1

V. Calimala, Map 4C4

V.d. Calzaiuoli, 62, 63, Map 5C4

Florence gazetteer

216

General index

General index

219

General index

220

General index

General index

FLORENCE AND TUSCANY

LEGEND

Area Maps

0   5   10   15   20 Km

=O= Superhighway (with access point)
=== Main Road-Four Lane Highway
=== Other Main Road
—— Secondary Road
—— Minor Road
—— Scenic Route
SS73 Road Number
--- Ferry
=== Railway
✈ Airport
✈ Airfield
▦ International Boundary
=== Province Boundary
⌂ Abbey, monastery
⁝ Ancient site, ruin
♜ Castle
⛱ Good Beach
12 Adjoining Page No.

City Maps

▇ Major Place of Interest
▨ Other Important Building
▢ Built-up Area
▨ Park
† † Cemetery
† † Named church, church
✡ Synagogue
✚ Hospital
𝑖 Information Office
⊠ Post Office
◔ Police Station
⬤ Parking Lot
→ One Way Street